SATBAYEV U

NEW SCHOOL OF ECONOMICS

AP® CALCULUS I

© *Sergey Khrushchev*

foreword by
Prof. Paul Nevai
the Ohio State University

Almaty

2019

Contents

Foreword

by

Paul Nevai
Emeritus Professor of Mathematics
The Ohio State University

It is my immense pleasure and tremendous honor to introduce Professor Sergey Khrushchev's textbooks entitled *AP®. Calculus I & II*. These volumes are designed to prepare the students for the *Advanced Placement Calculus exams* (google it).

Sergey and I have known each other since our childhood. More precisely, we met when we both enrolled at LGU (it was then called Leningrad State University but today it has a different name) in 1966. There were around 300 math majors making up our class and Sergey was viewed as one of the top three students. It was clear already then that Sergey will have a bright career as a research mathematician working in areas related to calculus or, using a fancier terminology, mathematical analysis.

After graduation Sergey and I took different paths. He started to work in an area that could be best characterized as function theory, whereas I worked in approximation theory and orthogonal polynomials (OPs). Then, around 1990, our paths miraculously crossed again when Sergey wrote a somewhat routine paper on OPs. I was less than enthused but, nevertheless, we remained in touch. Then Sergey had a few turbulent years while the Soviet Union fell apart and the new Russian society was taking shape. During this time, Sergey suddenly fully immersed himself in OPs and within half a decade he produced a long research paper that was of the quality that even Gauß (the guy who, at the age of 7, added up the integers from 1 to 100 almost instantaneously — although this is more like a myth than a historical fact) or Euler (the 2.71 guy who is buried in the hometown of Sergey) would have envied. His work was followed by an extraordinary monograph on continued fractions.

In the meantime, Sergey became involved in education as well. First he moved to Turkey, then to (North) Cyprus, and finally to Kazakhstan (where he had some family connections).

It is a rare instance when one person is able to combine the qualities of an outstanding research mathematician, a universal scholar, and that of an talented educator. Some names that come to my mind are Paul Halmos, Isidor P. Natanson, George Pólya, Vladimir I. Smirnov, Elias M. Stein, and Antoni Zygmund (all are googlable). Sergey is one of those rare breeds.

This book is based on Sergey's lectures. I wish I could tell the prospective readers that go on and enjoy. However, mathematics cannot be enjoyed without a substantial amount of suffering. As it has been observed many times, math is not a spectator sport. The reader will have to be prepared for many hours of hard work that will include numerous frustratingly futile efforts until the proverbial eureka moment sheds light on ideas that allow a problem to be understood and solved. Then comes the joy. Sometimes.

I will stop now to intimidate the readers any further, and, instead, wish the best luck for them to master the delicious secrets of calculus.

Preface

Principle 1. *Never to accept anything as true that I did not **incontrovertibly** know to be so; that is to say, carefully to avoid both prejudice and premature conclusions; and to include nothing in my judgements other than that which presented itself to my mind so clearly and distinctly, that I would have no occasion to doubt it.*

Principle 2. *To divide all the difficulties under examination into as many parts as possible, and as many as were required to solve them in the best way.*

Principle 3. *To conduct my thoughts in a given order, beginning with the **simplest** and most easily understood objects, and gradually ascending, as it were step by step, to the knowledge of the most **complex**; and **positing** an order even on those which do not have a natural order of precedence.*

Principle 4. *To undertake such complete enumerations and such general surveys that I would be sure to have left nothing out.*

Descartes R., "Discourse on the Method" 1637

This book follows my lectures on Advanced Placement Calculus given in the International School of Economics of Kazakh-British Technical University in Almaty, Kazakhstan. In 2011-2017 first-year students of the ISE together with AP Calculus studied AP Statistics, AP Microeconomics, AP Macroeconomics. At the end of the first year after the internal, they passed external exams running and graded by College Board, Washington. In case of successful pass, they became students of the International Program of University of London. The program followed that of London School of Economics and was directed those times by a team of the LSE.

AP Calculus exams consist of four parts. Currently, the first part includes 30 multiple choice questions and lasts 60 minutes. No calculators are allowed on this portion of the exam. The second part has 15 questions with calculators for 45 minutes. Then two free response questions for 30 minutes are given with calculators. Finally, students get four free response questions for 60 minutes. Calculators are not allowed. Examination papers are sent to Washington, where they are graded.

There is a long list of calculators allowed by College Board. However, I would recommend TI-Nspire™CS CAS by Texis Instruments. In fact, this calculator is a mini computer with color display and touch pad. It saves students time during the exams, and this is extremely important. In addition, it can be used in AP Statistics. It also has a serious support of Linear Algebra.

The average scores and the number of total exams throughout the World for the last five years is presented below.

Calculus AB	2012	2013	2014	2015	2016
Score 5	67 630	67 783	72 511	66 411	76 654
Total Exams	268 086	283 418	294 706	304 318	308 668
Mean Score	2.97	2.96	2.94	2.86	2.96

It is clear from these data that only approximately 25% of students of AP Calculus get the highest score in global exams. The main reason for this is that the theoretical part, which makes the whole course consistent and clear, is ignored by the overwhelming majority of students. They believe that careful study of practical problems solutions only will lead to a good result. However, it is not the case since such an approach makes impossible to follow the Principles of Descartes, one of the founders of Calculus, stated as the epigraph, see [4].Being short in time during real exams students make simple mistakes and lose precious points.

The key to a success in AP Calculus exams is knowledge of the theory (including all proofs) coupled with a serious practice. The system of the ISE worked as follows. Each of two semesters has 15 weeks. The first semester is devoted to Differential Calculus (Part I of this book), whereas the second to Integral Calculus (Part II). Each week students have 3 lecture hours, where not only theory is discussed but also typical problems are solved. There are also 2 hours of practice with assistants, when students regularly write quizzes. Finally, students write home works in class for one hour. Home works are announced on the site, and students may solve problems together, but they must write solutions in class individually.

In the first semester students have one midterm, one mock, and the final exam. In the second semester, an extra mock exams is added. The problems are more difficult than those of College Board.

As soon as this system was implemented in 2012 – 13 the results of College Board exams were improved. Every year 80−90 students of the ISE get the average score 3.7 − 4.1 of 5 possible, and approximately 50% get the highest score 5. The official statistics of College Board for the ISE is given in the following table.

Calculus AB	2012	2013	2014	2015	2016
5	17	23	42	39	31
4	10	13	10	15	19
3	8	9	9	16	18
2	7	3	3	3	5
1	12	7	5	14	7
Total Exams	54	56	69	87	80
Mean Score	3.24	3.76	4.17	3.71	3.78

This book contains in equal proportions a theoretical part, a practical part, and, finally, real exams in the AP format given in the ISE in 2015 − 16. The exams, as well as the solutions, are organized as addendums at the end of this book.

In his great discovery of Differential and Integral Calculus Newton seriously used "La Géométrie" by Descartes (1637), [3], and "Arithmetica Infinitorum" by Wallis (1656), see [10].

Traditionally, every Calculus course begins with the so-called Pre-Calculus part. In this book, it is replaced with Descartes' theory of tangents, and Descartes Analytic Geometry developed initially in "La Géométrie". So, the main object of Differential Calculus appears at the very beginning. This part includes some applications as well. It is concluded with Horner's Rule for evaluating values of polynomials and with a proof of Descartes' Rule of Signs using it. In short, Chapter 1 is a differential calculus for polynomials.

Descartes' theory of tangents can easily be illustrated by the example of parabola $y = x^2$. The point $x = 1, y = 1$ is placed on its graph. Lines passing through $(1, 1)$ have equations $y = k(x − 1) + 1$, $x = 1$. The vertical line $x = 1$ is not the tangent. So, the equation of the tangent is $y = k(x − 1) + 1$ for some k. This k can be found by replacing y with $y = k(x − 1) + 1$ in the equation of the parabola $y = x^2$. The obtained quadratic equation

$$x^2 − k(x − 1) − 1 = 0 \Leftrightarrow x^2 − kx + k − 1 = 0$$

must have a multiple root $x = 1$. This happens if and only if the discriminant of the quadratic equation is zero:

$$D = k^2 − 4(k − 1) = (k − 2) = 0 \Leftrightarrow k = 2.$$

Hence $y = 2x − 1$ is the equation of the tangent to $y = x^2$ at $(1, 1)$.

In contrast to Descartes' approach, Newton considered the slope of a tangent as the instantaneous rate of change, which is the limit of the average rates defined by secants to the curve.

In applications, the difference between the static Descartes approach and dynamical approach of Newton is well demonstrated by a particular case of the following Newton's problem given in Newton's Lectures on Algebra (1673-1683), see [11]. By the way, this is a typical problem for Calculus AP exams, which always presents in examination questions in one or another form.

Problem. If 58 cattle should eat up a meadow in 30 days, and 80 cattle in 19 days, and if the grass grows at a uniform rate, how many cattle will eat this meadow in 6 days?

Solution: Let $V(0)$ be the initial volume of grass grown up on the meadow and let v be the volume of the grass grown up per day. Then v is the rate at which the grass grows. Each cattle eats c grass per day. So, we obtain two equations of balance:

$$-\begin{cases} V(0) + 30v & = 58 \cdot 30 \cdot c \\ V(0) + 19v & = 80 \cdot 19 \cdot c \end{cases} \Rightarrow (30 - 19)v = (58 \cdot 30 - 80 \cdot 19)c,$$

implying the relationship between the rate v of the grass growth and the rate c of the grass consumption by each cattle, namely $v = 20c$. From the first equation we find that

$$V(0) = 58 \cdot 30 \cdot c - 30v = 30(58 - 20)c = 1140c.$$

Let n be the number of cattle which will eat the meadow in 6 days. Then the equation of the balance is

$$V(0) + 6v = 6nc \Leftrightarrow 1140c + 120c = 6cn \Leftrightarrow n = 210. \quad \square$$

In fact, Descartes method can be extended not only to polynomials but also to rational functions and even to algebraic implicit functions. In 1638, Descartes in his letter to Fermat posed a problem of finding the equation of the line which is tangent to Descartes' Folium

$$x^3 + y^3 = 9xy.$$

Descartes' solution is recovered in Problem 3.59. Fermat found his own method, which was close ideologically to later Newton's dynamical method. However, the important idea of rate of change was not present in Fermat's solution.

Descartes' Folium is a key example in Differential Calculus. It is not accidental that Descartes sent to Fermat namely this equation. Justification the shape of its plot requires the knowledge of all theoretical tools which are usually tested in College Board exams. Therefore, it is important for students to study the solution to Problem 5.76.

Being so successful in so many cases Descates' method, however, fails for logarithms. These are very important functions since according to Weber-Fenchler law people feel the outside world through logarithms. The reason for this is that people's abilities to react to outside signals are very limited. Therefore, logarithms eliminate not important signals in favor of fast growing signals of exponential character.

It is the Weber-Fenchler law which stands behind any banking system. Since people feel logarithmically the interest rates are calculated as fixed proportions of invested sums of money rather than fixed additive parts of investments. This topic is related to the number $e = 2.71828\ldots$ playing an important role in Calculus. The number e is the base of the natural logarithm $\ln x$. Logarithmic and exponential growths are crucial for AP Calculus exams.

Limits and continuity are present in Chapter 3. The intermediate value property of continuous functions is always present in AP Calculus exams. A monotonic function is continuous if and only if it has the intermediate value property. This fact is used to prove the continuity of elementary functions.

Remarkable limits, which are tested in AP Calculus exams, are used to find the formulas for the derivatives of elementary functions.

A special attention is paid to graphs plotting. From the very beginning, we promote the method of plotting graphs by special points. The solution to Problem 2.2 demonstrates the idea of this method. One can easily recover an approximate shape of the graph of a function using its small parts about vertical and oblique asymptotes as well as about x-intercepts. The complete graph can be obtained just by connection of the plotted part with simple smooth curves. This is the result of the principle, saying that a simple formula implies a simple graph. The list of special points is extended later by critical points, see section 5.5. Since a function is usually monotonic between neighboring critical points, the task of graph plotting is significantly simplified. The final stage is to determine the directions of concavity and the inflection points, see section 5.6. Examples of graph plotting are given in section 5.7.

Problems on related rates are considered on concrete examples in section 4.5. Fifteen such problems are solved. They actually exhaust the list of all possible problems which one can face on exams.

The example of Descartes' Folium shows that implicit functions in one variable appeared at the very beginning of Differential Calculus. Implicit functions in several variables are important for a number of courses related to optimization. Therefore, a complete theory of implicit functions in one variable is present in this book. Elementary examples can be found in section 2.3. In section 3.5 a theorem on existence of continuous implicit functions is proved. This theorem is a good illustration, by the way, of the Intermediate Value Theorem. Differentiability of implicit functions is investigated in section 5.8.

I included a small section on Darboux' Theorem since it is related to the Intermediate Value Property, and shows that not every function is a derivative of another function. It is also useful in the AP Calculus exams.

A convex up function is defined in AP Calculus as a function with increasing derivative. To save student's examination time I present other equivalent criteria.

The theory of convex functions is used later to consider important applications of Calculus to Economics. These applications include the theory of an efficient firm, elasticity of demand, and Lorenz curves.

This book can be also useful for Cambridge International AS and A Level Mathematics exams.

$AP^{®}$ is a trademark registered and/or owned by the College Board, which was not involved in the production of and does not endorse this product. There are no conflicts of interests in this book. All references are cited.

Acknowledgment

I am grateful to Professor Iskander Beisembetov, rector of Kazakh-British Technical University (KBTU), who invited me to the International School of Economics in 2011, which was the best scientific and educational place I had ever seen before. All materials for these two books were collected and tested during 2013-2017. I am also grateful to Iskander Beisembetov for a possibility to finish these books already in Satbayev University in Almaty.

Sergey Khrushchev
Professor of Mathematics
The New School of Economics
Satbayev Technical University
050013 Almaty, Kazakhstan
e-mail: sergey.khrushchev@yahoo.com

Part I   Differential Calculus

Chapter 1

Descartes' Analytic Geometry

Abstract

This chapter presents basic ideas of Descartes' Analytic Geometry playing a crucial role in Calculus. We study Descartes method of tangents to
algebraic curves, especially for polynomial curves. Horner's Rule for polynomials is given. Descartes' Rule of Signs is proved.

Keywords: slope, run, rise, point-slope equation, slope-intercept equation, general
linear equation, tangent, circle, hyperbola, ellipse, parabola, long division of polynomials, Horner's rule, roots, local maximum, local minimum, Descartes' Rule of
Signs.

1.1. Lines

The theory of tangents was first present systematically in La Géométrie (1637),
[3].Descartes' idea was to arrange a natural correspondence between points of
plane and pairs of numbers in order to reduce geometrical problems to algebraic
ones. This method, called later the method of coordinates, is illustrated by the
picture below. On a plane, we construct two directed straight perpendicular lines.
The first horizontal line is called the x-axis. The second vertical line is called the
y-axis. We claim that the set of points on the plane with coordinates x, y related by
the formula $y = ax + b$ represent a line. Indeed, if x runs from x_0 to x_2, then y rises
from

$$y_0 = ax_0 + b \ \text{ to } \ y_2 = ax_2 + b \Rightarrow y_2 - y_0 = a(x_2 - x_0).$$

Also, if x runs from x_1 to x_2, then y rises from

$$y_1 = ax_1 + b \ \text{ to } \ y_2 = ax_2 + b \Rightarrow y_2 - y_1 = a(x_1 - x_0).$$

This implies that the right triangles $\triangle Ax_2C$ and $\triangle BDC$ are similar. Hence the angles $\angle CAx_2$ and $\angle CBD$ are equal, implying that the points A, B, C are placed on one line.

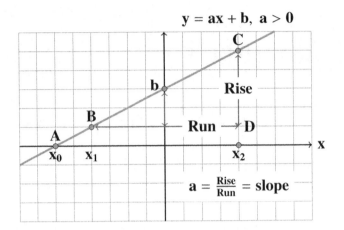

An important parameter of a line considered as a tangent to some curve is its slope a. The slope can be recovered from line's equation $y = ax + b$ as a coefficient a at x. If line's slope is known, then the line is uniquely determined by the coordinates (x_0, y_0) of some of its points. Given a slope a and a point (x_0, y_0) on the line, its equation can be recovered by the formula:

$$y = a(x - x_0) + y_0.$$

This equation is called the **point-slope** equation of a line.

Dealing with tangent it is necessary to recover their equations by various data given. These include line's recovery by two its points.

Given the coordinates (x_0, y_0) and (x_1, y_1) of two different points on the line, we can determine **Run** and **Rise**. This leads to a formula for the **slope**:

$$\mathbf{slope} = \frac{y_1 - y_0}{x_1 - x_0} = a \Rightarrow \boxed{y = \frac{y_1 - y_0}{x_1 - x_0}(x - x_0) + y_0}.$$

There are two important equations of a line:

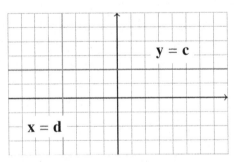

Notice that the vertical line $x = d$ cannot be recovered by the **Run-Rise** method presented above. To include all possibilities it is convenient to introduce a **General Linear Equation**:

$$Ax + By = C,$$

where both A and B cannot be equal to zero.

To get the standard equation of a line one can just solve the above equation in y (if $B \neq 0$):

$$y = -\frac{A}{B}x + C.$$

The equation

$$y = ax + b$$

is called the **slope-intercept** equation of a line, since a is its slope, and b is its y-intercept.

The following theorem is one of the key theorems for AP Tests. It allows one easily to recover the slope of a perpendicular line to a given one.

Theorem 1.1. *Let* $y = kx + b$ *be the equation of a non-horizontal line* $(k \neq 0)$. *Then* $y = k_1 x + b_1$ *is the equation of a perpendicular line if and only if*

$$\boxed{k_1 \cdot k = -1}.$$

Proof. We consider the case of two lines $y = kx + b$ and $y = k_1 x + b_1$ which intersect at a point P in the first quadrant $(x > 0, y > 0)$. They are perpendicular if and only if $\angle CPA = 90°$. Since $\angle ABP = 90°$, we conclude that $\angle BAP + \angle BPA = 90°$. Since $\angle BPA + \angle CPB = \angle CPA$, we see that

$$\angle CPA = \angle CPB + 90° - \angle BAP = 90° \Leftrightarrow \angle CPB = \angle BAP.$$

In other words, this happens if and only if two right triangles $\triangle CPB$ and $\triangle BAP$ are similar. Applying the similarity test by two sides and one angle, we see that $\triangle CPB \sim \triangle BAP$ if and only if

$$\frac{|BP|}{|BA|} = \frac{|BC|}{|BP|} \Leftrightarrow -\frac{1}{k_1} = k \Leftrightarrow k \cdot k_1 = -1.$$

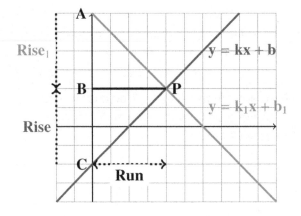

□

Problem 1.2. Given a vertex $(2, -2)$ and the diagonal $x + 2y = 0$ of a square find equations of sides of the square.

Solution:

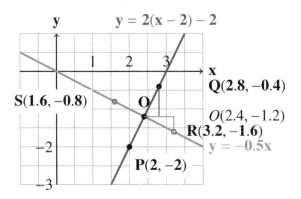

The point $P(2, -2)$ is not placed on the line $y = -0.5x$. By Theorem 1.1 the slope of a perpendicular line is $k_1 = -1/k = 2$. It follows that the second diagonal is placed on the line $y = 2(x - 2) + 2$. These two lines intersect at the center $O(2.4, -1.2)$ of the square. Considering P and O, we obtain that **Run** $= 2.4 - 2 = 0.4$, **Rise** $= -1.2 - (-2) = 0.8$. It follows that the x coordinate of the opposite vertex Q is $2.4 + 0.4 = 2.8$, whereas the y coordinate is $-1.2 + 0.8 = -0.4$. Observing that two right triangles shown on the picture are equal, we easily find the coordinates of other two vertexes S and R. Using point-slope equations we find equations of lines containing the sides of the square:

$$Q \to S : \quad \frac{\textbf{Rise}}{\textbf{Run}} = \frac{0.4}{1.2} = \frac{1}{3} \quad \boxed{y = \frac{1}{3}(x - 1.6) - 0.8, \quad 1.6 \le x \le 2.8};$$

$$S \to P : \quad \frac{\textbf{Rise}}{\textbf{Run}} = \frac{-1.2}{0.4} = -3 \quad \boxed{y = -3(x - 1.6) - 0.8, \quad 1.6 \le x \le 2};$$

$$P \to R : \quad \frac{\textbf{Rise}}{\textbf{Run}} = \frac{0.4}{1.2} = \frac{1}{3} \quad \boxed{y = \frac{1}{3}(x - 2) - 2, \quad 2 \le x \le 3.2};$$

$$R \to Q : \quad \frac{\textbf{Rise}}{\textbf{Run}} = \frac{-1.2}{0.4} = -3 \quad \boxed{y = -3(x - 2.8) - 0.4, \quad 2.8 \le x \le 3.2}.$$

$\square$

1.2. Quadratic Equations

A quadratic equation is the equation of the form

$$ax^2 + bx + c = 0,$$

where a, b, c are numbers, $a \ne 0$ and x is an unknown quantity. Any quadratic equation can be solved by the method of full squares:

$$0 = ax^2 + bx + c = a\left(x^2 + 2 \cdot \frac{b}{2a} \cdot x + \left(\frac{b}{2a}\right)^2\right) - \frac{b^2 - 4ac}{4a}$$

$$= a\left(x + \frac{b}{2a}\right)^2 - \frac{D}{4a}, \quad \boxed{\textbf{D} = \textbf{b}^2 - \textbf{4ac}} \Rightarrow \boxed{\textbf{x}_{1,2} = \frac{-\textbf{b} \pm \sqrt{\textbf{D}}}{\textbf{2a}}}.$$

Important partial case: $b = 2p$. Then

$$x_{1,2} = \frac{-b \pm \sqrt{D}}{2a} = \frac{-2p \pm \sqrt{4p^2 - 4ac}}{2a} = \frac{-\textbf{p} \pm \sqrt{p^2 - ac}}{\textbf{a}}.$$

Theorem 1.3. *Given the quadratic polynomial* $ax^2 + bx + c$, $a \ne 0$ *the following are equivalent:*

- $x_1 = x_0$;

- $ax^2 + bx + c = a(x - x_0)^2$;

- $D = b^2 - 4ac = 0$.

1.3. Lines and Circles

Euclidian Geometry gives a simple algorithm to plot tangents to a circle from a given point P outside of this circle. We plot an auxiliary circle based on OP as a diameter. This circle intercepts the circle O at two points. Then the line through P and T is a **tangent** to the circle O.

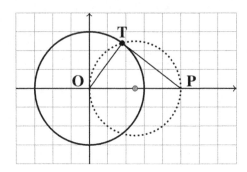

The above construction is based on the fact that the diameter OP of the circle is seen from any point T of this circle under angle $90°$. In particular, $OT \perp TP$ for the point of intercept T. This method is beautiful but cannot be extended to other curves.

Let us consider now a more general Descartes's approach. We are given a circle of radius 3 centered at $O(3,3)$ and a point $P(7,7)$ outside of this circle. An equation of a line through $P(7,7)$ with slope k is given by the point-slope equation

$$y = k(x - 7) + 7.$$

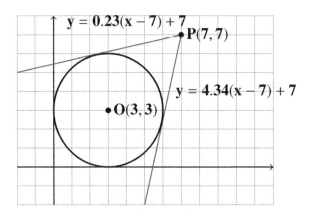

By Pythagorean theorem the circle is defined by the equation

$$(x - 3)^2 + (y - 3)^2 = 9.$$

Since the tangent has only one point in common with the circle the slope k of the tangent $y = k(x - 7) + 7$ is a number for which the system

$$\begin{cases} (x - 3)^2 + (y - 3)^2 & = 9 \\ k(x - 7) + 7 & = y \end{cases}$$

has a unique solution (x, y), which is the tangency point of this line and the circle. Substituting $y - 3 = kx + 4 - 7k$ into the first equation, we obtain that

$$9 = (x - 3)^2 + [kx + 4 - 7k]^2 = 9 + (1 + k^2)x^2 + 2[k(4 - 7k) - 3]x + (4 - 7k)^2 \Leftrightarrow$$
$$(1 + k^2)x^2 + 2[k(4 - 7k) - 3]x + (4 - 7k)^2 = 0.$$

The later quadratic equation has only one solution in x if and only if its reduced discriminant is zero:

$$0 = [k(4 - 7k) - 3]^2 - (1 + k^2)(4 - 7k)^2 = 7k^2 - 32k + 7.$$

We obtain two values for k:

$$k_1 = \frac{16 - \sqrt{207}}{7} \approx 0.230358, \quad k_2 = \frac{16 + \sqrt{207}}{7} \approx 4.34107.$$

1.4. Hyperbola

A classical hyperbola is the curve defined by the equation $yx = 1$.

Problem 1.4. Classify points of the coordinate plane by the number of tangents to the hyperbola $yx = 1$ passing through them.

Solution: Any vertical line $x = x_0$, $x_0 \neq 0$, intersects the hyperbola at unique point $(x_0, 1/x_0)$, implying that the hyperbola is placed in the first, $x > 0, y > 0$, and the third, $x < 0, y < 0$, quadrants of the coordinate plane. We apply Descartes' method to find all points on tangents to the hyperbola. The point-slope equation of a tangent to the hyperbola through (x_0, y_0) is given by $y = k(x - x_0) + y_0$. The point of tangency is determined by the system

$$\begin{cases} y & = k(x - x_0) + y_0 \\ yx & = 1 \end{cases} \Leftrightarrow \boxed{kx^2 + (y_0 - kx_0)x - 1 = 0}.$$

It is clear that $x = 0$ is not a solution of the boxed equation. Given x_0, y_0, k, this equation has a unique solution in x if and only if the discriminant $(y_0 - kx_0)^2 + 4k$ is 0. Notice that if $k = 0$ then $y_0 = 0$. However, the horizontal line $y = 0$ has no points in common with the hyperbola. It follows that all slopes of the tangents to the hyperbola are negative. Now, we solve the equation

$$0 = (y_0 - kx_0)^2 + 4k = k^2 x_0^2 - 2(x_0 y_0 - 2)k + y_0^2$$

in k. If $x_0 = 0$, then $y_0^2 = -4k$, implying that $k = -y_0^2/4$. So, for the points on the y-axis except for the origin $(0,0)$ there is only one tangent to the hyperbola. For $x_0 = y_0 = 0$ there is no tangent at all. If $x_0 \neq 0$, then

$$k = \frac{(x_0 y_0 - 2) \pm \sqrt{(x_0 y_0 - 2)^2 - x_0^2 y_0^2}}{x_0^2} = \frac{(x_0 y_0 - 2) \pm 2\sqrt{1 - x_0 y_0}}{x_0^2}.$$

If $y_0 = 0$, then one of the solutions is $k = 0$, which corresponds to no tangent. This formula shows that there is only one tangent for any point (x_0, y_0) on the coordinate axes except for the origin $(0,0)$. It also shows that there is only one tangent for any point (x_0, y_0) placed on the hyperbola $xy = 1$. The slope of this tangent is given by

$$\boxed{k = -\frac{1}{x_0^2}}.$$

There is no tangent at all through (x_0, y_0) if $x_0 y_0 > 1$, and there are two tangents if $x_0 \neq 0$ and $x_0 y_0 < 1$. The results of our calculations are plotted below. □

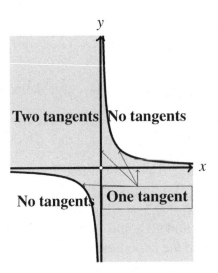

1.5. Parabola

A parabola is a curve defined by the equation $y = ax^2 + bx + c$, $a \neq 0$. Let x_1 and x_2 be the roots of the quadratic equation $ax^2 + bx + c = 0$, $a \neq 0$. Then

$$ax^2 + bx + c = a(x - x_1)(x - x_2).$$

The above factorization leads to **Vieta's Formulas**:

$$x_1 + x_2 = -\frac{b}{a}, \quad x_1 x_2 = \frac{c}{b}$$

These formulas are especially useful in computations with functions, which are symmetric in x_1 and x_2:

$$x_1^2 + x_2^2 = (x_1 + x_2)^2 - 2x_1 x_2 = \frac{b^2}{a^2} - \frac{2c}{a} = \frac{b^2 - 2ac}{a^2}.$$

The advantage of such calculations is that they do not involve radicals.

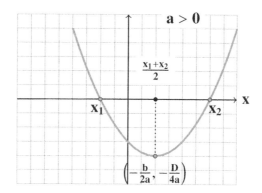

Vieta's formulas allow one to locate easily the vertex of a parabola as soon as the roots are known. The picture above shows that the roots are placed symmetrically with respect to the x-coordinate of parabola's vertex. Therefore, this x-coordinate is given by

$$\frac{x_1 + x_2}{2} = -\frac{b}{2a}.$$

The y-coordinate of the vertex can be found by a direct calculation:

$$y = a\left(\frac{x_1 + x_2}{2}\right)^2 + b\frac{x_1 + x_2}{2} + c = \frac{b^2}{4a} - \frac{b^2}{2a} + c = -\frac{D}{4a}. \tag{1.1}$$

By (1.1) the quadratic equation $ax^2 + bx + c = 0$ has no real roots if and only if $D < 0$.

Problem 1.5. Find the equation of the tangent to the curve $y = x^2$ at point $(1, 1)$.

Solution: Since $1 = 1^2$, the point $(1, 1)$ is on the curve $y = x^2$. A point-slope equation of a line through $(1, 1)$ is given by $y = k(x - 1) + 1$. This line is tangent to $y = x^2$ if and only if the quadratic equation in x

$$x^2 = k(x - 1) + 1 \Leftrightarrow x^2 - kx + k - 1 = 0$$

has only one solution $x_1 = 1$. By Vieta's formulas $k - 1 = x_1 x_2$, which shows that $x_2 = x_1 = 1$ if and only if $k = 2$. $\qquad\square$

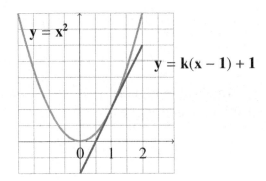

Theorem 1.6. *Let* $y = ax^2 + bx + c$, $a < 0$, *be a parabola. Then for any closed interval* $[e, f]$

$$\max_{e \le x \le f} y(x) = \begin{cases} y\left(-\frac{b}{2a}\right), & \text{if } e \le -\frac{b}{2a} \le f \\ y(e), & \text{if } -\frac{b}{2a} \le e \\ y(f), & \text{if } f \le -\frac{b}{2a} \end{cases}$$

Proof. The proof is shown on the graph:

$$y = ax^2 + by + c$$

□

Problem 1.7. Market research shows that consumers will buy x thousand units of a particular machine when the unit price is

$$p(x) = -x + 50$$

dollars. The cost of producing the x thousand units is

$$C(x) = 0.5x^2 + 20x + 54.$$

For what value of x is the production of these machines the most profitable?

(A) 2 (B) 10 (C) 11 (D) 12 (E) 18

Solution: The revenue is

$$R(x) = x \cdot p(x) = -x^2 + 50x$$

thousand dollars, and the profit is

$$\Pi(x) = R(x) - C(x) = -x^2 + 50x - (0.5x^2 + 20x + 54) = -1.5x^2 + 30x - 54 =$$
$$- 1.5(x^2 - 20x + 36) = -1.5(x - 2)(x - 18).$$

It follows that the graph of the profit is a parabola with the vertex directed upwards. The x-coordinate of the vertex of the parabola is

$$x = \frac{2 + 18}{2} = 10 \Rightarrow \textbf{Answer: B}.$$

1.6. Long Division of Polynomials and Horner's Rule

A polynomial is an algebraic expression of the form

$$P(x) = a_n x^n + a_{n-1} x^{n-1} + \cdots + a_1 x + a_0,$$

where the coefficients $a_0, a_1, \ldots, a_n$, $a_n \neq 0$ are real numbers and x is an unknown quantity. In the AP problems the coefficients are usually integers. The nonnegative integer n is called the **degree** of the polynomial P and is denoted by $n = \deg(P)$. Notice that the degree of a nonzero constant polynomial $P(x) \equiv a_0 \neq 0$ is 0, and the degree of 0 is $-\infty$.

Theorem 1.8 (Long Division of Polynomials). *Let $P(x)$ be a polynomial (the dividend) and $D(x)$ be another nonzero polynomial (the divisor). Then there are unique polynomials $Q(x)$ (a quotient) and $R(x)$ (a remainder) such that*

(**a**) $\deg(R) < \deg(D)$;

(**b**) $P(x) = D(x) \cdot Q(x) + R(x).$

The theorem is proved by the **Long Division of Polynomials**, which is a simple extension of a usual division algorithm for decimal integers:

$$a_n 10^n + a_{n-1} 10^{n-1} \cdots + a_1 10 + a_0.$$

The proof is present in books of Algebra. Here we illustrate it by a concrete example of the dividend $P(x) = 2x^3 - 5x^2 + 7$ and the divisor $D(x) = x - 2$. The algorithm of Long Division works as follows. We place $P(x)$ written as $2x^3 - 5x^2 + 0 \cdot x + 7$ (so that all powers of x are present in the expression) between two horizontal lines ant put the divisor $D(x) = x - 2$ on the left separated with) from $P(x)$. To cancel $2x^3$ in $P(x)$ we put $2x^2$ above $2x^3$ and multiply it by $D(x) = x - 2$. The result of this multiplication is written below $P(x)$. We make a substraction and obtain the polynomial $-x^2 + 0 \cdot x$. We write $-x$ above $-5x^2$ and multiply it by $D(x) = x - 2$. The process is continued until we obtain the reminder $R(x) = 3$.

Long Division

$$
\begin{array}{r}
2x^2 \quad -x \quad -2 \\
\hline
x-2)\overline{2x^3 \quad -5x^2 \quad +0\cdot x \quad +7} \\
\underline{2x^3 \quad -4x^2} \\
\underline{-x^2 \quad +0\cdot x} \\
\underline{-x^2 \quad +2\cdot x} \\
\underline{-2\cdot x \quad +7} \\
\underline{-2\cdot x \quad +4} \\
3
\end{array}
$$

Synthetic Division

$$
\begin{array}{r|rrrr}
2| & 2 & -5 & 0 & 7 \\
  &   & 4 & -2 & -4 \\
\hline
  & 2 & -1 & -2 & \mathbf{3}
\end{array}
$$

$$2x^3 - 5x^2 + 7 = (x - 2)(2x^2 - x - 2) + 3.$$

In case the divider is a polynomial $x - a$, the above algorithm of Long Division can be shorten to **Horner's Rule** or to **Synthetic Division** of polynomials.

$$
\begin{array}{r|rrrr}
2| & 2 & -5 & 0 & 7 \\
\hline
 & 2
\end{array}
\Rightarrow
\begin{array}{r|rrrr}
2| & 2 & -5 & 0 & 7 \\
 & & 4 \\
\hline
 & 2
\end{array}
\Rightarrow
\begin{array}{r|rrrr}
2| & 2 & -5 & 0 & 7 \\
 & & 4 \\
\hline
 & 2 & -1
\end{array}
\Rightarrow
$$

$$
\begin{array}{r|rrrr}
2| & 2 & -5 & 0 & 7 \\
 & & 4 & -2 \\
\hline
 & 2 & -1
\end{array}
\Rightarrow
\begin{array}{r|rrrr}
2| & 2 & -5 & 0 & 7 \\
 & & 4 & -2 \\
\hline
 & 2 & -1 & -2
\end{array}
\Rightarrow
\begin{array}{r|rrrr}
2| & 2 & -5 & 0 & 7 \\
 & & 4 & -2 & -4 \\
\hline
 & 2 & -1 & -2
\end{array}
\Rightarrow
$$

$$
\begin{array}{r|rrrr}
2| & 2 & -5 & 0 & 7 \\
 & & 4 & -2 & -4 \\
\hline
 & 2 & -1 & -2 & \mathbf{3}
\end{array}
\Rightarrow 2x^3 - 5x^2 + 7 = (x - 2)(2x^2 - x - 2) + 3.
$$

In the first line above we write $a = 2$ and separate this value by a vertical line from the coefficients $2 \ -5 \ 0 \ 7$ of the polynomial $2x^3 - 5x^2 + 7$. On the second step we put down the leading coefficient 2 under the second line. Then we multiply this coefficient by 2 and put the result under the first line below the second coefficient. On the third step we write $-5 + 4 = -1$ below -4 and again multiply it by 2. The result of this multiplication is put below 0. We continue this process until all fields in the table are completed. Then the first numbers in the last line give us the coefficients of the divisor, i.e. $2x^2 - x - 2$, and the utmost right number 3 is a reminder.

Here is an explanation why this scheme works.

$$
\begin{array}{c|cccc}
c & a_3 & a_2 & a_1 & a_0 \\
\hline
 & & a_3c & a_3c^2 + a_2c & a_3c^3 + a_2c^2 + a_1c \\
\hline
 & a_3 & a_3c + a_2 & a_3c^2 + a_2c + a_1 & \mathbf{a_3c^3 + a_2c^2 + a_1c + a_0}
\end{array}
$$

$$P(c) = (c\,(c\,(a_3c + a_2) + a_1) + a_0).$$

$$
\begin{array}{c|cccc}
3 & 2 & -7 & 0 & 5 \\
\hline
 & & 6 & -3 & -9 \\
\hline
 & 2 & -1 & -3 & -4
\end{array}
$$

$$\mathbf{2x^3 - 7x^2 + 5 = (x - 3)(2x^2 - x - 3) - 4.}$$

1.7. Roots of Polynomials

Definition 1.9. A number a is called a **root** of a polynomial $P(x)$ if $P(a) = 0$.

Lemma 1.10. *A real number a is a root of a polynomial $P(x)$ if and only if $P(x)$ can be factored as $P(x) = (x - a)Q(x)$.*

Proof. If P can be factored then $P(a) = (a - a)Q(a) = 0 \cdot Q(a) = 0$, implying that a is a root of $P(x)$. Suppose now that $P(a) = 0$. We apply the Long Division of Polynomials to the dividend $P(x)$ and the divisor $x - a$. Then

$$P(x) = (x - a) \cdot Q(x) + R(x),$$

where $\deg(R) < \deg(x - a) = 1$. It follows that $R(x) \equiv R(a)$. Hence

$$P(x) = (x - a) \cdot Q(x) + R(a).$$

Now put $x = a$ in the equality above. We obtain

$$0 = P(a) = (a - a) \cdot Q(x) + R(a) = R(a).$$

Since $R(a) = 0$ we conclude that $P(x) = (x - a) \cdot Q(x)$. $\square$

Theorem 1.11. *Any polynomial $P(x)$ can be uniquely factored into the product*

$$P(x) = (x - x_1)(x - x_2) \cdot (x - x_r)Q(x), \qquad (1.2)$$

where x_1, x_2, ..., x_r are the real roots of $P(x)$ not necessarily distinct, and the polynomial $Q(x)$ has no real roots at all.

Proof. By Lemma 1.10 the theorem is true for $r = 1$. Suppose that the statement of the theorem is true for any polynomial with exactly r real roots and consider a polynomial $P(x)$ with $r + 1$ real roots. By Lemma 1.10 the polynomial $P(x)$ can be factored as $(x - x_{r+1})Q(x)$, where Q is a polynomial. It is clear that Q has r real roots only (counting multiple roots). By the induction hypothesis it is factored into the product of a required type. Hence P is also factored as required. By the Principle of Mathematical Induction the proof is completed.   □

If $r > 1$ and $x_1 = x_2$, then $P(x) = (x - x_1)^2 Q_1(x)$, where Q_1 is a polynomial. In such a case the root x_1 is called a **multiple** root of P.

Corollary 1.12. *The number of roots of any polynomial cannot exceed its degree.*

Proof.

$$\textbf{degree}(P) = r + \textbf{degree}(Q) \quad □ \qquad (1.3)$$

Theorem 1.13 (The Intermediate Value Theorem for Polynomials)**.** *Let $P(x)$ be a polynomial such that $P(a)P(b) < 0$ for a pair of real numbers $a < b$. Then there is a number c in (a, b) such that $P(c) = 0$.*

Proof. See Corollary 3.53 and Theorem 3.34 for a rigorous proof. Here we present a proof, which was considered as correct in Descartes' times. Namely, we assume that $P(a) < 0$ and $P(b) > 0$. Then the points $A = (a, P(a))$ and $B = (b, P(b)$, see the picture below, are placed on the opposite sides of a "river" flowing along the x-axis. To get from the point A to B along the curve $y = P(x)$ one is forced to cross the river at some point c in the interval (a, b) as stated.   □

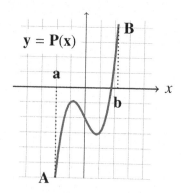

Theorem 1.14. *If $P(x)$ is a polynomial which does not have real roots, then* $\deg(P) = 2k$ *is an even number.*

Proof. Suppose to the contrary that a polynomial $P(x)$ has no roots and $\deg(P) = n$ is an odd number. Then for any x, $|x| > 1$, we have

$$P(x) = x^n \left(a_n + \frac{a_{n-1}}{x} + \frac{a_{n-2}}{x^2} + \cdots + \frac{a_0}{x^n} \right).$$

Let $M = \max(|a|_k, 0 \le k \le n)$. Since we assume that $|x| > 1$, we obtain that

$$\left| \frac{a_{n-1}}{x} + \frac{a_{n-2}}{x^2} + \cdots + \frac{a_0}{x^n} \right| \le \frac{|a_{n-1}|}{|x|} + \cdots + \frac{|a_0|}{|x|^n} \le \frac{n \cdot M}{|x|}.$$

Since $\deg(P) = n$, we see that $a_n \ne 0$. Therefore, for $|x| > (2n \cdot M)/|a_n|$ the sign of $P(x)$ coincides with the sign of $a_n x^n$. If n is odd, the signs are opposite for x and $-x$ if $|x| > (2n \cdot M)/|a_n|$. By the Intermediate Value Theorem the polynomial $P(x)$ has a real root which is a contradiction. □

Corollary 1.15. *The number of real roots of a polynomial $P(x)$ either is equal to its degree n or is less than n by an even number.*

Proof. Apply Theorem 1.14 and (1.3). □

1.8. Tangents to Polynomial Curves

Theorem 1.16. *Let*

$$p(x) = a_n x^n + a_{n-1} x^{n-1} + \cdots + a_1 x + a_0, \quad a_n \ne 0,$$

be a polynomial of degree n. Then the slope k of the tangent to the graph of $y = p(x)$ at $(x_0, p(x_0))$ equals

$$k = n a_n x_0^{n-1} + (n-1) a_{n-1} x_0^{n-2} + \cdots + 2 a_2 x_0 + a_1.$$

Proof. By Theorem 1.3 a line $y = k(x - x_0) + p(x_0)$ is tangent to the curve $y = p(x)$, where p is a quadratic polynomial, if the quadratic polynomial

$$p(x) - k(x - x_0) - p(x_0)$$

has a multiple root at x_0. We may hope that the same criterion holds for any polynomial as well. To prove this we observe that for $m = 1, 2, \ldots, n$

$$x^m - x_0^m = (x - x_0)(x^{m-1} + x_0 x^{m-2} + \cdots + x_0^{m-1}).$$

Multiplying both sides by a_m and summing up, we obtain

$$p(x) - p(x_0) = (x - x_0) \sum_{m=1}^{n} a_m(x^{m-1} + x_0 x^{m-2} + \cdots + x_0^{m-1}). \qquad (1.4)$$

It follows that if

$$k = \sum_{m=1}^{n} a_m(x^{m-1} + x_0 x^{m-2} + \cdots + x_0^{m-1})\Big|_{x=x_0} = \sum_{m=1}^{n} a_m \cdot m \cdot x_0^{m-1},$$

then the polynomial

$$p(x) - p(x_0) - k(x - x_0)$$

has a multiple root $x = x_0$. $\qquad\square$

Definition 1.17. A real number x_0 is called a point of a **local maximum** for a polynomial $P(x)$ if there is $\delta > 0$ such that $P(x) \leq P(x_0)$ for every x in the interval $(x_0 - \delta, x_0 + \delta)$.

A real number x_0 is called a point of a **local minimum** for a polynomial $P(x)$ if there is $\delta > 0$ such that $P(x) \geq P(x_0)$ for every x in the interval $(x_0 - \delta, x_0 + \delta)$.

If $P(x) = x^2$, then $x = 0$ is a point of local minimum for the polynomial x^2. If $P(x) = -x^2$, then $x = 0$ is a point of local maximum for $-x^2$.

Theorem 1.18 (Fermat). *If x_0 is a point of local maximum or minimum for a polynomial $P(x)$, then the tangent line to the curve $y = P(x)$ at $(x_0, P(x_0))$ is horizontal.*

Proof. Let x_0 be a point of local minimum for a polynomial $P(x)$. Then the polynomial $P(x) - P(x_0)$ is nonnegative on some interval $(x_0 - \delta, x_0 + \delta)$, $\delta > 0$. By Theorem 1.11 we obtain that

$$P(x) - P(x_0) = (x - x_0)^r Q(x), \quad \text{where} \quad Q(x_0) \neq 0.$$

Since $Q(x_0) \neq 0$, the sign of $Q(x)$ is one and the same for all x in some interval $(x_0 - \delta, x_0 + \delta)$, $\delta > 0$. There are two cases: either r is odd or even. If r is odd then the sign of $(x - x_0)^r$ is changed from $-$ to $+$ when x passes through x_0. It follows that $P(x) - P(x_0)$ cannot be positive on both halves of the interval $(x_0 - \delta, x_0 + \delta)$. Hence r is even. Since $P(x) - P(x_0)$ vanishes at $x = x_0$, we see that $r = 2s$, $s \geq 1$. In other words, the line $y = P(x_0)$ is tangent to the curve $y = P(x)$ at $(x_0, P(x_0)$ as stated. $\qquad\square$

The example of the polynomial $P(x) = x^6 - 7x^4 + 14x^2 - x - 6$ illustrates Fermat's theorem:

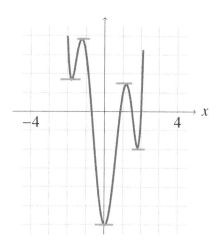

Let us observe that at each point of local maximum a polynomial curve changes its direction from up to down, and at each point of local minimum it changes direction from down to up. Given a polynomial $P(x)$ let **CD**(P) be the number of direction changes. Then

$$\mathbf{CD}(P) \leq \deg(P) - 1.$$

Indeed, by Theorems 1.16 and 1.18 the polynomial

$$Q(x) = na_n x^{n-1} + (n-1)a_{n-1}x^{n-1} + \cdots + 2a_2 x + a_1$$

vanishes at points of local maximum or local minimum. Since $\deg(Q) = \deg(P) - 1$, the result follows by Corollary 1.15.

Problem 1.19. Each graph shown below is a polynomial curve. Answer the following questions for each graph:

(a) What is the minimum degree of a polynomial that could have the graph?

(b) Is the leading coefficient of the polynomial negative or positive?

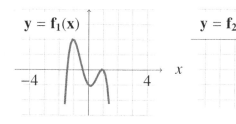

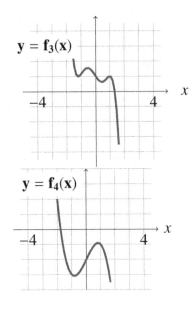

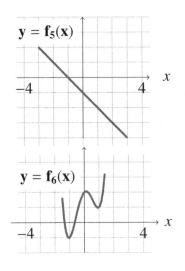

Solution: We have

$$\mathbf{CD}(f_1(x)) = 3 \Rightarrow \deg(f_1) \geq 4; \quad a_n < 0;$$

$$\mathbf{CD}(f_2(x)) = 1 \Rightarrow \deg(f_2) \geq 2; \quad a_n < 0;$$

$$\mathbf{CD}(f_3(x)) = 4 \Rightarrow \deg(f_3) \geq 5; \quad a_n < 0;$$

$$\mathbf{CD}(f_4(x)) = 2 \Rightarrow \deg(f_4) \geq 3; \quad a_n < 0;$$

$$\mathbf{CD}(f_5(x)) = 0 \Rightarrow \deg(f_5) = 1; \quad a_n < 0;$$

$$\mathbf{CD}(f_6(x)) = 3 \Rightarrow \deg(f_1) \geq 4 \quad a_n > 0;.$$

1.9.   Derivatives of Polynomials

Theorem 1.16 shows that the slope of the tangent to the graph $y = p(x)$ of a polynomial $p(x)$ is the polynomial in the x-coordinate of the tangency point given by

$$p^{(1)}(x) = na_n x^{n-1} + (n-1)a_{n-1}x^{n-2} + \cdots + 2a_2 x + a_1. \tag{1.5}$$

Definition 1.20. Given a polynomial $p(x)$ the polynomial (1.5) is called the **derivative** of p. It satisfies

$$\deg\left(p^{(1)}\right) = \deg(p) - 1.$$

Taking consecutive derivatives of p, we find a finite sequence of polynomials

$$
\begin{aligned}
p^{(1)}(x) &= na_n x^{n-1} + (n-1)a_{n-1}x^{n-2} + \cdots + 2a_2 x + a_1 \\
p^{(2)}(x) &= n(n-1)a_n x^{n-2} + (n-1)(n-2)a_{n-1}x^{n-3} + \cdots + 2a_2 \\
&\vdots \qquad \vdots \qquad\qquad\qquad \vdots \\
p^{(n)}(x) &= n \cdot (n-1) \cdot 2 \cdot 1 \cdot a_n
\end{aligned}
\tag{1.6}
$$

It is clear that $p^{(n+1)}(x) \equiv 0$. So, all derivatives of orders greater than n are zeros. Putting $x = 0$ in (1.6), we find that

$$a_0 = \frac{p^{(0)}(0)}{0!}, \quad a_1 = \frac{p^{(1)}(0)}{1!}, \quad a_2 = \frac{p^{(2)}(0)}{2!}, \quad \dots \quad a_n = \frac{p^{(n)}(0)}{n!},$$

where $k! = 1 \cdot 2 \cdot \dots \cdot n$, $0! = 1$, and $p^{(0)}(x) \equiv p(x)$.

Lemma 1.21. *If p and q are two polynomials such that $p^{(1)}(x) = q^{(1)}(x)$ for every x, and a is an arbitrary real number, then $p(x) = q(x) + p(a) - q(a)$.*

Proof. We have $p^{(1)}(x) - q^{(1)}(x) = (p - q)^{(1)}(x) = 0$, which implies by (1.5) that $p - q$ is a constant polynomial. Putting $x = a$, we find the constant. □

Theorem 1.22. *Let p and q be two polynomials of degree not exceeding n and let $p^{(k)}(a) = q^{(k)}(a)$ for some real number a and $k = 0, 1, \dots, n$, Then $p(x) = q(x)$ for every x.*

Proof. We prove the Theorem by induction on n. By Lemma 1.21 the Theorem is true for $n = 1$. Suppose that it is true for n and prove it for $n + 1$. If $p^{(k)}(a) = q^{(k)}(a)$ for $k = 0, 1, \dots, n + 1$, then $p_1^{(k)}(a) = q_1^{(k)}(a)$ for $k = 0, 1, \dots, n$, where we denote by p_1 and q_1 the derivatives of p and q correspondingly. It follows that $p_1(x) = q_1(x)$ for every x by the induction hypothesis. By Lemma 1.21

$$p(x) = q(x) + p(a) - q(a) = q(x).$$

This completes the proof of the Theorem. □

Corollary 1.23. *If p is a polynomial of degree n and a is a real number, then*

$$p(x) = p(a) + \frac{p^{(1)}(a)}{1!}(x - a) + \frac{p^{(2)}(a)}{2!}(x - a)^2 + \dots + \frac{p^{(n)}(a)}{n!}(x - a)^n. \quad (1.7)$$

Proof. Apply Theorem 1.22 to the polynomials in both sides of (1.7). □

Corollary 1.24. *If p is a polynomial of degree n, a is a real number and*

$$p(a) > 0, \quad p^{(1)} \geq 0, \quad p^{(2)} \geq 0, \quad \dots, \quad p^{(n)} \geq 0,$$

then every real root x_r of the polynomial $p(x)$ satisfies the inequality $x_r < a$.

Proof. If $x \geq a$, then $p(x) > 0$ by (1.7). □

Corollary 1.25. *If p is a polynomial of degree n, a is a real number and the sequence*

$$p(a) > 0, \quad p^{(1)} \leq 0, \quad p^{(2)} \geq 0, \quad \dots,$$

alternates, then every real root x_r of the polynomial $p(x)$ satisfies the inequality $x_r > a$.

Proof. Apply Lemma 1.24 to the polynomial $p(-x)$. □

Problem 1.26. Let
$$p(x) = x^6 - 7x^4 + 14x^2 - x - 2.$$

Using higher derivatives of p determine a finite interval $[a, b]$ containing all real zeros of p.

Solution: We evaluate all nonzero derivatives of $p(x)$ at $x = 2$:

$$p(x) = x^6 - 7x^4 + 14x^2 - x - 2 \Rightarrow$$

2|	1	0	-7	0	14	-1	-2
		2	4	-6	-12	4	6
	1	2	-3	-6	2	3	**4**

$$p^{(1)}(x) = 6x^5 - 28x^3 + 28x - 1 \Rightarrow$$

2|	6	0	-28	0	28	-1
		12	24	-8	-16	24
	6	12	-4	-8	12	**23**

$$p^{(2)}(x) = 30x^4 - 84x^2 + 28 \Rightarrow$$

2|	30	0	-84	0	28
		60	120	72	144
	30	60	36	72	**172**

$$p^{(3)}(x) = 120x^3 - 168x \Rightarrow$$

2|	120	0	-168	0
		240	480	624
	120	240	312	**624**

$$p^{(4)}(x) = 360x^2 - 168 \Rightarrow p^{(4)}(2) = \mathbf{1312}$$
$$p^{(5)}(x) = 720x \Rightarrow p^{(5)}(2) = \mathbf{2880}$$
$$p^{(6)}(x) = 720 \Rightarrow p^{(6)}(2) = \mathbf{720}$$

Similarly, we have

$$p(-2) = 8, \quad p^{(1)}(-2) = -25, \quad p^{(2)}(-2) = 172, \quad p^{(3)}(-2) = -624,$$
$$p^{(4)}(-2) = 1272, \quad p^{(5)}(-2) = -1440, \quad p^{(6)}(x) - 720.$$

It follows that real roots of $p(x)$ are located in the interval $(-2, 2)$. □

1.10. Polynomial Curves

Problem 1.27. Each curve shown below is the graph of one of the following functions:

(a) $y = x - 2$ (b) $y = x^3 - 2x - 2$ (c) $y = x^5 - 5x^3 + 4x - 2$

(d) $y = x^2 - 2x - 2$ (e) $y = 2x^4 - 4x^2 + x - 2$ (f) $y = x^6 - 7x^4 + 14x^2 - x - 2$

Identify the functions with their graphs. Justify your answer.

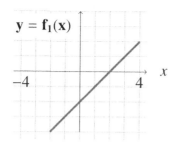

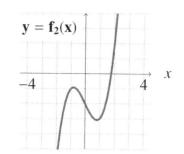

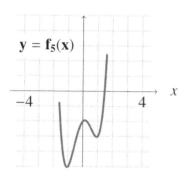

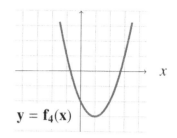

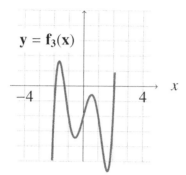

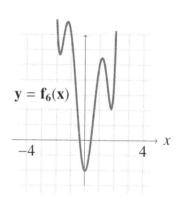

Solution: Using the graphs, we evaluate

$$f_1(0) = -2, \ f_2(0) = -2, \ f_3(0) = -2, \ f_4(0) = -2, \ f_5(0) = -2, \ f_6(0) = -2.$$

Since we cannot distinguish these polynomial by their values at $x = 0$, we must apply a more detailed analysis. We eliminate the linear polynomial $y = x - 2$ whose graph is a straight line. It follows that **(a)** $\leftrightarrow$ **1**.

Next, the polynomial in **(d)** is quadratic. Hence its graph is a parabola and we may identify it with **(d)** $\leftrightarrow$ **4**.

The polynomial in **(b)** has degree three. Its roots are $-\sqrt{2}, \ 0, \ \sqrt{2}$. There is only one graph with three x-intercepts. It is **2**. Moreover these x-intercepts in fact coincide with the roots of **(b)**. Hence **(b)** $\leftrightarrow$ **2**.

We analyse now graph **3**. It has **five** x-intercepts. It follows that the degree of the polynomial corresponding to this graph is at least 5. Now we observe that

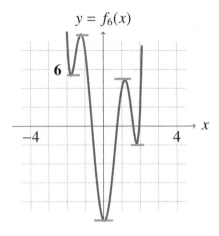

Figure 1.1: Analysis of graph **6**.

the graph goes down as x moves left, meaning that the polynomial is negative for such values of x. Similarly, the graph goes up as x moves right. It follows that the degree of the polynomial is odd and cannot be less than 5. There is only one polynomial in the list satisfying such properties. It is **(c)**. Hence **(c)** $\leftrightarrow$ **3**.

We analyse graph **6**. There are FIVE points on the graph, where the tangent is horizontal, i.e. the slope of the tangent vanishes at FIVE distinct points, see Fig 1.1. By Descartes the slope of the tangent is given by the derivative of the corresponding polynomial. We have the choice between **(e)** and **(f)**. The derivative of the polynomial in **(e)** has degree 3:

$$y' = 4 \cdot 2x^3 - 2 \cdot 4x + 1.$$

Therefore, this polynomial cannot have five different roots. We conclude that **(e)** $\leftrightarrow$ **5**, **(f)** $\leftrightarrow$ **6**.

1.11. Descartes' Rule of Signs

In his Geometry (1637), see [3], Descartes considers the polynomial

$$(x + 5)(x - 2)(x - 3)(x - 4) = (x + 5)(x^3 - 9x^2 + 26x - 24) =$$
$$x^4 - 4x^3 - 19x^2 + 106x - 120,$$

which has one negative root and three positive roots. The sequence of coefficients of this polynomial has one case of the sign permanence (at x^3) and three sign changes (at x^4, x^2, x).

We denote by $Z^+(p)$ the number of positive roots of a polynomial p counted with multiplicities. For the Descartes polynomial p we have $Z^+(p) = 3$. It is clear from Descartes' example that $Z^+(p)$ is somehow related to the number of sign changes of the coefficients of p.

Any sequence of real coefficients of a polynomial

$$p(x) = a_0 + a_1 x + a_2 x^2 + \cdots + a_n x^n, \ a_0 a_n \neq 0,$$

determines a sequence $\{\varepsilon_k\}_{k=0}^n$ of $+$ and $-$ of length $n + 1$ by the following rules:

$$\varepsilon_k = \begin{cases} + & \text{if } a_k > 0 \\ - & \text{if } a_k < 0 \\ \varepsilon_{k-1} & \text{if } a_k = 0 \end{cases}$$

The algorithm above is well-defined, since we assume that $a_0 a_n \neq 0$.

Definition 1.28. We say that a sequence $\{\varepsilon_k\}_{k=0}^n$ has a **sign variation** at $k < n$ if $\varepsilon_k \neq \varepsilon_{k+1}$. We say that $\{\varepsilon_k\}_{k=0}^n$ has a **sign permanence** at $k < n$ if $\varepsilon_k = \varepsilon_{k+1}$. We denote by **Var**$(p)$ the total number of sign variations in $\{\varepsilon_k\}_{k=0}^n$ and by **Per**(p) the total number of **sign permanence** in $\{\varepsilon_k\}_{k=0}^n$.

Since at every k, $0 \leq k < n$, there is either a sign variation, or a sign permanence, an important formula follows:

$$\text{Var}(p) + \text{Per}(p) = n. \tag{1.8}$$

Lemma 1.29. *Let*

$$p(x) = a_0 + a_1 x + a_2 x^2 + \cdots + a_n x^n, \ \ a_0 a_n \neq 0, \tag{1.9}$$

be a polynomial of degree n such that $p(r) = 0$ for some $r > 0$. Then the polynomial $P(x) = p(rx)$ satisfies

$$P(1) = 0, \ \ \text{Var}(P) = \text{Var}(p), \ \ Z^+(P) = Z^+(p).$$

Proof. The signs of the coefficients of P coincide with those of p, implying that $\text{Var}(P) = \text{Var}(p)$. It is clear that $P(x) = 0$ if and only if $p(rx) = 0$. This implies that $Z^+(P) = Z^+(p)$ as stated. $\square$

Theorem 1.30. *Let p, $p(0) \neq 0$, be a polynomial with real coefficients. Then $Z^+(p) \leq \text{Var}(p)$.*

Proof. We prove Theorem 1.30 by induction on $n = \deg(p)$. If $a > 0$ and $b > 0$, then

$$x + a \longleftrightarrow ++, \quad x - b \longleftrightarrow +-,$$

showing that either $0 = Z^+(p) = \text{Var}(p)$ or $1 = Z^+(p) = \text{Var}(p)$, which proves the theorem for $n = 1$. If a polynomial

$$p(x) = a_2 x^2 + a_1 x + a_0$$

has no positive roots, then there is nothing to prove. If it has some root $r > 0$, then Lemma 1.29 shows that we may assume that $r = 1$. Since $p(1) = 0$, Horner's Rule gives

$$
\begin{array}{c|ccc}
1 & a_2 & a_1 & a_0 \\
\hline
 & & a_2 & a_1 + a_2 \\
\hline
 & a_2 & a_1 + a_2 & \mathbf{a_0 + a_1 + a_2 = 0}
\end{array}
$$

$$p(x) = (x - 1)(a_2 x + a_2 + a_1).$$

Since $a_0 + a_1 + a_2 = 0$, there is at least one sign change in $\{a_0, a_1, a_2\}$, which corresponds to the root $x = 1$. The polynomial p has the second positive root if and only if the polynomial $a_2 x + a_2 + a_1$ has this root. It follows that there is a sign change in the sequence $\{a_2, a_2 + a_1\}$, which is only possible if there is a sign change in $\{a_2, a_1\}$.

Suppose that Theorem 1.30 holds for any polynomial of degree not exceeding $n - 1$ and consider a polynomial

$$p(x) = a_0 + a_1 x + a_2 x^2 + \cdots + a_n x^n, \quad a_0 a_n \neq 0, \tag{1.10}$$

of degree n. If p has no positive roots, then there is nothing to prove. If $p(r) = 0$ for some $r > 0$, then by Lemma 1.29 we may assume without loss of generality that p in (1.9) satisfies $p(1) = 0$. It follows that

$$p(x) = (x - 1)q(x), \quad q(x) = b_0 + b_1 x + b_2 x^2 + \cdots + b_{n-1} x^{n-1},$$

where $\deg(q) = n - 1$ and $Z^+(q) \leq \text{Var}(q)$ by the induction hypothesis. By Horner's Rule

$$b_{n-1} = a_n, \quad b_{n-2} = a_n + a_{n-1}, \quad b_0 = a_n + a_{n-1} + \cdot + a_1.$$

Any sign change in the sequence $\{b_{n-1}, \ldots, b_0\}$ is preceded by a sign change in $\{a_n, \ldots, a_0\}$. Since $b_{n-1} + \cdots + b_0 = 0$, there is at least one extra sign change in $\{a_n, \ldots, a_0\}$, which corresponds to the root $x = 1$. Since the number of sign variations in $\{a_n, \ldots, a_0\}$ and $\{a_0, \ldots, a_n\}$ is the same, we obtain that

$$Z^+(p) = Z^+(q) + 1 \leq \text{Var}(q) + 1 \leq \text{Var}(p),$$

as stated. $\qquad\qquad\qquad\qquad\qquad\qquad\qquad\qquad\qquad\qquad\qquad\qquad\qquad\square$

The following example illustrates the proof of Theorem 1.30.

Example 1.31. Proof of Theorem 1.30 on the example of the polynomial

$$p(x) = x^5 - 3x^4 + 2x^3 + x^2 - 3x + 2.$$

Proof. Since $p(1) = 0$, we obtain by Horner's Rule that

$$
\begin{array}{r|rrrrrr}
1 & 1 & -3 & 2 & 1 & -3 & 2 \\
  &   & 1 & -2 & 0 & 1 & -2 \\
\hline
  & 1 & -2 & 0 & 1 & -2 & \mathbf{0}
\end{array}
$$

$$p(x) = (x - 1)q(x) = (x - 1)(x^4 - 2x^3 + 0 \cdot x^2 + x - 2).$$

The sign change at $b_4 = 1$ of $q(x)$ corresponds to the sign change at $a_5 = 1$; the sign change at $b_3 = -2$ corresponds to the sign change at $a_4 = -3$; the sign change at $b_1 = 1$ corresponds to the sign change at $a_2 = 1$. The extra sign change in the coefficients of p appears at $a_1 = -3$, since the sum of coefficients of q is zero. □

Theorem 1.32 (The First Descartes' Theorem). *If*

$$p(x) = a_0 + a_1 x + a_2 x^2 + \cdots + a_n x^n, \ a_0 a_n \neq 0,$$

is a polynomial with only real roots, then **Var**(p) *is the number of positive roots of p and* **Per**(p) *is the number of negative roots of p.*

Proof. There is a simple relation between **Per**(p) and **Var**$(p(-x))$:

$$\mathbf{Var}(p(-x)) \leq \mathbf{Per}(p).$$

Any consecutive pair of $++$ or $--$ turns into a sign change for $p(-x)$ since there is a sign of a coefficient at an odd degree in such a pair. However, this pair is not transformed into a sign change if the coefficient at the odd degree is zero. Therefore, we have inequality and not equality.

Since the number of negative roots $Z^-(p)$ equals the number $Z^+(p(-x))$ of positive roots of $p(-x)$, we conclude by Theorem 1.30 that

$$Z^-(p) + Z^+(p) \leq \mathbf{Var}(p(-x)) + \mathbf{Var}(p) = \mathbf{Per}(p) + \mathbf{Var}(p) = \deg(p). \quad (1.11)$$

In our case $Z^-(p) + Z^+(p) = \deg(p)$. It follows that all inequalities in (1.11) are in fact equalities which completes the proof. □

Theorem 1.33 (**Descartes' Rule of Signs**). *The number* $Z^+(p)$ *of positive roots of the algebraic equation* $p(x) = 0$ *equals* $V(p) - 2k$, *where k is a nonnegative integer.*

Proof. Without loss of generality we may assume that

$$p(x) = x^n + a_{n-1}x^{n-1} + \cdots + a_1 x + a_0, \quad a_0 \neq 0.$$

By Theorem 1.11 the polynomial p is a finite product of $Z^+(p)$ linear terms $x - x_i$, $x_i > 0$, a number of linear terms $x + y_j$, $y_i > 0$, and of a polynomial $q(x)$ which has no zeros. The leading term of $q(x)$ is 1. Since for big values of $|x|$ the polynomial $q(x)$ behaves as $x^{\deg(q)}$, we conclude by Theorem 1.13 that $q(x)$ is everywhere positive and, in particular, $q(0) > 0$.

A simple evaluation of the sign of the free term of the product of linear polynomials and $q(x)$ shows that

$$(-1)^{Z^+(p)} = \text{sign}(a_0).$$

Suppose that $a_0 > 0$. Then each change of sign from $+$ to $-$ must be followed by the change from $-$ to $+$, implying that $\text{Var}(p)$ is even. Suppose that $a_0 < 0$. Then each change of sign from $-$ to $+$ must be followed by the change from $+$ to $-$, implying that $\text{Var}(p)$ is odd since $a_n = 1$. It follows that

$$(-1)^{Z^+(p)} = (-1)^{\text{Var}(p)} \Rightarrow Z^+(p) = \text{Var}(p) - 2k.$$

By Theorem 1.30 $Z^+(p) \leq \text{Var}(p$, which completes the proof. $\qquad\square$

Problems

Prob. 1 — Find the slope of the line through the points $(-2, 5)$ and $(3, -1)$.

(A) -1.2 (B) 1.2 (C) $-\dfrac{5}{6}$ (D) $\dfrac{5}{6}$ (E) **none of these**

Prob. 2 — Find the equation of the line that through the points $(3, -2)$ and $(1, 6)$.

(A) $y - 4x = 10$ (B) $y = -4x + 10$ (C) $4y + x = 25$ (D) $4y - x = 23$

Prob. 3 — Let L be the line $4x + 3y = 3$. Find an equation of a line through $Q(2, -3)$ perpendicular to L.

(A) $y = -0.75x - 1.5$ (B) $3y - 4x = 10$ (C) $y = 4x - 3$ (D) $y = 0.75x - 4.5$

Prob. 4 — Find an equation of the line through $(2, -1)$ which is perpendicular to the line $y = 2x + 1$.

(A) $y = -0.5x - 1$ (B) $2y + x = 1$ (C) $2y + x = 1$ (D) $y = -0.5x$

Prob. 5 — A line through $(1, 2)$ with slope -2 is perpendicular to another line through $(1, 1)$. Find the equations of both lines.

Prob. 6 — Determine whether the points $(1, 2)$, $(2, 4)$, and $(0, 6)$ form the vertices of a right triangle.

Prob. 7 — Find the slope k of a line through $(2, -1)$ which makes with the coordinate axes a triangle with area 4.

$$\text{(A) } -0.5 \quad \text{(B) } 0.5 \quad \text{(C) } 1 \quad \text{(D) } -1 \quad \text{(E) none of these}$$

Prob. 8 — Find equations of tangent lines to the curve $2x^2 - 5y^2 = 3$, passing through $P(1, 0)$.

Prob. 9 — Find equations for tangents to the curve $(x - 2)^2 + (y - 2)^2 = 1$ passing through the origin.

Prob. 10 — Determine the set of points on the coordinate plane covered by tangents to the curve $4x^2 - 9y^2 = 1$.

Prob. 11 — The tangent to the hyperbola $yx = 1$ at $x_0 > 0$ makes the triangle with the coordinate axes. The area of this triangle is

$$\text{(A) } 2x_0 \quad \text{(B) } \frac{2}{x_0} \quad \text{(C) } 2 \quad \text{(D) } 4 \quad \text{(E) none of these}$$

Prob. 12 — Two postmen A and B separated by 59 miles begin their trips towards each other. A covers 7 miles every 2 hours, whereas B makes 8 miles every 3 hours. What a distance will be covered by A before he meets B if B began his trip 1 hour later than A?

$$\text{(A) } 24 \quad \text{(B) } 35 \quad \text{(C) } 37 \quad \text{(D) } 39 \quad \text{(E) none of these}$$

Prob. 13 — A whiz-bang is moving so that its height over the ground level is given by the following formula $H(t) = -t^2 + 8t + 43$. For how long will it be 50 feet over the ground?

$$\text{(A) } 6 \text{ sec} \quad \text{(B) } 3 \text{ sec} \quad \text{(C) } 5.5 \text{ sec} \quad \text{(D) } 2.5 \text{ sec} \quad \text{(E) } 5 \text{ sec}$$

Prob. 14 — Find the quotient and the reminder of the division of the dividend $x^3 - 2x^2 - 4$ by the divisor $x - 3$.

Prob. 15 — Using Horner's Rule evaluate the value of the polynomial

$$P(x) = x^5 - 2x^4 + 3x^3 - 5x^2 + 3x + 1 \text{ at } x = 3.$$

Prob. 16 — Using Horner's Rule evaluate the value of the polynomial

$$P(x) = x^5 - 2x^4 - 10x^3 + 30x^2 + 65x - 120 \text{ at } x = 2.$$

Prob. 17 — Using Horner's Rule find the roots of the polynomial

$$P(x) = x^3 - x^2 - 10x + 6 = 0.$$

Repeat the proof of Descartes' Rule of signs for this polynomial from Newton's Arithmetics.

Prob. 18 — (Newton) Descartes' Rule of signs says that the equation

$$x^3 + px^2 + 3p^2x - q = 0, \quad p > 0, q > 0, \tag{1.12}$$

has one positive root and at most three negative roots. Descartes' Rule also says that the equation

$$(x - 2p)(x^3 + px^2 + 3p^2x - q) = x^4 - px^3 + p^2x^2 - (2p^3 + q)x + 2pq = 0$$

has at most four positive roots and no negative roots. Show that the equation (1.12) has one positive root and two complex roots.

Prob. 19 — (Laguerre) If a sequence $b_0, b_1, \ldots, b_m$ has V sign changes and the sequence

$$b_0, \ b_0 + b_1, \ b_0 + b_1 + b_2, \ \ldots, \ b_0 + \cdots + b_{m-1} \tag{1.13}$$

has W sign changes and $b_0 + \cdots + b_m = 0$, then $W + 1 = V - 2k$, where k is a nonnegative integer.

Prob. 20 — A bookstore can get a book from a publisher at a cost of \$15 per copy. It is estimated that if the bookstore sells the book for p dollars per copy, approximately $20(25 - p)$ copies will be sold each month. Find bookstore's monthly profit as a function of price, graph this function, and use the graph to estimate the optimal selling price.

Prob. 21 — A real estate company manages 250 apartments. All the apartments can be rented at a price of \$1 000 per month, but for each \$100 increase in the monthly rent, there will be five additional vacancies more.

(*a*)Find the total monthly revenue R obtained from renting apartments as a function of the monthly rental price p per unit.

(*b*)Sketch the graph of the revenue function found in part (*a*).

(*c*)What monthly rental price p should the company charge in order to maximize total revenue? What is the maximum revenue?

Prob. 22 — The curve is defined by

$$x^2 + 6x - 12y + 33 = 0.$$

(**a**)Determine the type of this curve (parabola, ellipse or hyperbola).

(**b**)Find the foci (focus) of this curve.

(**c**)Determine its direction in the coordinate system.

(**d**)Sketch the graph of this curve.

Prob. 23 — The curve $16y^2 + 32y - 4x^2 - 24x = 84$ determines

(**A**) an ellipse (**B**) a parabola (**C**) an y – directed hyperbola

(**D**) an x – directed hyperbola (**E**) empty curve.

Prob. 24 — Find the number of real roots of the equation:

$$x^3 - 3x - 1 = 0.$$

Chapter 2

Functions and Graphs

Abstract

Euler's theory of functions and the method of graphs plotting by special points and by the principle 'simple formula - simple graph' are demonstrated. The theory of logarithms and exponents are explained by the Weber-Fechner law. The notions of superpositions of a pair of functions as well as of the inverse functions are discussed. Trigonometric and inverse trigonometric functions are introduced.

Keywords: function, domain, range, natural domain, graphs, vertical line test, horizontal, vertical, and oblique asymptotes, implicit functions, conic sections, reflective properties of parabola and ellipse, exponents, logarithms, inverse function, horizontal line test, increasing and decreasing functions, trigonometric functions, radians and degrees, period, inverse trigonometric functions,

2.1. Functions

Dealing with applications we usually consider two variables, one of which is independent and another dependent. For instance, if s denotes the distance covered by a moving car, then t denotes the time elapsed from the moment when this car started its movement. In this model time t is an independent variable and s a dependent variable. At any moment t the distance s covered by this very moment is determined uniquely by t.

Leonard Euler, one of the creators of Calculus, introduced in 18th century a convenient notation: $s = f(t)$, which says that s is a **function** of t. In practice,

31

functions are usually given by concrete formulas:

$$s = t^2 - 1, \quad s = \frac{t^2 - 1}{t + 1}, \quad s = 10\sin(t + 1).$$

Euler's notation allows one to concentrate on study of general properties of functions.

Later Euler's approach was made even more systematic. Together with a function $y = f(x)$ one also considers its **domain** $\mathcal{D} = \mathcal{D}(f)$, and its **range** $\mathcal{R} = \mathcal{R}(f)$.

The domain $\mathcal{D}(f)$ is defined as a set of points x, to which f may be applied. It is usually determined together with f. In the above example with car the domain is the closed interval $[0, T]$, where T is the time of observation.

As soon as $\mathcal{D}(f)$ is defined one associates with **every** number x in $\mathcal{D}(f)$ a unique number denoted by $f(x)$. The set of all numbers $f(x)$, when x runs over $\mathcal{D}(f)$, makes up the range $\mathcal{R}(f)$ of the function $y = f(x)$.

In our example above $\mathcal{R}(s)$ is the set of all possible distances maid by the car during the time of observation.

If $y = f(x)$ is determined by some concrete formula, then one may talk on the so-called **natural domain** of f. The natural domain is the set of all x such that the formula defining f makes sense.

By some reasons, which we cannot discuss at this very moment, the natural domains and ranges of all functions, defined by formulae, are finite unions of intervals on the real axis.

There is also a way, which is quite common in AP tests, to represent functions by tables. For example, daily air temperature measurements at a meteorological station are organised in the following table.

t	8	9	10	11	12	13	14	15	16	17	18
T	-5	-4	-2	-1	-0.5	1	3	3.5	4	1	-2

Here the temperature T (in degrees of Celsius) depends on time t (in hours). It is assumed that the function $T = T(t)$ is unknown except for the values specified in the table.

If one faces a problem associated with a function defined by a table, then sometimes it is useful to represent this function with a tabular graph as follows.

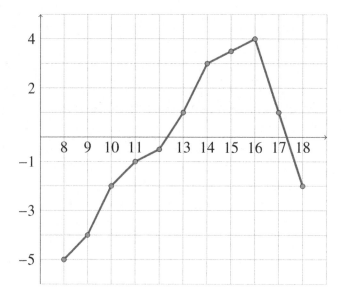

This plotting allows one answer many questions assuming that $T(t)$ is linear between the points given in the table.

2.2. Graphs

It is common to study functions by their graphs.

Definition 2.1. The **graph** $G(f)$ of a function $y = f(x)$ is the line on the coordinate plane, which is made by the points $(x, f(x))$, when x ranges over $\mathcal{D}(f)$.

Functions are often represented as combinations of elementary functions such as polynomials, exponents, logarithms etc. Therefore, the skill of plotting the graphs basing on known graphs is important for AP Calculus Tests. In this section of the textbook, you find a number of tricks, which are helpful for this.

In practice, graphs are also used to define functions. You may be asked if a given line on a plane is a graph of some function. In such a case apply the **vertical line test**.

Theorem 2.2 (The Vertical Line Test). *A a subset Γ of the coordinate plane is the graph of some function if and only if every vertical line $x = a$ intersects Γ at most at one point.*

Proof. Since points of any graph have the form $(a, f(a))$, the proof of the test is evident. Indeed, assume that Γ is a graph of $y = f(x)$. Any vertical line $x = a$ either intersects Γ or not. If it intersects the graph, then $(a, f(a))$ is on $x = a$. There may be no other point of Γ in this intersection, since f associates only one element $f(a)$ with every $a \in \mathcal{D}(f)$.

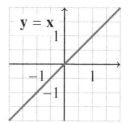 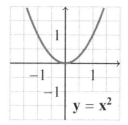 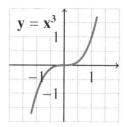

Figure 2.1: Three important graphs.

If the vertical line $x = a$ intersects the line Γ at most at one point, then $f(a)$ is the number such that $(a, f(a)) \in \Gamma$. □

Since in average students have only two minutes for each multiple-choice question, and fifteen minutes for each free response question, plotting graphs by randomly chosen points is the way to fail the exam. There are two different methods to plot graphs fast. The first is based on a database of standard graphs like graphs of parabolas, hyperbolas and other basic graphs. Then using simple rules of graphs transformation one can plot many other graphs. The second approach is based on plotting the graph by its parts about particular points such as, for example, the y and x intercepts. This method uses the principle "simple formula - simple graph". Here are three important graphs which one always must keep in mind solving problems of AP Tests, see Fig 2.1.

Problem 2.3. Using the standard graph of the parabola $y = x^2$, plot the graph of the function $y = -(x + 2)^2 + 1$.

Solution: We can obtain the graph of the given function in two steps. First, we reflect the graph of $y = x^2$ with respect to the coordinate x-axis. Second, we shift the graph obtained one unit up and two units left so that the vertex of the parabola will be at $(-2, 1)$.

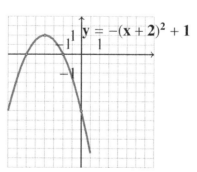

This graph can also be plotted by the second method. The x-intercepts of the graph are $x = -3$ and $x = -1$. Hence the vertex of the parabola has coordinates $(-2, 1)$.

The y-intercept is $(0, -3)$. Now, we just connect four marked points of the graph by a smooth line.   □

Problem 2.4. Sketch the graph of the function

$$y = \frac{x^2 - 4x + 3}{x^2 + x - 2}.$$

Solution: We observe that

$$x^2 - 4x + 3 = (x - 1)(x - 3), \quad x^2 + x - 2 = (x + 2)(x - 1).$$

It follows that

$$\frac{x^2 - 4x + 3}{x^2 + x - 2} = \frac{(x - 1)(x - 3)}{(x + 2)(x - 1)} = \frac{x - 3}{x + 2} = 1 - \frac{5}{x + 2}. \tag{2.1}$$

The domain of the function is $x \neq 1$, $x \neq -2$. We plot the graph by its behaviour about particular points using the principle "Simple Formula – Simple Graph".

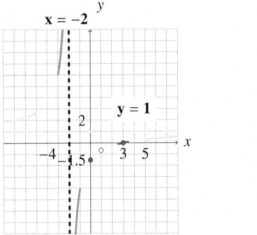 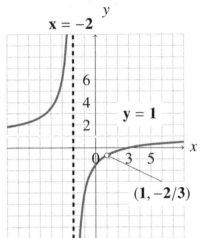

By (2.1) we see that the values of $y(x)$ are very close to $y = 1$ if x is big. Moreover, we can easily see that $y(x) > 1$ if $x < -2$ and $y(x) < 1$ if $x > -2$. These observations alow us to plot two parts of the graph indicated on the figure above. The function $y(x)$ is not determined at $x = -2$. If $x < -2$, then $y(x) > 1$ and is big provided x is close to -2. Similarly, $y(x) < 0$ and assumes negative values for $x > -2$ if x is close to -2. This gives us two extra parts of the graph. Since $y(0) = -1.5$, we conclude that the point $(0, -1.5)$ is on the graph. By (2.1) we see that $y(3) = 0$ and moreover, $y(x) \approx 0.5(x - 3)$ about $x = 3$. Finally, the point $(1, -2/3)$ must be excluded from the graph since $x = 1$ is not in the natural domain of $y(x)$. Connecting by simple smooth lines the parts of the graph constructed on the left figure, we obtain the graph of $y(x)$ on the right.   □

The line $y = 1$ is called the **horizontal asymptote** for the function $y = y(x)$ in Problem 2.4. The line $x = -2$ is called the **vertical asymptote** for $y = y(x)$, see the formal definitions 3.12 and 3.17 below.

Problem 2.5. Sketch the graph of the function

$$y = \frac{x^3 - 2x^2 + 10}{x^2 - x + 5}.$$

Solution: First we observe that the discriminant $1 - 20 = -19$ of the divisor $x^2 - x + 5$ is negative. This shows that the natural domain of the function $y(x)$ is the set of all real numbers $(-\infty, +\infty)$. We apply the Long Division of polynomials:

$$
\begin{array}{r}
x \quad -1 \\
\hline
x^2 - x + 5 \overline{)x^3 \quad -2x^2 \quad +0 \cdot x \quad +10} \\
\underline{x^3 \quad -x^2 \quad +5x} \\
-x^2 \quad -5x \quad +10 \\
\underline{-x^2 \quad +x \quad -5} \\
-6 \cdot x \quad +15
\end{array}
$$

It follows that

$$\frac{x^3 - 2x^2 + 10}{x^2 - x + 5} = x - 1 + \frac{-6x + 15}{x^2 - x + 5}. \tag{2.2}$$

This formula shows that the graph of $y(x)$ is placed above the line $y = x - 1$ if $x < 2.5$ and is placed below this line if $x > 2.5$. The graph of $y(x)$ and the line $y = x - 1$ have only one common point $(2.5, 1.5)$. Since $y(0) = 2$ we find the second important point $(0, 2)$ on the graph of $y(x)$. By (2.2) the graph of $y(x)$ is close to the line $y = x - 1$ if $|x|$ is big enough. This gives us two segments of the graph.

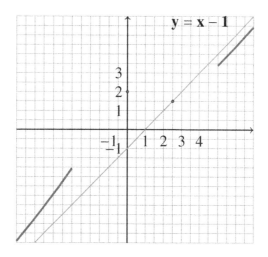

It remains to draw a smooth curve through $(0, 2)$, $(2.5, 1.5)$ which connects two segments pictured above. As result we obtain something like this:

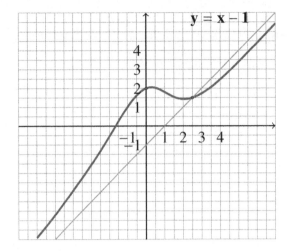

At this very moment we cannot justify completely the plot shown above. One of the goals of Differential Calculus is to develop theory which allows one to justify such plotting. But even with this theory at hand it is important first to draw the graph approximately and only after that justify everything with Differential Calculus. □

The line $y = x - 1$ is called the **oblique** asymptote for $y = y(x)$.

2.3. Implicit Functions

In AP Calculus implicit functions are families of functions defined by one formula. For example, let us consider the equation of a circle $x^2 + y^2 = 4$.

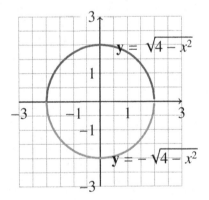
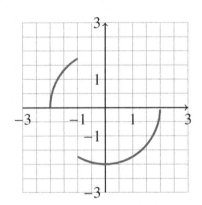

It determines an implicit function $y = y(x)$, which is represented by two branches as shown on the left picture. Notice that formally there are infinitely many branches,

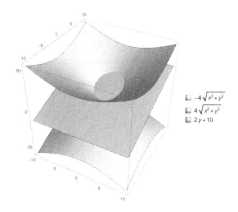

Figure 2.2: Ellipse as the intersection of a cone and a plane.

see an example on the right picture. However, since the main problem of Calculus is the study of tangents, branches are represented by 'continuous curve'.

Not every formula represents an implicit function. For instance, there are no points on the coordinate plane satisfying $x^2 + y^2 + 1 = 0$.

A general linear equation $Ax + By = C$ of a line determines an implicit function which may be represented explicitly if $B \neq 0$.

Let us consider the surface in the coordinate space defined by the formula

$$z^2 = a^2(x^2 + y^2), \ a > 0.$$

Every horizontal plane $z = c$ intersects this surface by the circle $x^2 + y^2 = c^2/a^2$ centered at the origin with radius $|c|/a$. It follows that this surface is nothing but a cone. It can be obtained by rotation of the line $z = ax$ about the z-axis.

The intersection of the cone with the coordinate plane

$$Kx + Ly + Mz = N$$

can be obtained by eliminating variable z if $M \neq 0$. Substituting the expression of z in x and y into the equation of the cone we obtain that this line is described by

$$Ax^2 + Bxy + Cy^2 + Dx + Ey + F = 0.$$

The equations of this form represent conic sections as soon as A, B, C are not all zeros and the equations do not degenerate.

Appollonius (262-200 B.C.) wrote a book titled "On Conic Sections" in which he showed that there are only three types of conic sections: ellipse (Fig 2.2), hyperbola (Fig 2.4) and parabola (Fig 2.3).

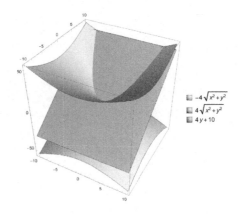

Figure 2.3: Parabola as the intersection of a cone and a plane.

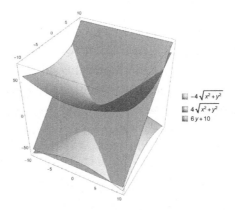

Figure 2.4: Hyperbola as the intersection of a cone and a plane.

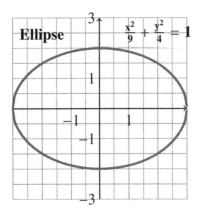 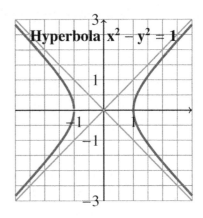

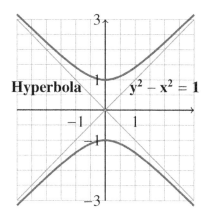 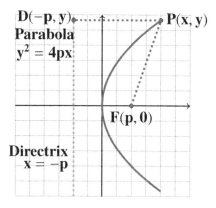

Theorem 2.6. *The parabola defined by the equation $y^2 = 4px$, $p > 0$, coincides with the set of all points equidistant from the directrix ($x = -p$) and the focus $(p, 0)$ of the parabola.*

Proof.

$$|DP|^2 = (x + p)^2 = x^2 + 2xp + p^2 = (x - p)^2 + 4px = (x - p)^2 + y^2 = |PF|^2 \qquad \square$$

Theorem 2.7 (Reflective Property of a Parabola). *The line tangent to a parabola at a point P makes equal angles with the line through P and parallel to the axis of symmetry and the line through P and the focus of the parabola.*

Proof. By Theorem 2.6 $FP = PD$. The dotted line through P is the bisectrix of $\angle FPD$. Since $|FQ| < |QD|$ for any point $Q \neq P$, we see that the bisectrix may have only one point in common with the parabola.

$$x^2 = 4py$$

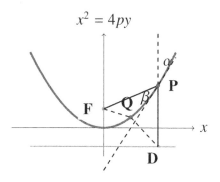

Similar arguments work for points above P. It follows that the bisectrix is tangent to the parabola at P. Then $\alpha = \beta$ by the theorem on vertical angles and the definition of bisectrix. $\qquad \square$

Reflective Property of a Parabola is used in mirrored parabolic troughs to focus sun beams on a pipe with fluid passing through the focus. The fluid is directed to a heat exchanger. The steam obtained is used to turn turbines generating electricity.

Problem 2.8. Find the equation of the directrix and the coordinates of the vertex and focus of the parabola given by the equation

$$3x + 2y^2 + 8y - 4 = 0.$$

Solution: Rewrite the equation so that the y terms are on one side of the equation, and then complete the square on y:

$$2y^2 + 8y = -3x + 4$$
$$2(y^2 + 4y) = -3x + 4$$
$$2(y^2 + 4y + 4) = -3x + 4 + 8$$
$$2(y + 2)^2 = -3(x - 4)$$
$$(y + 2)^2 = -1.5(x - 4).$$

We find the coordinates of the vertex of the parabola and p:

$$\textbf{vertex} = (4, -2) \quad 4p = -\frac{3}{2} \Rightarrow p = -\frac{3}{8}$$

Hence the parabola opens to the left.
The coordinates of the focus are:

$$\left(4 + \left(-\frac{3}{8}, -2\right)\right) = \left(\frac{29}{8}, -2\right)$$

The equation of the directrix is

$$x = 4 - \left(-\frac{3}{8}\right) = \frac{35}{8}$$

□

2.4. An Application of Conic Sections

In 1988 Jurij Franko at the Slovenian ski company, Elan, developed shaped skis which made it possible to perform carve turns at low speed and short turn radius, see Fig 2.5.

The side-cuts of shaped skis have a form of a parabola. Therefore, if the skis move downhill under angle they move along the corresponding branch of the parabola with the directrix directed to the steepest descent of the mountain terrain. Since this branch of the parabola is going right/left and down the speed increases but not significantly. Notice that elliptic skis will tend to be directed perpendicular to the steepest descent, whereas the hyperbolic skis tend to approach the asymptote of the hyperbola. This results in significant speed increase especially on steep

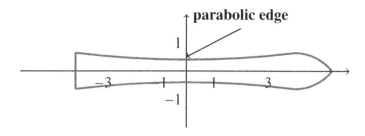

Figure 2.5: Carving Skis.

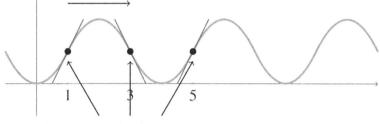

Figure 2.6: Carving Path of Parabolic Skis.

slopes, see Fig 2.7, since they move very close to straight lines. Fig 2.7 shows that hyperbolic skis move in the direction of the asymptote almost 50% of the path. Therefore, only parabolic skis give a possibility to move as a train on rails. Since all three types of conic sections can be easily obtained by cutting cones with planes, the ski-cuts in the form of conic sections are not so difficult to make. The above analysis shows that the parabolic skis are the best choice, see Fig 2.6.

$$y = \begin{cases} x^2 & \text{if } -1 \le x \le 1; \\ -(x-2)^2 + 2 & \text{if } 1 \le x \le 3; \\ (x-4)^2 & \text{if } 3 \le x \le 5; \\ -(x-6)^2 + 2 & \text{if } 5 \le x \le 7; \\ (x-8)^2 & \text{if } 7 \le x \le 9; \\ \dots \dots \dots \end{cases} \tag{2.3}$$

The formula for the path of carving is given in (2.3). Such functions defined by multi-line formulas are very common in Calculus AP Tests.

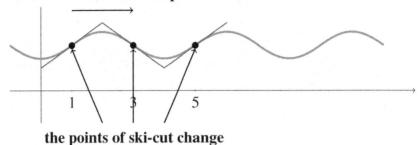

the points of ski-cut change

Figure 2.7: The Path of Hyperbolic Skis.

2.5. Exponents and Logarithms

Suppose that \$1000 are invested at 5% interest compounded annually. To determine the value of this investment in one year we apply the formula

$$I_1 = 1000\left(1 + \frac{5}{100}\right) = 1000 \cdot 1.05 = 1050.$$

If the interest rate is fixed then the value of the investment in n years equals

$$I_n = 1000\left(1 + \frac{5}{100}\right)^n = 1000 \cdot 1.05^n. \tag{2.4}$$

Definition 2.9. A sequence $\{I_n\}_{n \geq 0}$ is called a **geometric sequence** if

$$I_n = C \cdot a^n \tag{2.5}$$

for some a, $a > 0$, $a \neq 1$ and for some constant C, $C \neq 0$.

Any geometric sequence is a function defined on the set $\mathbb{N}$ of all natural numbers. If $C = 1$ then this function satisfies the functional equation

$$a^{x+y} = a^x \cdot a^y. \tag{2.6}$$

Using this formula, we extend the exponential function $y = a^x$ to the set of all integers $\mathbb{Z}$:

$$a^{-n} = \frac{1}{a^n}, \quad n \in \mathbb{N}, a^0 = 1,$$

so that the functional equation (2.6) holds true for all integer x and y. Applying surds to both sides of (2.6), we see that

$$\sqrt[q]{a^{x+y}} = \sqrt[q]{a^x} \cdot \sqrt[q]{y}.$$

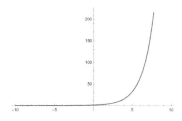

Figure 2.8: Exponential function $y = 2^x$.

Hence if we define $a^{\frac{x}{q}} = \sqrt[q]{a^x}$, then the exponential function extends to the set of all rational numbers so that (2.6) holds for rational x and y.

If x is irrational, then we can approximate x by cutting its decimal fraction at appropriate places. For instance,

$$x = \sqrt{2} = 1.41421356237309504880168872421\ldots \Rightarrow$$
$$2^{\sqrt{2}} \approx 2^{1.414213562373} \approx 2.665144142690.$$

The rigorous theory of real numbers, which is beyond the scope of AP Calculus, justifies this method.

To plot the graph of $y = 2^x$ we evaluate 2^n for $n = 0, 1, \ldots, 10$. The result is present in the table

n	0	1	2	3	4	5	6	7	8	9	10
2^n	1	2	4	8	16	32	64	128	256	512	1024

Now if we try to plot the graph of $y = 2^x$ in the coordinate axis with 1 cm step, then the width of the graph will be 10 cm, whereas the hight 1024 cm, which is greater than 10 meters. It follows that such a graph cannot be included in this book. The fast growth of the exponential function a^x, $a > 1$, suits well for description of catastrophic processes. In practice, the graph of $y = a^x$ is plotted with re-scaling of the y-coordinates, see Fig 2.8.

Notice, that this conclusion means, by the way, that the common bank practice of calculating interests, see (2.4), has a catastrophic character. The reason why this happens is explained by **logarithms** and by the Weber-Fechner law.

It is seen from Fig 2.8 that any horizontal line $y = c$, $c > 0$, intersects the graph of $y = 2^x$ only at one point. In other words, the equation $2^x = y$ has a unique solution in x for every $y > 0$. The correspondence $y \rightarrow x$ in the equation $y = 2^x$ defines a very important function called **logarithm**. Since we consider x as an independent variable, we replace y with x and x with y in the correspondence shown above.

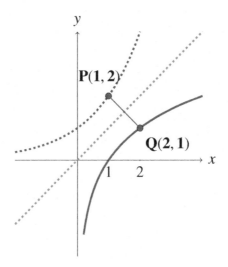

Figure 2.9: The Graph of $y = \log_2 x$.

The logarithm is defined for every a, $a > 0$, $a \neq 1$. We can restate the above definition in terms of the formula:

$$a^{\log_a x} = x.$$ (2.7)

Here $\log_a x$ is the only number satisfying (2.7).

The Weber-Fechner law says that the human being response to physical phenomena obeys the logarithmic law, see [9]. This ability of human beings makes them less sensitive to the changes of the outside world by converting the outside impulses of exponential growth into a linear scale and reduces the reactions to the most significant ones. A human being cannot control too many parameters at the same time and the Weber-Fechner law is a consequence of this fact. From the point of view of Mathematics this means that any outside event $h(t)$ is transformed into $\log_2 h(t)$ by the organs of feelings. The Weber-Fechner law provides a simple explanation why the interest rate of an investment is defined by an exponential function. That is the only function, which allows an investor to notice some growth of the investment made. Applying logarithms to the formula (2.4), we obtain that

$$\log_{10} I_n = 3 + n \log_{10} 1.05.$$

So the investor 'feels' the increment of $n \log_{10} 1.05$, which his/her investment got in one year.

The graph of $y = \log_2 x$ is the symmetric reflection of the graph $y = 2^x$ with respect to the line $y = x$. The symmetric reflection appears only because we make the substitution $y \leftrightarrow x$ in the definition of the logarithm. On the Graph this substitution looks like $(x, y) \leftrightarrow (y, x)$, see the points P and Q on Fig 2.9.

Theorem 2.10 (Rules of Logarithms). *Let a > 0, a ≠ 1. Then for any positive numbers x and y*

1. **ProductRule** : $\log_a xy = \log_a x + \log_a y$;

2. **QuotientRule** : $\log_a \dfrac{x}{y} = \log_a x - \log_a y$;

3. **ReciprocalRule** : $\log_a \dfrac{x}{y} = \log_a x - \log_a y$;

4. **PowerRule** : $\log_a x^y = y \log_a x$;

Proof. We prove only the **Product Rule**. Other rules can be proved similarly. By (2.6) we have:

$$a^{\log_a xy} = xy = a^{\log_a x} \cdot a^{\log_a y} = a^{\log_a x + \log_a y}$$

Since a^x takes any positive value only once, we conclude that the **Product Rule** holds. □

Theorem 2.11 (Euler's Change of Base Formula). *Let a and b be positive numbers neither of which equals 1. And let x > 0. Then*

$$\boxed{\log_a x = \frac{\log_b x}{\log_b a}}.$$

Proof. By (2.7) we have

$$b^{\log_b x} = x = a^{\log_a x} = \left(b^{\log_b a}\right)^{\log_a x} = b^{(\log_b a)(\log_a x)} \Leftrightarrow$$

$$\log_b x = (\log_b a)(\log_a x) \Leftrightarrow \log_a x = \frac{\log_b x}{\log_b a}. \qquad □$$

Equations of tangent lines to exponential and logarithmic functions cannot be obtained by Descarte's method. Let us illustrate this on the example of $y = 2^x$ and the point $(0, 1)$, which is on the graph of this function. To find the equation of the tangent line at $(0, 1)$ we must find such a number k that the equation

$$0 = 2^x - (kx + 1) = 2^x - 1 - kx$$

has a multiple root at $x = 0$. This equation is not algebraic and, therefore, Descartes' method fails.

By this very reason both functions $y = a^x$ and $y = \log_a x$ in some courses of Calculus are called 'early transcendental'. The main purpose of Differential Calculus is to develop methods to find equations of tangents for transcendental curves.

2.6. Inverse Functions

Definition 2.12. If f and g are functions, the **composite** $f \circ g$ (''f composed with g'') is defined by

$$f \circ g(x) = f(g(x)).$$

The domain $f \circ g$ consists of x in $\mathcal{D}(g)$ such that $g(x)$ is in $\mathcal{D}(f)$.

For example, let $f(x) = 2^x$ and $g(x) = -x^2$. Then $f \circ g(x) = 2^{-x^2}$. The domain of $f \circ g$ is $\mathbb{R}$. If $f(x) = \log_2 x$ and $g(x) = -x^2$, then $f \circ g(x)$ has no sense for every x in $\mathbb{R}$. In this case $f \circ g$ is an 'empty function'.

Definition 2.13. A function g is called an inverse function for a function f if

(a) $\mathcal{D}(g) = \mathcal{R}(f)$;

(b) $g \circ f(x) = x$ for every x in $\mathcal{D}(f)$.

For example, by (2.7) $y = a^x$ is the inverse function for $y = \log_a x$. By the Power Rule the function $y = \log_a x$ is the inverse function for $y = a^x$.

Theorem 2.14. *If an inverse function exists, then it is unique.*

Proof. Let g_1 and g_2 be inverse functions for f. Then $\mathcal{D}(g_1) = \mathcal{D}(g_2) = \mathcal{R}(f)$. So, if y is a number in $\mathcal{R}(f)$, then $y = f(x)$ for some x in $\mathcal{D}(f)$. By the definition of an inverse function

$$g_1(y) = g_1 \circ f(x) = x = g_2 \circ f(x) = g_2(y).$$

It follows that g_1 and g_2 have equal domains and take equal values at equal points. $\square$

The inverse function for a function $f(x)$ is denoted by $f^{-1}(x)$ or simply f^{-1}. Do not confuse this function with $1/f(x)$.

Definition 2.15. A function f is called one-to-one if it has the inverse function.

For example, the function $y = x$ is one-to-one and the function $y = x^2$ is not.

Theorem 2.16 (The Horizontal Line Test). *A function $y = f(x)$ is one-to-one if and only if every horizontal line intersects its graph at most once.*

Proof. The horizontal line through $(0, y)$ intersects the graph of f at a point (x, y) if and only if y is in $\mathcal{R}(f)$. If this point of intersection is unique, then $g(y) = x$ is the inverse function. If the inverse function exists, then the point of intersection exists and unique and is given by $(g(y), y)$. $\square$

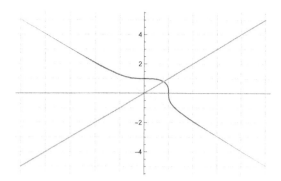

Figure 2.10: The inverse function to $y = \sqrt[3]{1 - x^3}$.

Problem 2.17. Plot the graph and find the inverse function to

$$y = \sqrt[3]{1 - x^3}.$$

Solution: To prove that the inverse function exists, we solve the equation $y = \sqrt[3]{1 - x^3}$ in x:

$$y = \sqrt[3]{1 - x^3} \Leftrightarrow y^3 = 1 - x^3 \Leftrightarrow x^3 = 1 - y^3 \Leftrightarrow x = \sqrt[3]{1 - y^3}.$$

Applying the substitution $x \leftrightarrow y$, we obtain that the inverse function is the function $y = \sqrt[3]{1 - x^3}$ itself.

To plot the graph of $y = \sqrt[3]{1 - x^3}$ we observe that

$$y = \sqrt[3]{1 - x^3} = x\sqrt[3]{\frac{1}{x^3} - 1} = -x\sqrt[3]{1 - \frac{1}{x^3}} \sim -x,$$

if $|x|$ is big.

Observing that $-x < \sqrt[3]{1 - x^3}$ for every x, we conclude that the graph of $y = \sqrt[3]{1 - x^3}$ is placed above its asymptote $y = -x$. Since this function is the inverse for itself, its graph must be symmetric with respect to the line $y = x$. The graph intersects the line $y = x$ at the point $(1/\sqrt[3]{2}, 1/\sqrt[3]{2})$. See the graph on Fig 2.10.   □

Problem 2.18. Find the inverse function for

$$y = \log_2(x + \sqrt{x^2 + 1})$$

and plot its graph.

Solution:

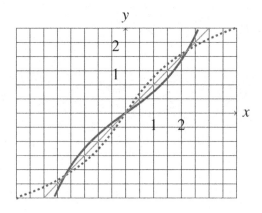

We solve the equation $y = \log_2(x + \sqrt{x^2 + 1})$ in x:

$$y = \log_2(x + \sqrt{x^2 + 1}) \Leftrightarrow 2^y - x = \sqrt{x^2 + 1} \Leftrightarrow (2^y - x)^2 = 1 + x^2 \Leftrightarrow$$

$$2^{2y} - 2 \cdot x \cdot 2^y + x^2 = 1 + x^2 \Leftrightarrow x = \frac{2^y - 2^{-y}}{2}.$$

It follows that

$$y = \frac{2^x - 2^{-x}}{2}$$

is the inverse function. Since $y(-x) = -y(x)$, the graph of y is symmetric with respect to the center $(0, 0)$ of the coordinates. Since $y(0) = 0$ and $y(x) \sim 0.5 \cdot e^x$ for big positive x, the graph can be obtained by the principle "Simple Formula - Simple Graph. $\qquad\square$

Definition 2.19. let $y = f(x)$ be a function with a domain $\mathcal{D}$ symmetric with respect to the point $x = 0$. Then f is called **even** if $f(x) = f(-x)$ for every x in $\mathcal{D}$, and is called **odd** if $f(x) = -f(-x)$ for every x in $\mathcal{D}$

Both functions in Problem 2.18 are odd. For the direct function this follows from the calculations:

$$y(-x) = \log_2(\sqrt{x^2 + 1} - x) = \log_2 \frac{(\sqrt{x^2 + 1} - x)(\sqrt{x^2 + 1} + x)}{\sqrt{x^2 + 1} + x} =$$

$$\log_2 \frac{((\sqrt{x^2 + 1})^2 - x^2)}{\sqrt{x^2 + 1} + x} = \log_2 \frac{1}{\sqrt{x^2 + 1} + x} = -\log_2(\sqrt{x^2 + 1} + x) = -y(x).$$

Since the graph of the inverse function is symmetric with respect to the line $y = x$, it must be odd too.

The notions of even and odd functions are useful in plotting graphs since they reduce the amount of work required.

Definition 2.20. A function $y = f(x)$ is called **strictly increasing (increasing)** if for any two numbers x_1 and x_2 in $\mathcal{D}(f)$

$$x_1 < x_2 \Rightarrow f(x_1) < f(x_2) \quad (f(x_1) \leq f(x_2)).$$

A function $y = f(x)$ is called **strictly decreasing (decreasing)** if $-f(x)$ is **strictly increasing (increasing)**.

Definition 2.21. A function $y = f(x)$ is called **strictly monotonic (monotonic)** if it is either **strictly increasing (increasing)** or **strictly decreasing (decreasing)**.

Theorem 2.22. *Let $f(x)$ be a strictly monotonic function. Then it has the inverse function.*

Proof. We apply the Horizontal Line Test. If a horizontal line $y = c$ intersects the graph of $y = f(x)$ more than at one point, then there exist two different x_1 and x_2 in $\mathcal{D}(f)$ such that $f(x_1) = f(x_2) = c$. Since $x_1 \neq x_2$, we have either $x_1 < x_2$ or $x_2 < x_1$. Both cases lead to a contradiction. It follows that the Horizontal Line Test holds and f^{-1} exists. □

It is not true that only strictly monotonic functions have the inverse. Let

$$f(x) = \begin{cases} x & \text{if } x \text{ is rational} \\ -x & \text{if } x \text{ is irrational} \end{cases}$$

Then obviously $f \circ f(x) = x$ for every x. It follows that $f^{-1} = f$.

2.7. Trigonometric Functions

Calculus AP exams require very basic trigonometry. In trigonometry angles are directed:

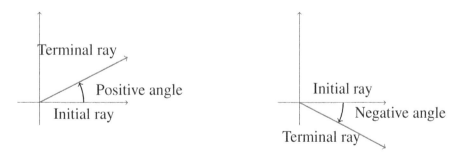

An angle is directed from the **initial** ray to the **terminal** ray. Positive angles are directed **counterclockwise**. Trigonometric angles are measured in linear scale

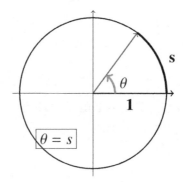

Figure 2.11: The Radian Measure.

in degrees and radians. The degree scale is determined by conditions that the zero angle (the initial ray is not rotated and is equal to the terminal ray) has 0° and the full angle (the initial ray is rotated counterclockwise and coincides with the terminal ray) has 360°. In the degree scale the straight angle (one half of the full angle) has 180° and the right angle (one quarter of the full angle) has 90°.

The degree scale goes back to Babylon and is not in a good correspondence with formulas of Calculus. The reason is that the number 360 assigned to the full angle is accidental. One of the main problems of Mathematics in ancient times was to measure the length of a circle of radius r. Elementary Geometry says that the area of the domain bounded by a circle of radius r equals πr^2, whereas its length equals $2\pi r$. Here π is an universal constant. Its precise value attracted the attention of a great number of mathematicians. Nowadays, with computers one can easily evaluate π with quite a high accuracy:

$$\pi \approx 3.14159265358979323846264338327950288419711693993751.$$

By Theorem 1.16 the slope of the tangent to the curve $y = \pi r^2$ at r is $y = 2\pi r$. Since Differential Calculus studies the slopes of tangents to curves, it looks reasonable to measure angles by the length s of the arc which the angle cuts from the **unit** circle centered at the vertex of the angle.

Definition 2.23. An angle of one **radian** is the angle subtended by the unit circle arc of length one, see Fig 2.11.

It follows that the full angle equals 2π radians. Since both scales are linear, we can easily switch from degrees to radians and vice versa by the following formulas:

$$\textbf{degrees} = \textbf{radians} \times \frac{180}{\pi} \qquad \textbf{radians} = \textbf{degrees} \times \frac{\pi}{180}.$$

Since time given for AP Calculus exams is restricted, it is a good idea to learn the table below by heart.

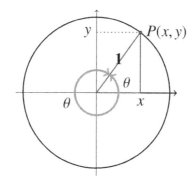

Figure 2.12: The Reference Triangle.

Degrees	30	45	60	90	120	135	150	180
Radians	$\frac{\pi}{6}$	$\frac{\pi}{4}$	$\frac{\pi}{3}$	$\frac{\pi}{2}$	$\frac{2\pi}{3}$	$\frac{3\pi}{4}$	$\frac{5\pi}{6}$	π

Trigonometric functions are defined by the reference triangle. This is the right triangle with one vertex at the origin and another one at the point of intersection of the terminal ray with the unit circle. Notice that one reference triangle corresponds to an infinite number of trigonometric angles. These angles differ from each other by an integer number of full turns. The vertex $P(x, y)$ can be at any point of the unit circle. Using the reference triangle, see Fig 2.12, we define

$$\boxed{x = \cos\theta, \quad y = \sin\theta}.$$

The reference triangles show that $\cos\theta$ is even and $\sin\theta$ is odd.

Definition 2.24. A function $f(x)$ defined on $\mathbb{R}$ is called **periodic** if there is a positive number T such that

$$f(x + T) = f(x)$$

for every value of x. This number T is called a period of f. The smallest such value P of T, if exists, is called the **fundamental period** of f.

Any constant function $f(x) \equiv c$ is periodic, but neither of them has the fundamental period. The functions $\sin\theta$ and $\cos\theta$ are periodic since by definition

$$\sin(\theta + 2\pi) = \sin\theta, \quad \cos(\theta + 2\pi) = \cos\theta.$$

Lemma 2.25. *If T is a period for $f(x)$, then*

$$f(x) = f(x + n \cdot T)$$

for every x in $\mathbb{R}$ and every integer n.

Proof. If n is a positive integer, then

$$f(x) = f(x + 1 \cdot T) = f(x + 2 \cdot T) = \cdots = f(x + n \cdot T).$$

If $-n$ is a positive integer, then

$$f(x - n \cdot T) = f(x - (n - 1) \cdot T) = \cdots = f(x - T) = f(x) \qquad \square$$

Theorem 2.26. *If P is the fundamental period of $f(x)$ and T is any positive period of $f(x)$, then there exists a positive integer n such that $T = n \cdot P$.*

Proof. Since P is the fundamental period of $f(x)$ and T is its period, we conclude that $P \leq T$. If $P = T$, then the proof is finished. If $P < T$, then there exists a unique positive integer n such that $nP \leq T < (n+1)P$. If $nP \neq T$, then the number $S = (n+1)P - T$ satisfies $0 < S < P$ and by Lemma 2.25 is a period of $f(x)$, which contradicts the assumption that P is the fundamental period of $f(x)$. It follows that $nP = T$ as stated. $\qquad \square$

Here is the table of particular values of $\sin \theta$ and $\cos \theta$.

Degrees	30	45	60	90	120	135	150	180
Radians	$\dfrac{\pi}{6}$	$\dfrac{\pi}{4}$	$\dfrac{\pi}{3}$	$\dfrac{\pi}{2}$	$\dfrac{2\pi}{3}$	$\dfrac{3\pi}{4}$	$\dfrac{5\pi}{6}$	π
$\sin \theta$	$\dfrac{1}{2}$	$\dfrac{\sqrt{2}}{2}$	$\dfrac{\sqrt{3}}{2}$	1	$\dfrac{\sqrt{3}}{2}$	$\dfrac{\sqrt{2}}{2}$	$\dfrac{1}{2}$	0
$\cos \theta$	$\dfrac{\sqrt{3}}{2}$	$\dfrac{\sqrt{2}}{2}$	$\dfrac{1}{2}$	0	$-\dfrac{1}{2}$	$-\dfrac{\sqrt{2}}{2}$	$-\dfrac{\sqrt{3}}{2}$	-1

Theorem 2.27. *The fundamental period of $\sin \theta$ is 2π.*

Proof. The reference triangle shows that the function $\sin \theta$ strictly increases on the interval $[0, \pi/2]$ and strictly decreases on the interval $[\pi/2, \pi]$. Since $\sin 0 = 0$, this implies that any period is greater or equal π. It cannot be π since $\sin \pi/2 = 1$ and $\sin(\pi + \pi/2) = -1$. It cannot be greater than π and smaller than 2π since $\sin 0 = 0$ and $\sin(0 + T) < 0$ for $\pi < T < 2\pi$. Since 2π is a period, it is the fundamental period. $\qquad \square$

Using reference triangle, we can easily see that

$$\sin\left(\theta + \frac{\pi}{2}\right) = \cos \theta. \qquad (2.8)$$

It follows that the fundamental period of $\cos \theta$ is also 2π.

Using the table of values for $\sin x$, we make the data plot of these points. Connecting them with a smooth curve, we obtain a sketch of the graph of $y = \sin x$.

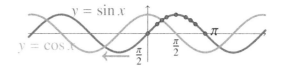

Figure 2.13: The Graphs of $y = \sin x$ and $y = \cos x$.

The graph of $y = \cos x$ is the right shift of the graph of $y = \sin x$ by $\pi/2$, see (2.8) and 2.13.

There is a deep formula discovered by Euler:

$$e^{i\theta} = \cos\theta + i\sin\theta. \tag{2.9}$$

Here e is the number

$$e = 2.71828182845904523536028747135266249775724709370000\ldots.$$

Number e originates in formulas for interest rates compounded continuously and will be discussed in more details later. Number i is a root of the quadratic equation $x^2 + 1 = 0$, which has no solutions in real numbers. It is a complex number. This topic is beyond Calculus AP, but it explains an important relationship of trigonometric functions with exponential functions. If we put $\theta = \pi$ in (2.9), then we obtain the following formula

$$e^{i\pi} = -1.$$

It relates the three most important fundamental constants of Analysis: e, π and i. Euler's formula also shows that

$$\sin\theta = \frac{e^{i\theta} - e^{-i\theta}}{2i}, \quad \cos\theta = \frac{e^{i\theta} + e^{-i\theta}}{2}.$$

Formula (2.9) is very useful to recover the trigonometric formulas for $\cos(x + y)$ and $\sin(x + y)$:

$$\begin{cases} \cos(x + y) & = \cos x \cos y - \sin x \sin y \\ \sin(x + y) & = \sin x \cos y + \sin y \cos x \end{cases} \tag{2.10}$$

Indeed,

$$\cos(x + y) + i\sin(x + y) = e^{i(x+y)} = e^{ix} \cdot e^{iy} = (\cos x + i\sin x) \cdot (\cos y + i\sin y) =$$
$$= \cos x \cos y + i^2 \sin x \sin y + i(\sin x \cos y + \sin y \cos x) =$$
$$\cos x \cos y - \sin x \sin y + i(\sin x \cos y + \sin y \cos x).$$

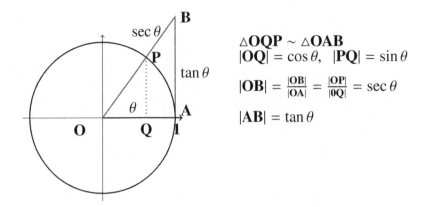

Figure 2.14: $\sec\theta$ and $\tan\theta$.

Let us put $y := -y$ in the first equation of (2.10) and subtract the equation obtained from the initial one. Then

$$\cos(x + y) - \cos(x - y) = -2\sin x \sin y.$$

Substituting

$$\begin{cases} x + y & = A \\ x - y & = B \end{cases} \Leftrightarrow \begin{cases} x & = \frac{A+B}{2} \\ y & = \frac{A-B}{2} \end{cases},$$

we obtain the following formula

$$\cos A - \cos B = -2\sin\frac{A+B}{2}\sin\frac{A-B}{2}. \tag{2.11}$$

Similarly,

$$\cos A + \cos B = 2\cos\frac{A+B}{2}\cos\frac{A-B}{2},$$
$$\sin A + \sin B = 2\sin\frac{A+B}{2}\cos\frac{A-B}{2}, \tag{2.12}$$
$$\sin A - \sin B = 2\cos\frac{A+B}{2}\sin\frac{A-B}{2}.$$

Besides $\sin x$ and $\cos x$ the following four trigonometric functions are also important in AP Calculus:

$$\tan\theta = \frac{\sin\theta}{\cos\theta} \quad \cot\theta = \frac{\cos\theta}{\sin\theta}$$
$$\csc\theta = \frac{1}{\sin\theta} \quad \sec\theta = \frac{1}{\cos\theta}$$

With $\sec\theta$ one can easily measure the distance $|OP|$ to the top B of a high object as soon as the distance to its bottom A is known. Similarly, $\tan\theta$ is useful to determine the height $|AB|$, see Fig 2.14.

The following formulas are important:

$$1 = \sin^2 x + \cos^2 x \qquad \cos 2x = \cos^2 x - \sin^2 x \qquad \sin 2x = 2 \sin x \cos x$$

$$\sec^2 x = 1 + \tan^2 x \qquad \csc^2 x = 1 + \cot^2 x \qquad \tan 2x = \frac{2 \tan x}{1 - \tan^2 x}$$

2.8. Inverse Trigonometric Functions

Definition 2.28. For $-1 \le x \le 1$ arcsin x is the angle in $[-\pi/2, \pi/2]$ such that

$$\sin(\arcsin x) = x,$$

and arccos x is the angle in $[0, \pi]$ such that

$$\cos(\arccos x) = x.$$

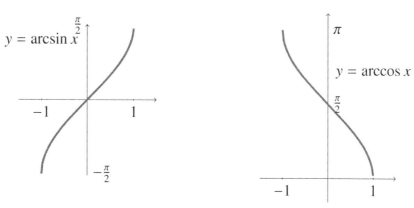

The restriction of $y = \sin x$ to the closed interval $[-\pi/2, \pi/2]$ is the inverse function for $y = \arcsin x$. Similarly, the restriction of $y = \cos x$ to the closed interval $[0, \pi]$ is the inverse function for $y = \arccos x$. Therefore, many courses of Calculus make use of the following notations

$$\sin^{-1} x = \arcsin x, \quad \cos^{-1} x = \arccos x.$$

Definition 2.29. For $x \in \mathbb{R}$ arctan x is the angle in $(-\pi/2, \pi/2)$ satisfying

$$\tan(\arctan x) = x.$$

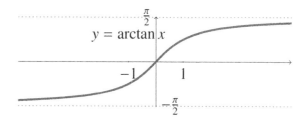

Definition 2.30. For $x \in \mathbb{R}$ arccot$x$ is the angle in $(0, \pi)$ satisfying

$$\cot(\text{arccot}x) = x.$$

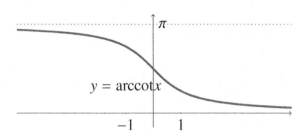

Problems

Prob. 25 — Determine the natural domain of the function $y = \sqrt{6 + x - x^2}$.

Prob. 26 — Sketch the graph of the function: $y = \cos 2(x - 1)$.

Prob. 27 — Sketch the graph of the implicit function: $4y^2 - x - 24y + 35 = 0$.

Prob. 28 — Which of the following represents the graph of $f(x)$ moved to the left:

(A) $f(x - 3)$ (B) $f(x) - 3$ (C) $f(x + 3)$ (D) $f(x) + 3$.

Prob. 29 — Find equations of tangent lines to the curve $2x^2 - 5y^2 = 3$, passing through the point $P(1.5; 0.6)$.

Prob. 30 — Find equations for tangents to the curve $(x - 2)^2 + (y - 2)^2 = 2$ passing through the origin.

Prob. 31 — Find equations of tangents to the curve $9x^2 + 4y^2 = 72$ through the point $P(8; 18)$.

Prob. 32 — Find equations of tangent lines to the curve $2y^2 - 4y - x + 4 = 0$ passing through the origin.

Prob. 33 — Find equations of tangent lines to the circle $x^2 + y^2 = 9$ passing through $P(2; -4)$. Find equations of normal lines to the circle at the points of tangency.

Prob. 34 — Sketch the graph of the function

$$y = x + \frac{1}{x}.$$

Prob. 35 — Sketch the graph of the function

$$y = \frac{x^2}{1 + x}.$$

Prob. 36 — Sketch the graph of the function (Witch of Agnesi):

$$y = \frac{4}{1 + x^2}.$$

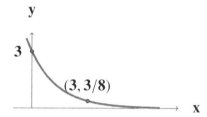

Prob. 37 — The graph of $y = Ca^x$ is plotted above. Find C and a.

Prob. 38 — Simplify

$$\log_3\left(\frac{64}{125}\right) = \textbf{(A)}\ \frac{4}{5}\ \ \textbf{(B)}\ -1\ \ \textbf{(C)}\ 6\log_3 2 - 3\log_3 5\ \ \textbf{(D)}\ \frac{6\log_3 2}{3\log_3 5}\ \ \textbf{(E)}\ \frac{5}{4}$$

Prob. 39 — Simplify

$$\log_3\left(\frac{1}{x} + \frac{1}{x^2}\right) = \textbf{(A)}\ -3\log_3 x\ \ \textbf{(B)}\ \log_3(x+1) - \log_3 x^2$$

$$\textbf{(C)}\ \log_3(x+1) - 2\log_3 x\ \ \textbf{(D)}\ \log_3 1\ \ \textbf{(E)}\ \log_3(x - x^2)$$

Prob. 40 — If $f(x) = 2x - 1$ and $g(x) = x + 3$, which of the following gives the value of the composition $f \circ g$ at point $x = 2$?

$$\textbf{(A)}\ 2\ \ \textbf{(B)}\ 6\ \ \textbf{(C)}\ 7\ \ \textbf{(D)}\ 9\ \ \textbf{(E)}\ 10$$

Prob. 41 — Show that the composition of two polynomials is a polynomial too.

Prob. 42 — Find the inverse function of $y = 3x - 2$.

Prob. 43 — Find the inverse of the function

$$y = \begin{cases} x & \text{if } x \le 0 \\ x^2 & \text{if } x > 0 \end{cases}$$

Prob. 44 — Find the inverse function of $y = \log_2(1 - 2^{-x})$.

(A) $y = \log_2\left(\dfrac{1}{1 - 2^x}\right)$ (B) $y = \log_2(1 - 2^x)$ (C) $y = \log_2(2^x - 1)$

(D) $y = \log_2\left(\dfrac{1}{2^x - 1}\right)$ (E) **does not exist**

Prob. 45 — Find the inverse function of $f(x) = \frac{2x+1}{x+3}$.

(A) $y = \dfrac{x + 3}{2x + 1}$ (B) $y = \dfrac{2x + 1}{x + 3}$ (C) $y = \dfrac{1 - 3x}{x - 2}$

(D) $x = \dfrac{1 - 3y}{y - 2}$ (E) **does not exist**

Prob. 46 — Find the inverse function to the function $y = 4 \arcsin \sqrt{1 - x^2}$.

Prob. 47 — Find the inverse function to the function

$$y = 1 + \frac{2^x - 2^{-x}}{2^x + 2^{-x}}.$$

Prob. 48 — Prove that any function defined in the symmetric interval $(-a, a)$ is a sum of an even function and odd function.

Prob. 49 — The population of a city is 375 000 and is increasing 2.25% per year. In how many years the population will exceed one million? ($\lg 375 \approx 2.574$, $\lg 1.0225 \approx 0.00966$)

(A) 20   (B) 30   (C) 40   (D) 45   (E) 50

Prob. 50 — Let $f(x) = 3 - \ln(x + 2)$. What of the following is the range of f?

(A) $(-\infty, +\infty)$ (B) $(-\infty, 0)$ (C) $(-2, +\infty)$ (D) $(0, +\infty)$ (E) $(0, 5, 3)$

Prob. 51 —

$$\tan \frac{4\pi}{3} = \text{(A)} \ -\sqrt{3} \ \text{(B)} \ \frac{\sqrt{3}}{3} \ \text{(C)} \ \sqrt{3} \ \text{(D)} \ -\frac{\sqrt{3}}{3} \ \text{(E)} \ -2$$

Prob. 52 — The function $\sin^{-1} x = \arcsin x$ is defined for

(**A**) $-\dfrac{\pi}{2} \leq x \leq \dfrac{\pi}{2}$ (**B**) $0 \leq x \leq \pi$ (**C**) $-\pi \leq x \leq \pi$

(**D**) $-1 \leq x \leq 1$ (**E**) $0 \leq x \leq 2\pi$

Prob. 53 — The period of $y = \sin\left(\dfrac{x}{2}\right)$ is

(**A**) $\dfrac{\pi}{2}$ (**B**) 4π (**C**) 2π (**D**) 8π (**E**) $\dfrac{\pi}{4}$

Prob. 54 — Which of the following gives the solution of $\tan x = -1$ in $\pi < x < \dfrac{3\pi}{2}$?

(**A**) $-\dfrac{\pi}{4}$ (**B**) $\dfrac{\pi}{4}$ (**C**) $\dfrac{\pi}{3}$ (**D**) $\dfrac{3\pi}{4}$ (**E**) **no solutions**

Prob. 55 — Find the solutions of the equation $\cos x - \sin x = 1$ in $[0, 2\pi)$.

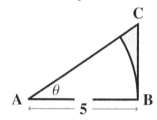

Prob. 56 — The shaded area in the figure above is the complement of the sector of a circle of radius 5 inches lying inside the right triangle $\triangle ABC$ with the angle θ. Express this shaded area as a function S of θ assuming that θ is expressed in radians.

(**A**) $S = 25(\tan\theta - \theta)$ (**B**) $S = 25(\sin\theta - \theta)$ (**C**) $S = 12.5(\sin\theta - \theta)$

D $S = 12.5(\cos\theta - \theta)$ **E** $12.5(\tan\theta - \theta)$

Prob. 57 — Apply the double-angle formula to prove:

$$\cos\frac{\pi}{16} = \frac{1}{2}\sqrt{2 + \sqrt{2 + \sqrt{2}}}$$

Chapter 3

Limits and Continuity

Abstract

The notion of limit as instantaneous rate of Change. Theorems on limits. Limits and asymptotes. Chains of intervals and Cauchy sequences. Continuous functions and Intermediate Value Theorem. Continuity of implicit functions. Demand and Supply Functions. The graph of Descartes' folium. Euler's number e and Financial Mathematics. Remarkable limits.

Keywords: average velocity, instantaneous rate of change, limit of a sequence, chain of intervals, Cauchy sequence, continuous function, intermediate value property, removable discontinuity, non-removable discontinuity, absolute maximum, absolute minimum, Extreme Value Theorem, separately continuous functions, equilibrium price, equilibrium equation, Sandwich Theorem,

3.1. Instantaneous Rate of Change

Newton essentially modified Descartes' method of tangents. He implemented a dynamical approach to this question. Suppose that a point moves along a straight line with variable velocity. At moment $t = 0$ it is at the origin. By time t its distance to the origin is given by the formula $s = 0.5 \cdot t^2$. Here 0.5 is a physical constant, which is measured in meters/sec^2 and t is time measured in seconds.

Now we find the equation of the tangent line to the graph of $s = 0.5t^2$ at $t_0 = 1$ using Newton's dynamical approach. If $t > t_0$, then the chord through $(t_0, s(t_0))$ and $(t, s(t))$ has the slope

$$\frac{s(t) - s(t_0)}{t - t_0} = 0.5\frac{t^2 - t_0^2}{t - t_0} = 0.5(t + t_0).$$

61

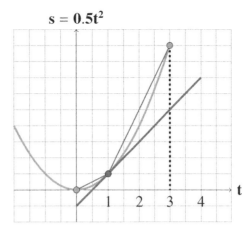

$$s = 0.5t^2$$

Figure 3.1: The Instantaneous Rate of Change.

From dynamical point of view it is nothing but the **average velocity** of the particle for the time interval $[t_0, t]$. When t approaches t_0, i.e. $t \to t_0$, the slope of the chord $0.5(t + t_0)$ approaches the slope of the tangent $0.5(t_0 + t_0) = t_0$, which coincides with the result obtained by Descartes' method.

Definition 3.1. Let f be a function defined on an interval $(a - \Delta, a + \Delta)$, $\Delta > 0$, except for possibly at a. Then

$$\lim_{x \to a} f(x) = L,$$

if for every $\varepsilon > 0$ there is $\delta = \delta(\varepsilon) > 0$ such that

$$0 < |x - a| < \delta(\varepsilon) \Rightarrow |f(x) - L| < \varepsilon. \tag{3.1}$$

In terms of the above definition we can write

$$\lim_{t \to t_0} \frac{s(t) - s(t_0)}{t - t_0} = t_0. \tag{3.2}$$

The function

$$f(t) = \frac{s(t) - s(t_0)}{t - t_0},$$

which evaluates the slope of the chord through two points, is not defined at $t = t_0$. This is the main reason why f in the definition of the limit is allowed to be not defined at $x = a$. By the same reason, $0 < |x - a|$ in (3.1). To justify (3.2) we notice that

$$\left| \frac{s(t) - s(t_0)}{t - t_0} - t_0 \right| = |0.5(t + t_0) - t_0| = 0.5|t - t_0| < \varepsilon,$$

if $|t - t_0| < \delta(\varepsilon) = 2\varepsilon$.

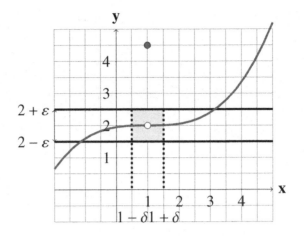

Figure 3.2: Graphical Definition of Limit.

Definition 3.2. If $y = f(x)$ is a function defined on an interval $(a - \Delta, a + \Delta)$ such that the following limit

$$\lim_{x \to a} \frac{f(x) - f(a)}{x - a} = f'(a)$$

exists, then the number $f'(a)$ is called the **instantaneous rate of change** of f at $x = a$, see Fig 3.1.

The instantaneous rate of change of a function is nothing but the slope of the tangent to the curve $y = f(x)$ at $x = a$. The method of limits allows us to evaluate slopes of tangents to graphs as soon as we can find (3.2). Since the implication (3.1) is an unusual statement for Elementary Mathematics, we illustrate it graphically.

The function shown on Fig 3.2 satisfies $\lim_{x \to 1} f(x) = 2$, since for every $\varepsilon > 0$ there is $\delta > 0$ such that the horizontal strip $2 - \varepsilon < y < 2 + \varepsilon$ being intersected with the vertical strip $1 - \delta < x < 1 + \delta$ (the gray area on the graph) contains all points of the graph of $f(x)$ except, possibly, point $(1, f(1))$, $f(1) = 4.5$.

Definition 3.3. Dealing with limits the following terminology is useful. We say that a property of a function f holds **about** a point a if there is $\Delta > 0$ such that this property holds in $(a - \delta, a + \Delta)$.

Theorem 3.4. *If* $\lim_{x \to a} f(x)$ *exists and is finite, then* f *is bounded about* a.

Proof. Put $\varepsilon = 1$ in the definition of limit. Then $\Delta = \delta(1)$. □

Theorem 3.5. *If* $\lim_{x \to a} f(x) = L$ *exists and positive, then* f *is positive about* a *except for, possibly, at* $x = a$ *itself.*

Proof. Put $\varepsilon - L/2$ in the definition of limit. Then $\Delta = \delta(L/2)$. □

Theorem 3.6. *For every function f the existence of the instantaneous rate of change at a implies the existence of limit:*

$$\lim_{x \to a} \frac{f(x) - f(a)}{x - a} = f'(a) \Rightarrow \lim_{x \to a} f(x) = f(a).$$

Proof. By Theorem 3.4 there is a positive constant M such that

$$\left| \frac{f(x) - f(a)}{x - a} \right| < M \quad \text{about} \quad a.$$

Let $\varepsilon > 0$. Then

$$|f(x) - f(a)| = \left| \frac{f(x) - f(a)}{x - a} \right| \cdot |x - a| < M \cdot |x - a|.$$

So, if $\delta(\varepsilon) = \varepsilon/M$, then

$$|x - a| < \delta \Rightarrow |f(x) - f(a)| < \varepsilon. \qquad \square$$

There is a useful notion of one-sided limits, which is helpful in AP Calculus tests.

Definition 3.7. Let f be a function defined on an interval (a, b), $a < b$. Then $\lim_{x \to a^+} f(x) = L$, if for every $\varepsilon > 0$ there is $\delta = \delta(\varepsilon) > 0$ such that

$$0 < x - a < \delta(\varepsilon) \Rightarrow |f(x) - L| < \varepsilon. \qquad (3.3)$$

Definition 3.8. Let f be a function defined on an interval (b, a), $b < a$. Then $\lim_{x \to a^-} f(x) = L$, if for every $\varepsilon > 0$ there is $\delta = \delta(\varepsilon) > 0$ such that

$$0 < a - x < \delta(\varepsilon) \Rightarrow |f(x) - L| < \varepsilon. \qquad (3.4)$$

Theorem 3.9. *Let $\Delta > 0$ and f be a function defined on an interval $(a - \Delta, a + \Delta)$ except for, possibly, the point a. Then $\lim_{x \to a} f(x) = L$ if and only if*

$$\lim_{x \to a^-} f(x) = \lim_{x \to a^+} f(x) = L.$$

Proof. It follows directly from the definitions. $\qquad \square$

3.2. Limits and Infinity

Definition 3.10. Let f be a function defined on some interval $[A, +\infty)$. We say that $f(x)$ has the limit L as x approaches **plus infinity** and write

$$\lim_{x \to +\infty} f(x) = L$$

if for every number $\epsilon > 0$ there exists a corresponding number M such that for all x

$$x > M \Rightarrow |f(x) - L| < \epsilon.$$

Let f be a function defined on some interval $(-\infty, B]$. We say that $f(x)$ has the limit L as x approaches **minus infinity** and write

$$\lim_{x \to -\infty} f(x) = L$$

if for every number $\epsilon > 0$ there exists a corresponding number N such that for all x

$$x < N \Rightarrow |f(x) - L| < \epsilon.$$

Theorem 3.11. *We have*

$$\lim_{x \to +\infty} f(x) = L \Leftrightarrow \lim_{x \to 0^+} f\left(\frac{1}{x}\right) = L,$$

$$\lim_{x \to -\infty} f(x) = L \Leftrightarrow \lim_{x \to 0^-} f\left(\frac{1}{x}\right) = L.$$

Proof. Obvious. □

Definition 3.12. A line $y = b$ is called a **horizontal asymptote** of the graph of a function $y = f(x)$ if either $\lim_{x \to +\infty} f(x) = b$ or $\lim_{x \to -\infty} f(x) = b$

Example 3.13. The graph of

$$y = \frac{2x + 1}{\sqrt{x^2 + 1}}$$

has two horizontal asymptotes: $y = 2$ and $y = -2$.

Indeed,

$$\lim_{x \to \pm\infty} \frac{2x + 1}{\sqrt{x^2 + 1}} = \lim_{x \to \pm\infty} \frac{x}{|x|} \frac{2 + 1/x}{\sqrt{1 + 1/x^2}} = \begin{cases} 2 & \text{if } x \to +\infty \\ -2 & \text{if } x \to -\infty. \end{cases}$$

Definition 3.14. A line $y = ax + b$ with $a \neq 0$ is called an **oblique asymptote** of the graph for $y = f(x)$ if either

$$\lim_{x \to +\infty} (f(x) - ax - b) = 0 \quad \text{or} \quad \lim_{x \to -\infty} (f(x) - ax - b) = 0.$$

Example 3.15. The graph of

$$y = \sqrt{x^2 + 1}$$

has two oblique asymptotes: $y = x$ and $y = -x$.

Indeed,

$$\sqrt{x^2 + 1} = |x| \sqrt{1 + \frac{1}{x^2}} \Rightarrow \begin{cases} \lim_{x \to -\infty} \left(\sqrt{x^2 + 1} - (-x) \right) = 0, \\ \lim_{x \to +\infty} \left(\sqrt{x^2 + 1} - (x) \right) = 0. \end{cases}$$

Since the number of directions along the x-axis towards infinity is bounded by two, there are at most two horizontal or oblique asymptotes.

Definition 3.16. Let f be a function defined on some interval $(a, a + \Delta)$, $\Delta > 0$. We say that $f(x)$ has the limit $+\infty$ as $x \to a^+$ and write $\lim_{x \to a^+} f(x) = +\infty$ if for every number $M > 0$ there exists a corresponding number $\delta > 0$ such that $a < x < a + \delta \Rightarrow f(x) > M$.

Let f be a function defined on some interval $(a, a+\Delta)$, $\Delta > 0$. We say that $f(x)$ has the limit $-\infty$ as $x \to a^+$ and write $\lim_{x \to a^+} f(x) = -\infty$ if for every number $N < 0$ there exists a corresponding number $\delta > 0$ such that $a < x < a + \delta \Rightarrow f(x) < N$.

The limits

$$\lim_{x \to a^-} f(x) = -\infty, \quad \lim_{x \to a^-} f(x) = +\infty$$

are defined similarly.

Definition 3.17. A line $x = a$ ia a **vertical asymptote** of the graph of a function $y = f(x)$ if at least one of the following limits exist:

$$\begin{cases} \lim_{x \to a^+} f(x) = +\infty, \\ \lim_{x \to a^+} f(x) = -\infty, \\ \lim_{x \to a^-} f(x) = +\infty, \\ \lim_{x \to a^-} f(x) = -\infty. \end{cases} \tag{3.5}$$

Example 3.18. Is it true that the vertical line $x = 0$ is the vertical asymptote for

$$f(x) = \frac{\sin(1/x)}{x}?$$

Since $\sin(1/x) = +1$ for $x = (2\pi \cdot n + \pi/2)^{-1}$, and $\sin(1/x) = -1$ for $x = (2\pi \cdot n - \pi/2)^{-1}$, $n = 1, 2, 3, \ldots$, neither of the limits in (3.5) exists for $y = f(x)$, implying that the line $x = 0$ is not a vertical asymptote of the graph of $y = f(x)$.

3.3. The Limit of a Sequence and Real Numbers

There is an important notion of limit, namely the limit of a sequence. Let f be a function defined only for positive integers. Then this function can be represented in the table form as the table of values $f(n)$, $n = 1, 2, \ldots$. To shorten notations one denotes a sequence of values as $\{f(n)\}_{n\geq 1}$, or most often as $\{a_n\}_{n\geq 1}$ or $(a_n)_{n\geq 1}$. For example,

$$1, \frac{1}{2}, \frac{1}{3}, \ldots \quad \text{is denoted by} \quad \left\{\frac{1}{n}\right\}_{n\geq 1}.$$

Definition 3.19. Given a sequence $\{a_n\}_{n\geq 1}$ we say that it has a limit A:

$$\lim_n a_n = A,$$

if for every $\varepsilon > 0$ there is an integer $N(\varepsilon)$ such that

$$n > N(\varepsilon) \Rightarrow |a_n - A| < \varepsilon.$$

Since there is only one direction towards infinity in the set of all positive integers, the direction of approaching infinity is not indicated in the notation $\lim_n a_n$. With every sequence $\{a_n\}_{n\geq 1}$ one can relate the following function on $[1, +\infty)$:

$$f(x) = a_n \quad \text{if} \quad n \leq x < n + 1, \quad n = 1, 2, 3, \ldots.$$

It is easy to see that

$$\lim_n a_n = \lim_{x \to +\infty} f(x)$$

as soon as one of the above limits exists.

Definition 3.20. A **chain of intervals** is a sequence of embedded **closed** intervals $[a_n, b_n]$:

$$a_1 \leq a_2 \leq \cdots \leq a_n \leq \cdots \leq b_n \leq \cdots \leq b_2 \leq b_1,$$

such that $\lim_n (b_n - a_n) = 0$.

Theorem 3.21. *Given any chain of embedded closed intervals $[a_n, b_n]$ there exists at most one real number which belongs to each interval of the chain.*

Proof. Suppose to the contrary that there are two distinct numbers $c < d$ such that

$$a_n \leq c < d \leq b_n \Rightarrow 0 < d - c \leq b_n - a_n \to 0,$$

which is a contradiction.   □

It is proved in rigorous theory of real numbers that for any chain of intervals there is a real number c which is contained in every interval of the chain. This theory is beyond the scope of AP Calculus. However, it is useful to understand how this number c can be found.

If one uses a calculator to find the value of $\sqrt{2}$, then a calculator gives the answer 1.41421. Increasing the accuracy of calculations, one can get a better result 1.414213562373. In the first case the calculator in fact shows that the precise value of $\sqrt{2}$ is placed between two rational numbers, i.e. is in the interval

[1.41421, 1.41422]. The length of this interval 10^{-5} is called the mistake of approximation. In the second case the calculator shows that the precise value of $\sqrt{2}$ is in a smaller closed interval of length 10^{-12}. Increasing the accuracy of a calculator we obtain a chain of intervals each of which contains $\sqrt{2}$. Therefore, the statement that any chain of closed intervals contains exactly one real number is equivalent to the assumption that the set of real numbers has no 'holes'.

It is important to notice that the intervals in the chain must be closed. For instance, the chain of open intervals $\{(0, 1/n)\}_{n \geq 1}$ has no real number in common.

Definition 3.22. An increasing sequence $\{c_n\}$ is called bounded above if there is a finite number C such that $c_n \leq C$ for every integer n. A decreasing sequence $\{c_n\}$ is called bounded below if if there is a finite number C such that $C \leq c_n$ for every integer n.

Theorem 3.23. *Any increasing (decreasing) sequence $\{c_n\}$ bounded above (below) has a finite limit.*

Proof. It is clear that $\{-c_n\}$ is decreasing and bounded below if $\{c_n\}$ is increasing and bounded above. So, we can consider only the case of increasing sequences bounded above. We put $a_1 = c_1$ and $b_1 = C$. Then all elements of $\{c_n\}$ are in the closed interval $[a_1, b_1]$. Since $[a_1, b_1]$ is a union of two closed intervals $[a_1, 0.5(a_1 + b_1)]$ and $[0.5(a_1 + b_1), b_1]$ with only one point $0.5(a_1 + b_1)$ in common, either all members of the sequence $\{c_n\}$ are placed in the first half of $[a_1, b_1]$, or there are infinitely many in the second. In the first case we put $a_2 = a_1$, $b_2 = 0.5(a_1 + b_1)$. In the second case we put $a_2 = 0.5(a_1 + b_1)$, $b_2 = b_1$. Repeating this construction by induction, we obtain a chain of closed intervals $[a_k, b_k]$ such that each of them contains infinitely many members of $\{c_n\}$. Since the sequence $\{c_n\}$ increases, this means that every interval $[a_k, b_k]$ contains all members of $\{c_n\}$ except for a finite number of first terms. Let c be a unique number which is common to all the intervals in the chain. Let $\varepsilon > 0$. Since $\lim_k(b_k - a_k) = 0$, there is $k = k(\varepsilon)$ such that $b_k - a_k < \varepsilon$. Since by our construction all numbers c_n as well as c are in $[a_k, b_k]$ for every $n > N$, we see that

$$-\varepsilon < -(b_k - a_k) \leq c - c_n \leq b_k - a_k < \varepsilon.$$

It follows that $|c_n - c| < \varepsilon$ for $n > N$. Hence $\lim_n c_n = c$. $\qquad\square$

Definition 3.24. A sequence $\{x_n\}$ is called a **Cauchy sequence** if for every $\varepsilon > 0$ there is a positive integer $N(\varepsilon)$ such that

$$n, m > N(\varepsilon) \Rightarrow |x_n - x_m| < \varepsilon. \tag{3.6}$$

Every Cauchy sequence is placed in some finite closed interval. Indeed, put $\varepsilon = 1$ in Definition 3.24. Then for $n > N = N(1)$ we have

$$-1 + x_{N+1} < x_n < x_{N+1} + 1$$

So, all terms of $\{x_n\}$ are in the closed interval $[x_{N+1}-1, x_{N+1}+1]$ except for, possibly, of a finite number terms x_n for $n = 1, \ldots, N$. Enlarging the closed interval, if necessary, we obtain the desired finite interval $[a, b]$.

Theorem 3.25. *Any Cauchy sequence has a limit.*

Proof. Let $[a_1, b_1]$ be a closed interval which contains all terms $\{x_n\}$. We divide $[a_1, b_1]$ into **three** closed segments $[a_1, c]$, $[c, d]$, $[d, b_1]$ of equal lengths. The points of two intervals $[a_1, c]$ and $[d, b_1]$ are on the distance exceeding $(b_1-a_1)/3 > 0$. It follows that at least one of them contains only a finite number of terms of $\{x_n\}$. We remove it and obtain a closed interval $[a_2, b_2]$ of length $2(b_1 - a_1)/3$, which contains all but a finite number of terms of $\{x_n\}$. Continuing this process by induction we obtain a sequence of embedded closed intervals $[a_n, b_n]$, each of which contains all terms of $\{x_n\}$ except for a finite number of them. Since the lengths of the intervals $[a_n, b_n]$ satisfy

$$b_n - a_n = \left(\frac{2}{3}\right)^{n-1} (b_1 - a_1) \underset{n}{\to} 0,$$

there is only one real number c, which belongs to each $[a_n, b_n]$.

Let $\varepsilon > 0$. Then there is $M(\varepsilon)$ such that for every $m > M(\varepsilon)$

$$c - \varepsilon < a_m < c < b_m < c + \varepsilon.$$

Let $m = M(\varepsilon) + 1$. Since only finite number of terms of $\{x_n\}$ are placed outside of $[a_m, b_m]$, there is N such that $a_m \le x_n \le b_m$ for $n > N$. In other words,

$$n > N \Rightarrow |c - x_n| < \varepsilon. \qquad \square$$

Cauchy sequences are used when it is difficult or even impossible to find a formula for the limit c. In this book, they are used in the proof of Picard's Theorem on existence solutions to differential equations.

3.4.   Continuous Functions

There is an important class of functions, satisfying $\lim_{x \to c} f(x) = f(c)$. These functions are helpful for limits evaluations.

Definition 3.26. Let f be a function defined on an interval $[a, b]$. Then f is said to be **continuous** at c in (a, b) if $\lim_{x \to c} f(x) = f(c)$. It is said to be **continuous** at a and b if, correspondingly,

$$\lim_{x \to a^+} f(x) = f(a), \quad \lim_{x \to b^-} f(x) = f(b)$$

In AP Calculus the definition of a continuous function is often illustrated by the following obvious test.

Theorem 3.27. *A function* $y = f(x)$ *is continuous at* $x = c$ *if and only if the following three conditions hold simultaneously:*

(1) *The function* f *is defined on an open interval which contains c.*

(2) *The limit* $\lim_{x \to c} f(x) = L$ *exists.*

(3) $f(c) = L.$

Notice that at the end points a and b the test is applied with the corresponding one-sided limits.

Definition 3.28. A function f defined on a closed interval $[a, b]$ is said to have the **intermediate value** property if for every y between $f(a)$ and $f(b)$ the equation $y = f(x)$ has at least one solution x in the open interval (a, b).

Theorem 3.29. *Let* f *be a strictly monotonic function on a closed interval* $[a, b]$ *with intermediate value property. Then* f *is continuous at every point c of* $[a, b]$.

Proof. The idea of the construction is shown on Fig 3.3. Suppose that f strictly increases and $a < c < b$. Then $f(a) < f(c) < f(b)$. Let ε be any positive number satisfying $\varepsilon < \min(f(c) - f(a), f(b) - f(c))$. Then

$$f(a) < f(c) - \varepsilon < f(c) < f(c) + \varepsilon < f(b).$$

By the intermediate value property of f there are s, t in (a, b) such that

$$f(c) - \varepsilon = f(s), \quad f(c) + \varepsilon = f(t).$$

Since f is strictly increasing, we conclude that $s < c < t$. We define $\delta(\varepsilon)$ to be $\min(c - s, t - c)$. By the monotonic property of f we obtain

$$s \leq c - \delta(\varepsilon) < x < c + \delta(\varepsilon) \leq t \Rightarrow f(s) < f(x) < f(t) \Rightarrow |f(x) - f(c)| < \varepsilon.$$

Hence $\lim_{x \to a} f(x) = f(c)$, implying that f is continuous at c as stated. The cases $c = a$ and $c = d$ are considered similarly. $\square$

Corollary 3.30. *Given* $\alpha \in \mathbb{R}, \alpha \neq 0$, *and* $0 < a \neq 1$, *the following elementary functions are continuous at every point of their natural domain:*

$$y = x^\alpha, \quad y = a^x, \quad y = \log_a x \quad \tan x, \quad \cot x.$$

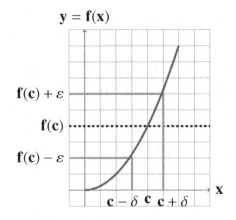

Figure 3.3: Continuity of Monotonic Functions with Intermediate Value Property.

Corollary 3.31. *Suppose that for a function f defined on a closed interval $[a, b]$ one can find a finite number of points*

$$a = a_0 < a_1 < \cdots < a_n = b,$$

such that the restriction of f to any closed interval $[a_{k-1}, a_k]$, $k = 1, \ldots, n$, satisfies the intermediate value property and is monotonic. Then f is continuous at any point of $[a, b]$.

Proof. By Theorem 3.29 the function f is continuous at c if $c \neq a_k$. By Theorem 3.29 $\lim_{x \to a_k^-} f(x) = \lim_{x \to a_k^+} f(x) = f(a_k)$, which completes the proof.   □

.

Corollary 3.32. *Trigonometric functions $y = \sin x$, $y = \cos x$, are continuous on $\mathbb{R}$.*

Proof. Since $y = \sin x$ is periodic with fundamental period 2π, it is sufficient to prove the continuity of $y = \sin x$ on the closed interval $[0, 2\pi]$. The function $y = \sin x$ is strictly monotonic and has the intermediate value property on the intervals:

$$[0, \pi/2], \quad [\pi/2, 3\pi/2], \quad [3\pi/2, 2\pi].$$

Hence, it is continuous. Since $\cos x = \sin(\pi/2 - x)$, the function $y = \cos x$ is continuous too.   □

Basic elementary functions have the intermediate value property. This fact coupled with the monotonicity of these functions was used to establish their continuity.

The following lemma is a technical tool which will be used to study the intermediate value property.

Lemma 3.33. *Let f be a continuous function on a closed interval $[a, b]$ and $\{[a_n, b_n]\}_{n \geq 1}$ be a chain of intervals in $[a, b]$ with c being a common point for all of them. Then for every $\varepsilon > 0$ there is $N(\varepsilon)$ such that*

$$n > N(\varepsilon) \text{ and } a_n \leq x \leq b_n \Rightarrow f(c) - \varepsilon < f(x) < f(c) + \varepsilon.$$

Proof. Since f is continuous at c, for every $\varepsilon > 0$ there is $\delta = \delta(\varepsilon) > 0$ such that

$$c - \delta < x < c + \delta \Rightarrow f(c) - \varepsilon < f(x) < f(c) + \varepsilon. \tag{3.7}$$

Since $\{[a_n, b_n]\}_{n \geq 1}$ is a chain with common point c, there is $N(\delta)$ such that

$$n > N(\delta) \Rightarrow c - \delta < a_n < b_n < c + \delta. \tag{3.8}$$

Combining (3.7) and (3.8) we complete the proof. $\square$

Theorem 3.34 (The Intermediate Value Theorem). *Every continuous function on a closed interval $[a, b]$ has the intermediate value property.*

Proof. Let $a_1 = a$, $b_1 = b$, and y be any real number between $f(a_1)$ and $f(b_1)$. If $y = f(e_1)$, where e_1 is the middle of $[a_1, b_1]$, then the proof is completed. If not, then y is a number between either $f(a_1)$ and $f(e_1)$, or between $f(e_1)$ and $f(b_1)$. We denote by $[a_2, b_2]$ any interval of the mentioned two, for which y is placed between $f(a_2)$ and $f(b_2)$. If we continue by induction, then we either find a solution in a finite number of steps, or obtain a chain of closed intervals $[a_n, b_n]$. This sequence is indeed a chain, since the intervals with greater indices are contained in the intervals with smaller indices, and

$$b_n - a_n = \frac{b - a}{2^{n-1}}.$$

Let c be a common point of this chain of intervals. Then by Lemma 3.33 for every $\varepsilon > 0$ there is a positive integer N such that

$$n > N \Rightarrow \begin{cases} c - \delta & < a_n < c + \delta \\ c - \delta & < b_n < c + \delta \end{cases} \Rightarrow \begin{cases} f(c) - \varepsilon & < f(a_n) < f(c) + \varepsilon \\ f(c) - \varepsilon & < f(b_n) < f(c) + \varepsilon \end{cases}$$

Since y is between $f(a_n)$ and $f(b_n)$, this implies that

$$f(c) - \varepsilon < y < f(c) + \varepsilon$$

for every $\varepsilon > 0$. Hence $y = f(c)$. $\square$

It is not true that any function satisfying the intermediate value property is continuous. Here is an example.

Example 3.35. Let f be a function on the interval $[0, 1]$ such that $f(0) = 1$, $f(1) = 0$, and for $0 < x < 1$

$$f(x) = \begin{cases} x & \text{if } x \text{ is rational;} \\ x^2 & \text{if } x \text{ is irrational.} \end{cases} \tag{3.9}$$

Then $y = f(x)$ is discontinuous at any point of its domain, but it satisfies the intermediate value property.

The function f is discontinuous at $x = 0$ and $x = 1$, since

$$\lim_{x \to 0^+} f(x) = 0 \neq f(0), \quad \lim_{x \to 1^-} f(x) = 1 \neq f(1).$$

Every c in $[0, 1]$ can be approximated arbitrary close by rational as well as irrational numbers. So, $f(x)$ approaches c along rational numbers and c^2 along irrational numbers. Since $c \neq c^2$ for every c, $0 < c < 1$, the function $y = f(x)$ is discontinuous at any point of $(0, 1)$. Still f has the intermediate value property. Indeed, if y, $0 < y < 1$ is rational, then $f(y) = y$. If $0 < y < 1$ is irrational, then $c = \sqrt{y}$ is irrational as well and $f(c) = y$.

However, if we consider strictly monotonic functions only, then continuity and intermediate value property are equivalent.

Theorem 3.36. *A strictly monotonic function on $[a, b]$ is continuous if and only if it has intermediate value property.*

Proof. If a monotonic function has intermediate value property, then it is continuous by Theorem 3.29. If a strictly monotonic function is continuous then it has intermediate value property by Theorem 3.34. □

If f is a strictly monotonic continuous function on a closed interval $[a, b]$, then its range $\mathcal{R}(f)$ is a closed interval $[m_f, M_f]$, where M_f is the maximal value of f and m_f is the minimal value of f on $[a, b]$. For monotonic f these numbers equal the valued of $f(x)$ at $x = a$ and $x = b$.

If f is an arbitrary continuous function on $[a, b]$, then by the Intermediate value theorem given a pair of values $y_1 < y_2$ in $\mathcal{R}(f)$, the whole interval (y_1, y_2) is in $\mathcal{R}(f)$. It follows that $\mathcal{R}(f)$ is an interval as well and, therefore, $\mathcal{R}(f) = \langle m_f, M_f \rangle$. Here M_f is the least number such that

$$f(x) \leq M_f \text{ for every } x, \ a \leq x \leq b.$$

Similarly, m_f is the greatest number such that

$$f(x) \geq m_f \text{ for every } x, \ a \leq x \leq b.$$

The following theorem shows that in fact $\mathcal{R}(f) = [m_f, M_f]$.

Theorem 3.37 (Extreme Value Theorem). *A continuous function f on a closed bounded interval $[a, b]$ attains a maximum and minimum value at least once. In other words, there are numbers c and d in $[a, b]$ such that*

$$m_f = f(c) \leq f(x) \leq f(d) = M_f \ \text{for all } \ x \ \text{in} \ [a, b].$$

Proof. We prove that there is a number d in $[a, b]$ such that $f(d) = M_f$. If e is the middle of $[a, b]$, then

$$\mathcal{R}(f) = \langle m_f, M_f \rangle = f([a, e]) \cup f([e, b])$$

is a union of two intervals, at least one of which has the right end at M_f. We chose this interval and denote it by $[a_1, b_1]$. Clearly,

$$b_1 - a_1 = \frac{b - a}{2}.$$

Repeating this construction, we obtain by induction a chain of embedded intervals $\{[a_n, b_n]\}_{n \geq 1}$, satisfying

$$b_n - a_n = \frac{b - a}{2^n},$$

and the right end of the interval $f([a_n, b_n])$ is M_f. Let d be the only real number common to all intervals of the chain constructed. Since f is continuous at d, we obtain by Lemma 3.33 that for every $\varepsilon > 0$ there is a positive integer n such that the interval $f([a_n, b_n])$ is contained in the interval $[f(d) - \varepsilon, f(d) + \varepsilon]$. In particular, this is true for the right end of $f([a_n, b_n])$, which is M_f. It follows that M_f is finite and satisfies

$$f(d) - \varepsilon \leq M_f \leq f(d) + \varepsilon.$$

Since $\varepsilon > 0$ is an arbitrary small positive number, we conclude that $M_f = f(d)$ as stated. To prove the second statement we apply the proof given above to the continuous function $-f$. $\square$

Definition 3.38. Any point d in $[a, b]$, satisfying $f(d) = M_f$, is called a point of **absolute maximum** of f on $[a, b]$. Any point c in $[a, b]$, satisfying $f(c) = m_f$, is called a point of **absolute minimum** of f on $[a, b]$.

Theorem 3.39 (Continuity of the Inverse Function). *Suppose that f is a continuous function on a closed interval $[a, b]$ such that there is a function g satisfying $g(f(x)) = x$ for every x in $[a, b]$. Then f is strictly monotonic on $[a, b]$ and g being restricted to the closed interval with the end-points $f(a)$ and $f(b)$ is the continuous inverse function for f.*

Proof. We first prove that all values $f(x)$ for x in $[a, b]$ lie between $f(a)$ and $f(b)$. Suppose to the contrary that there is c in (a, b) such that $f(c) > \max(f(a), f(b))$ or $f(c) < \min(f(a), f(b))$. In the first case we consider any number y, satisfying

$$\max(f(a), f(b)) < y < f(c).$$

By Theorem 3.34 there is x_1 in (a, c) and x_2 in (c, b) such that $f(x_1) = f(x_2) = y$. Observing that

$$x_1 = g(f(x_1)) = g(y) = g(f(x_2)) = x_2,$$

we obtain a contradiction. The second case is considered similarly.

Suppose that $f(a) < f(b)$ and that $a \le x_1 < x_2 \le b$. Since

$$x_1 = g(f(x_1)) = g(f(x_2)) = x_2,$$

the case $f(x_1) = f(x_2)$ is not possible. If $f(x_1) > f(x_2)$, then there is y between $f(x_1)$ and $f(x_2)$. By the first part of the proof

$$f(a) \le f(x_2) < y < f(x_1) \le f(b).$$

By Theorem 3.34 there is x_3 in (a, x_1) and x_4 in (x_2, b) such that $f(x_3) = f(x_4) = y$. It follows that $x_3 = g(f(x_3)) = g(f(x_4)) = x_4$, which is a contradiction. Hence $f(x_1) < f(x_2)$. $\square$

Corollary 3.40. *The inverse trigonometric functions*

$$y = \arcsin x, \quad y = \arccos x, \quad y = \arctan x, \quad y = \text{arccot}\, x,$$

are continuous.

Theorem 3.41. *Let f be a continuous function on $[a, b]$ and g be a continuous function on $[c, d]$ such that $\mathcal{R}(f)$ is contained in $[c, d]$. Then the function $y = g \circ f(x) = g(f(x))$ is continuous on $[a, b]$.*

Proof. If e is a number in $[a, b]$, then $f(e)$ is a number in $[c, d]$. Since g is continuous at $f(e)$, for every $\varepsilon > 0$ there is $\delta(\varepsilon) > 0$ such that

$$\begin{cases} |y - f(e)| < \delta(\varepsilon) \\ c \le y \le d \end{cases} \Rightarrow |g(y) - g(f(e))| < \varepsilon.$$

Since f is continuous at e, for $\delta(\varepsilon)$ there is $\delta_1(\varepsilon)$ such that

$$\begin{cases} |x - e| < \delta_1(\varepsilon) \\ a \le x \le b \end{cases} \Rightarrow |f(x) - f(e)| < \varepsilon.$$

It follows that

$$\begin{cases} |x - e| < \delta_1(\varepsilon) \\ a \le x \le b \end{cases} \Rightarrow |g(f(x)) - g(f(e))| < \varepsilon,$$

implying that $f(g(x))$ is continuous at e. $\square$

Problem 3.42. A continuous function $f(x)$ on $[0, 11]$ takes values specified in the following table.

x	0	2	5	10	11
$f(x)$	-2	4	k	5	-2

For which values of the parameter k the equation $f(x) = 2$ has at least four solutions in $(-1, 11)$?

(A) $2 < k < 5$ (B) $k < 2$ (C) $k > 5$ (D) $k = 2$ (E) $k = 5$.

Solution:

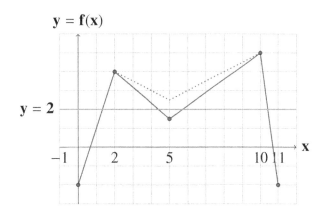

If $k < 2$ then by the Intermediate Value Theorem the equation $f(x) = 2$ has at least one root on each of the four intervals: $(0, 2)$, $(2, 5)$, $(5, 10)$, $(10, 11)$. The example shown on the graph above indicates that this may be not the case if $k \geq 2$. **Answer: B**

Problem 3.43. (a) Suppose that a function $y = f(x)$ is continuous on the closed interval $[0, 1]$ and that $0 \leq f(x) \leq 1$ for every x in $[0, 1]$. Show that there exists a number c in $[0, 1]$ such that $f(c) = c$.

(b) If the product $f(x) \cdot g(x)$ is continuous at $x = 0$, must $f(x)$ and $g(x)$ be continuous at $x = 0$? Give reasons for your answer.

(c) Give an example of functions $f(x)$ and $g(x)$, both continuous at $x = 0$, for which the superposition $f \circ g$ is not continuous at $x = 0$.

(d) Is it true that a continuous function that is never zero on an interval never changes sign on that interval? Give reasons for your answer.

Solution: (a) If $f(0) = 0$ or $f(1) = 1$ then $c = 0$ or $c = 1$. If $f(0) > 0$ and $f(1) < 1$, then the continuous function $h(x) = f(x) - x$ satisfies $h(0) > 0$ and

$h(1) < 0$ which implies by the Intermediate Value Theorem that there is c in $(0, 1)$ such that $h(c) = 0$ and, therefore, $f(c) = c$.

(**b**) We define

$$f(x) = \begin{cases} 1 & \text{if } x \text{ is irrational} \\ 0 & \text{if } x \text{ is rational} \end{cases} \qquad g(x) = \begin{cases} 0 & \text{if } x \text{ is irrational} \\ 1 & \text{if } x \text{ is rational} \end{cases} \tag{3.10}$$

Then both $f(x)$ and $g(x)$ are not continuous at any point a. However, the product $f(x) \cdot g(x) \equiv 0$ is continuous everywhere.

(**c**) Let

$$f(x) = \begin{cases} 1 & \text{if } x \geq 1 \\ -1 & \text{if } x < 1 \end{cases} \qquad g(x) = x + 1.$$

Clearly, both $f(x)$ and $g(x)$ are continuous at $x = 0$. But

$$f(g(x)) = f(x + 1) = \begin{cases} 1 & \text{if } x \geq 0 \\ -1 & \text{if } x < 0 \end{cases}$$

is not continuous at $x = 0$.

(**d**) It is true. Suppose that $f(x_1)$ and $f(x_2)$, where $x_1 < x_2$ are points in the interval, have opposite signs. Applying the Theorem on Intermediate Values to $y = f(x)$ and the interval $[x_1, x_2]$ we find c in (x_1, x_2) such that $f(c) = 0$, which is a contradiction.

3.5.   Continuity of Implicit Functions

An important class of functions included in AP Calculus exams is the class of implicit functions. We already considered some simple examples in section 2.3. Here is one more example. Let us consider the folium of Descartes

$$x^3 + y^3 - 9xy = 0. \tag{3.11}$$

It is easy to see that $x = 2, y = 4$ is a solution to the equation (3.11). An important question is to decide if there exists a continuous function $y = y(x)$ defined about $x = 2$ which satifies (3.11) and the condition $y(2) = 4$.

The example of the equation

$$x^2 + y^2 - 4x - 8y + 20 = (x - 2)^2 + (y - 4)^2 = 0$$

shows that the point with the coordinates $x = 2, y = 4$ is the only point on the plane which satisfies it. So, we have to decide when such a function $y = y(x)$ exists and when it does not exist.

Definition 3.44. A function $f(x, y)$ in two variables defined on an open square centered at (a, b) is called **separately** continuous at (a, b) if

$$\lim_{x \to a} f(x, b) = \lim_{y \to b} f(a, y) = f(a, b).$$

The function $f(x, y)$ is called **continuous** at (a, b) if for every $\varepsilon > 0$ there is $\delta > 0$ such that

$$|x - a| < \delta \ \text{ and } \ |y - b| < \delta \Rightarrow |f(x, y) - f(a, b)| < \varepsilon.$$

It is clear that every continuous function at (a, b) is separately continuous at (a, b). The converse is not true as a simple example shows:

$$f(x, y) = \begin{cases} \frac{xy}{x^2+y^2} & \text{if } (x, y) \neq (0, 0); \\ 0 & \text{if } (x, y) = (0, 0). \end{cases}$$

Indeed, the restriction of $f(x, y)$ to the line $y = x$ is discontinuous at $x = 0$:

$$f(x, x) = \begin{cases} \frac{1}{2} & \text{if } x \neq 0; \\ 0 & \text{if } x = 0. \end{cases}$$

Theorem 3.45. *Let $f(x, y)$ be a function such that*

(1) *$f(x, y)$ is separately continuous at every point of a closed square centered at (a, b) with the side length $2d$;*

(2) *for every x, $|x - a| \leq d$, the function $y \to f(x, y)$ is strictly monotonic on $[b - d, b + d]$;*

(3) *$f(a, b) = 0$.*

Then there is δ, $0 < \delta \leq d$ and a unique continuous function $y = y(x)$ defined on $(a - \delta, a + \delta)$ which satisfies the equations $f(x, y(x)) = 0$, $y(a) = b$.

Remark Notice that $f(x, y) = (x - 2)^2 + (y - 4)^2$ is separately continuous everywhere. However, for every x the function $y \to f(x, y)$ represents a parabola, which is not monotonic about $y = 4$.

The function $f(x, y) = x^3 + y^3 - 9xy$ is separately continuous everywhere. If $3 < y_1 < y_2$, then

$$f(x, y_2) - f(x, y_1) = y_2^3 - y_1^3 - 9x(y_2 - y_1) = (y_2 - y_1)(y_1^2 + y_2^2 + y_1 y_2 - 9x) > 0$$

if $x \leq 3$, implying that $y \to f(x, y)$ is strictly monotonic on $(3, +\infty)$ for $x \leq 3$.

In the first example there is no function $y = y(x)$ satisfying $f(x, y) = 0$ about $x = 2$, whereas in the second one there is a continuous function $y = y(x)$ on $(1, 3)$ satisfying $f(x, y(x)) = 0$ for $1 < x < 3$.

The following theorem proved in [12], shows that in fact Theorem 3.45 deals with continuous functions. We give its proof following [8].

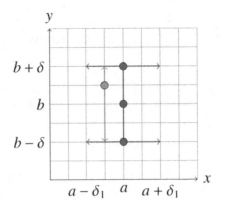

Figure 3.4: Separate Continuity.

Theorem 3.46. *If $f(x, y)$ is separately continuous at every point of a closed square $\max(|x - a|, |y - b|) \leq d$ centered at (a, b) and for every x the function $y \to f(x, y)$ is monotonic on $[b - d, b + d]$, then $f(x, y)$ is continuous at (a, b).*

Proof. By separate continuity, given $\varepsilon > 0$ there exists $\delta > 0$ such that

$$|y - b| \leq \delta \Rightarrow |f(a, y) - f(a, b)| < \varepsilon/2.$$

In other words, any value of f on the vertical blue segment on Fig 3.4 deviates from $f(a, b)$ less than by $\varepsilon/2$. Applying separate continuity of $f(x, y)$ at $(a, b + \delta)$ and $(a, b - \delta)$, we find a positive δ_1 such that

$$|x - a| \leq \delta_1 \Rightarrow |f(x, b + \delta) - f(a, b + \delta)| < \varepsilon/2,$$
$$|x - a| \leq \delta_1 \Rightarrow |f(x, b - \delta) - f(a, b - \delta)| < \varepsilon/2,$$

which means that the deviation of any value of f on two horizontal blue segment from $f(a, b \pm \delta)$ does not exceed $\varepsilon/2$. It follows that

$$|f(x, b \pm \delta) - f(a, b)| \leq |f(x, b \pm \delta) - f(a, b \pm \delta)| + |f(a, b \pm \delta) - f(a, b)| < \varepsilon/2 + \varepsilon/2 = \varepsilon,$$

where the choice of signs $\pm$ is one and the same. Take any point (x, y) satisfying

$$\max(|x - a|, |y - b|) < \min(\delta, \delta_1)$$

and draw a vertical segment through it. Since the function $f(x, y)$ is monotonic on this segment, the value $f(x, y)$ is placed between $f(x, b - \delta)$ and $f(x, b + \delta)$. Hence we conclude that $|f(x, y) - f(a, b)| < \varepsilon$. $\square$

Proof of Theorem 3.45. Since $y \to f(a, y)$ is strictly monotonic and continuous on the interval $[b - d, b + d]$, it vanishes only at $y = b$ and takes the values of opposite sign at $b - d$ and $b + d$. Let

$$\varepsilon = 0.5 \min(|f(a, b - d)|, |f(a, b + d)|).$$

Since $x \to f(x, b \pm d)$ are both continuous at $x = a$, there is $\delta_1 > 0$ such that

$$|x - a| < \delta_1 \Rightarrow |f(x, b \pm d) - f(a, b \pm d)| < \varepsilon.$$

It follows that $y \to f(x, y$ takes the values of opposite signs at $y = b - d$ and $y = b + d$. Since this function is strictly monotonic, it vanishes only once somewhere at $(b - d, b + d)$, which correctly defines the required function $y(x)$ on the open interval $(a - \delta_1, a + \delta_1)$.

To prove that $y(x)$ is continuous at $x = a$, we take a positive $\varepsilon < d$ and observe that

$$f(a, b - \varepsilon)f(a, b + \varepsilon) < 0 \Rightarrow \varepsilon_1 = \min(|f(a, b - \varepsilon)|, |f(a, b + \varepsilon)|) > 0.$$

By separate continuity of f at $(a, b - \varepsilon)$ and $(a, b + \varepsilon)$, there is $\delta_1 > 0$ such that

$$|x - a| < \delta_1 \Rightarrow \begin{cases} |f(a, b - \varepsilon) - f(x, b - \varepsilon)| & < \varepsilon_1 \\ |f(a, b + \varepsilon) - f(x, b + \varepsilon)| & < \varepsilon_1 \end{cases}.$$

It follows that

$$f(x, b - \varepsilon)f(x, b + \varepsilon) < 0$$

if $|x - a| < \delta_1$. By the Intermediate Value Theorem, we see that

$$|x - a| < \delta_1 \Rightarrow b - \varepsilon < y(x) < b + \varepsilon,$$

implying the continuity of $y(x)$ at $x = a$. Decreasing d if necessary, we can put the center of the square at any point of the curve $y = y(x)$ and apply the same arguments. $\square$

A nice review of the theory of separate continuous functions is given in [2].

3.6. Demand and Supply Functions

Monotonic and inverse function have important applications in Economics. Fig 3.5 demonstrates a typical buy-sell model. The graph $q = q^S(p)$ displays the number of products the producer may supply for the given price p. The function $q = q^S(p)$ is strictly increasing. The graph $q = q^D(p)$ displays the number of products consumers may buy for the given price p. The function $q = q^D(p)$ is strictly decreasing. Both functions are assumed to satisfy the intermediate value property. Therefore, they are continuous.

Theorem 3.47 (Equilibrium Theorem). *Given demand $q^D(p)$ and supply $q^S(p)$ functions the equation*

$$q^D(p) = q^S(p) \tag{3.12}$$

has a unique solution $p = p_e$.

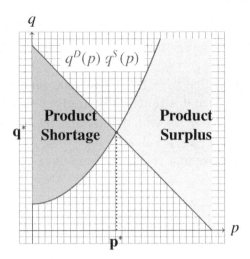

Figure 3.5: The Demand-Supply Functions.

Proof. Since both $q^D(p)$ and $q^S(p)$ are continuous, the function

$$f(p) = q^D(p) - q^S(p)$$

is continuous as well. If the product is distributed for free, the demand exceeds the supply, which implies that $f(0) < 0$. If commodity's price p_m is too high, then $q^D(p_m) = 0$, implying that $f(p_m) > 0$. By the intermediate Value Theorem there is a price p^* in the interval $(0, p_m)$ satisfying (3.12). Since $q^D(p)$ strictly decreases and $q^S(p)$ strictly increases, equation (3.12) has only one solution. $\square$

The solution p_e to (3.12) is called the **equilibrium** price and equation (3.12) is called the **equilibrium equation**. The area between the curves $q = q^D(p)$ and $q = q^S(p)$ for $0 < p < p^*$ corresponds the product shortage, whereas the area between the same curves for $p < p^* < p_m$ corresponds the product surplus, see Fig 3.5.

Problem 3.48. The quantity demanded on a Samsung smart-phone is 5000 per week when the unit price is $800. For each decrease in the unit price of $20 below $800, the quantity demanded increases by 50 units. The supplier will not market any smart-phone if the unit price is $300 or lower. But at a unit price of $500, they are willing to make available 2500 units in the market. The supply equation is also known to be linear. Find the demand and supply equation. Find the equilibrium point for the demand and supply.

Solution: Let $q^D(p)$ be the number of smart-phones demanded at price p. Since $q^D(p - 20) = q^D(p) + 50$ for every p, the demand function $q = q^D(p)$ is

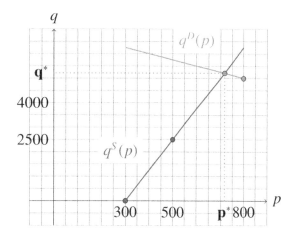

Figure 3.6: The Demand-Supply Equations.

linear. The slope of its graph is

$$\frac{q^D(800) - q^D(780)}{800 - 780} = \frac{5000 - 5050}{20} = -2.5.$$

It follows that $q^D(p) = -2.5p + b$, where b is an unknown constant. To find b we write

$$5000 = q^D(800) = -2.5 \cdot 800 + b = -2000 + b \Rightarrow b = 7000 \Rightarrow$$

$$\boxed{q^D(p) = -2.5p + 7000}.$$

Let $q^S(p)$ be the number of smart-phones supplied at price p. Then since $q^S(300) = 0$ and $q^S(500) = 2500$, the formula for $q^S(p)$ can be obtained by the point-slope equation:

$$\boxed{q^S(p) = 12.5(p - 300)}.$$

The equilibrium prise p^* is the price such that $q^D(p^*) = q^S(p^*)$, see Fig 3.5. This happens if and only if

$$-2.5p^* + 7000 = 12.5(p^* - 300) \Leftrightarrow 15p^* = 10750 \Leftrightarrow p^* = \frac{2150}{3} = 716.67.$$

$\square$

Both, the demand and supply functions are monotonic. By Theorem 2.22 they both have inverse functions. Since the variables here have dimensions (p is measured in dollars and q in number of units sold), in this case we do not replace p with

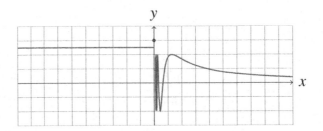

Figure 3.7: Essential discontinuity.

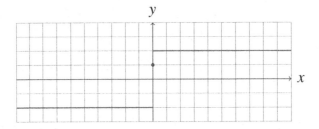

Figure 3.8: Non removable discontinuity.

q and vice versa. Instead we determine the inverse direct and demand functions by the formulas:

$$q^D(p) = -2.5p + 7000 \Rightarrow p^D(q) = -\frac{1}{2.5}(q - 7000);$$

$$q^S(p) = 12.5(p - 300) \Rightarrow p^S(q) = \frac{1}{12.5}q + 300.$$

3.7.   Classification of Points of Discontinuity

Definition 3.49. Let f be a function defined on an open interval containing a point a except, possibly, at a point a itself. Then a is called a point of a **removable discontinuity** of a function f if a value $f(a)$ may be assigned at $x = a$ in a such a way that f becomes continuous at $x = a$. Otherwise, a point a is called a point of a **non-removable discontinuity** of f.

The graphs on Fig 3.7 and Fig 3.8 show examples of non-removable discontinuities, whereas the graph on Fig 3.9 gives an example of a removable discontinuity. By Theorem 3.27 a point a is a point of removable discontinuity if and only if

$$\lim_{x \to a^-} f(x) = \lim_{x \to a^+} f(x).$$

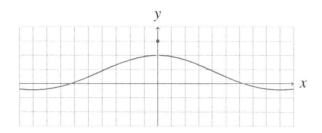

Figure 3.9: Removable discontinuity.

If f is not defined for $x < a$ or $x > a$, then a is a point of removable discontinuity if and only if the limit on the opposite side of a exists. There are two types of non-removable discontinuity. The first is shown on Fig. 3.8.

Definition 3.50. Let f be a function defined on an open interval containing a point a except, possibly, at a point a itself. Then a is called a **jump discontinuity** if both limits

$$\lim_{x \to a^-} f(x) \quad \text{and} \quad \lim_{x \to a^+} f(x) \tag{3.13}$$

exist are finite and not equal.

Definition 3.51. Let f be a function defined on an open interval containing a point a except, possibly, at a point a itself. Then a is called an **essential discontinuity** of f if at least one of the limits in (3.13) either does not exist or is infinite.

Fig 3.7 demonstrate the graph of a function which has an essential discontinuity at $x = 0$. Every point on the real line is a point of essential discontinuity for both functions f and g defined in (3.10). The function f with the Intermediate Value property defined in (3.9) on $[0, 1]$ has essential discontinuity at every point of the open interval $(0, 1)$. At $c = 0$ and $c = 1$ it has removable discontinuities.

3.8. Three Theorems on Limits

The following three important theorems considerably simplify the task of concrete limits evaluation. They follow the structure of elementary functions and are often used in Calculus AP exams.

Theorem 3.52 (Algebraic Rules for Limits)**.** *Let $\Delta > 0$ and f and g be two functions defined on $(a - \Delta, a + \delta)$ except for, possibly, at a. Suppose that*

$$\lim_{x \to a} f(x) = A, \quad \lim_{x \to a} g(x) = B.$$

Then

(a) $\lim_{x \to a}(f(x) + g(x)) = A + B$.

(b) $\lim_{x \to a}(f(x) \cdot g(x)) = A \cdot B$.

(c)

$$\lim_{x \to a} \frac{g(x)}{f(x)} = \frac{B}{A}, \quad \text{if } A \neq 0.$$

Proof. We prove (**c**). Two other statements are proved similarly. Since $A \neq 0$ and $\lim_{x \to a} f(x) = A$, we may take $\varepsilon = 0.5|A|$ in (3.1) and find $\delta_1 > 0$ such that

$$0 < |x - a| < \delta_1 \Rightarrow |f(x) - A| < 0.5|A| \Rightarrow |f(x)| > 0.5A.$$

Assuming that $0 < |x - a| < \delta_1$, we obtain

$$\left| \frac{g(x)}{f(x)} - \frac{B}{A} \right| = \frac{|g(x)A - f(x)B|}{|A||f(x)|} \leq \frac{2}{A^2}|g(x)A - f(x)B| =$$

$$\frac{2}{A^2}|(g(x) - B)A - (f(x) - A)B| \leq \frac{2}{|A|}|g(x) - B| + \frac{2|B|}{A^2}|f(x) - A|.$$

$$(3.14)$$

Since $\lim_{x \to a} f(x) = A$ and $\lim_{x \to a} g(x) = B$, given any $\varepsilon > 0$ we can find $0 < \delta_2 = \delta_2(\varepsilon) < \delta_1$ such that

$$0 < |x - a| < \delta_2 \Rightarrow \begin{cases} |f(x) - A| & < \frac{A^2}{4|B|}\varepsilon \\ |g(x) - B| & < \frac{|A|}{4}\varepsilon. \end{cases}$$

Combining this with (3.14), we obtain

$$\left| \frac{g(x)}{f(x)} - \frac{B}{A} \right| < \frac{2}{|A|}\frac{|A|}{4}\varepsilon + \frac{2|B|}{A^2}\frac{A^2}{4|B|}\varepsilon = \varepsilon$$

as soon as $0 < |x - a| < \delta_2$. $\qquad\square$

Corollary 3.53. *Every polynomial is continuous at any real point.*

Proof. Apply Theorem 3.52. $\qquad\square$

Corollary 3.54. *If $p(x) = a_n x^n + \cdots + a_0$ is a polynomial, then*

$$p'(x_0) = \lim_{x \to x_0} \frac{p(x) - p(x_0)}{x - x_0} = na_n x_0^{n-1} + \cdots + a_1.$$

Proof. By (1.4) and Theorem 3.52

$$\lim_{x \to x_0} \frac{p(x) - p(x_0)}{x - x_0} = \lim_{x \to x_0} \sum_{m=1}^{n} a_m(x^{m-1} + x_0 x^{m-2} + \cdots + x_0^{m-1}) = \sum_{m=1}^{n} m a_m x_0^{m-1}. \qquad \square$$

Problem 3.55. Investigate the function

$$f(x) = \frac{x^2 + 5x + 6}{x^2 - 4}$$

on removable discontinuities.

Solution: Since $x^2 + 5x + 6 = (x + 2)(x + 3)$ and $x^2 - 4 = (x + 2)(x - 2)$, we obtain that

$$f(x) = \frac{(x + 2)(x + 3)}{(x + 2)(x - 2)} = \frac{x + 3}{x - 2} \quad \text{for} \quad x \neq -2. \tag{3.15}$$

The number -2 is not in the natural domain of $f(x)$. By (3.15) and the Algebraic Rules for limits

$$\lim_{x \to -2^-} f(x) = \lim_{x \to -2^-} \frac{x + 3}{x - 2} = -\frac{1}{4} = \lim_{x \to -2^+} \frac{x + 3}{x - 2} = \lim_{x \to -2^+} f(x).$$

It follows that -2 is a removable discontinuity of f. By the Algebraic Rules $f(x)$ is continuous at any point $x \neq 2$. Since

$$\lim_{x \to 2^-} f(x) = -\infty, \quad \lim_{x \to 2^+} f(x) = +\infty,$$

the point $x = 2$ is the point of essential discontinuity of f. $\qquad \square$

Theorem 3.56 (Composition of Limits). *Let $\Delta_f > 0$, f be a function defined on $(a - \Delta_f, a + \Delta_f)$ except for, possibly, at a, such that $\lim_{x \to a} f(x) = b$, and the equation $f(x) = b$ has no solutions in $(a - \Delta_f, a)$ or in $(a, a + \Delta_f)$. Let $\Delta_g > 0$, g be a function defined on $(b - \Delta_g, b + \Delta_g)$ except for, possibly, at b, such that $\lim_{x \to b} g(x) = c$. Then*

$$\lim_{x \to a} g(f(x)) = c.$$

Proof. Let $\varepsilon > 0$. Since $\lim_{x \to b} g(x) = c$, there is $\delta = \delta(\varepsilon)$ such that $\delta(\varepsilon) < \Delta_g$ and

$$0 < |y - b| < \delta(\varepsilon) \Rightarrow |g(y) - c| < \varepsilon.$$

Since $\lim_{x \to a} f(x) = b$, there is $\delta_1(\varepsilon) < \Delta_f$ such that

$$0 < |x - a| < \delta_1(\varepsilon) \Rightarrow |f(x) - b| < \delta(\varepsilon).$$

Since the equation $f(x) = b$ has no solutions neither in $(a - \delta_1(\varepsilon), a)$, nor in $(a, a + \delta_1(\varepsilon))$, we conclude that

$$0 < |x - a| < \delta_1(\varepsilon) \Rightarrow 0 < |f(x) - b| < \delta(\varepsilon) \Rightarrow |g(f(x)) - c| < \varepsilon. \qquad \square$$

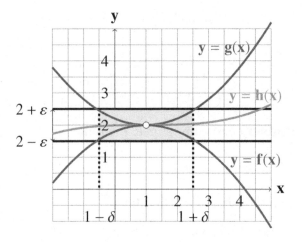

Figure 3.10: Sandwich Theorem.

Theorem 3.57 (Sandwich Theorem). *Let* $\Delta > 0$ *and* f, g, *and* h *be functions defined on* $(a - \Delta, a + \Delta)$ *except for, possibly, at a. Suppose that*

$$\lim_{x \to a} f(x) = \lim_{x \to a} g(x) = A,$$

and

$$f(x) \leq h(x) \leq g(x), \quad \text{for } x, \ 0 < |x - a| < \Delta.$$

Then $\lim_{x \to a} h(x) = A$.

Proof. See Fig 3.10. Given $\varepsilon > 0$ we find $\delta(\varepsilon) > 0$ such that

$$0 < |x - a| < \delta(\varepsilon) \Rightarrow \left\{ \begin{array}{l} A - \varepsilon \leq g(x) \leq A + \varepsilon \\ A - \varepsilon \leq f(x) \leq A + \varepsilon \end{array} \right. .$$

Since the graph of $y = h(x)$ is placed between the graphs of $y = g(x)$ and $y = f(x)$, we see that

$$0 < |x - a| < \delta(\varepsilon) \Rightarrow |h(x) - A| < \varepsilon. \qquad \square$$

Problem 3.58. Sketch the graph of the Descartes' Folium

$$y^3 + x^3 - 9xy = 0. \tag{3.16}$$

Proof. See Fig 3.11. If $x < 0$ and $y \leq 0$, then (3.16) has no solutions, since for such values the left-hand part of (3.16) is negative whereas the right-hand part is non-negative. It follows that if the solution $y(x)$ exists for x, $x < 0$, then it must be positive. Let us fix x, $x < 0$ and consider an equivalent algebraic equation in y:

$$y^3 + 0 \cdot y^2 - 9xy + x^3 = 0. \tag{3.17}$$

Equation (3.17) has only one sign change. By Descates' Rule of Signs, see Theorem 1.33, the number of positive roots of (3.17) equals $V(p) - 2k = 1 - 2k$, where k is a nonnegative integer. Since the number of roots in non-negative, we conclude that $k = 0$. Hence for every x, $x < 0$, equation (3.17) has a unique positive root $y(x)$.

The function $f(x, y) = y^3 - 9xy + x^3$ is separately continuous everywhere. Both function $y \to -9xy$, $y \to y^3$ increase if $x < 0$, implying that $y \to f(x, y)$ is strictly monotonic for every $x < 0$. By Theorem 3.45 the function $y(x)$ is continuous on $(-\infty, 0)$.

Since $f(x, 0) = x^3 < 0$ and $f(x, -x) = 9x^2 > 0$, by the Intermediate Value Theorem the function $y(x)$ satisfies

$$0 < y(x) < -x \text{ if } x < 0. \tag{3.18}$$

Since $f(x, 0) = x^3 < 0$ and $f(x, x^2/9) = 9^{-3}x^6 > 0$, by the Intermediate Value Theorem the function $y(x)$ satisfies

$$0 < y(x) < \frac{1}{9}x^2 \text{ if } x < 0. \tag{3.19}$$

Applying Theorem 3.57, we obtain that

$$\lim_{x \to 0^-} y(x) = 0 \text{ and } \lim_{x \to 0^-} \frac{y(x)}{x} = 0. \tag{3.20}$$

Dividing both parts of (3.16) by x^3, and denoting $A = y/x$, we obtain that

$$A^3 + 1 = \frac{9}{x} \cdot A \Rightarrow A + 1 = \frac{9}{x} \frac{A}{A^2 - A + 1}.$$

Since $A < 0$, we have

$$0 < \frac{9}{|x|} \frac{-A}{A^2 - A + 1} = A + 1 < \frac{9}{|x|}.$$

By Theorem 3.57,

$$\lim_{x \to -\infty} \frac{y(x)}{x} = -1. \tag{3.21}$$

This indicates that the graph of $y(x)$ may have an asymptote $y = -x + b$. To determine if this is indeed the case and find b we introduce a function $y_1(x)$ such that $y(x) = -x + y_1(x)$. By (3.18) and (3.21), we obtain that

$$x < y_1(x) < 0, \quad \lim_{x \to -\infty} \frac{y_1(x)}{x} = 0. \tag{3.22}$$

The algebraic equation $(-x + y_1)^3 + x^3 - 9x(-x + y_1) = 0$ is equivalent to

$$y_1^3 - 3xy_1^2 + (3x^2 - 9x)y_1 + 9x^2 = 0. \tag{3.23}$$

Dividing both parts of (3.23) by x^2, we get

$$\left(\frac{y_1^2(x)}{x^2} - 3\frac{y_1(x)}{x} + 3 - \frac{9}{x}\right)y_1(x) = -9 \tag{3.24}$$

Passing to the limit, see (3.22), we find that

$$\lim_{x\to-\infty} y_1(x) = -3. \tag{3.25}$$

It follows that $y = -x - 3$ is an oblique asymptote for the graph of $y = y(x)$ at $x = -\infty$.

To show that the graph of $y(x)$ is placed above the oblique asymptote $y = -x-3$ we put $y_1 = -3 + y_2$ and substitute this into (3.23). We obtain the following algebraic equation for y_2:

$$y_2^3 - 3(x + 3)y_2^2 + 3(x^2 + 3x + 9)y_2 - 27 = 0,$$

which has one sign change for $x \le -3$ and three sign changes for $-3 < x < 0$. In both cases there is at least one positive root. Since y_1 is the only real root of (3.23), we conclude that y_2 is positive, which means that $y(x) > -x - 3$ for $x < 0$.

By the second formula of (3.20) the curve $y(x)$ is tangent to the x-axis from the left at $x = 0$.

We observe that substitutions $x := y$, $y := x$ do not change equation (3.17). This means that the graph of (3.17) is symmetric with respect to the line $y = x$, which intersects the folium of Descartes at $(0,0)$ and $(4.5, 4.5)$.

For $x > 0$ the number of sign variations of the polynomial $f(x, y)$ is two. By Descartes' Rule of signs the equation (3.17) either has two positive roots or none. To determine when there are two positive roots we evaluate

$$f\left(x, \frac{x}{\sqrt[3]{2}}\right) = \frac{3x^2}{2}\left(x - 3\sqrt[3]{4}\right),$$

which is negative for x in the open interval $(0, 3\sqrt[3]{4})$. Since $f(x, 0) = x^3 > 0$, we see that There is a root $y_2(x)$, satisfying

$$0 < y_2(x) < \frac{x}{\sqrt[3]{2}} < x.$$

By the symmetry there is another positive root $y_3(x)$, satisfying $y_3(x) > x$.

To prove that any vertical line with the x-intercept x satisfying $x > 3\sqrt[3]{4}$ does not intersects the folium of Descartes we fix a point (x, y) on this curve with positive coordinates and denote by t the quotient y/x. Substituting $y = tx$ into (3.17), we find that

$$x = \frac{9t}{t^3 + 2} \overset{t=s\cdot 2^{-1/3}}{=} \frac{3s}{s^3 + 2}3\sqrt[3]{4} = 3\sqrt[3]{4}\cdot\left\{1 - \frac{(s-1)^2(s+2)}{s^3 + 2}\right\} < 3\sqrt[3]{4}$$

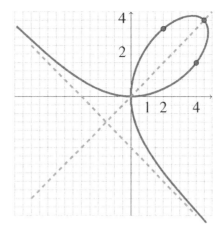

Figure 3.11: The Folium of Descartes.

as stated.

Taking into account that the points $(0,0)$, $(2,4)$, $(4,2)$, $(4.5,4.5)$, $(3\sqrt[3]{4}, 3\sqrt[3]{2})$, $(3\sqrt[3]{2}, 3\sqrt[3]{4})$ are on the folium of Descartes, we connect them by a simple loop. The lower branch for $x > 0$ is obtained by the symmetric reflection. It is clear that $y = -x - 3$ is an oblique asymptote for this part of the folium. More details will be justified later using Implicit Differentiation.   □

Problem 3.59. Using Descartes' Method of tangents find the equation of the tangent to Descartes' Folium

$$y^3 + x^3 = 9xy$$

at a generic point (a, b) of the Folium.

Solution: Following Descartes' Rule of tangents we replace y in the equation of the Folium with a point-slope equation $y = k(x - a) + b$ passing through a point (a, b) on the Folium. The numbers a and b satisfy the equation $b^3 - 9ab + a^3 = 0$ and the resulting equation is

$$0 = (k(x - a) + b)^3 - 9x(k(x - a) + b) + x^3 =$$
$$k^3(x - a)^3 + 3k^2(x - a)^2 b + 3k(x - a)b^2 + b^3 - 9kx(x - a) - 9xb + x^3 =$$
$$p(x)(x - a)^2 + 3k(x - a)b^2 - 9ka(x - a) - 9(x - a)b + x^3 - a^3 + b^3 - 9ab + a^3 =$$
$$p(x)(x - a)^2 + (x - a)\left(3kb^2 - 9ka - 9b + x^2 + ax + a^2\right).$$

The right-hand part of the equation is divisible by $(x - a)^2$ if and only if

$$3kb^2 - 9ka - 9b + 3a^2 = 0 \Rightarrow k = \frac{3b - a^2}{b^2 - 3a}.$$

The point $(4, 2)$ is on the Folium. Then

$$k = \frac{6 - 16}{4 - 12} = \frac{5}{4} \Rightarrow y = \frac{5}{4}x - 3. \quad \square$$

3.9.   Financial Mathematics and $e = 2.71828\ldots$

The interest rate of 5% compounded annually is evaluated by the formula (2.4). To see what is the interest rate of 5% compounded quarterly, we observe that banks operate on a market competitively. It follows that interest rate for equal time intervals must be equal. So, if the interest rate is r% for the full year, then the quarterly compounded interest is $\frac{r}{4}$%. Four quarters make a full year. Hence, if the initial investment was I_0, then the balance of the account in one year is

$$I_0\left(1 + \frac{1}{4} \cdot \frac{r}{100}\right)^4 = I_0\left(1 + \frac{0.01 \cdot r}{4}\right)^4.$$

Similarly, the balance by the end of a year of an account with interest rate r% compounded monthly is

$$I_0\left(1 + \frac{0.01 \cdot r}{12}\right)^{12}.$$

If the interest rate is compounded daily, then the formula for the balance takes the form

$$I_0\left(1 + \frac{0.01 \cdot r}{365}\right)^{365}.$$

Example 3.60. Suppose \$1 000 is invested at the annual interest rate of 5%. Evaluate the balance in one year, if the interest is compounded

(a) Annually: $1000(1 + 0.05) = 1050$.

(b) Quarterly: $1000(1 + 0.05/4)^4 = 1050.9453369141$.

(c) Monthly: $1000(1 + 0.05/12)^{12} = 1051.1618978821$.

(d) Daily $1000(1 + 0.05/365)^{365} = 1051.267496479$.

Calculations in Example 3.60 indicate that the limit

$$\lim_n\left(1 + \frac{s}{n}\right)^n, \quad 0 \leq s \leq 1,$$

exists.

Theorem 3.61. *The following limit exists:*

$$\lim_{x \to +\infty} \left(1 + \frac{1}{x}\right)^x = e = 2.7182818284590....$$

This theorem claims that the interest rate of 100% compounded **continuously** increases the initial investment ≈ 2.72 times. Notice that the interest rate of 100% compounded annually only doubles the initial investment.

We split the proof of Theorem 3.61 into a number of simple steps.

Theorem 3.62 (Newton's Binomial Formula)**.** *Given real numbers a, b and a positive integer n the following formula holds true:*

$$(a + b)^n = a^n + na^{n-1}b^1 + \frac{n(n-1)}{2!}a^{n-2}b^2 + \frac{n(n-1)(n-2)}{3!}a^{n-3}b^3 + \cdots + b^n.$$

Proof. This formula is proved by induction on n.

$$n = 1 : \ a^1 + b^1 = (a+b)^1,$$
$$n = 2 : \ a^2 + 2a^1b^1 + b^2 = (a+b)^2,$$
$$n = 3 : \ a^3 + 3a^2b + 3ab^2 + b^3 = (a+b)^3.$$

Let us assume that Newton's Binomial Formula holds for a positive integer n. Then

$$(a + b)^{n+1} = (a + b) \cdot \left\{a^n + na^{n-1}b^1 + \frac{n(n-1)}{2!}a^{n-2}b^2 + \cdots + b^n\right\} =$$

$$
\begin{array}{cccccc}
a^{n+1}+ & na^nb^1+ & \frac{n(n-1)}{2!}a^{n-1}b^2+ & \cdots + & ab^n+ & \\
\updownarrow & \updownarrow & \updownarrow & \updownarrow & \updownarrow & \updownarrow \\
& ba^n+ & na^{n-1}b^2+ & \frac{n(n-1)}{2!}a^{n-2}b^3+ & \cdots + & b^{n+1}
\end{array}
$$

Observing that

$$n + 1 = n + 1$$
$$\frac{n(n-1)}{2!} + n = \frac{(n+1)n}{2!}$$
$$\frac{n(n-1)(n-2)}{3!} + \frac{n(n-1)}{2!} = \frac{(n+1)(n)(n-1)}{3!} \quad \text{etc}$$

we complete the proof by the Principle of Mathematical Induction. $\qquad\square$

Corollary 3.63. *For any real x and positive integer n the following formula holds true:*

$$\left(1 + \frac{x}{n}\right)^n = 1 + x + \frac{x^2}{2!}\left(1 - \frac{1}{n}\right) + \frac{x^3}{3!}\left(1 - \frac{1}{n}\right)\left(1 - \frac{2}{n}\right) + \cdots +$$
$$\frac{x^n}{n!}\left(1 - \frac{1}{n}\right)\left(1 - \frac{2}{n}\right)\cdots\left(1 - \frac{n-1}{n}\right).$$

(3.26)

Proof. Put $a = 1$, $b = x/n$ in Newton's Binomial Formula. $\square$

Suppose that $x = 1$. Since each term in (3.26) is positive, does not decrease with growth of n, and the number of positive terms increases, The formula (3.26) shows that the sequence

$$\left(1 + \frac{1}{n}\right)^n$$

increases. Moreover, the same formula shows that this sequence is bounded above:

$$\left(1 + \frac{1}{n}\right)^n \leq 2 + \frac{1}{2!} + \frac{1}{3!} + \cdots + \frac{1}{n!} \leq 2 + \frac{1}{2} + \frac{1}{2^2} + \cdots + \frac{1}{2^{n-1}} < 2 + \frac{0.5}{1 - 0.5} = 3.$$

By Theorem 3.23 any increasing sequence bounded above has a finite limit. Therefore, the limit $\lim_n (1 + 1/n)^n$ exists. If $n \leq x < n + 1$ then

$$\left(1 + \frac{1}{n+1}\right)^n \leq \left(1 + \frac{1}{x}\right)^x \leq \left(1 + \frac{1}{n}\right)^{n+1}.$$

The proof of Theorem is completed by Sandwich Theorem. $\square$

Corollary 3.64.
$$e = 2 + \frac{1}{2!} + \frac{1}{3!} + \cdots + \frac{1}{n!} + \cdots .$$

Proof. Let m be a positive integer. Then by (3.26) with $n > m$ and $x = 1$ we have

$$2 + \frac{1}{2!}\left(1 - \frac{1}{n}\right) + \cdots + \frac{1}{m!}\left(1 - \frac{1}{n}\right)\left(1 - \frac{2}{n}\right)\cdots\left(1 - \frac{m-1}{n}\right) < \left(1 + \frac{1}{n}\right)^n < e.$$

Passing in this inequality to the limit, we obtain that

$$2 + \frac{1}{2!} + \frac{1}{3!} + \cdots + \frac{1}{m!} < e.$$

The sequence on the left is increasing and bounded by e. It follows that

$$2 + \frac{1}{2!} + \frac{1}{3!} + \cdots + \frac{1}{n!} + \cdots \le e.$$

By by (3.26) with $x = 1$ we obtain that

$$\left(1 + \frac{1}{n}\right)^n \le 2 + \frac{1}{2!} + \frac{1}{3!} + \cdots + \frac{1}{n!} + \cdots .$$

Passing to the limit in n, we complete the proof. □

Notice that

$$2 + \frac{1}{2!} + \frac{1}{3!} + \frac{1}{4!} + \frac{1}{5!} + \frac{1}{6!} + \frac{1}{7!} + \frac{1}{8!} + \frac{1}{9!} + \frac{1}{10!} = \frac{9864101}{3628800},$$

which provides a very good approximation 2.7182818 to the number e.

3.10. Remarkable Limits

Theorem 3.65 (The First Remarkable Limit).

$$\lim_{x \to 0} \frac{e^x - 1}{x} = 1.$$

Proof. By (3.26) we have for positive x:

$$1 + x \le \left(1 + \frac{x}{n}\right)^n < 1 + x + \frac{x^2}{2!} + \cdots + \frac{x^n}{n!}.$$

Since

$$n! = 1 \cdot 2 \cdot 3 \cdot \cdots \cdot n \ge \underbrace{2 \cdot \cdots \cdot 2}_{n-1} = 2^{n-1},$$

we conclude by the formula for the sum of geometric progression, assuming that $0 < x < 2$:

$$\frac{x^2}{2!} + \cdots + \frac{x^n}{n!} \le \frac{x^2}{2} + \frac{x^3}{2^2} + \cdots + \frac{x^n}{2^{n-1}} =$$

$$\frac{x^2}{2}\left(1 + \frac{x}{2} + \cdots + \frac{x^{n-2}}{2^{n-2}}\right) = \frac{x^2}{2} \frac{1 - \left(\frac{x}{2}\right)^{n-1}}{1 - \frac{x}{2}} < \frac{x^2}{2 - x}.$$

It follows that for $0 < x < 2$ and any positive integer n

$$1 + x \le \left(1 + \frac{x}{n}\right)^n < 1 + x + \frac{x^2}{2 - x}. \tag{3.27}$$

Passing to the limit in n, we obtain

$$1 + x \le e^x \le 1 + x + \frac{x^2}{2 - x}.$$

It follows that

$$1 \le \frac{e^x - 1}{x} \le 1 + \frac{x}{2 - x}.$$

By Sandwich Theorem this implies

$$\lim_{x \to 0^+} \frac{e^x - 1}{x} = 1.$$

Finally,

$$\lim_{x \to 0^-} \frac{e^x - 1}{x} = \lim_{x \to 0^+} \frac{e^{-x} - 1}{-x} = \lim_{x \to 0^+} e^{-x} \cdot \lim_{x \to 0^+} \frac{e^x - 1}{x} = 1,$$

since the function $y = e^{-x}$ is continuous at $x = 0$. $\qquad\square$

Corollary 3.66. *The instantaneous rate of change of $y = e^x$ at $x = x_0$ is e^{x_0}.*

Proof. We have

$$\lim_{x \to x_0} \frac{e^x - e^{x_0}}{x - x_0} = e^{x_0} \lim_{x \to x_0} \frac{e^{x - x_0} - 1}{x - x_0} = e^{x_0} \cdot \lim_{y \to 0} \frac{e^y - 1}{y} = e^{x_0}. \qquad\square$$

Theorem 3.67 (The Second Remarkable Limit).

$$\lim_{x \to 0} \frac{\ln(1 + x)}{x} = 1.$$

Proof. Let $x = e^t - 1$. Then $x = 0$ if and only if $t = 0$. Since the function $e^t - 1$ is continuous, we conclude that $\lim_{t \to 0} x(t) = 0$. It follows that

$$\lim_{x \to 0} \frac{\ln(1 + x)}{x} = \lim_{t \to 0} \frac{\ln(1 + e^t - 1)}{e^t - 1} = \lim_{t \to 0} \frac{t}{e^t - 1} = \frac{1}{\lim_{t \to 0} \dfrac{e^t - 1}{t}} = \frac{1}{1} = 1. \qquad\square$$

Corollary 3.68. *The instantaneous rate of change of $y = \ln x$ at $x = x_0$ is $1/x_0$.*

Proof. We have

$$\lim_{x \to x_0} \frac{\ln x - \ln x_0}{x - x_0} = \lim_{x \to x_0} \frac{\ln\left(\dfrac{x}{x_0}\right)}{x - x_0} = \lim_{x \to x_0} \frac{1}{x_0} \frac{\ln\left(1 + \dfrac{x - x_0}{x_0}\right)}{\dfrac{x - x_0}{x_0}} \overset{y = \frac{x - x_0}{x_0}}{=\!=}$$

$$\frac{1}{x_0} \lim_{y \to 0} \frac{\ln(1 + y)}{y} = \frac{1}{x_0}.$$

$\qquad\square$

Corollary 3.69.

$$\lim_{x \to +\infty} \left(1 - \frac{1}{x}\right)^x = \frac{1}{e}.$$

Proof.

$$\lim_{x \to +\infty} \left(1 - \frac{1}{x}\right)^x = \frac{\lim_{x \to +\infty} \left(1 - \frac{1}{x^2}\right)^x}{\lim_{x \to +\infty} \left(1 + \frac{1}{x}\right)^x} = \frac{\lim_{x \to +\infty} e^{x \ln\left(1 - \frac{1}{x^2}\right)}}{\lim_{x \to +\infty} \left(1 + \frac{1}{x}\right)^x}. \qquad (3.28)$$

Since the function $y = e^x$ is continuous,

$$\lim_{x \to +\infty} e^{x \ln\left(1 - \frac{1}{x^2}\right)} = e^{\lim_{x \to +\infty} x \ln\left(1 - \frac{1}{x^2}\right)}.$$

By Theorem 3.67

$$\lim_{x \to +\infty} x \ln\left(1 - \frac{1}{x^2}\right) = \lim_{x \to +\infty} \frac{-1}{x} \cdot \frac{\ln\left(1 - \frac{1}{x^2}\right)}{-\frac{1}{x^2}} \overset{y = -1/x^2}{=}$$

$$\lim_{x \to +\infty} \frac{-1}{x} \cdot \lim_{y \to 0} \frac{\ln(1 + y)}{y} = 0 \cdot 1 = 0.$$

Finally, combining in (3.28) these calculations with Theorem 3.61, we obtain the result stated. $\qquad \square$

Theorem 3.70 (The Third Remarkable Limit). *Let $\alpha \in \mathbb{R}$. Then*

$$\lim_{x \to 0} \frac{(1 + x)^\alpha - 1}{x} = \alpha.$$

Proof. If $\alpha = 0$, then the formula is obvious. Suppose that $\alpha \neq 0$. Then

$$\lim_{x \to 0} \frac{(1 + x)^\alpha - 1}{x} = \lim_{x \to 0} \frac{e^{\alpha \ln(1 + x)} - 1}{x} \overset{y = \alpha \ln(1 + x)}{=} \lim_{y \to 0} \frac{e^y - 1}{e^{y/\alpha} - 1} =$$

$$\alpha \cdot \lim_{y \to 0} \frac{e^y - 1}{y} \cdot \lim_{y \to 0} \frac{y/\alpha}{e^{y/\alpha} - 1} = \alpha.$$

$\qquad \square$

Corollary 3.71. *The instantaneous rate of change of $y = x^\alpha$, where $\alpha \neq 0$, at $x = x_0$ is $\alpha x^{\alpha - 1}$.*

Proof.

$$\lim_{x \to x_0} \frac{x^\alpha - x_0^\alpha}{x - x_0} = x_0^{\alpha - 1} \lim_{x \to x_0} \frac{\left(\frac{x}{x_0}\right)^\alpha - 1}{\frac{x}{x_0} - 1} = x_0^{\alpha - 1} \lim_{x \to x_0} \frac{\left(1 + \frac{x}{x_0} - 1\right)^\alpha - 1}{\frac{x}{x_0} - 1} \overset{y = \frac{x}{x_0} - 1}{=}$$

$$x_0^{\alpha - 1} \lim_{y \to 0} \frac{(1 + y)^\alpha - 1}{y} = \alpha x_0^{\alpha - 1}.$$

$\qquad \square$

Theorem 3.72 (The Fourth Remarkable Limit).

$$\lim_{x \to 0} \frac{\sin x}{x} = 1.$$

Proof. If we apply the formula (2.9), then

$$1 = \lim_{x \to 0} \frac{e^{ix} - 1}{ix} = \frac{1}{i} \lim_{x \to 0} \frac{\cos x - 1}{x} + \lim_{x \to 0} \frac{\sin x}{x} \Rightarrow \lim_{x \to 0} \frac{\sin x}{x} = 1.$$

This calculation shows that even this remarkable limit is related in fact to the First Remarkable Limit. However, justification of these arguments is beyond this course. Therefore, we provide another proof.

To begin with we observe that the ratio $(\sin x)/x$ is an even function with the natural domain $x \neq 0$. Therefore, it is enough to prove that

$$\lim_{x \to 0^+} \frac{\sin x}{x} = 1.$$

Now, we plot the reference triangle $\triangle POQ$ for $\sin x$ and the tangent axis AB for $\tan x$. We evaluate the areas (see Fig 3.12):

$$\frac{\sin x}{2} = \text{Area}(\triangle POA) < \text{Area}(\text{Sector}(OAP)) = \frac{x}{2} < \text{Area}(\triangle OAB) = \frac{\tan x}{2}.$$

It follows that

$$1 < \frac{x}{\sin x} < \frac{1}{\cos x} \Rightarrow \boxed{\cos x < \frac{\sin x}{x} < 1}. \tag{3.29}$$

By Corollary 3.32 $\lim_{x \to 0} \cos x = \cos 0 = 1$. The proof is completed by Theorem 3.57. $\qquad\square$

Corollary 3.73. *The instantaneous rate of change of $y = \sin x$ at $x = x_0$ is $\cos x_0$.*

Proof. By (2.12) and Theorem 3.72

$$\lim_{x \to x_0} \frac{\sin x - \sin x_0}{x - x_0} = \lim_{x \to x_0} 2 \cos \frac{x + x_0}{2} \sin \frac{x - x_0}{2} \cdot \frac{1}{x - x_0} =$$

$$\lim_{x \to x_0} \cos \frac{x + x_0}{2} \cdot \lim_{x \to x_0} \frac{\sin \frac{x - x_0}{2}}{\frac{x - x_0}{2}} \overset{y = \frac{x - x_0}{2}}{=} \cos \frac{x_0 + x_0}{2} \cdot \lim_{y \to 0} \frac{\sin y}{y} = \cos x_0,$$

as stated. $\qquad\square$

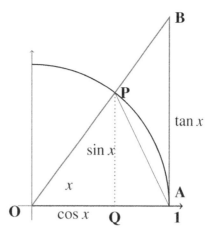

Figure 3.12: Areas of the sector and triangles.

3.11.   Exercises

Exercise 3.74. Find each limit, if it exists:

$$(a) \ \lim_{x \to a^-} f(x) \quad (b) \ \lim_{x \to a^+} f(x) \quad (c) \ \lim_{x \to a} f(x)$$

for $f(x) = \sqrt[3]{x^3 - 1}$, $a = 1$.

Solution: The function $z = \sqrt[3]{y}$ is monotonic on $\mathbb{R}$ and the equation $z = \sqrt[3]{y}$ has a unique solution $y = z^3$ for every z. By Theorem 3.29 the function $z = \sqrt[3]{y}$ is continuous in y everywhere. Therefore,

$$\lim_{x \to 1} f(x) = \sqrt[3]{\lim_{x \to 1}(x^3 - 1)}.$$

By Theorem 3.52 we obtain that $\lim_{x \to 1}(x^3 - 1) = 1^3 - 1 = 0$.
    Answer: $\lim_{x \to 1^-} f(x) = \lim_{x \to 1^+} f(x) = \lim_{x \to 1} f(x) = 0$.   □

Exercise 3.75. Sketch the graph of $f(x)$ and find each limit, if it exists:

$$(a) \ \lim_{x \to 1^-} f(x) \quad (b) \ \lim_{x \to 1^+} f(x) \quad (c) \ \lim_{x \to 1} f(x)$$

$$f(x) = \begin{cases} x^2 + x + 1 & \text{if } x < 1 \\ 5 - 2x & \text{if } x \geq 1 \end{cases}$$

Solution:

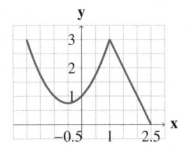

For $x < 1$ the graph of $y = f(x)$ coincides with the parabola

$$y = x^2 + x + 1 = (x + 0.5)^2 + 0.75.$$

For $x > 1$ the graph of $y = f(x)$ coincides with the line $y = 5 - 2x$ passing through $(1, 3)$ and $(2.5, 0)$. So, we have by Theorem 3.52:

$$\lim_{x \to 1^-} f(x) = \lim_{x \to 1}(x^2 + x + 1) = 3 = \lim_{x \to 1}(5 - 2x) = \lim_{x \to 1^-} f(x).$$

By Theorem 3.9 the limit $\lim_{x \to 1} f(x)$ exists and equals 3.   □

Exercise 3.76. Evaluate the limit

$$\lim_{x \to 0} \frac{x(1 - \cos(-2x))}{x^3 + x^2}.$$

   Solution: We have

$$1 - \cos(-2x) = 1 - \cos(2x) = \cos^2 x + \sin^2 x - (\cos^2 x - \sin^2 x) = 2 \sin^2 x.$$

Then, applying Theorem 3.52 and Theorem 3.72, we obtain

$$\lim_{x \to 0} \frac{x(1 - \cos(-2x))}{x^3 + x^2} = \lim_{x \to 0} \frac{2 \sin^2 x}{x^2 + x} = 2 \lim_{x \to 0} \left(\frac{\sin x}{x} \right)^2 \frac{x^2}{x^2 + x} =$$

$$2 \cdot 1^2 \lim_{x \to 0} \frac{x}{x + 1} = 2 \cdot 1 \cdot 0 = 0.$$

□

Exercise 3.77. Evaluate the limit:

$$\lim_{x \to 0} \frac{1 - \cos(1 - \cos x)}{x^4}.$$

   Solution: By Corollary 3.32 the function $y = \cos x$ is continuous at $x = 0$ and $1 - \cos x \neq 0$ for $0 < |x| < \pi/2$. Then by Theorem 3.56 and Theorem 3.52:

$$\lim_{x \to 0} \frac{1 - \cos(1 - \cos x)}{x^4} = \lim_{x \to 0} \frac{1 - \cos(1 - \cos x)}{(1 - \cos x)^2} \cdot \frac{(1 - \cos x)^2}{x^4} \overset{y = 1 - \cos x}{=}$$

$$\lim_{y \to 0} \frac{1 - \cos y}{y^2} \cdot \lim_{x \to 0} \left(\frac{1 - \cos x}{x^2} \right)^2 = \left(\lim_{x \to 0} \frac{1 - \cos x}{x^2} \right)^3.$$

Since by Theorem 3.72

$$\frac{1 - \cos x}{x^2} = \frac{2 \sin^2\left(\frac{x}{2}\right)}{x^2} = \frac{1}{2} \frac{\sin^2\left(\frac{x}{2}\right)}{\left(\frac{x}{2}\right)^2} \xrightarrow[x \to 0]{} \frac{1}{2},$$

the required limit equals $1/8$. $\square$

Exercise 3.78. Evaluate the limit:

$$\lim_{x \to \infty} \left(\frac{x^2 + 1}{x^2 - 1}\right)^{x^2}.$$

Solution: By Theorem 3.61 and Corollary 3.69

$$\lim_{x \to \infty} \left(\frac{x^2 + 1}{x^2 - 1}\right)^{x^2} = \lim_{x \to \infty} \frac{\left(1 + \frac{1}{x^2}\right)^{x^2}}{\left(1 - \frac{1}{x^2}\right)^{x^2}} = \frac{\lim_{x \to \infty}\left(1 + \frac{1}{x^2}\right)^{x^2}}{\lim_{x \to \infty}\left(1 - \frac{1}{x^2}\right)^{x^2}} \overset{y = x^2}{=} \frac{\lim_{y \to +\infty}\left(1 + \frac{1}{y}\right)^{y}}{\lim_{x \to \infty}\left(1 - \frac{1}{y}\right)^{y}} =$$

$$\frac{e}{1/e} = e^2.$$

$\square$

Exercise 3.79. Evaluate the limit:

$$\lim_{x \to +\infty} \left(\cos \sqrt{x + 1} - \cos \sqrt{x}\right).$$

Solution: By (2.11)

$$\cos \sqrt{x + 1} - \cos \sqrt{x} = -2 \sin \frac{\sqrt{x + 1} + \sqrt{x}}{2} \sin \frac{\sqrt{x + 1} - \sqrt{x}}{2} =$$

$$-2 \sin \frac{\sqrt{x + 1} + \sqrt{x}}{2} \sin \frac{1}{2\left(\sqrt{x + 1} + \sqrt{x}\right)} \overset{y = \frac{1}{2\left(\sqrt{x+1} + \sqrt{x}\right)}}{=} -2 \sin \frac{1}{y} \sin y.$$

Since $y \to 0^+$ if $x \to +\infty$, we obtain that

$$\lim_{x \to +\infty} \left(\cos \sqrt{x + 1} - \cos \sqrt{x}\right) = \lim_{y \to 0^+} \left(-2 \sin \frac{1}{y}\right) \cdot \sin y.$$

Finally, since for $y > 0$

$$-2 \sin y \le \left(-2 \sin \frac{1}{y}\right) \cdot \sin y \le 2 \sin y,$$

and since $\lim_{y \to 0} \sin y = 0$, we conclude by Theorem 3.57 that the limit exists and equals 0. $\square$

Exercise 3.80. Evaluate the limit

$$\lim_{x \to 0} \frac{2x - \arctan x}{2x + \arctan x}.$$

Solution:

$$\lim_{x \to 0} \frac{2x - \arctan x}{2x + \arctan x} \overset{x = \tan y}{=} \lim_{y \to 0} \frac{2 \tan y - y}{2 \tan y + y} = \lim_{y \to 0} \frac{2 \sin y - y \cos y}{2 \sin y + y \cos y} =$$

$$\lim_{y \to 0} \frac{2 \sin y}{2 \sin y + y \cos y} - \lim_{y \to 0} \frac{y \cos y}{2 \sin y + y \cos y} =$$

$$\lim_{y \to 0} \frac{2 \frac{\sin y}{y}}{2 \frac{\sin y}{y} + \cos y} - \lim_{y \to 0} \frac{\cos y}{2 \frac{\sin y}{y} + \cos y} = \frac{2}{2 + 1} - \frac{1}{2 + 1} = \frac{1}{3}. \quad \square$$

Exercise 3.81. Show that the function $y = (x - a)^3(x - b)^4 + x$ takes the value $(a + b)/2$ for some positive value of x.

Solution: The function $y(x)$ is continuous and $y(a) = a$, $y(b) = b$. Since the value $(a + b)/2$ is between a and b by the Intermediate Value Theorem $f(c) = (a + b)/2$ at some point between a and b. $\quad \square$

Problems

Prob. 58 — Evaluate

$$\lim_{x \to 0} \frac{\sqrt{x + 4} - 2}{\sin 5x} =$$

(A) $\dfrac{1}{5}$ (B) $\dfrac{1}{10}$ (C) $\dfrac{1}{20}$ (D) 2 (E) **nonexistent**

Prob. 59 — Find

$$\lim_{x \to e^+} \frac{[1 + \sin(x - e)]^{\frac{e}{x - e}}}{\frac{1}{x + 3e - x}}.$$

(A) e^{e-1} (B) e (C) 0 (D) 1 (E) **nonexitent**

Prob. 60 — Find

$$\lim_{x \to 0} (\cos x)^{\cot^2 2x} =$$

(A) $-e$ (B) 1 (C) 0 (D) $e^{-\frac{1}{8}}$ (E) **none of these**

Prob. 61 — Evaluate

$$\lim_{x \to 0} (1 + \tan x)^{\dfrac{x^2}{\sin^2 2x}} =$$

(A) 0 (B) 4 (C) 1 (D) 3 (E) **none of these**

Prob. 62 — Evaluate

$$\lim_{x \to \pi} \frac{\sin \pi - \sin x}{\pi - x} =$$

(A) 0 (B) -1 (C) 1 (D) ∞ (E) **nonexistent**

Prob. 63 — Evaluate

$$\lim_{x \to \infty} \frac{3x^2 - 2x - 1}{x^3 + 4} =$$

(A) 3 (B) $\dfrac{3}{4}$ (C) $-\dfrac{1}{4}$ (D) 0 (E) **nonexistent**

Prob. 64 — Evaluate

$$\lim_{x \to 4^-} \frac{3}{x + 2^{\dfrac{1}{x - 4}}} =$$

(A) 0 (B) $\dfrac{3}{4}$ (C) $-\dfrac{3}{4}$ (D) $\dfrac{3}{2}$ (E) **nonexistent**

Prob. 65 — Evaluate

$$\lim_{x \to 3^+} \sqrt{9 - x^2} =$$

(A) 3 (B) 0 (C) -3 (D) 1 (E) **nonexistent**

Prob. 66 — Evaluate

$$\lim_{x \to \infty} \frac{\sin^2(x - 9)}{(x - 3)^2} =$$

(A) 1 (B) 3 (C) 9 (D) 0 (E) **nonexistent**

Prob. 67 — Evaluate

$$\lim_{x \to \pi/2} \left(\frac{\sin x}{\cos^2 x} - \tan^2 x \right) =$$

(A) $\dfrac{1}{2}$ (B) -1 (C) 0 (D) 1 (E) ∞

Prob. 68 — Which of the following statements is or are true?

I $\lim_{x \to +\infty} \frac{\sin x}{x} = 1$

II $\lim_{x \to -3} \frac{x^2+5x+6}{x^2+x-6} = \frac{1}{5}$

III $\lim_{x \to 4} \frac{2-\sqrt{x}}{4-x} = \frac{1}{4}$

(A) I and II only (B) I and III only (C) II and III only (D) I, II, and III

Prob. 69 — Which of the following is continuous at x = 0 ?

I. $f(x) = |x|$ II. $f(x) = e^x$ III. $f(x) = \ln(e^x - 1)$

(A) I only (B) II only (C) II and III only

(D) I and; II only (E) **none of these**

Prob. 70 — The graph of a function f is reflected across the x-axis and then shifted up 2 units. Which of the following describes this transformation on f?

(A) $-f(x)$ (B) $f(x) + 2$ (C) $-f(x+2)$ (D) $-f(x-2)$ (E) $-f(x) + 2$

Prob. 71 — Which of the following functions is not continuous for all real numbers x?

(A) $f(x) = x^{1/3}$ (B) $f(x) = \dfrac{2}{(x+1)^4}$ (C) $f(x) = |x+1|$

(D) $f(x) = \sqrt{1+e^x}$ (E) $f(x) = \dfrac{x-3}{x^2+9}$

Prob. 72 — Which of the following is NOT necessary to establish in order to show that a function $f(x)$ is continuous at the point $x = c$?

(A) $f(c)$ exists;

(B) Domain of $f(x)$ is all real numbers;

(C) $\lim_{x \to c} f(x) = f(c)$;

(D) $\lim_{x \to c} f(x)$ exists;

(E) All of these are necessary.

Prob. 73 —

$$\lim_{x \to 1} \frac{\ln x}{x} =$$

(A) 0 (B) 1 (C) e (D) $-e$ (E) **nonexistent**

Prob. 74 — Evaluate

$$\lim_{x \to \infty} \frac{x^3 - 4x + 1}{2x^3 - 5} =$$

(A) $-\dfrac{1}{5}$ (B) $\dfrac{1}{2}$ (C) $\dfrac{2}{3}$ (D) 1 (E) **nonexistent**

Prob. 75 — For what value of k does

$$\lim_{x \to 4} \frac{x^2 - x + k}{x - 4} \quad \text{exist?}$$

(A) 7 (B) 3 (C) -4 (D) -12 (E) **No such value exists**

Prob. 76 — Suppose f is defined as

$$f(x) = \begin{cases} \dfrac{|x| - 2}{x - 2} & \text{if } x \neq 2 \\ k & \text{if } x = 2. \end{cases}$$

Then the value of k for which $f(x)$ is continuous for all real values of x is

(A) -1 (B) 0 (C) 1 (D) -2 (E) **No such value exists**

Prob. 77 — The function

$$G(x) = \begin{cases} x - 5 & \text{if } x > 2 \\ -5 & \text{if } x = 2 \\ 5x - 13 & \text{if } x < 2 \end{cases}$$

is not continuous at $x = 2$ because

(A) $G(2)$ is not defined (B) $\lim\limits_{x \to 2} G(x)$ does not exist

(C) $\lim\limits_{x \to 2} G(x) \neq G(2)$ (D) $G(2) \neq -5$ (E) **None of the above**

Prob. 78 — Evaluate

$$\lim_{x \to -2} \frac{\sqrt{2x + 5} - 1}{x + 2} =$$

(A) 1 (B) 0 (C) $+\infty$ (D) $-\infty$ (E) **Does not exist**

Prob. 79 — The Intermediate Value Theorem states that given a continuous function f defined on the closed interval $[a, b]$ for which 0 is between $f(a)$ and $f(b)$, there exists a point c between a and b such that

(A) $c = a - b$ (B) $f(a) = f(b)$ (C) $f(c) = 0$ (D) $f(0) = c$ (E) $c = 0$

Prob. 80 — If $f(x) = x^3 - 10x + 10000$, show that there is a value c such that $f(c) = e$.

Prob. 81 — Extend Theorem 3.29 to monotonic functions.
Hint: Apply one-sided limits.

Prob. 82 — Given that the demand and supply curves are

$$q^S(p) = 0.2p^2 + 0.3p - 1, \quad q^D(p) = 10 - p - 0.05p^2,$$

find the equilibrium price and quantity, and sketch the curves for $1 \le p \le 10$.

Prob. 83 — The function

$$f(x) = 2^x - \frac{|x - 3|}{x - 3} \text{ has}$$

(A) a removable discontinuity at $x = 3$ (B) an infinite discontinuity at $x = 3$

(C) a jump discontinuity at $x = 3$ (D) no discontinuities

(E) a removable discontinuity at $x = 0$ and an infinite discontinuity at $x = 3$.

Prob. 84 — Find the values of c so that the function

$$f(x) = \begin{cases} c^2 - x^2 & \text{if } x < 2 \\ x + c & \text{if } x \ge 2 \end{cases}$$

is continuous everywhere.

(A) $-3, -2$ (B) $2, 3$ (C) $2, -3$ (D) $3, -2$ (E) **No such values exist**

Prob. 85 — Let f be the function defined by the following formulas:

$$f(x) = \begin{cases} \sin x & \text{if } x < 0 \\ x^2 & \text{if } 0 \le x < 1 \\ 2 - x & \text{if } 1 \le x < 2 \\ x - 3 & \text{if } 2 \le x \end{cases}$$

For what values of x is f NOT continuous?

(A) 0 only (B) 1 only (C) 2 only (D) 0 and 2 only (E) 0, 1, and 2

Prob. 86 — Let f be a continuous function on the closed interval $[-3,6]$. If $f(-3) = -1$ and $f(6) = 3$, then the Intermediate Value Theorem guarantees that

(A) $f(0) = 0$

(B) The slope of the graph of f is $\dfrac{4}{9}$ somewhere between -3 and 6

(C) $-1 \le f(x) \le 3$ for all x between -3 and 6

(D) $f(c) = 1$ for at least one c between -3 and -6

(E) $f(c) = 1$ for at least one c between -1 and 3

Prob. 87 — The function f is continuous on the closed interval $[0,2]$ and has values that are given in the table below.

x	0	1	2
$f(x)$	1	k	2

The equation $f(x) = 0.5$ must have at least two solutions in the interval $[0,2]$ if $k =$

(A) 0 (B) $\dfrac{1}{2}$ (C) 1 (D) 2 (E) 3

Prob. 88 — Which of the following points of discontinuity of

$$f(x) = \frac{x(x-1)(x-2)(x+1)^2(x-3)^2}{x(x-1)(x-2)^2(x+1)^2(x-3)^2}$$

is not removable?

(A) $x = -1$ (B) $x = 0$ (C) $x = 1$ (D) $x = 2$ (E) $x = 3$

Prob. 89 — If f is continuous on $[-4,4]$ such that $f(-4) = 11$ and $f(4) = -11$, then which must be true?

(A) $f(0) = 0$ (B) $\lim\limits_{x \to 2} f(x) = 8$ (C) $\lim\limits_{x \to 3} f(x) = \lim\limits_{x \to -3} f(x)$

(D) f is not defined at $x = 0$ (E) there is $c \in [-4,4]$ such that $f(c) = 8$

Prob. 90 — If f is continuous on $[1,8]$ and some values of f are given in the table below

x	1	3	5	8
$f(x)$	-2	4	10	6

then which of the following must be true?

    I. $f(x) = 3$ has a solution in $[1, 8]$

   II. $f(x) = 0$ has a solution in $[1, 8]$

  III. $f(x) = 9$ has a solution in $[1, 8]$

    (A) I only **(B)** II only **(C)** II and III only

    (D) I and; II only **(E) none of these**

Prob. 91 — A hiker leaves the base of a mountain at 6:00 A.M. and takes a path to the mountain top. He arrives at the summit at 6:00 P.M. The next morning he leaves at 6:00 A.M. down the path he climbed up and comes to the mountain base at 6:00 P.M. Both ways were made nonstop. Is there a point on the path that the hiker will cross exactly the same time of day on both days? How many such points may exist?

Prob. 92 — Evaluate the limit:

$$\lim_{x \to 0}(1 + \tan^2 \sqrt{x})^{\frac{1}{2x}}.$$

Prob. 93 — Are there values k such that

$$f(x) = \begin{cases} 2kx - 3 \text{ for } x > 2 \\ 3kx + 5k \text{ for } x \le 2 \end{cases}$$

is continuous?

Prob. 94 — Find the number of real roots of the equation:

$$x^3 - 15x + 1 = 0.$$

Chapter 4

Differentiation Rules

Abstract

The Rules of Differentiation. Logarithmic Derivatives. Derivatives of Inverse Functions. Tangents and Normals. Linearization and Leibnitz differentials. Related Rates.

Keywords: rational functions, the chain rule, relative rate of change, percentage rate of change, differential, marginal cost,

4.1. Basic Rules

Theorem 4.1 (The Sum Rule). *If u and v are differentiable functions at $x = c$, then $u + v$ is differentiable at $x = c$ and*

$$(u + v)'(c) = u'(c) + v'(c).$$

Proof. Apply the definition of the derivative and the Sum Rule for limits. □

Theorem 4.2 (The Product Rule). *If u and v are differentiable functions at $x = c$, then uv is differentiable at $x = c$ and*

$$(u \cdot v)'(c) = u'(c) \cdot v(c) + u(c) \cdot v'(c).$$

Proof. Since

$$u(c+\Delta x)v(c+\Delta x)-u(c)v(c) = u(c+\Delta x)\left\{v(c + \Delta x) - v(c)\right\}+v(c)\left\{u(c + \Delta x) - u(c)\right\},$$

we obtain that

$$(u \cdot v)'(c) = \lim_{\Delta x \to 0} \frac{u(c + \Delta x)v(c + \Delta x) - u(c)v(c)}{\Delta x} =$$

$$\lim_{\Delta x \to 0} u(c + \Delta x) \lim_{\Delta x \to 0} \frac{v(c + \Delta x) - v(c)}{\Delta x} + v(c) \lim_{\Delta x \to 0} \frac{u(c + \Delta x) - u(c)}{\Delta x} =$$

$$u(c)v'(c) + v(c)u'(c) = u'(c)v(c) + u(c)v'(c)$$

as stated. □

Theorem 4.3 (The Quotient Rule). *If u and v are differentiable functions at $x = c$ and $v(c) \neq 0$, then u/v is differentiable at $x = c$ and*

$$\left(\frac{u}{v}\right)'(c) = \frac{u'(c) \cdot v(c) - u(c) \cdot v'(c)}{v^2(c)}. \tag{4.1}$$

Proof. Since v is differentiable at c, it is continuous at c. Since $v(c) \neq 0$, we obtain that $\lim_{\Delta x \to 0} v(c + \Delta x) = v(c) \neq 0$, implying that $v(c + \Delta x) \neq 0$ if Δx is sufficiently small. Since

$$\frac{u(c + \Delta x)}{v(c + \Delta x)} - \frac{u(c)}{v(c)} = \frac{\{u(c + \Delta x) - u(c)\} v(c) - u(c) \{v(c + \Delta x) - v(c)\}}{v(c + \Delta x)v(c)},$$

we obtain (4.1) by Theorem 3.52. □

The following corollary is useful in practical calculations.

Corollary 4.4 (The Reciprocal Rule). *If v is differentiable at $x = c$ and $v(c) \neq 0$, then*

$$\left(\frac{1}{v}\right)' = -\frac{v'}{v^2}.$$

Proof. Put $u \equiv 1$ in (4.1). □

Theorem 4.5 (The Chain Rule). *Let g be a function defined about c which is differentiable at c. Let f be a function defined about $g(c)$ and be differentiable at $g(c)$. Then the superposition $f \circ g$ is defined about c, is differentiable at c and*

$$(f \circ g)'(c) = f'(g(c)) \cdot g'(c).$$

Proof. Since f is defined about $g(c)$, there is $\varepsilon > 0$ such that f is defined on the interval $I = (g(c) - \varepsilon, g(c) + \varepsilon)$. Since g is differential at c, it is continuous at c. Therefore, there is $\delta > 0$ such that $g(x)$ is in I for every x satisfying $|x - c| < \delta$. It follows that $f \circ g$ is defined on $(c - \delta, c + \delta)$.

Table 4.1: Derivatives of Basic functions.

n	$f(x)$	$f'(x)$	n	$f(x)$	$f'(x)$
1	x^α	$\alpha x^{\alpha-1}$	**2**	x^2	$2x$
3	$\dfrac{1}{x}$	$-\frac{1}{x^2}$	**4**	$\sqrt{x}$	$\frac{1}{2\sqrt{x}}$
5	e^x	e^x	**6**	$\ln x$	$\frac{1}{x}$
7	a^x	$a^x \ln a$	**8**	$\log_a x$	$\frac{1}{x\ln a}$
9	$\ln\left(x + \sqrt{x^2+1}\right)$	$\frac{1}{\sqrt{x^2+1}}$	**10**	$\ln\left(x + \sqrt{x^2-1}\right)$	$\frac{1}{\sqrt{x^2-1}}$
11	$\sin x$	$\cos x$	**12**	$\cos x$	$-\sin x$
13	$\tan x$	$\sec^2 x$	**14**	$\cot x$	$-\csc^2 x$

Let us consider on $(c - \delta, c + \delta)$ an auxiliary function

$$F(x) = \begin{cases} \dfrac{f(g(x)) - f(g(c))}{g(x) - g(c)} & \text{if } g(x) \neq g(c) \\ f'(g(c)) & \text{if } g(x) = g(c) \end{cases}$$

Then

$$\lim_{x \to c} F(x) = f'(g(c))$$

by Theorem 3.56. It follows that

$$(f \circ g)'(c) = \lim_{x \to c} F(x) \cdot \frac{g(x) - g(c)}{x - c} = f'(g(c)) \cdot g'(c). \qquad \square$$

The results of section 3.10 are included in Table 4.1. Table 4.1 includes also some useful lines, which are justified in problems below.

Using Differentiation Rules and Table 4.1 we can find derivatives of many functions.

Definition 4.6. A function f is called **rational** if it can be represented as a quotient of two polynomials $f(x) = P(x)/Q(x)$. The set of all rational functions in x is denoted by $\mathbb{R}(x)$. Here $\mathbb{R}$ denotes the set of real numbers which are taken as coefficients in polynomials $P(x)$ and $Q(x)$.

It is clear that $\mathbb{R}(x)$ is closed with respect to algebraic operations, as well as with respect to compositions of functions. By Theorems 4.1, 4.2, 4.3 the set $\mathbb{R}(x)$ is closed under differentiation.

It is important to observe that the transcendent function $y = \ln x$ has a rational derivative.

Problem 4.7. Evaluate the derivative of $y = a^x$, $a > 0$, $a \neq 1$.

Solution:

$$y' = \left(e^{x\ln a}\right)' \overset{\text{Th. 4.5}}{=} \left(e^{x\ln a}\right)\ln a = a^x \ln a. \quad \square$$

Problem 4.8. Evaluate the derivative of $y = \log_a x$, $a > 0$, $a \neq 1$.

Solution:

$$y' = \left(\frac{\ln x}{\ln a}\right)' = \frac{1}{x\ln a}. \quad \square$$

Problem 4.9. [5, p. 85]. Evaluate the derivative of $y = \frac{1}{x}\sqrt{a^2 - x^2}$.

Solution:

$$y' \overset{\text{Th. 4.2}}{=} \left(\frac{1}{x}\right)'\sqrt{a^2 - x^2} + \frac{1}{x}\left(\sqrt{a^2 - x^2}\right)' \overset{\text{Th. 4.5}}{=}$$

$$-\frac{\sqrt{a^2 - x^2}}{x^2} + \frac{1}{x}\cdot\frac{(a^2 - x^2)'}{2\sqrt{a^2 - x^2}} = -\frac{\sqrt{a^2 - x^2}}{x^2} - \frac{1}{\sqrt{a^2 - x^2}} =$$

$$-\frac{a^2 - x^2}{x^2\sqrt{a^2 - x^2}} - \frac{x^2}{x^2\sqrt{a^2 - x^2}} = -\frac{a^2}{x^2\sqrt{a^2 - x^2}}.$$

Problem 4.10. [5, 86]. Evaluate the derivative of $y = \frac{x}{x+\sqrt{1+x^2}}$.

Solution:

$$y' \overset{\text{Th. 4.3}}{=} \frac{1\cdot\left(x+\sqrt{1+x^2}\right) - x\left(x+\sqrt{1+x^2}\right)'}{\left(x+\sqrt{1+x^2}\right)^2} \overset{\text{Th. 4.1}}{=}$$

$$\frac{x+\sqrt{1+x^2} - x - x\left(\sqrt{1+x^2}\right)'}{\left(x+\sqrt{1+x^2}\right)^2} = \frac{x+\sqrt{1+x^2} - x - \dfrac{x^2}{\sqrt{1+x^2}}}{\left(x+\sqrt{1+x^2}\right)^2} =$$

$$\frac{1}{\left(x+\sqrt{1+x^2}\right)^2\sqrt{1+x^2}}.$$

The calculations can be simplified if one observes that

$$y = \frac{x\left(x-\sqrt{1+x^2}\right)}{\left(x+\sqrt{1+x^2}\right)\left(x-\sqrt{1+x^2}\right)} = -x^2 + x\sqrt{1+x^2}.$$

Then

$$y' = -2x + \sqrt{1 + x^2} + \frac{x^2}{\sqrt{1 + x^2}} = -2x + \frac{1 + 2x^2}{\sqrt{1 + x^2}}. \quad \square$$

Notice that

$$\frac{1}{\left(x + \sqrt{1 + x^2}\right)^2 \sqrt{1 + x^2}} = \frac{\left(x - \sqrt{1 + x^2}\right)^2}{\sqrt{1 + x^2}} = -2x + \frac{1 + 2x^2}{\sqrt{1 + x^2}}.$$

This example shows that the results of differentiation obtained with a calculator may differ from the answers provided in exams.

Problem 4.11. [5, p. 101]. Evaluate the derivative of
$y = \ln(1 + x^2)$.

Solution:

$$y' \overset{\text{Th. 4.5}}{=} \frac{(1 + x^2)'}{1 + x^2} = \frac{2x}{1 + x^2}. \quad \square$$

Problem 4.12. [5, p. 101]. Evaluate the derivative of $y = \ln(x + \sqrt{1 + x^2})$.

Solution:

$$y' \overset{\text{Th. 4.5}}{=} \frac{1 + \left(\sqrt{1 + x^2}\right)'}{x + \sqrt{1 + x^2}} = \frac{1 + \dfrac{x}{\sqrt{1 + x^2}}}{x + \sqrt{1 + x^2}} = \frac{1}{\sqrt{1 + x^2}}. \quad \square$$

Problem 4.13. Evaluate the derivative of $y = x^x$.

Solution:

$$y' = \left(e^{x \ln x}\right)' = e^{x \ln x}(x \ln x)' = x^x \left(\ln x + 1 \cdot \frac{1}{x}\right) = x^x (\ln x + 1). \quad \square$$

Problem 4.14. [5, p. 117]. Evaluate the derivative of $y = \tan x$.

Solution:

$$y' = \left(\frac{\sin x}{\cos x}\right)' \overset{\text{Th. 4.3}}{=} \frac{\cos^2 x + \sin^2 x}{\cos^2 x} = \frac{1}{\cos^2 x} = 1 + y^2. \quad \square$$

Problem 4.15. [5, p. 121]. Evaluate the derivative of $y = e^{\sin x}$.

Solution:

$$y' \overset{\text{Th. 4.5}}{=} e^{\sin x}(\sin x)' = e^{\sin x} \cos x. \quad \square$$

Problem 4.16. Evaluate the derivative of $y = \sec x = \frac{1}{\cos x}$.

Solution:

$$y' \overset{\text{TCor. 4.4}}{=} -\frac{(\cos x)'}{\cos^2 x} = \sec x \tan x. \quad \square$$

Theorem 4.17 (Logarithmic Derivative). *Let u_i, $i = 1, \ldots, n$, be differentiable functions at $x = c$. Then*

$$(u_1 \cdot u_2 \cdot \cdots \cdot u_n)' = u_1 \cdot u_2 \cdot \cdots \cdot u_n \left(\frac{u_1'}{u_1} + \frac{u_2'}{u_2} + \cdots + \frac{u_n'}{u_n} \right).$$

Proof. By Theorem 4.5 we have assuming that u is negative about $x = c$:

$$(\ln -u)' = \frac{-u'}{-u} = \frac{u'}{u}$$

It follows that

$$(\ln |u|)' = \frac{u'}{u}$$

if $u(c) \neq 0$. Since

$$\ln |u_1 \cdot u_2 \cdot \cdots \cdot u_n| = \ln |u_1| + \ln |u_2| + \cdots + \ln |u_n|,$$

the result follows by Theorem 4.1. $\qquad \square$

Corollary 4.18. *Let u_i, $i = 1, \ldots, n$ be differentiable functions at $x = c$. Then*

$$(u_1 \cdot u_2 \cdot \cdots \cdot u_n)' = u_1' \cdot u_2 \cdot \cdots \cdot u_n + u_1 \cdot u_2' \cdot \cdots \cdot u_n + \cdots + u_1 \cdot u_2 \cdot \cdots \cdot u_n'.$$

Problem 4.19. Evaluate the derivative of $y = (a + x)(b + x)(c + x)$.

Solution:

$$y' = (a + x)(b + x)(c + x) \left[\frac{1}{a + x} + \frac{1}{b + x} + \frac{1}{c + x} \right]. \quad \square$$

Logarithmic derivatives are also used to evaluate **Relative and Percentage Rates of Change**. The relative rate of change of a quantity $Q(x)$ with respect to x is given by the ratio

$$\begin{bmatrix} \text{Relative rate of} \\ \text{change of } Q(x) \end{bmatrix} = \frac{Q'(x)}{Q(x)} = (\ln Q(x))'.$$

The corresponding percentage rate of change of $Q(x)$ with respect to x is

$$\begin{bmatrix} \text{Percentage rate of} \\ \text{change of } Q(x) \end{bmatrix} = 100\frac{Q'(x)}{Q(x)} = 100 (\ln Q(x))'.$$

Problems

Prob. 95 — Find derivatives of the following functions in x:

$$y = \sqrt[3]{x}, \quad y = x\sqrt[3]{x^2}, \quad y = \frac{1}{\sqrt[3]{x^2}}, \quad y = \frac{1}{x\sqrt[3]{x^2}} \quad y = \frac{1}{\sqrt[2]{1-x^2}}.$$

Prob. 96 — Find derivatives of the following functions in x:

$$y = \sqrt[2]{a + bx + cx^2}, \quad y = \sqrt[3]{(a^4 - x^4)^2}, \quad y = \sqrt[3]{a + b\sqrt{bx} + x}.$$

Prob. 97 — Find derivatives of the following functions in x:

$$y = \sqrt[4]{x}, \quad y = x^2\sqrt[3]{x^2}, \quad y = \frac{1}{\sqrt[4]{x}}, \quad y = \frac{1}{x\sqrt[4]{x^3}}.$$

Prob. 98 — Find derivatives of the following functions in x:

$$y = \frac{1}{x + \sqrt{a^2 - x^2}}, \quad y = \sqrt[4]{\left(1 - \frac{1}{\sqrt{x}} + \sqrt[3]{(1-x^2)^2}\right)^3}.$$

Prob. 99 — Let $p = p(x)$ and $q = q(x)$ be functions in x and m, n be positive numbers. Find the derivatives of the following functions:

$$y = \frac{p^m}{q}, \quad y = \frac{p}{q^n}, \quad y = \frac{p^m}{q^n}, \quad y = \frac{1}{p^m q^n}.$$

Prob. 100 — Find derivatives of the following functions in x:

$$y = \frac{1}{2}\ln\frac{1+x}{1-x}, \quad y = \ln\frac{\sqrt{1+x} + \sqrt{1-x}}{\sqrt{1+x} - \sqrt{1-x}}.$$

Prob. 101 — Evaluate the derivative of the function:

$$y = \ln(x + \sqrt{x^2 - 1}) - \ln\left(\frac{1}{x} + \sqrt{1 + \frac{1}{x^2}}\right)$$

Prob. 102 — Evaluate the derivative of the function:

$$y = x - \ln(2e^x + 1 + \sqrt{e^{2x} + 4e^x + 1}).$$

Prob. 103 — Evaluate the derivative of the function:

$$y = \ln \tan \frac{x}{2} - (\cot x)\ln(1 + \sin x) - x.$$

Prob. 104 — Given positive integers m, n, find derivatives of the following functions in x:

$$y = \ln^n x, \quad y = x^m \ln^n x, \quad y = \ln \ln x.$$

Prob. 105 — Find derivatives of the following functions in x:

$$y = (1 + x^2)^{\sin x}, \quad y = x10^{\sqrt{x}}, \quad y = 2^{\frac{x}{\ln x}}.$$

Prob. 106 — Given positive integers m, n, find derivatives of the following functions in x:

$$y = x^m e^x, \quad y = e^{(e^x)}, \quad y = x^{\ln x}, \quad y = (2x)^{\sqrt{x}}.$$

Prob. 107 — Find derivatives of the following functions in x:

$$y = \ln(x - \cos x), \quad y = \tan \frac{1 - e^x}{1 + e^x}, \quad y = \log_3(x^2 - \sin x).$$

Prob. 108 — Find derivatives of the following functions in x:

$$y = \frac{2\cos x}{\sqrt{\cos 2x}}, \quad y = \sqrt[x]{(x+1)^2}, \quad y = \sqrt{x \sin x \sqrt{1 - e^x}}.$$

Prob. 109 — Find derivatives of the following functions in x:

$$y = \sin^2\left(\frac{1 - \ln x}{x}\right), \quad y = \frac{1}{\sqrt{1 + \sin^2 x}}.$$

Prob. 110 — If $y = \ln(x\sqrt{x^2 + 1})$ then $y'(x) =$

$$\textbf{(A) } 1 + \frac{x}{1 + x^2} \quad \textbf{(B) } 1 + \frac{x}{x\sqrt{1 + x^2}} \quad \textbf{(C) } \frac{2x^2 + 1}{x\sqrt{1 + x^2}}$$

$$\textbf{(D) } \frac{2x^2 + 1}{x(1 + x^2)} \quad \textbf{(E) } \frac{x^2 + x + 1}{x(1 + x^2)}$$

Prob. 111 — Which of the following functions are not differentiable at $x = 2/3$? Justify your answer.

$$I. \ f(x) = \sqrt[3]{x - 2} \quad II. \ g(x) = |3x - 2| \quad III. \ h(x) = |9x^2 - 4|.$$

(**A**) *I* only (**B**) *II* only (**C**) *I* and *II* only

(**D**) *II* and *III* only (**E**) *I* and *III* only

Prob. 112 — Let

$$f(x) = \begin{cases} \dfrac{x^2 + x}{x} & \text{if } x \neq 0 \\[2mm] 1 & \text{if } x = 0 \end{cases}$$

Which of the following statements are true of f?

    I f is defined at $x = 0$.

  II $\lim_{x \to 0} f(x)$ exists.

  III f is differentiable at $x = 0$.

(**A**) *I* only (**B**) *II* only (**C**) *I, II* only

(**D**) *II, III* only (**E**) *I, II* and *III*.

Prob. 113 — If $f(x) = 3\sqrt[3]{x^2} + x^2$, then $f'(8) =$

(**A**) 2 (**B**) 17 (**C**) $\dfrac{8}{3}$ (**D**) $\dfrac{2}{3}$ (**E**) 15

Prob. 114 — If $g(x) = \dfrac{5x^2 + x}{5x^2 - x}$, then $g'(x) =$

(**A**) 5 (**B**) $\dfrac{10x^2 + 1}{10x^2 - 1}$ (**C**) $\dfrac{-10}{(5x - 1)^2}$ (**D**) $\dfrac{-4x^2}{(x^2 - x)^2}$ (**E**) $\dfrac{5x^2 - x}{(x^2 - x)^2}$

Prob. 115 — If $f(x) = \sqrt{x^2 + \sqrt{x}}$, then $f'(x) =$

(**A**) $\dfrac{1}{4\sqrt{x}\sqrt{x^2 + \sqrt{x}}}$ (**B**) $\dfrac{x\sqrt{x} + 1}{2\sqrt{x}\sqrt{x^2 + \sqrt{x}}}$ (**C**) $\dfrac{1}{4\sqrt{x^2 + \sqrt{x}}}$

(**D**) $\dfrac{4x\sqrt{x} + 1}{4\sqrt{x}\sqrt{x^2 + \sqrt{x}}}$ (**E**) $\dfrac{-1}{2\sqrt{x}\sqrt{x^2 + \sqrt{x}}}$

Prob. 116 — If $f(x) = x^2 \sqrt{2x + 1}$, then $f'(x) =$

(A) $\dfrac{-2x^2 - x}{\sqrt{2x + 1}}$ (B) $\dfrac{5x^2 + 2x}{\sqrt{2x + 1}}$ (C) $\dfrac{-4x^2 + 2x}{2\sqrt{2x + 1}}$

(D) $\dfrac{5x^2 + 2x}{2\sqrt{2x + 1}}$ (E) $\dfrac{-5x^2 - 2x}{\sqrt{2x + 1}}$

Prob. 117 — If $f(x) = \cos^2 x$, find $f'''(x)$.

(A) $4\sin 2x$ (B) $2\sin 2x$ (C) $\sin 2x$ (D) $4\cos 2x$ (E) $-\cos 2x$

Prob. 118 — If $f(x) = 3^{2x}$, find $f'(x) =$

(A) $\dfrac{3^{2x}}{\ln 9}$ (B) $\dfrac{3^{2x}}{\ln 3}$ (C) $\dfrac{3^{2x}}{2}$ (D) $2 \cdot 9^x \cdot \ln(3)$ (E) $2(3^{2x-1})$

Prob. 119 — If the function $f(x)$ is differentiable and

$$f(x) = \begin{cases} ax^3 - 6x & \text{if } x \le 1 \\ bx^2 + 4 & \text{if } x > 1 \end{cases}$$

then $a =$

(A) 0 (B) 1 (C) -14 (D) -24 (E) 26

Prob. 120 — If the function

$$f(x) = \begin{cases} 3ax^2 + 2bx + 1 & \text{if } x \le 1 \\ ax^4 - 4bx^2 - 3x & \text{if } 1 < x \end{cases}$$

is differentiable for all real values of x, then $b =$

(A) $-\dfrac{11}{4}$ (B) $\dfrac{1}{4}$ (C) $-\dfrac{7}{16}$ (D) 0 (E) $-\dfrac{1}{4}$

Prob. 121 — It is expected that in t months from now, the population of a certain city will be $P = t + 4t^{3/2} + 1\,000$.

(a) Find the rate of change of the population in six months from now.

(b) Find the percentage rate of change of the population in six months from now. Sketch the graph of the percentage rate as a function of time (calculators are allowed).

(c)Determine the behaviour of the percentage rate of change of the population in the long run (that is for big t).

Prob. 122 — The gross annual earnings of a company is modelled by $A(t) = 0.2t^2 + 1.6t + 3$, where $A(t)$ is measured in ten thousand dollars in t years passed since its formation in 2015.

(a)At what rate were the gross annual earnings of the company growing with respect to time in 2017?

(b)At what percentage rate were the gross annual earnings growing with respect to time in 2017? Draw the graph of the percentage rate as a function of time (you may use a calculator).

(c)Determine the percentage rate of change of the gross annual earnings in the long run.

4.2. Derivatives of Inverse Functions

By Theorem 3.39 the inverse function to a continuous function $f(x)$ on $[a,b]$ is continuous. The following theorem says that the inverse function is differentiable as soon as the original function is differentiable.

Theorem 4.20. *Let $f(x)$ be a differentiable function on $[a,b]$ with the inverse function g satisfying $g(f(x)) = x$ for every x in $[a,b]$. Then g is differentiable on the interval with end points at $f(a)$ and $f(b)$ at every point $f(c)$ such that $f'(c) \neq 0$, and, moreover,*

$$g'(f(c)) = \frac{1}{f'(c)}. \tag{4.2}$$

Proof. Since f is differentiable on $[a,b]$, it is continuous on $[a,b]$. By Theorem 3.39 the function g is strictly monotonic and continuous and f is strictly monotonic as well. By the Intermediate Value Theorem they both take any intermediate value exactly once. Let $a < c < b$ be a number between a and b. Then for every y between $f(a)$ and $f(b)$ there exists exactly one x in $[a,b]$ such that $y = f(x)$. With this notation in mind we have $g(f(x)) = x$, $g(f(c)) = c$, and

$$\frac{g(y) - g(f(c))}{y - c} = \frac{x - c}{f(x) - f(c)}.$$

Passing to the limit $y \to c$, we obtain (4.2) if $f'(c) \neq 0$. Using one-side limits we complete the proof for $c = a$ and $c = b$ in a similar way. $\qquad\square$

Remark. The example of $f(x) = x^3$ shows that the condition $f'(c) \neq 0$ is important for differentiability of g at $f(c)$. In this case $g(x) = \sqrt[3]{x}$ is not differentiable at $x = 0$.

Example 4.21. The derivative of the inverse to $y = x^5 + 2x - 1$.

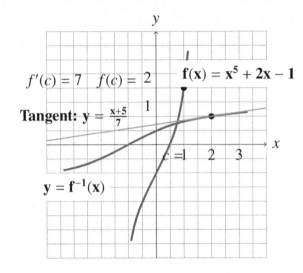

Problem 4.22. Find the derivative of $y = \arcsin x$.

Solution: By the definition of $\arcsin x$ this function is defined on $[-1, 1]$ as the inverse function for the restriction of $y = \sin x$ to the interval $[\pi/2, \pi/2]$. Since $(\sin x)' = \cos x \neq 0$ on $(-\pi/2, \pi/2)$, the function $\arcsin x$ is differentiable on $(-1, 1)$ by Theorem 4.20. We can find the derivative by the Chain Rule applied to the identity

$$x = \sin(\arcsin x) \Rightarrow 1 = \cos(\arcsin x) \cdot (\arcsin x)' \Rightarrow$$

$$(\arcsin x)' = \frac{1}{\cos(\arcsin x)} = \frac{1}{\sqrt{1 - \sin^2(\arcsin x)}} = \frac{1}{\sqrt{1 - x^2}}.$$

□

Problem 4.23. Find the derivative of $y = \arctan x$.

Solution: We differentiate the identity $x = \tan(\arctan x)$ in x by the Chain Rule. Then

$$1 = (\tan(\arctan x))' = \sec^2(\arctan x)(\arctan x)'.$$

But

$$\sec^2 \theta = 1 + \tan^2 \theta \Rightarrow \sec^2(\arctan x) = 1 + x^2.$$

Thus

$$(\arctan x)' = \frac{1}{1 + x^2}.$$

Problems

Prob. 123 — Evaluate the derivatives:

$$y = \arctan \frac{1}{x} \ , y = \arctan \frac{1+x}{1-x}, \quad y = \arccos \ \sqrt{x} \ .$$

Prob. 124 — Evaluate the derivatives:

$$y = \arctan(\ln x) + \ln(\arctan x) \ . y = \arcsin \left(2x \sqrt{1 - x^2} \right).$$

Prob. 125 — Evaluate the derivatives:

$$\arctan \frac{2x}{1 - x^2}, \quad \arctan \frac{\sqrt{1 + x^2} - 1}{x}.$$

Prob. 126 — Evaluate the derivatives:

$$y = \arcsin x \sqrt{1 + x^2} \ , y = \frac{\arccos x}{\sqrt{1 - x^2}}.$$

Prob. 127 — If $f(x) = 3x^2 - x$ and $g(x) = f^{-1}(x)$, then $g'(10)$ could be

(A) 59 **(B)** $\dfrac{1}{59}$ **(C)** 11 **(D)** $\dfrac{1}{11}$ **(E)** $\dfrac{1}{10}$

Prob. 128 — Prove that the equation $y^3 + y = x$ has a unique differentiable solution $y(x)$ and find its derivative at $x = 2$.

Prob. 129 — Determine the domain of the inverse function for $y = x + e^x$ and find its derivative.

4.3. Tangents and Normals.

Definition 4.24. A line through a point (x_0, y_0) of a curve is called **normal** to the curve at (x_0, y_0) if it is perpendicular to the tangent to this curve at (x_0, y_0).

If the tangent has a point-slope equation $y = k(x - x_0) + y_0$ and $k \neq 0$, then by Theorem 1.1 the point-slope equation of the normal is given by

$$y = -\frac{1}{k}(x - x_0) + y_0. \tag{4.3}$$

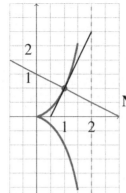

$$y^2(2-x) = x^3$$

Tangent: y = 2x − 1

Normal: y = −0.5x + 1.5

Figure 4.1: Cissoid of Diocles.

Problem 4.25. Find the equation of the normal line to the Cissoid of Diocles $y^2(2-x) = x^3$ at $(1, 1)$, see Fig 4.1.

Solution: Since

$$y = \sqrt{\frac{x^3}{2-x}}$$

for $y > 0$, $0 \le x < 2$, the function $y(x)$, $y(1) = 1$, is differentiable on $(0, 2)$. Differentiating the identity $y^2(2-x) = x^3$ in x, we obtain that

$$2y(x)y'(x)(2-x) - y^2 = 3x^2 \Rightarrow y'(x) = \frac{3x^2 + y^2}{2y(2-x)}.$$

Since $y(1) = 1$, we find that $y'(1) = 2$. It follows that the equation of the normal at $(1, 1)$ is given by $y = -0.5x + 1.5$. □

Definition 4.26. Two curves are called orthogonal at a point of their intercept if the tangent of one curve is perpendicular to the tangent of another curve.

Problem 4.27. Show that the curves $2x^2 + 3y^2 = 5$ and $y^2 = x^3$ are orthogonal at the points of intercepts, see Fig 4.2.

Solution: Both curves are symmetric with re4spect to the x-axis. Therefore, we may consider their parts in the upper half-plane. The first is the part of the ellipse which is the graph of $y_1 = \frac{1}{\sqrt{3}}\sqrt{5 - 2x^2}$. The second is the graph of $y_2(x) = \sqrt{x^3}$. The function $y_1(x)$ strictly decreases and $y_2(x)$ strictly increases. Both functions are continuous on $[0, \sqrt{2.5}]$. Since

$$y_1(0) - y_2(0) = \frac{1}{\sqrt{3}}\sqrt{5}, \quad y_1(1) - y_2(1) = 0,$$

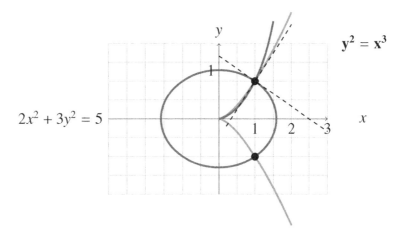

Figure 4.2: Orthogonal curves.

there is only one point of intercept, namely, $(1, 1)$ in the upper half-plane. Differentiating the equations of the curves in x, we obtain

$$4x + 6y_1y_1' = 0 \Rightarrow y_1'(1) = -\frac{2}{3},$$

$$2y_2y_2' = 3x^2 \Rightarrow y_2'(1) = \frac{3}{2}.$$

Since $y_1'(1)y_2'(1) = -1$, the curves are orthogonal at $(1, 1)$.

Theorem 4.28. *Let $y(x)$ be a function differentiable at $x = a$. Then the tangent to the graph of $y(x)$ at $x = a$ intercepts the x-axis and y-axis at the points*

$$x = a - \frac{y(a)}{y'(a)}, \quad y = y(a) - ay'(a). \tag{4.4}$$

Proof. To obtain the first equation put $y = 0$ in the equation of the tangent $y = y'(a)(x-a)+y(a)$. To obtain the second equation put $y = 0$ in the same equation. □

Problems

Prob. 130 — Find the line through the origin which is orthogonal to the hyperbola $xy = 1$ at the points of intercepts.

Prob. 131 — The tangent to the hyperbola $yx = 1$, $y > 0$, at $x = a$ makes a right triangle with the coordinate axis. Find its area.

4.4. Linearization and Leibniz Differentials

Theorem 4.29. *Let f be a continuous function defined about c, and L be a linear function. Then*

$$\lim_{\Delta x \to 0} \frac{f(c + \Delta x) - L(c + \Delta x)}{\Delta x} = 0 \tag{4.5}$$

if and only if f is differentiable at c and

$$L(c + \Delta x) = f'(c)\Delta x + f(c). \tag{4.6}$$

Proof. Suppose that a linear function L satisfies (4.5). Then by the Product Rule for limits we have

$$\lim_{\Delta x \to 0} f(c + \Delta x) - L(c + \Delta x) = \lim_{\Delta x \to 0} \frac{f(c + \Delta x) - L(c + \Delta x)}{\Delta x} \cdot \lim_{\Delta x \to 0} \Delta x = 0 \cdot 0,$$

implying that

$$f(c) = \lim_{\Delta x \to 0} f(c + \Delta x) = \lim_{\Delta x \to 0} L(c + \Delta x) = L(c).$$

Since L is linear, there is a real number k such that $L(x + \Delta x) = k \cdot \Delta x + f(c)$. Then

$$\lim_{\Delta x \to 0} \frac{f(c + \Delta x) - f(c)}{\Delta x} =$$
$$\lim_{\Delta x \to 0} \frac{f(c + \Delta x) - L(c + \Delta x)}{\Delta x} + \lim_{\Delta x \to 0} \frac{L(c + \Delta x) - L(c)}{\Delta x} = 0 + k = k.$$

It follows that f is differentiable at c and $k = f'(c)$.

Suppose now that f is differentiable at c and put $L(c + \Delta x) = f'(c)\Delta x + f(c)$. Then

$$\lim_{\Delta x \to 0} \frac{f(c + \Delta x) - L(c + \Delta x)}{\Delta x} = \lim_{\Delta x \to 0} \frac{f(c + \Delta x) - f(c)}{\Delta x} - f'(c) = 0,$$

as stated. $\qquad\qquad\square$

Theorem 4.29 says that the tangent to the graph of $y = f(x)$ at $x = c$ is the best linear approximation.

Definition 4.30. Given a differentiable function $f(x)$ at $x = c$, the linear function

$$L(x) = f'(c)(x - c) + f(c)$$

is called the **linearization** of f at c.

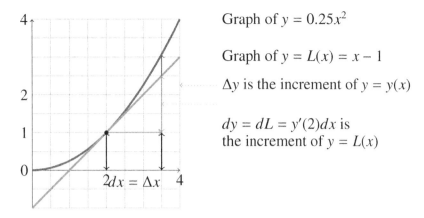

Graph of $y = 0.25x^2$

Graph of $y = L(x) = x - 1$

Δy is the increment of $y = y(x)$

$dy = dL = y'(2)dx$ is
the increment of $y = L(x)$

Figure 4.3: Linearization

Theorem 4.29 justifies Descartes' method of tangents for explicit functions. Indeed, to find $f'(c)$ we substitute $y = L(x)$ in the left-hand part of the equation $y - f(x) = 0$ to obtain $L(x) - f(x)$. Then $f'(c)$ is the slope of that $L(x)$ which satisfies

$$\lim_{x \to c} \frac{f(x) - L(x)}{x - c} = 0.$$

For polynomials $f(x)$ it is the same as to say that $f(x) - L(x)$ has a multiple root at $x = c$.

If both values $f(c)$ and $f'(c)$ are known, then the linearization of f at c can be used to find the values $f(x)$ for x close to c by the formula

$$f(x) \approx L(x). \tag{4.7}$$

Fig 4.3 illustrates the method of linearization. In this case $f(x) = 0.25x^2$. Then $f(2) = 1$ and $f'(2) = 1$. It follows that $L(x) = x - 1$. So, we obtain, in particular, that $3.0625 = f(3.5) \approx L(3.5) = 2.5$. The mistake of the approximation is less that 0.6.

Problem 4.31. Using linearization evaluate $\sqrt{4.1}$:

(**A**) 2.0248 (**B**) 2.025 (**C**) 2.01 (**D**) 2.024 (**E**) 2.015

Solution: We have $c = 4$, implying that

$$f'(c) = \frac{1}{2\sqrt{x}}\bigg|_{x=4} = 0.25, \quad f(c) = 2.$$

Hence

$$2.0248456731317\ldots = f(4.1) \approx L(4.1) = 0.25 \cdot 0.1 + 2 = 2.025.$$

Although (**A**) gives the precise value, the correct answer is (**B**). $\square$

Definition 4.32. The linearization of f at x is the sum of the homogeneous part $f'(x)\Delta x$ and a constant part $f(x)$. The homogeneous part is called the **differential** of the function $y = f(x)$ and is denoted by

$$dy = df = f'(x)\Delta x.$$

Notations d comes from the first letter of the Latin *differentia* [7, p. 524]. For a fixed x_0 the graph of a differentiable function f has the tangent at $(x_0, f(x_0))$, which is nothing but the graph of the linearization $L(x)$. When x_0 is increased by Δx the function f gets the increment $\Delta f = f(x_0 + \Delta x) - f(x_0)$, whereas the linearization being linear gets the increment $\Delta L = f'(x_0)\Delta x$. For $f(x) = x$ we obviously have $dx = 1 \cdot \Delta x \Rightarrow dx = \Delta x$. Therefore, we may write

$$dy = df = f'(x)dx.$$

Problem 4.33. Using differentials evaluate $\sqrt{4.1}$:

Solution: We have

$$d\sqrt{x} = \frac{dx}{2\sqrt{x}} \Rightarrow d\sqrt{x}\bigg|_{\substack{x=4 \\ dx=0.1}} = \frac{0.1}{2\sqrt{4}} = 0.25 \Rightarrow$$

$$f(4.01) \approx \sqrt{x}\bigg|_{x=4} + d\sqrt{x}\bigg|_{\substack{x=4 \\ dx=0.1}} = 2.025.$$

Theorem 4.34 (Differential Rules). *Let u and v be differentiable functions. Then*

1 $d(u \pm v) = du \pm dv$;

2 $d(uv) = udv + vdu$;

3 $d\left(\dfrac{u}{v}\right) = \dfrac{vdu - udv}{v^2}$, *if $v \neq 0$.*

Proof. Apply the Differential Rules and the formulas $du = u'dx$, $dv = v'dx$. $\quad\square$

Problem 4.35. A pyramid has a square base of 180 m. An engineer stands at the midpoint of pyramid's side and views its apex through a theodolite. The angle of elevation ϕ is found to be $58°$. How accurate must this angle measurement be to keep the error in the height h of the pyramid between -1 m and $+1$ m?

Solution: First we find the relationship between the height h and the angle of observation ϕ:

$$h = 90 \tan \phi \Rightarrow \boxed{\Delta h \approx dh = \frac{90\,d\phi}{\cos^2 \phi}}.$$

We are given that $\phi = 58°$ and that under this angle the mistake $|dh|$ must be less than 1. Then

$$|d\phi \text{ radians}| = \frac{\cos^2 58° \frac{\pi}{180}}{90} |dh| = \frac{\cos^2 \frac{29\pi}{90}}{90}$$

is the upper bound of the mistake in radians. It follows that the bound of the mistake in degrees is

$$|d\phi \text{ degrees}| \leq \frac{180}{\pi} \frac{\cos^2 \frac{29\pi}{90}}{90} = \frac{2 \cos^2 \frac{29\pi}{90}}{\pi}$$

Using differentials, we find that

$$\cos^2 \frac{\pi}{3} - \cos^2 \frac{29\pi}{90} \approx \left(\cos^2 x\right)' \Big|_{x=\pi/3} \cdot \frac{\pi}{90} = -\frac{\pi\sqrt{3}}{180}.$$

It follows that

$$\cos^2 \frac{29\pi}{90} \approx \frac{1}{4} + \frac{\pi\sqrt{3}}{180}.$$

Then

$$|d\phi \text{ degrees}| \leq \frac{1}{2\pi} + \frac{\sqrt{3}}{90} \approx 0.18 \text{ degrees.} \quad \square$$

Problem 4.36. A factory produces $Q(L) = 600L^{2/3}$ units, where L is the labor force used. Use linearization to estimate the percentage increase in labor that is required to increase output by 1%.

Solution: The goal is to get

$$1\% = \frac{\Delta Q}{Q} \cdot 100\% \Leftrightarrow \frac{\Delta Q}{Q} = 0.01.$$

Since

$$\frac{\Delta Q}{Q} \approx \frac{Q'\Delta L}{Q} = \frac{400 \cdot L^{-1/3}\Delta L}{600 \cdot L^{2/3}} = \frac{2}{3}\frac{\Delta L}{L},$$

we obtain that

$$\frac{\Delta L}{L} \approx \frac{3}{2} \cdot \frac{\Delta Q}{Q} = 1.5 \cdot 0.01 = 0.015 \Rightarrow \textbf{percentage increase in labor} = 1.5\%. \quad \square$$

If $C(x)$ is the production cost of x widgets, then

$$\Delta C = C(x+1) - C(x) \tag{4.8}$$

is the production cost of the $x + 1$th widget provided x widgets were produced. In Economics the derivative $C'(x)$ is called the **marginal cost**. The marginal cost equals $dC = C'(x)dx$, where $dx = (x + 1) - x = 1$. If x is big enough the marginal cost is a good approximation to $\Delta C \approx C'(x)dx = C'(x)$, see (4.8)

Problem 4.37. The dollar cost of producing x washing machines is $C(x) = 500 + 100x - 0.2x^2$.

(a) Find the average cost of producing the first 100 washing machines.

(b) Find the marginal cost when 100 washing machines are produced.

(c) Suppose that 100 machines were produced. Compare the marginal cost with the cost of producing one more washing machine by a direct calculation.

Solution: (a)

$$\frac{C(x)}{x} = \frac{500}{x} + 100 - 0.2x \Rightarrow \frac{C(100)}{100} = 5 + 100 - 20 = \$85.$$

(b)

$$C'(x) = 100 - 0.4x \Rightarrow C'(100) = 100 - 40 = \$60.$$

(c)

$$C(101) - C(100) = 100(101 - 100) - 0.2(101 - 100)(101 + 100) =$$
$$100 - 40.2 = \$59.8. \quad \square$$

Problems

Prob. 132 — If $y = x^7 + 7x$, find the value of dy when $x = 1$ and $dx = 0.2$.

Prob. 133 — For $y = x^2 - x$ find dy and Δy at $x = 1$, if $dx = 0.1$.

Prob. 134 — Using linearization evaluate $\arctan(1.01)$.

Prob. 135 — Evaluate $\ln \tan(46°30')$.

Prob. 136 — If $y = \tan x$, $x = \pi$, and $dx = 0.5$, what does dy equal?

(**A**) -0.25 (**B**) -0.5 (**C**) 0 (**D**) 0.5 (**E**) 0.25

Prob. 137 — Find an approximate solution to the equation $11 \sin x - 12 \cos x = 0$.

Prob. 138 — Using the linearization or differentials estimate $\ln(e^2 + 0.1)$.

Prob. 139 — Estimate Δy if $y = \frac{2-x}{1+x}$ $x_0 = 1$ $dx = 0.1$.

Prob. 140 — For $y = x(x^2 + 1)^{-1}$, find dy and use it to approximate Δy if x decreases from 1 to 0.98.

Prob. 141 — Let $f(x) = x^3 - x^2 + x - 1$ and $g(x) = x^5 + 2x$. Use differentials to approximate the change in $g(f(x))$ if x changes from 1 to 1.01.

Prob. 142 — For $y = \ln(x^2 + 1)$, find dy and use it to approximate Δy if x changes from 0 to 0.1.

Prob. 143 — Let f be the function given by $f(x) = x^2 - 2x + 3$. The tangent line to the graph of f at $x = 2$ is used to approximate values of $f(x)$. Which of the following is the greatest value of x for which the error resulting from this tangent line approximation is less than 0.5?

$$\textbf{(A) } 2.4 \quad \textbf{(B) } 2.5 \quad \textbf{(C) } 2.6 \quad \textbf{(D) } 2.7 \quad \textbf{(E) } 2.8$$

Prob. 144 — Using differentials approximate $\sqrt[5]{1.06}$.

Prob. 145 — What is the largest percentage error in the measurement of the radius of a sphere, if the error in the evaluation of its surface area must be no greater than 10%?

4.5. Related Rates

Related Rates is a section of AP Calculus course dealing with problems considering the dynamic of related variables. Mathematically this problems can be described as follows. Two variables $x = x(t)$ and $y = y(t)$ are related by an equation

$$f(x, y) = 0. \qquad (4.9)$$

The position x_0 of $x(t)$ at some moment $t = t_0$ is given as well as the rate of change $x'(t_0)$. It is required to find the rate of change $y'(t_0)$.

The main difficulty which students of AP Calculus face here is that the equation (4.9) is not given usually explicitly. Rather it is stated indirectly in words. Therefore, a right approach to these problems is to eliminate actually all words and replace the problem with its graph. After that (4.9) can be easily recovered. Finally, this equation must be differentiated in t after the substitution $x = x(t)$, $y = y(t)$. We illustrate this approach on examples.

Problem 4.38 (Filling a Conical Tank). Water runs into a conical tank at the rate 10ft^3/min. The tank stands point down and has a height of 12 ft and a base radius 6 ft. How fast is the water level rising when the water is 6 ft deep?

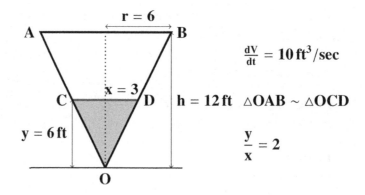

Figure 4.4: A Conical Tank

Solution: The Graph of the Problem is pictured on Fig 4.4. The problem says that the volume V of water in the conic tank is related with the height y of the water level. At any moment water fills a cone with radius of the base x and the height y. The volume is $V = \frac{1}{3}\pi x^2 y$. We may exclude x using the similarity of triangles $\triangle OAB \sim \triangle OCD$:

$$\frac{y}{x} = \frac{12}{6} = 2 \Rightarrow x = \frac{y}{2}.$$

Then the equation related two variables V and y is:

$$\boxed{V = \frac{\pi}{12}y^3}.$$

Now we differentiate the Equation of Related Variables

$$\frac{dV}{dt} = \frac{\pi}{12} \cdot 3 \cdot y^2 \cdot \frac{dy}{dt} \Rightarrow \boxed{\frac{dV}{dt} = \frac{\pi}{4}y^2 \cdot \frac{dy}{dt}}.$$

Finally putting here $y = 6$ and $dV/dt = 10$, we obtain that

$$10 = \frac{\pi}{4} \cdot 36 \cdot \frac{dy}{dt} \Rightarrow \frac{dy}{dt} = \frac{10}{9\pi} \approx \boxed{0.35 \, \text{ft/sec}}.$$

Problem 4.39 (A Rising Balloon). An air balloon is rising straight up from a level field. It is tracked by a range finder located 200 ft from the liftoff point. At some moment the range finder fixes that the elevation angle is $\pi/6$ and it is increasing at the rate of 0.1 rad/min. How fast is the balloon rising at that very moment?

Solution: The Graph of the Problem is pictured on Fig 4.5. The related variables are h, the height of the balloon, and *theta*, the angle in the range finder. The equation relating the variables is:

$$\frac{h}{200} = \tan\theta \Rightarrow \boxed{h = 200\tan\theta}.$$

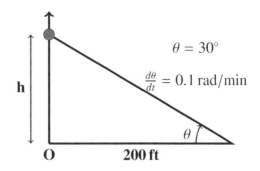

Figure 4.5: A Rising Balloon

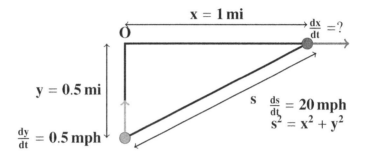

Figure 4.6: Police Case

Differentiating the equation in t we obtain

$$\frac{dh}{dt} = \frac{200}{\cos^2\theta}\frac{d\theta}{dt}.$$

Since $\theta = 30°$, we obtain that $\cos^2\theta = \frac{3}{4}$. Finally

$$\frac{dh}{dt} = 200 \cdot \frac{4}{3} \cdot 0.1 = \boxed{26.67\text{ft/min}}.$$

Problem 4.40 (Police Case). A police patrol car is moving from the south to a right-angled intersection of country roads at 50mph. The police officer notices that a taxi cab in front turned the corner and is now moving straight east. When the police car is 0.5 mi south of the intersection and the taxi cab is 1mi to the east, the police officer determines with radar that the distance between them and the car is increasing 20 mph. What is the speed of the taxi cab?

Solution: The Graph of the Problem is shown on Fig 4.6. The coordinate center O is placed at the intersection. Then the position of the taxi cab is given by its x coordinate, which is the distance to O. The position of police patrol car is

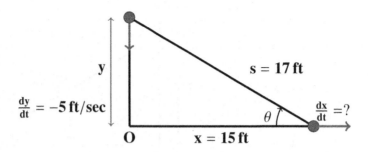

Figure 4.7: A Sliding Ladder

given by its y-coordinate, which is the distance to O with sign minus. The distance s between the cars, x, and y are related by the equation:

$$s^2 = x^2 + y^2.$$

We differentiate this equation and obtain

$$2s\frac{ds}{dt} = 2x\frac{dx}{dt} + 2y\frac{dy}{dt} \Rightarrow \boxed{\frac{ds}{dt} = \frac{1}{\sqrt{x^2 + y^2}}\left(x\frac{dx}{dt} + y\frac{dy}{dt}\right)}$$

Putting:

$$x = 1, \ y = -0.5, \ \frac{dy}{dt} = 50, \ \frac{ds}{dt} = 20,$$

we obtain

$$20 = \frac{1}{\sqrt{1^2 + 0.5^2}}\left(\frac{dx}{dt} + 0.5 \cdot (-50)\right).$$

Answer:

$$\frac{dx}{dt} = 20\sqrt{1.25} + 25 \approx \boxed{47.36 \text{ mph}}.$$

Problem 4.41 (A Sliding Ladder). The top of a 17- ft ladder is sliding against a house wall. At the moment the ladder's base is 15 ft from the wall, it is moving down at the rate of 5 ft/sec. How fast is the bottom of the ladder sliding at this moment? At what rate is the area of the triangle formed by the ladder, wall and ground changing at this very moment? At what rate is the angle θ between the ladder and the ground changing at this moment?

Solution: The Graph of the Problem is shown on Fig 4.7 The equation, which relates y and x is given by:

$$x^2(t) + y^2(t) = 269 \Rightarrow \begin{array}{l} x(t) = 15 \Rightarrow y(t) = 8; \\ y\dfrac{dy}{dt} + x\dfrac{dx}{dt} = 0. \end{array}$$

It follows that

$$\frac{dx}{dt}\bigg|_{y=8} = -\frac{y}{x}\frac{dy}{dt}\bigg|_{\substack{x=15 \\ y=8}} = -\frac{8}{15}\cdot(-5)\text{ ft/sec} = \boxed{\frac{8}{3}\text{ ft/sec}}.$$

The area A of the triangle is $0.5\cdot x\cdot y$. Then

$$\frac{dA}{dt} = \frac{1}{2}\frac{d(xy)}{dt} = \frac{1}{2}(x'y + xy')\bigg|_{\substack{x=15 \\ y=8}} = \frac{1}{2}\left(\frac{8}{3}\cdot 8 - 5\cdot 15\right) = \boxed{-\frac{161}{6}\text{ ft}^2/\text{sec}}.$$

By the Chain Rule:

$$\left(1 + \tan^2\theta\right)\frac{d\theta}{dt} = \frac{d\tan\theta}{dt} = \frac{y'x - yx'}{x^2}$$

It follows that

$$\frac{d\theta}{dt} = \frac{y'x - yx'}{x^2\left(1 + \frac{y^2}{x^2}\right)} = \frac{y'x - yx'}{x^2 + y^2}$$

$$\frac{d\theta}{dt}\bigg|_{\substack{x=15 \\ y=8}} = \frac{y'x - yx'}{x^2 + y^2}\bigg|_{\substack{x=15 \\ y=8}} = \frac{-5\cdot 15 - 8\cdot 8/3}{64 + 225} = \boxed{-\frac{1}{3}\text{ rad/sec}}.$$

Problem 4.42 (Particle Motion). A particle moves from left to right along the parabolic curve $y = \sqrt{-x}$ in such a way that its x-coordinate (in meters) increases at the rate of 18 m/sec. How fast is the angle of inclination θ of the line joining the particle to the origin changing when $x = -4$?

Solution:

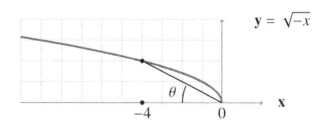

$$\tan\theta = \frac{\text{green}}{\text{red}} = \frac{y}{-x} = (-x)^{1/2},\quad \theta = \theta(t)\quad x = x(t).$$

We have

$$\left(1 + \tan^2\theta\right)\frac{d\theta}{dt} = \frac{1}{\cos^2\theta}\frac{d\theta}{dt} = \frac{d\tan\theta}{dt} = \frac{d(-x)^{-1/2}}{dt} =$$

$$-0.5\cdot(-x)^{-3/2}\cdot(-1)\cdot\frac{dx}{dt} = 0.5(-x)^{-3/2}\frac{dx}{dt}.$$

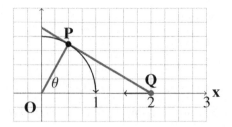

Figure 4.8: Moving along a Circle

$$x = -4 \Rightarrow y = 2, \ \tan\theta = 0.5.$$

$$\frac{d\theta}{dt} = \left(1 + \tan^2\theta\right)^{-1} 0.5(-x)^{-3/2}\frac{dx}{dt} = \frac{4}{5} \cdot \frac{1}{2} \cdot \frac{1}{8}(16) = \boxed{\frac{4}{5}}.$$

Problem 4.43 (A point moving along parabola). At which point of the parabola $y^2 = 16x$ the y-coordinate increases exactly four times faster than the x-coordinate?

Solution: We notice that $x = x(t)$ and $y = y(t)$ are two functions related by

$$y(t)^2 = 16x(t).$$

Differentiating this equation in t we get

$$2y\frac{dy}{dt} = 16\frac{dx}{dt} \Rightarrow \frac{\frac{dy}{dt}}{\frac{dx}{dt}} = \frac{8}{y}.$$

Now $8/y = 4$ if and only if $y = 2$. Since the point moves along the parabola we find

$$x = \frac{y^2}{16} = \frac{1}{4}. \quad \square$$

Problem 4.44 (Moving along a circle). A particle P moves clockwise at a constant rate along the unit circle centered at the origin. The particle's initial position is $(0, 1)$ on the y-axis and its final destination is the point $(1, 0)$ on the x-axis. Once the particle is in motion, the tangent line at P intersects the x-axis at a point Q (which moves over time). If it takes the particle 60 sec to travel from start to finish, how fast is the point Q moving along the x-axis when its distance to the origin is 2?

Solution: The graph of the Problem is shown on Fig 4.8. Let θ be the size of the angle $\angle QOP$. Since the particle travels from start to finish in 60 sec, it is traveling along the circle at a constant rate of $\pi/2$ radians in 1 min, or $\pi/2$ rad/min. In other words, $d\theta/dt = -\pi/2$, with t being measured in minutes. The negative sign appears because θ is decreasing over time. Let $x(t)$ be the distance at time t from Q to the origin. Then

$$x \cos \theta = 1 \Rightarrow x = \frac{1}{\cos \theta} \Rightarrow \frac{dx}{dt} = \frac{\tan \theta}{\cos \theta} \frac{d\theta}{dt} = -\pi \frac{\tan \theta}{2 \cos \theta}.$$

If $x = 2$, then $\cos \theta = 1/2$ and $\tan \theta = \sqrt{\sec^2 \theta - 1} = \sqrt{3}$. It follows that

$$\frac{dx}{dt} = \frac{-\pi \sqrt{3}}{2 \cdot 1/2} = -\pi \sqrt{3} \approx \boxed{-5.44 \text{ units/min}}. \quad \square$$

Problem 4.45 (Pollution and Fish Population). A plant located on the shore of a lake pollutes it and, therefore, influences the fish population. Ecologists found out an empirical formula related the number F of fish in the population and the level x of pollution measured in parts per million:

$$F = \frac{60\,000}{2 + \sqrt[3]{x^2}}.$$

When there are 10 000 fish left in the lake, the pollution is increasing at the rate of 2 ppm/year. At what rate is the fish population changing at this time?

Solution: We want to find dF/dt when $F = 10\,000$ and $dx/dt = 2$ First we find the volume of pollution corresponding to the level of population 10 000:

$$10\,000 = \frac{60\,000}{2 + \sqrt[3]{x^2}} \Rightarrow \mathbf{x = 8}.$$

Next, we find

$$\frac{dF}{dx} = \frac{62\,000 \cdot (-1)}{(2 + \sqrt[3]{x^2})^2} \frac{2}{3 \sqrt[3]{x}} = \frac{-124\,000}{3 \sqrt[3]{x}(2 + \sqrt[3]{x^2})^2}.$$

Finally,

$$\frac{dF}{dt} = \frac{dF}{dx} \cdot \frac{dx}{dt} = \frac{-124\,000}{3 \sqrt[3]{x}(2 + \sqrt[3]{x^2})^2} \frac{dx}{dt},$$

implying that

$$\left. \frac{dF}{dt} \right|_{dx/dt=2} = -\frac{124\,000}{3 \cdot 2 \cdot (2 + 4)^2} \cdot 2 \approx \boxed{114.85 \text{ fishes per year}}. \quad \square$$

Problem 4.46 (A Building Shadow). The shadow of a 100ft building on level ground is 60 ft long. At the moment in question, the angle θ the sun lights makes with the ground is increasing at the rate of $0.30°$ min. At what rate is the shadow decreasing?

Solution: Let x be the shadow length in ft. Then

$$\tan\theta = \frac{100}{x} \Rightarrow \left(1 + \tan^2\theta\right)\frac{d\theta}{dt} = \frac{d\tan\theta}{dt} = \frac{d}{dt}\frac{100}{x} = -\frac{100}{x^2}\frac{dx}{dt}.$$

$$\left.\frac{d\theta}{dt}\right|_{x=60\text{ ft}} = 0.30°/\text{min} = \frac{0.3\pi}{180}\text{ rad/min}, \ \left.\tan\theta\right|_{x=60\text{ ft}} = \frac{100}{60} = \frac{5}{3}.$$

$$\left.\frac{dx}{dt}\right|_{x=60\text{ ft}} = \left(1 + \frac{25}{9}\right)\cdot\frac{0.3\pi}{180}\text{ rad/min} : \left(\frac{-100\text{ ft}}{3600\text{ ft}^2}\right) \approx \boxed{-0.71\text{ ft}/min.} \quad \square$$

Problem 4.47 (Wind Chill Temperature). Wind chill F temperature is the temperature in calm air that has the same chilling effect on a person as that of a particular combination of temperature and wind. There is an empirical formula for the Wind Chill Temperature in the Fahrenheit scale:

$$F = 91.4 - (0.47 - 0.02w + 0.3\sqrt{w})\cdot(91.4 - T).$$

Here w is the wind speed (in mph) and T is the temperature in calm air (in degrees of Fahrenheit). If the temperature is currently 30°**F**, and is dropping at a rate of 3°**F** per hour, and if the wind is currently blowing at 6 mph, and is increasing at a rate of 1 mph, how quickly is the wind chill temperature changing?

Solution: Let t_0 be the time of interest. Using Differentiation Rules, we obtain:

$$\frac{dF}{dt} = \left(0.02\frac{dw}{dt} - \frac{0.3}{2\sqrt{w}}\frac{dw}{dt}\right)(91.4 - T) + (0.47 - 0.02w + 0.3\sqrt{w})\cdot\frac{dT}{dt} \Rightarrow$$

$$\left.\frac{dF}{dt}\right|_{t=t_0} = \left(0.02\cdot 1 - \frac{0.3}{2\sqrt{6}}\cdot 1\right)(91.4 - 30) + (-0.47 - 0.02\cdot 6 + 0.3\sqrt{6})\cdot(-3) =$$

$$- 0.041237\cdot 61.4 - 0.144847\cdot 3 \approx \boxed{-2.97°\text{F/hour.}} \quad \square$$

Problem 4.48 (Filling a Trough). A trough is 25 ft long and 5 ft wide across its top. The trough ends with isosceles triangles with height 5 ft on both sides. Water runs into the trough at the rate of 2 ft^3/min. How fast is the water level rising when it is 2 ft deep?

Solution: The Graph of the Problem (the perpendicular cross-section of the through) is shown on Fig 4.9. The volume $V(t)$ of water in the trough is the volume of a horizontally directed prism with length 25 ft. The water level $y(t)$ is the height of the base of the prism. Since $\triangle OAB \sim \triangle OCD$, we see that $y/x = 5/2.5 = 2$ Then the area of a perpendicular water cross-section is

$$\textbf{Area} = 0.5\cdot\textbf{base}\cdot y = xy = 0.5y^2 \Rightarrow V(t) = 25\cdot\textbf{Area} = 12.5\cdot y^2.$$

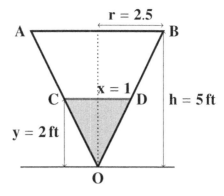

Figure 4.9: Filling a Trough

It follows that

$$2 = \frac{dV}{dt} = 25y\frac{dy}{dt} \Rightarrow \left.\frac{dy}{dt}\right|_{y=2} = \frac{2}{25 \cdot 2} = \boxed{\frac{1}{25}} \text{ ft/min.}$$

Problem 4.49 (Melting Ice). A spherical iron ball is coated with a layer of ice of uniform thickness. If the ice melts at the rate of 10 mL/min, how fast is the outer surface area of ice decreasing when the outer diameter (ball plus ice) is 20 cm?

   Solution:

$$V(t) = \frac{4}{3}\pi r^3 \Rightarrow -10 \text{ cm}^3/\text{min} = \frac{dV}{dt} = 4\pi r^2\frac{dr}{dt}.$$

It follows that

$$\left.\frac{dr}{dt}\right|_{r=10 \text{ cm}} = -\frac{10}{4 \cdot \pi \cdot 100} \text{ cm/min} = -\frac{1}{40\pi} \text{ cm/min.}$$

$$\frac{dA(r)}{dt} = \frac{d(4\pi r^2)}{dt} = 8\pi r\frac{dr}{dt} \Rightarrow$$
$$\left.\frac{dA(r)}{dt}\right|_{t=10 \text{ cm}} = 8\pi \cdot 10 \cdot \frac{-1}{40\pi} = \boxed{-2 \text{ cm}^2/\text{min}}. \quad \square$$

Problem 4.50. Oil is leaking from a tanker on the surface of a gulf and forms an oil slick whose volume increases at a constant rate of 4 000 cubic centimeters per minute. The oil spot is a right circular cylinder with both its radius and height changing with time. At the instant when the radius of the oil spot is 200 centimeters and the height is 0.2 centimeter, the radius is increasing at the rate of 1.5 centimeters per minute. At this instant, what is the rate of change of the height of the oil slick with respect to time, in centimeters per minute?

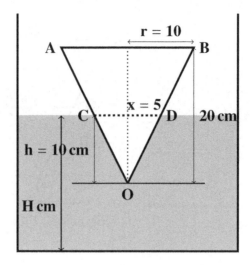

Figure 4.10: Displacing Water

Solution: By the Chain Rule:

$$4000 = \frac{dV}{dt} = \frac{d(\pi r^2 h)}{dt} = \pi r^2 \frac{dh}{dt} + 2\pi r h \frac{dr}{dt}.$$

Since at the described moment

$$r = 200, \ h = 0.2, \ \frac{dr}{dt} = 1.5,$$

we obtain that in this moment dh/dt satisfies:

$$4000 = \pi 200^2 \frac{dh}{dt} + 2\pi 200 \cdot 0.2 \cdot 1.5 \Rightarrow \frac{dh}{dt} = \frac{4000 - 120\pi}{40\,000\pi} \approx \boxed{0.029 \, \text{cm/min}}.$$

Problem 4.51. A cylindrical tank of radius 50 cm and height 150 cm is filled with water by 2/3 of the total volume. A cone of radius 10 cm and height 20 cm is lowered vertically, vertex down, into the water of the tank. The vertex of the cone approaches the bottom of the tank at a speed of 1 cm per second. How fast is the water level rising in the tank, when half the height of the cone is submerged?

Solution: The graph of the problem is shown on Fig 4.10. Let $h = h(t)$ be the distance from the vertex of the cone to the water level $H = H(t)$ in the cylinder of radius $R = 50$ cm. Then the radius of the base of the cone on the water level is $r = 0.5h$. The volume of water displaced by this part of the cone equals the volume $V(h)$ of this cone, i.e.

$$V(h) = \frac{1}{3}\pi \left(\frac{h}{2}\right)^2 h = \frac{\pi h^3}{12}.$$

It is easy to see that $V(20) < \pi 50^3$, implying that the water cannot be displaced by this cone from the tank. When the cone is submerged in water on depth $h = h(t)$, the water level becomes $H(t) > H(0)$. The volume of the cylinder of height $H(t)$ is $\pi R^2 \cdot H(t)$. This cylinder is filled with water of volume $\pi R^2 \cdot H(0)$ (the initial volume of water which remains constant during the whole process) and the empty part of the cone of height $h(t)$. Thus

$$\pi R^2 \cdot H(t) = \pi R^2 \cdot H(0) + V(h(t)) = \pi R^2 \cdot H(0) + \frac{\pi h(t)^3}{12},$$

or equivalently

$$H(t) - H(0) = \frac{h^3(t)}{12 \cdot R^2}.$$

Differentiating this identity in t, and taking into account that $R = 50$, we obtain

$$\frac{dH}{dt} = \frac{h^2}{4R^2}\frac{dh}{dt} = \frac{h^2}{10\,000}\frac{dh}{dt}.$$

Since the distance of the vertex of the cone to the bottom of the tank is $H(t) - h(t)$, we obtain that

$$-1 = \frac{dH}{dt} - \frac{dh}{dt} \Rightarrow \boxed{\frac{dh}{dt} = \frac{dH}{dt} + 1}.$$

It follows that

$$\frac{dH}{dt} = \frac{h^2}{10\,000}\left(1 + \frac{dH}{dt}\right) \Rightarrow \frac{dH}{dt} = \frac{h^2}{10\,000 - h^2}.$$

Finally,

$$\frac{dH}{dt}\bigg|_{h=10} = \frac{h^2}{10\,000 - h^2}\bigg|_{h=10} = \frac{100}{10\,000 - 100} =$$
$$\frac{1}{99} = 0.010101\ldots \approx \boxed{0.01\ \text{cm/sec}}. \quad \square$$

Problems

Prob. 146 — The radius r of a disc is a differentiable function of time t. Let A be the area of a disc of radius r. Write the equation that relates dA/dt and dr/dt.

Prob. 147 — The top of a 37ft ladder is leaned against a vertical wall. The top is slipping down the wall at the rate of 3ft per second. How fast is the bottom of the ladder slipping along the ground when the bottom of the ladder is 12ft away from the base of the wall?

Prob. 148 — Two commercial airplanes are flying at an altitude of 10 000 meters along straight-line perpendicular courses. The first airplane is approaching the intersection point at a speed of 900km/h. The second plane is approaching the intersection at 800km/h. At what rate is the distance between the planes changing when the first plane is 21 kilometers from the intersection point and the second plane is 21 kilometers from the intersection point?

Prob. 149 — At the top of a 60 feet high pole is placed a light. From the level of light a ball is dropped down. The ball is falling down 30 feet from the pole according to the Galileo's Law $s = 16t^2$. How fast is the shadow of the ball on the ground is moving one second later?

Prob. 150 — A boat is being pulled towards a dock by a rope connected to the bow of the boat. The dock is 12 feet higher than the bow of the boat. The rope is being pulled in at the rate of 5 feet per second. How fast is the boat approaching the dock when the length of rope between the dock and the boat is 35 feet?

Prob. 151 — A boy is playing with a kite, which is at a height of 100 feet. The wind is carrying the kite horizontally away from the boy at a speed of 15 feet per second. How fast must the kite string be let out when the string is 250 feet long?

Prob. 152 — Ship **A** is 20 miles west of point O and moving east at 20 miles per hour. Ship **B** is 30 miles north of O and moving south at 15 miles per hour. Are they approaching or separating after 1 hour, and at what rate?

Prob. 153 — A trough is 10 feet long. Its perpendicular cross section has the shape of an equilateral triangle 2 feet on each side. If water is being pumped in at the rate of $5 ft^3/min$, how fast is the water level rising when the water is 1 ft deep?

Prob. 154 — If a mothball evaporates at a rate proportional to its surface area πr^2, show that its radius decreases at a constant rate.

Prob. 155 — Let $u = u(t)$ be the number of people hired at time t in a given industry. Let $v = v(t)$ be the average production per person at time t. Find the rate of growth of the total production $y = uv$ if the labor force u is growing at the rate of 6% per year and the production per worker is growing at the rate of 2% per year.

Prob. 156 — A dinghy is pulled toward a dock by a rope from the bow through a ring on the dock 6 ft above the bow. The rope is hauled in at the rate of 2 ft sec.

   a.How fast is the boat approaching the dock when 10 ft of rope are out?

   b.At what rate is the angle changing at this instant.

Prob. 157 — A swimming pool is 40 feet long, 20 feet wide, 4 feet deep at the shallow end, and 9 feet deep at the deep end (see figure). Water is being pumped into the pool at the rate of 10 cubic feet per minute. How fast is the water level rising when there is 4 feet of water in the deep end?

Prob. 158 — A reporter is videotaping a race from a stand 250 ft from the track, following a racing car that is moving at $= 264$ ft/sec. How fast will reporter's camera angle θ be changing when the car is right in front of him? A second later?

Prob. 159 — An airplane is flying at a constant altitude of 8 000 meters above sea level as it approaches North Cyprus airport Ercan. The aircraft comes within the direct line of sight of a radar station located on the island. The radar indicates the initial angle between sea level and its line of sight to the aircraft is $30°$. How fast (in kilometers per hour) is the aircraft approaching Ercan, when first detected by the radar, if it is turning upward (counterclockwise) at the rate of 0.5 deg/sec in order to keep the aircraft at sight?

Prob. 160 — A railroad track crosses a highway at an angle of $60°$. A train is approaching the intersection at the rate of 40mi/h, and a car is approaching the intersection from the same side as the train, at the rate of 50mi/h. If, at a certain moment, the train and car are both 2 miles from the intersection, how fast is the distance between them changing?

Prob. 161 — A manufacturer supplies q thousand units of a commodity when its market price is p dollars per unit. The supply-demand equation is given implicitly

$$3p^2 - q^2 = 12.$$

How fast is the supply changing when the price is \$4 per unit and is increasing at the rate of 87 cents per month?

Prob. 162 — When the price of a certain commodity is p dollars per unit, customers demand x hundred units of the commodity, where

$$x^2 + 3px + p^2 = 79.$$

How fast is the demand x changing with respect to time when the price is \$5 per unit and is decreasing at the rate of 30 cents per month?

Chapter 5

Applications of Differentiation

Abstract

Rolle's Theorem. Lagrange's Theorem. Daeboux' Theorem. Taylor's Formula. Critical Points. Convexity and Inflection Points. The Shape of a Graph. The Shapes of Implicit Functions Graphs. Cost Functions, Revenue, Profit. Lorenz Curves. Elasticity of Demand. L'Hospital's Rule.

Keywords: Mean Value Theorem, Peano's form of reminder, Fermat's principle, concave up/down functions, inflection points, parametric plotting.

5.1. Rolle's Theorem

Theorem 5.1 (Rolle's Theorem)**.** *Suppose that* $y = f(x)$ *is **continuous** at **every** point of a **closed** interval* $[a, b]$ *and **differentiable** at every point of the **open** interval* (a, b)*. If* $f(a) = f(b)$*, then there is at least one number c in* (a, b) *such that* $f'(c) = 0$*.*

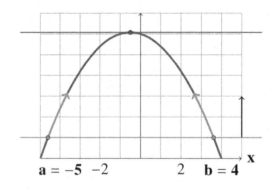

Figure 5.1: Rolle's Theorem

141

The graph of Fig 5.1 illustrates the idea of the proof. Line $y = 1$ intersects the graph of $y = f(x)$ at two points. When this horizontal line is moving up the points of intersection are getting closer and finally the horizontal line becomes the horizontal tangent.

Proof of Rolle's Theorem. If $f(x) = f(a) = f(b)$ for every x in (a, b), then $f'(x) = 0$ for $a < x < b$. If it is not the case, then either there is w in (a, b) such that $f(w) > f(a)$, or there is u in (a, b) such that $f(u) < f(a)$. In the first case by Theorem 3.37 there is a point c in (a, b) of absolute maximum. Then $f'(c) = 0$ by Theorem 5.36. The second case is considered similarly. □

Problem 5.2. Let

$$f(x) = \begin{cases} -0.3\dfrac{x^3 + 2x^2 - 19x - 20}{x + 1} & \text{if } x \neq -1 \text{ and } x \text{ is in } [-5, 4] \\ 6 & \text{if } x = -1 \end{cases}$$

Check if this function satisfies the conditions of Rolle's theorem.

Solution:

$$x^3 + 2x^2 - 19x - 20 = (x + 5)(x + 1)(x - 4) \Rightarrow f(x) = -0.3 \cdot (x + 5)(x - 4).$$

Notice that

$$-0.3 \cdot (x + 5)(x - 4)\Big|_{x=-1} = 6.$$

Hence $f(x) = -0.3 \cdot (x + 5)(x - 4)$ on $[-5, 4]$ and is differentiable everywhere in $(-5, 4)$. Since $f(-5) = f(4) = 0$, f satisfies all conditions of Rolle's Theorem. The graph of $y = f(x)$ is plotted above. □

Problem 5.3. Let $f(x) = x^{2/3} - x^{1/3}$ on the interval $[0, 1]$. Is it true that f satisfies the conditions of Rolle's Theorem?

Solution:
$$f(0) = 0, \quad f(1) = 1^{2/3} - 1^{1/3} = 1 - 1 = 0.$$

Since f is continuous on $[0, 1]$ and differentiable on $(0, 1)$, it satisfies the conditions of Rolle's Theorem. A direct calculation shows that

$$f'(x) = \frac{2}{3}x^{-1/3} - \frac{1}{3}x^{-2/3} = \frac{2x^{1/3} - 1}{3x^{2/3}} = 0 \Leftrightarrow x = \frac{1}{8}. \quad □$$

Problem 5.4. Let $f(x) = x(x - 1)(x - 2)(x - 3)$. Show that the equation $f'(x) = 0$ has three real roots.

Solution: We see that $f(0) = f(1) = f(2) = f(3) = 0$. By Rolle's Theorem f' must vanish on each of of the following three open intervals $(0, 1)$, $(1, 2)$, $(2, 3)$. So, f' has three distinct roots. Since f' is a polynomial of degree 3, these are all roots of f'. □

Corollary 5.5. *If $p(x)$ is a polynomial of degree n, $n > 1$, with n distinct roots, then its derivative $p'(x)$ is a polynomial which has $n - 1$ distinct roots.*

Proof. Apply the arguments used in Problem 5.4. □

Problem 5.6. Show that the equation $e^x = 1 + x$ has only one real root $x = 0$.

Solution: Suppose to the contrary that the equation $f(x) = e^x - 1 - x = 0$ has a solution $x_0 \neq 0$. Then $f(x)$ vanishes at the ends of the interval made by 0 and x_0. By Rolle's Theorem the equation $f'(c) = 0$ must have a nonzero solution $c \neq 0$. But $f'(x) = e^x - 1$ and $e^x - 1 = 0$ only if $x = 0$ which is a contradiction. □

Problem 5.7. Show that the equation $x^3 + x + 2 = 0$ has exactly one real solution.

Solution: The continuous function $f(x) = x^3 + x + 2$ takes the values of opposite signs at the ends of the interval $[-2, 0]$ ($f(-2) = -8$, $f(0) = 2$). By the Intermediate Value Theorem the graph of f intercepts the x-axis at some point a of the open interval $(-2, 0)$. Suppose that f has another root $b \neq a$. Since f is differentiable everywhere, by Rolle's theorem its derivative must vanish at some point c between a and b. However, this is impossible since the derivative of f is positive everywhere: $f'(x) = 3x^2 + 1 > 0$. □

t (hours)	12	13	15	16	18	19	20
$L(t)$(people)	80	160	170	120	160	40	0

Problem 5.8. The sale of concert tickets started at noon ($t = 12$) and ended in 8 hours. The number L of people waiting in line to purchase tickets at time t for $12 \leq t \leq 20$ is modeled by a differentiable function L. Sample values of $L(t)$ are shown in the table above.

(a) Use the table to estimate the instantaneous rate of change of the number of people waiting in line at $17 : 00$. Show the computations that lead to your answer. Indicate units of measure.

(b) Determine the fewest number of times t satisfying $L'(t) = 0$. Give reasons for your answer.

Solution: (a) Notice that 16 and 18 are the closest moments of time at which the values of $L(t)$ are known and such that $(16 + 18)/2 = 17$. The slope of the chord connecting the points $(16, 120)$ and $(18, 160)$ is a good approximation to the value of the instantaneous rate of change at $t = 17$:

Rate of change at $t = 17 \approx \dfrac{L(18) - L(16)}{18 - 16} = \dfrac{160 - 120}{2} = 20$ persons/ hour.

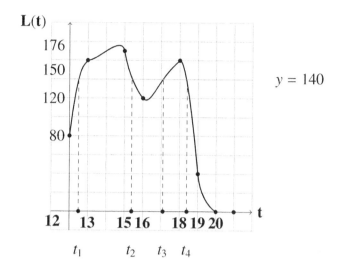

(**a**) Since $L(t) - 145$ is continuous on $[12, 20]$ and takes values of opposite signs at $t = 12$ and $t = 13$, at $t = 15$ and $t = 16$, at $t = 16$ and $t = 18$, at $t = 18$ and $t = 19$. By the Intermediate Value Theorem $L(t) - 140 = 0$ at least once in each of the intervals:

$$(12, 13), \quad (15, 16), \quad (16, 18), \quad (18, 19).$$

Hence, there are points $12 < t_1 < 13$, $15 < t_2 < 16$, $16 < t_3 < 18$, and $18 < t_4 < 19$ such that

$$L(t_1) = L(t_2) = L(t_3) = L(t_4) = 140.$$

Then by Rolle's Theorem

$$L'(s_1) = L'(s_2) = L'(s_3) = 0,$$

where $t_1 < s_1 < t_2 < s_2 < t_3 < s_3 < t_4$. The example plotted shows that there may be exactly three points on the graph of $L(t)$ with horizontal tangent. It follows that the correct answer is **three**. $\square$

Problems

Prob. 163 — Let
$$f(x) = \begin{cases} x^3 & \text{if } 0 \le x \le 1 \\ 2 - x & \text{if } 1 < x \le 2 \end{cases}$$

Is it true that f satisfies the conditions of Rolle's Theorem?

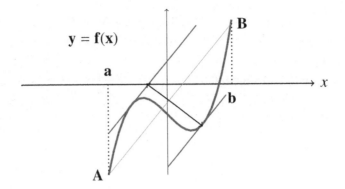

Figure 5.2: Lagrange's Theorem. A geometrical illustration.

Prob. 164 — Show that the equation $\ln(1 + x) = x$ has only one real root $x = 0$.

Prob. 165 — Show that all roots of the Legendre polynomial

$$P_n(x) = \frac{1}{2^n \cdot n!} \frac{d^n(x^2 - 1)^n}{dx^n}$$

are real and lie in the interval $(-1, 1)$.

5.2.   Lagrange's Theorem

Theorem 5.9 (Lagrange's Theorem). *Suppose that $y = f(x)$ is continuous on a closed interval $[a, b]$ and differentiable on the interval's interior (a, b). Then there is at least one point c in (a, b) at which*

$$\frac{f(b) - f(a)}{b - a} = f'(c).$$

In AP Calculus Lagrange's Theorem is referred to as the **Mean Value Theorem** (for derivatives). The reason is that Lagrange's Theorem states that the average velocity equals instantaneous velocity at least once during the time of observation.

The idea of the proof of Lagrange's Theorem is shown on Fig 5.2. One just moves the chord in the perpendicular direction until it becomes tangent to the curve. There is also an algebraic proof. Let

$$g(x) = f(x) - \frac{f(b) - f(a)}{b - a}(x - a).$$

Then $g(a) = f(a) = g(b)$. Applying Rolle's Theorem to the function $y = g(x)$, we obtain that

$$g'(c) = \frac{f(b) - f(a)}{b - a}$$

for some c in (a, b).

Example 5.10. The function $y = x^2$ is continuous for $0 \leq x \leq 2$ and differentiable for $0 < x < 2$. Since $f(0) = 0$ and $f(2) = 4$, the Mean Value Theorem says that $f'(x) = 2x$ at some point c in $(0, 2)$ must have value

$$\frac{f(2) - f(0)}{2 - 0} = \frac{4 - 0}{2 - 0} = 2.$$

It is easy to see that $c = 1$.

Example 5.11. If a car accelerating from zero goes 100 meters for 5 seconds, its average velocity for the 5-sec interval is $100/5 = 20$ m/ sec. The Mean Value Theorem says that at some point during the acceleration the speedometer must read exactly 72 km/h

Problem 5.12. Let

$$f(x) = \begin{cases} x^2 - x, & -2 \leq x \leq -1 \\ 2x^2 - 3x - 3, & -1 < x \leq 0 \end{cases}$$

Does f satisfy the conditions of the Mean Value Theorem?

Solution: The function $f(x)$ being defined by two polynomials is differentiable and therefore continuous everywhere except possibly the point $x = 1$. We have

$$\lim_{x \to -1^-} f(x) = \lim_{x \to -1^-} x^2 - x = 1 + 1 = 2,$$

$$\lim_{x \to -1^+} f(x) = \lim_{x \to -1^+} 2x^2 - 3x - 3 = 2 + 3 - 3 = 2,$$

implying that f is continuous at $x = -1$.

To investigate differentiability of $f(x)$ at $x = -1$ we evaluate two limits:

$$\lim_{x \to -1^-} \frac{f(x) - f(-1)}{x - (-1)} = \lim_{x \to -1^-} \frac{x^2 - x - 2}{x + 1} = -3,$$

$$\lim_{x \to -1^+} \frac{f(x) - f(-1)}{x - (-1)} = \lim_{x \to -1^+} \frac{2x^2 - 3x - 5}{x + 1} = -7 \neq -3,$$

implying that $f(x)$ is not differentiable at $x = -1$.

Problem 5.13. Let

$$f(x) = \begin{cases} 2x - 3, & 0 \leq x \leq 2 \\ 6x - x^2 - 7, & 2 < x \leq 3 \end{cases}$$

Does f satisfy the conditions of the Mean Value Theorem?

Solution:

$$f'(x) = \begin{cases} 2 & \text{if } 0 < x < 2 \\ 6 - 2x & \text{if } 2 < x < 3 \end{cases}$$

$$\lim_{x \to 2^-} \frac{f(2) - f(x)}{2 - x} = \lim_{x \to 2^-} f'(c_x) = 2.$$

$$\lim_{x \to 2^+} \frac{f(x) - f(2)}{x - 2} = \lim_{x \to 2^-} f'(c_x) = \lim_{x \to 2^-} (6 - 2c_x) = 6 - 2 \cdot 2 = 2.$$

It follows that $f(x)$ is differentiable on $(0, 3)$. It is continuous on $[0, 3]$. Hence f satisfies the conditions of the Mean Value Theorem.

The following simple lemma is useful for solutions of problems in AP Calculus exams.

Lemma 5.14. *Let $y = f(x)$ be a continuous function on a closed interval $[a, b]$ such that $f(a) = f(b)$. If there is a point c in (a, b) satisfying*

$$f(c) > f(a) = f(b),$$

then for every y in $(f(a), f(c))$ the equation $y = f(x)$ has at least two solutions x_1 and x_2 satisfying $a < x_1 < x_2 < b$.

Proof. Apply the Intermediate Value Theorem to the intervals $[a, c]$ and $[c, b]$. $\square$

Problem 5.15. A marathon racer ran a 26.2 *mi* marathon in 2.4 hours. Show that at least twice the marathon racer was running at exactly 10 mph, assuming the initial and final speeds are zero.

Solution: By the Mean Value Theorem there is $c \in (0, 2.4)$ such that

$$v(c) = \frac{26.2}{2.4} = 10.916\ldots > 10.$$

Since $v = v(t)$ is continuous on $[0, 2.4]$ and $v(0) = v(2.4) = 0$, there must be t_1 and $t_2, t_2 > t_1$ in $(0, 2.4)$ such that $v(t_1) = v(t_2) = 10$ by Lemma 5.14. $\square$

Problem 5.16 (The sine inequality). Show that for any numbers a and b, the sine inequality is true:

$$|\sin a - \sin b| \leq |a - b|.$$

Solution:

$$|\sin a - \sin b| = |(\sin)'(c)| \cdot |a - b| = |\cos(c)| \cdot |a - b| \leq |a - b|. \quad \square$$

Theorem 5.17. *If $f'(x) = 0$ at each point x of an open interval (a, b), then $f(x) = C$ for all x in (a, b), where C is a constant.*

Proof. If $a < x_1 < x_2 < b$, then by Lagrange's Theorem applied to the interval $[x_1, x_2]$ we have

$$f(x_2) - f(x_1) = f'(c)(x_2 - x_1) = 0.$$

Let $x_2 = 0.5(a + b)$. Then for every x in $(a, 0.5(a + b))$ we have that $f(x) = f(0.5(a + b))$. Let now $x_1 = 0.5(a + b)$. Then for every x in $(0.5(a + b), b)$ we have that $f(x) = f(0.5(a + b))$. $\qquad\square$

Corollary 5.18. *If $f'(x) = g'(x)$ at each point x of an open interval (a, b), then there exists a constant C such that $f(x) = g(x) + C$ for all x in (a, b). That is, $f - g$ is a constant function on (a, b).*

Definition 5.19. Given a function $f(x)$ on (a, b) a function $F(x)$ is called an **antiderivative** of f if

$$F'(x) = f(x) \text{ for every } x \text{ in } (a, b).$$

Corollary 5.18 says that if an antiderivative exists, then it is unique up to an additive constant. Theorem 5.22 below shows that not every function has an antiderivative.

Corollary 5.18 is also useful in the so-called PVA problems (Position-Velocity-Acceleration).

Problem 5.20. Assume that a body is falling freely from rest with acceleration 9.8 m/sec^2 and that its position $s(t)$ is measured positive downwards from the rest position. Find a formula for $s(t)$.

Solution: The velocity $v(t)$ of the body satisfies the equation $v' = 9.8$. Hence $v(t) = 9.8t + C$ where C is some constant by Corollary 5.18. But the body is falling from the rest state, which implies $v(0) = C = 0$. Next, again by Corollary 5.18

$$s'(t) = 9.8t \Rightarrow s(t) = 4.9t^2 + C.$$

Since $s(0) = 0$ we obtain that $s(t) = 4.9t^2$. $\qquad\square$

Problem 5.21. Suppose that $f(0) = 1$ and $f'(x) = 10$ for all x. Is it true that $f(x) = 10x + 1$ for all x? Give reasons for your answer.

Solution: We define

$$F(x) = f(x) - (10x + 1) \Rightarrow F'(x) = f'(x) - 10 = 0.$$

for every x. Then $F(x) = C$ by Theorem 5.17. But $F(0) = f(0) - 1 = 0$, implying $C = 0$. It follows that $f(x) = 10x + 1$.

Problems

Prob. 166 — The function $f(x) = \sqrt[5]{(x-2)^2}$ takes equal values at the ends of the interval $[0, 4]$. Can we apply Rolle's theorem on $[0, 4]$?

Prob. 167 — It took 20 sec for a mercury thermometer to rise from $-22°C$ to $100°C$ when it was taken from a freezer and placed in boiling water. Show that somewhere along the way the mercury was rising at the rate of $6.1°C/sec$.

Prob. 168 — The acceleration of gravity on the moon is $1.6m/sec^2$. If a rock is dropped from the top of a cliff, how fast will it be going just before it hits bottom 10 sec later?

Prob. 169 — A dynamical blast blows a heavy rock straight up with a launch velocity of 160 ft/sec. The rock reaches the height of

$$H(t) = 160t - 16t^2 \ \text{ft}$$

after t seconds.

- How high does the rock go?
- What are the velocity and speed of the rock when it is 256 ft above the ground on the way up? On the way down?
- What is the acceleration of the rock at any time t during its flight?
- When does the rock hit the ground?

Prob. 170 — Using Corollary 5.18 show that

$$\arctan \frac{2x}{1-x^2} = 2\arctan x + \begin{cases} -\pi & \text{if } x > 1 \\ 0 & \text{if } -1 < x < 1 \\ \pi & \text{if } x < -1 \end{cases}$$

Prob. 171 — Using Corollary 5.18 show that

$$\arctan \frac{\sqrt{1+x^2}-1}{x} = \frac{1}{2}\arctan x, \quad x \neq 0.$$

5.3. Darboux' Theorem

Suppose that a point is moving along the y-coordinate axis and its position is determined by a differentiable function $y = f(t)$. We consider a general situation, so that the derivative $f'(t)$ exists at any moment of time but is not necessarily continuous. The following example

$$f(t) = \begin{cases} t^2 \sin\left(\frac{1}{t}\right), & \text{if } t \neq 0 \\ 0, & \text{if } t \neq 0 \end{cases}$$

shows that this may happen. The derivative of this function exists everywhere but it is not continuous at $t = 0$.

A natural question arises. Suppose that a number y is placed between $f'(a)$ and $f'(b)$. Is it true that there is a moment of time c between a and b, such that the instantaneous velocity $f'(c)$ is y?

Theorem 5.22 (Darboux). *If $y = f(x)$ is differentiable function on $[a, b]$ and y is any value between $f'(a)$ and $f'(b)$, then there is c in (a, b) such that $f'(c) = y$.*

Proof. Without loss of generality we may assume that $f'(a) < f'(b)$ (replace f with $-f$ otherwise). Since f is differentiable at a as well as at b, given $\varepsilon > 0$ there is $\Delta x > 0$ such that the slopes of the chords

$$\frac{f(a + \Delta x) - f(a)}{\Delta x} \quad \text{and} \quad \frac{f(b) - f(b - \Delta x)}{\Delta x}$$

are inside the intervals

$$(f'(a) - \varepsilon, f'(a) + \varepsilon), \quad \text{and} \quad (f'(b) - \varepsilon, f'(b) + \varepsilon).$$

So, if $0 < \varepsilon < \min(y - f'(a), f'(b) - y)$, we obtain the inequalities:

$$\frac{f(a + \Delta x) - f(a)}{\Delta x} < y < \frac{f(b) - f(b - \Delta x)}{\Delta x}.$$

We consider now the slope

$$k(t) = \frac{f(t + \Delta x) - f(t)}{\Delta x}$$

of the sliding chord. The function $k(t)$ is continuous and

$$k(a) < y < k(b - \Delta x).$$

By the Intermediate Value Theorem there is t_0 such that $k(t_0) = y$. By Lagrange's theorem applied to f and the chord with the slope $k(t_0)$, there exists c such that $f'(c) = k(t_0) = y$ as stated. □

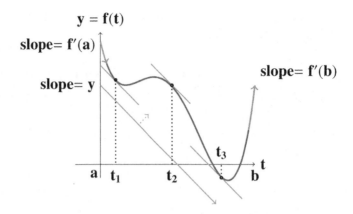

Figure 5.3: Instantaneous velocity equals y at $t = t_1, t_2, t_3$.

The proof of Darboux' Theorem presented above could be used to find the moments of time c when $f'(c) = y$ by the graph of f, see Fig 5.3.

The standard proof of Darboux' Theorem is shorter and beautiful but it is not so illustrative graphically as the given one. Let $g(t) = f(t) - yt$. Then $g'(a)$ and $g'(b)$ have opposite signs. If $g'(a) < 0$, then g decreases about a. Since in this case $g'(b) > 0$, the function $g(t)$ increases about b, this implies that g cannot have an absolute minimal value neither at a, nor at b. By Theorem 3.37 it has the absolute minimum at $t = c$, where $a < c < b$. By Theorem $0 = g'(c) = f'(c) - y$, which completes the proof. The case of $g'(a) > 0$, when $g'(b) < 0$, is considered similarly but in this case instead of the absolute minimum we search for the absolute maximum.

Problem 5.23. A car is moving at 60 km/h slowing down to 40 km/h according to road signs. The samples of the car velocities are given in the following table.

time in minutes	10	12	17	19	25	27
velocity in km/h	60	40	60	40	60	40

Show that there are at least five moments of time when the speedometer of the car shows 47 km/h.

Solution: Apply Darboux' Theorem to the following intervals of time

$$(10, 12), \ (12, 17), \ (17, 19), \ (19, 25), \ (25, 27). \quad \square$$

Lemma 5.24. *Let f be differentiable at every point of an open interval (a, b) and $a < c < b$. If the limit $\lim_{x \to c^+} f'(x) = K$ exists, then $K = f'(c)$. The same is true if $\lim_{x \to c^-} f'(x) = K$ exists.*

Proof. By Lagrange's Theorem

$$f'(c) = \lim_{x \to c^+} \frac{f(x) - f(c)}{x - c} = \lim_{x \to c^+} f'(c_x) = K$$

as stated. □

This shows that the derivative of a differentiable function on $[a, b]$ cannot have 'jumps'.

Problem 5.25. Let f be a differentiable function on $[-1, 1]$ satisfying the properties $f(-1) = -1$, $f(0) = 1$, $f(1) = 0$. Show that there is a point c in the interval $(-1, 1)$ such that $f'(c) = -0.25$.

Solution: By Lagrange's Theorem there are points $-1 < c_1 < 0 < c_2 < 1$ such that
$$2 = f(0) - f(-1) = f'(c_1), \quad -1 = f(1) - f(0) = f'(c_2).$$

Since $f'(c_2) < -0.25 < f'(c_1)$, the result follows by Darboux' Theorem. □

5.4. Taylor's Formula

Theorem 5.26. *Let $\delta > 0$ and a be a real number. Suppose that a function $f(x)$ is defined on $(a - \delta, a + \delta)$ and has the derivative $f^{(n+1)}(x)$ of order $n + 1$ at every point of this interval. Then for every Δx, $|\Delta x| < \delta$ there is θ in $(0, 1)$ such that*

$$f(a + \Delta x) = f(a) + \frac{f^{(1)}(a)}{1!}\Delta x + \cdots + \frac{f^{(n)}(a)}{n!}\Delta x^n + \frac{f^{(n+1)}(a + \theta\Delta x)}{(n + 1)!}\Delta x^{n+1}. \quad (5.1)$$

Formula (5.1) is called Taylor's formula. We give a proof of this theorem following [6, p. 89-90].

Proof of Theorem 5.26. We fix Δx and define a constant P so that

$$f(a + \Delta x) = f(a) + \frac{f^{(1)}(a)}{1!}\Delta x + \cdots + \frac{f^{(n)}(a)}{n!}\Delta x^n + \frac{P}{(n + 1)!}\Delta x^{n+1}.$$

We are going to show that $P = f^{(n+1)}(a + \theta\Delta x)$ for some θ in $(0, 1)$. For this purpose we define an auxiliary function $\phi(t)$ on the closed interval I with end points at a and $b = x + \Delta x$:

$$\phi(t) = f(b) - f(t) - \frac{(b - t)}{1!}f^{(1)}(t) - \cdots - \frac{(b - t)^n}{n!}f^{(n)}(t) - \frac{(b - t)^{n+1}}{(n + 1)!}P.$$

By the definition of P we have

$$\phi(a) = \phi(b) = 0.$$

Since $\phi(t)$ satisfies the conditions of Rolle's Theorem, there is c between a and b such that $\phi'(c) = 0$. A direct calculation shows that

$$0 = \phi'(t) = -f'(t) + f'(t) - \frac{(b-t)}{1!}f^{(2)}(t) + \frac{(b-t)}{1!}f^{(2)}(t) - \cdots -$$

$$\frac{(b-t)^n}{n!}f^{(n+1)}(t) + \frac{(b-t)^n}{n!}P = \frac{(b-t)^n}{n!}\left\{P - f^{(n+1)}(t)\right\} \Leftrightarrow P = f^{(n+1)}(t)$$

as stated. $\qquad\qquad\square$

Taylor's formula is a topic of AP Calculus BC. However, it is useful for solutions of some multiple-choice questions of Calculus AB. To begin with since $P^{(n+1)}(x) \equiv 0$ for every polynomial of degree n we obtain another proof of formula (1.7).

If $f(x) = e^x$ then $f^{(n)}(x) = e^x$ for every n. Applying (5.1) to this f and $a = 0$, $\Delta x = x$, we obtain for every positive integer n that

$$e^x = 1 + \frac{x}{1!} + \frac{x^2}{2!} + \cdots + \frac{x^n}{n!} + \frac{x^{n+1}}{(n+1)!}e^{\theta_n x}, \quad 0 < \theta_n < 1.$$

It is easy to see that if $n > k = \lceil |x| \rceil + 1$, then

$$0 \leq \frac{|x|^n}{n!} < |x|^k \left(\frac{|x|}{\lceil |x| \rceil + 1}\right)^{n-k} \underset{n \to +\infty}{\longrightarrow} 0,$$

implying that

$$e^x = 1 + \frac{x}{1!} + \frac{x^2}{2!} + \cdots + \frac{x^n}{n!} + \cdots = \lim_n \sum_{k=0}^{n} \frac{x^k}{k!} \qquad (5.2)$$

In particular, we obtain Corollary 3.64 if we put here $x = 1$.

Similarly, one can obtain the following formulas:

$$\sin x = x - \frac{x^3}{3!} + \frac{x^5}{5!} - \cdots + \frac{(-1)^n x^{2n+1}}{(2n+1)!} + \cdots$$

$$\cos x = 1 - \frac{x^2}{2!} + \frac{x^4}{4!} - \cdots + \frac{(-1)^n x^{2n}}{(2n)!} + \cdots \qquad (5.3)$$

$$\ln(1 + x) = \frac{x}{1} - \frac{x^2}{2} + \frac{x^3}{3} - \cdots + \frac{(-1)^{n-1} x^n}{n} + \cdots, \quad |x| < 1$$

$$\frac{1}{2}\ln\left(\frac{1+x}{1-x}\right) = \frac{x}{1} + \frac{x^3}{3} + \frac{x^5}{5} + \cdots + \frac{x^{2n+1}}{2n+1} + \cdots, \quad |x| < 1 \qquad (5.4)$$

For any real α and $|x| < 1$

$$(1 + x)^\alpha = 1 + \frac{\alpha}{1!}x + \frac{\alpha(\alpha - 1)}{2!}x^2 + \cdots + \frac{\alpha(\alpha - 1)\cdots(\alpha - n + 1)}{n!}x^n + \cdots . \quad (5.5)$$

In evaluation of limits it is often convenient to apply Taylor's Formula with Peano's form of remainder:

$$f(a + x) = f(a) + \frac{f^{(1)}(a)}{1!}x + \cdots + \frac{f^{(n)}(a)}{n!}x^n + o(x^n), \quad (5.6)$$

where $o(x^n)$ means that this reminder has the form $\varepsilon(x)x^n$, $\lim_{x\to 0} \varepsilon(x) = 0$. As formula (5.1) shows, this is indeed the case if The derivative $f^{(n+1)}$ is bounded about a.

Problem 5.27. Evaluate

$$\lim_{x\to 0} \frac{e^x \sin x - x(1 + x)}{x^3}.$$

Solution: By (5.2) and (5.3)

$$e^x \sin x = \left(1 + x + \frac{x^2}{2!} + \frac{x^3}{3!} + o(x^3)\right) \cdot \left(x - \frac{x^3}{3!} + o(x^3)\right) =$$

$$x + x^2 + \frac{x^3}{2} - \frac{x^3}{6} + o(x^3) = x + x^2 + \frac{x^3}{3} + o(x^3).$$

It follows that

$$e^x \sin x - x(1 + x) = \frac{x^3}{3} + o(x^3) \Rightarrow \lim_{x\to 0} \frac{e^x \sin x - x(1 + x)}{x^3} = \frac{1}{3}. \quad \square$$

Problem 5.28. Evaluate

$$\lim_{x\to +\infty} x^{3/2}\left(\sqrt{x + 1} + \sqrt{x - 1} - 2\sqrt{x}\right).$$

Solution: By (5.5) with $\alpha = 1/2$

$$x^{3/2}\left(\sqrt{x + 1} + \sqrt{x - 1} - 2\sqrt{x}\right) = x^2\left\{\sqrt{1 + \frac{1}{x}} + \sqrt{1 + \frac{1}{x}} - 2\right\} =$$

$$x^2\left\{\left(1 + \frac{1}{2x} + \frac{1/2(1/2 - 1)}{2x^2} + o\left(\frac{1}{x^2}\right)\right) + \left(1 + \frac{1}{2x} + \frac{1/2(1/2 - 1)}{2x^2} + o\left(\frac{1}{x^2}\right)\right) - 2\right\} =$$

$$x^2\left\{-\frac{1}{4x^2} + o\left(\frac{1}{x^2}\right)\right\} \xrightarrow{x\to +\infty} -\frac{1}{4}. \quad \square$$

Problem 5.29. Evaluate

$$\lim_{x \to 0} \frac{1}{x}\left(\frac{1}{x} - \cot x\right).$$

Solution: By (5.3) and (5.5) (put $m = -1$, $x := -x$)

$$\cot x = \frac{\cos x}{\sin x} = \frac{1 - \dfrac{x^2}{2} + o(x^2)}{x - \dfrac{x^3}{6} + o(x^3)} = \frac{1}{x}\left(1 - \frac{x^2}{2} + o(x^2)\right)\frac{1}{1 - \dfrac{x^2}{6} + o(x^2)} =$$

$$\frac{1}{x}\left(1 - \frac{x^2}{2} + o(x^2)\right)\left(1 + \frac{x^2}{6} + o(x^2)\right) = \frac{1}{x}\left(1 - \frac{x^2}{2} + \frac{x^2}{6} + o(x^2)\right) =$$

$$\frac{1}{x} - \frac{1}{3}x + o(x).$$

It follows that

$$\frac{1}{x}\left(\frac{1}{x} - \cot x\right) = \frac{1}{x}\left(\frac{1}{x} - \left(\frac{1}{x} - \frac{1}{3}x + o(x)\right)\right) = \frac{1}{3} + o(1) \underset{x \to 0}{\longrightarrow} \frac{1}{3}. \quad \square$$

Problem 5.30. Evaluate

$$\lim_{x \to 0} \frac{1 - (\cos x)^{\sin x}}{x^3}.$$

Solution: By (5.3) and (5.4)

$$\sin x \ln \cos x = \left(x - \frac{x^3}{6} + o(x^3)\right)\ln\left(1 - \frac{x^2}{2} + o(x^3)\right) =$$

$$\left(x - \frac{x^3}{6} + o(x^3)\right)\left(-\frac{x^2}{2} + o(x^3)\right) = -\frac{x^3}{2} + o(x^3).$$

It follows that

$$1 - (\cos x)^{\sin x} = 1 - e^{\sin x \ln \cos x} = 1 - e^{-\frac{x^3}{2} + o(x^3)} = 1 - \left(1 - \frac{x^3}{2} + o(x^3)\right) = \frac{x^3}{2} + o(x^3)$$

(see (5.2)). Hence the limit exists and equals $1/2$. $\quad \square$

Problems

Prob. 172 — Represent the polynomial $x^4 - 5x^3 + 5x^2 + x + 2$ as a polynomial in $x - 2$.

Prob. 173 — Using Taylor's formula show that

$$\arctan x = x - \frac{x^3}{3} + \frac{x^5}{5} - \cdots + \frac{(-1)^{n-1}x^{2n+1}}{2n+1} + \cdots \ , |x| < 1.$$

Prob. 174 — Using Taylor's formula show that

$$\arcsin x = x + \frac{1}{2}\cdot\frac{x^3}{3} + \frac{1\cdot 3}{2\cdot 4}\cdot\frac{x^5}{5} + \frac{1\cdot 3\cdot 5}{2\cdot 4\cdot 6}\cdot\frac{x^7}{7} + \cdots \ , |x| < 1.$$

Prob. 175 — Evaluate the limit

$$\lim_{x\to 0}\frac{\sin(\sin x) - x\sqrt[3]{1-x^2}}{x^5}.$$

Prob. 176 — Are there a and b such that $1 + \ln(1+ax) - \sqrt{1+bx} = o(x^3)$, $x \to 0$?

5.5. Critical Points

Theorem 5.31 (Monotonicity Test)**.** *Let f be continuous on $[a,b]$ and differentiable on (a,b).*

(**a**) *If $f'(x) > 0$ at each point x of (a,b), then f is strictly increasing on $[a,b]$.*

(**a**) *If $f'(x) < 0$ at each point x in (a,b), then f is strictly decreasing on $[a,b]$.*

Proof. If $a \le x_1 < x_2 \le b$, then by Lagrange's Theorem

$$f(x_2) - f(x_1) = f'(c)(x_2 - x_1), \quad \text{where } x_1 < c < x_2.$$

It follows that

$$f(x_2) - f(x_1) = \begin{cases} f'(c)(x_2 - x_1) > 0 & \text{in case } (\mathbf{a}) \\ f'(c)(x_2 - x_1) < 0 & \text{in case } (\mathbf{b}) \end{cases}$$ $\square$

Problem 5.32. For $x > 0$ prove the inequality

$$x - \frac{x^3}{6} < \sin x.$$

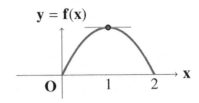

Figure 5.4: The critical point $x = 1$.

Solution: We have

$$f(x) = \sin x - \left(x - \frac{x^3}{6}\right) \Rightarrow f'(x) = \cos x - 1 + \frac{x^2}{2} = \frac{x^2}{2} - 2\sin^2\frac{x}{2}.$$

If $0 < y < \pi/2$, then $\sin y < y$ by (3.29). If $1 < \pi/2 \le y$, then again $\sin y \le 1 < y$. It follows that

$$f'(x) = 2\left\{\left(\frac{x}{2}\right)^2 - \sin^2\frac{x}{2}\right\} > 0,$$

implying that $f(x)$ increases by Theorem 5.31. Since $f(0) = 0$ and $f(x)$ is continuous on $[0, +\infty)$, we obtain the result. □

In general, the intervals of monotonicity of a function f are interlaced with the so-called critical points.

Definition 5.33. A point c of the domain $\mathcal{D}(f)$ of a function f is called an **interior** point if there is $\delta > 0$ such that the interval $(c - \delta, c + \delta)$ is in the domain $\mathcal{D}(f)$.

Definition 5.34. An interior point c of the domain $\mathcal{D}(f)$ of a function f such that either $f'(c) = 0$ or $f'(c)$ is undefined is called a **critical point** of f.

Fig 5.4 demonstrate a critical point, where $f'(c)$ is defined and Fig 5.5 where $f'(c)$ does not exist. Critical points may be partially classified using the following definition.

Definition 5.35. Let a function f be defined on $[a, b]$. It has a **local maximum** value at a point c in $[a, b]$ if $f(x) \le f(c)$ about c. It has a **local minimum** value at a point c in $[a, b]$ if $f(x) \ge f(c)$ about c.

Theorem 5.36 (Fermat). *Let* $y = f(x)$ *be a differentiable function and* c *be an interior point in* $\mathcal{D}(f)$ *of local maximum (or minimum) of* f. *Then* $f'(c) = 0$.

Proof. Let c be an interior point in $\mathcal{D}(f)$ of local maximum of f. Then

$$0 \le \lim_{x \to c^-} \frac{f(x) - f(c)}{x - c} = f'(c) = \lim_{x \to c^+} \frac{f(x) - f(c)}{x - c} \le 0 \Rightarrow f'(c) = 0.$$

The case of a local minimum is considered similarly. □

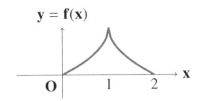

Figure 5.5: The critical point $x = 1$.

Problem 5.37 (Descartes' Paradox)**.** In 1638 Fermat sent to Descartes his rule of local maximum and minimum. Descartes responded with the following paradox, see Fig 5.6. Given a circle $x^2 + y^2 = r^2$ and $a > r$ find the point of the circle closest to $A(-a, 0)$. Since

$$f(x) = |AB|^2 = (x + a)^2 + y^2 = (x + a)^2 + r^2 - x^2 = 2ax + a^2 + r^2,$$

the derivative $f'(x) = 2a$ cannot vanish. However, $B(-r, 0)$ is the closest point to $A(-a, 0)$. Explain Descartes' Paradox.

Solution: The function $f(x)$ is linear and is defined on the interval $[-r, r]$. Its minimal value $(a-r)^2$ is taken at $x = -r$, whereas its maximal value $(a+r)^2$ is taken at $x = r$. The derivative must vanish at a point c of local minimum (maximum) only if c is an interior point of $\mathcal{D}(f)$. □

The following theorem is a convenient monotonicity test in situations when it is difficult or even impossible to determine the sign of $f'(x)$ on (a, b), see for example Problem 5.76.

Theorem 5.38. *Let f be continuous on $[a, b]$ and differentiable on (a, b). If $f(a) \neq f(b)$ and $f'(x) \neq 0$ for x in (a, b), then f is strictly monotonic on $[a, b]$.*

Proof. Without loss of generality we may assume that $f(a) < f(b)$. Otherwise, we may consider $-f$ instead of f. By Lagrange's Theorem, see Theorem 5.9, there is c in (a, b) such that

$$0 < \frac{f(b) - f(a)}{b - a} = f'(c).$$

If there is d in (a, b) such that $f'(d) < 0$, then by Darboux' Theorem 5.22 there is a point e between c and d such that $f'(e) = 0$, which is a contradiction. It follows that $f'(x) > 0$ for every x in (a, b). By Theorem 5.31 f is strictly increasing. □

On Fig 5.5 the slope of the tangent to the graph $y = f(x)$ is positive at any x, $0 < x < 1$, and is negative at any x, $1 < x < 2$. The function $y = f(x)$ increases on $(0, 1)$. The slope of the tangent to the graph $y = f(x)$ is negative at any x, $1 < x < 2$. The function $y = f(x)$ decreases on $(0, 1)$. On Fig 5.5 $x = 1$ is a point of local maximum but $f'(c)$ does not exist, since f is not differentiable at $x = 1$.

In case f is differentiable about a critical point c the cases of local maximum and local minimum can be distinguished by the following test.

Theorem 5.39. *Let f be continuous on $[a,b]$ and differentiable on (a,b) except for, possibly, a critical point c in $[a,b]$. Moving across $\mathbf{c}$ from left to right,*

(1) *if f' changes from **negative** to **positive** at c, then f has a local minimum at c;*

(2) *if f' changes from **positive** to **negative** at c, then f has a local maximum at c;*

(3) *if f' does **not change sign** at c (that is, f' is positive on both sides of c, or negative on both sides), then f has no local extremum at c;.*

Proof. In case (1) the function f decreases in some interval $(a - \delta, a)$, $\delta > 0$, and increases in some interval $(a, a + \delta_1)$ by Theorem 5.31. Since it is continuous at $x = a$, the point a is a point of local minimum. To prove (2) we apply (1) to $-f$. In case (3) the function f increases (decreases) on the both intervals $(a - \delta, a)$ and $(a, a + \delta_1)$. Since f is continuous at a, it is an increasing (decreasing) function about a. $\qquad\square$

Example 5.40. (1) The function $y = x^2$ has a local minimum at 0 ($y' = 2x$).

(2) The function $y = -x^2$ has a local maximum at 0 ($y' = -2x$).

(3) The function $y = x^3$ has no local extremum at 0 ($y' = 3x^2$).

Theorem 5.41 (The Second Derivative Test for Extrema). *Let $y = f(x)$ be a differentiable function on an open interval (a,b), which is twice-differentiable at c, where $f'(c) = 0$.*

(a) *If $f''(c) > 0$, then f has a local **minimum** at c.*

(b) *If $f''(c) < 0$, then f has a local **maximum** at c.*

Proof. (a) Since
$$0 < f''(c) = \lim_{x \to c} \frac{f'(x) - f'(c)}{x - c},$$
and $f'(c) = 0$ we conclude by Theorem 3.4 that
$$0 < \frac{f'(x) - f'(c)}{x - c} = \frac{f'(x)}{x - c}$$
about c. It follows that $f'(x) < 0$ for x in some interval $(c - \delta, c)$, and $f'(x) > 0$ for x in some interval $(c, c + \delta)$. The case (b) is considered similarly. $\qquad\square$

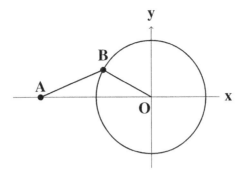

Figure 5.6: Descartes' Paradox.

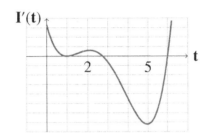

Figure 5.7: The graphs of $y = I'(t)$.

Remark 5.42. The Second Derivative Test for Local Extrema is an extension of the known **Parabola Test** for $f(x) = ax^2 + bx + c$, see Theorem 1.6.

1. If $f'(c) = 0$ and $a < 0$ (i.e the parabola directed downwards), then f has a local maximum at $x = c$.

2. If $f'(c) = 0$ and $a > 0$ (i.e the parabola directed upwards), then f has a local minimum at $x = c$.

Remark 5.43. By Theorem 3.37 any function f continuous on $[a, b]$ and differentiable in (a, b) except for a finite number of points has an absolute maximum value. By Theorem 5.36 $f'(c) = 0$ at any point of local maximum c, $a < c < b$. Therefore, to find the absolute maximum one can make the list of all critical points in (a, b), add to this list a, b and evaluate f at each of these points. The maximal value will be the absolute maximum of f on $[a, b]$. In practice this list contains usually not more than four points. The same is true for absolute minimum.

Theorem 5.44. *Let $R = R(q)$ be the revenue of a firm and $C = C(q)$ be its total cost function. Then at the value q maximizing the profit*

$$R'(q) = C'(q).$$

In economical terms this equations sounds as the marginal revenue equals the marginal cost.

Proof. Since the profit $\Pi(q)$ of the firm is $R(q) - C(q)$, the result follows by Fermat's Theorem, see Theorem 5.36. □

Problem 5.45. The value of an investment at time t is given by $I(t)$. The rate of change, $I'(t)$, of $I(t)$ is shown on Fig 5.7.

(a) What are the critical points of $I(t)$?

(b) Identify each critical point as a local maximum, a local minimum, or neither.

(c) Explain the financial significance of each of the critical points.

Solution:

The critical points of $I(t)$ are solutions to the equation $I'(t) = 0$, i.e. they are located at the points, where the tangent is horizontal. The graph of $y = I'(t)$ shows that these points are $t = 1$, $t = 2.75$, $t = 6$. Since $I'(t) > 0$ on $[0, 2.75]$ except for zero at $t = 1$, we conclude that $I(t)$ strictly increases on both intervals $[0, 1)$ and $(1, 2.75]$. Since f is continuous at $t = 1$, we conclude that

$$\lim_{t \to 1^-} I(t) = I(1) = \lim_{t \to 1^+} I(t).$$

It follows that $I(t) < I(1)$ for $t < 1$ and $I(t) > I(1)$ for $t > 1$. Hence $I(t)$ strictly increases on $[0, 2.75]$. The latter arguments are necessary since $I'(1) = 0$.

The derivative $I'(t)$ changes its signs at $t = 2.75$ and $t = 6$. Therefore, $I(t)$ decreases on $[2.75, 6]$ and increases for $t > 6$. By Theorem 5.39 $t = 2.75$ is a local maximum and $t = 6$ is a local minimum. The point $t = 1$ is neither a local maximum nor a local minimum. At the moment $t = 1$ the investment instantaneously stops its increase in value, though it starts increasing again immediately afterwards. At $t = 2.75$ the investment $I(t)$ takes its maximal value on $[0, 6]$ and begins decreasing. At $t = 6$ it starts increasing again. So, it is better to convert the investment $I(t)$ into money about the moment $t = 2.75$. However, it can be seen from the graph (Fig 5.8) that the investment drops fast down starting with approximately $t = 3$ but recovers in value later about $t = 7$. □

Problem 5.46. The cost $C(v)$ in dollars of use of a heavy lorry on a highway for one hour is determined by the formula:

$$c\left(432 + 0.001v^3\right),$$

where the speed v is measured in km/h and c is some constant. Find the optimal speed of transportation.

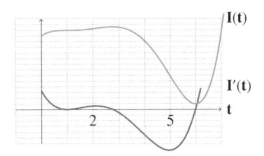

Figure 5.8: The graphs of $y = I(t)$ and $y = I'(t)$.

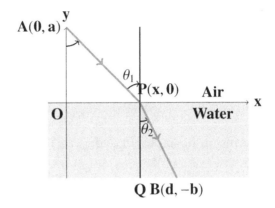

Figure 5.9: The Law of Refraction.

Solution: Let s be the distance of transportation. Then it will be covered in s/v hours, implying that the total cost $C(v)$ of transportation with speed v equals

$$C(v) = \frac{cs}{v}(432 + 0.001v^3) = cs\left(0.001v^2 + \frac{432}{v}\right).$$

We have

$$C'(v) = cs\left(0.002v - \frac{432}{v^2}\right) = 0 \Leftrightarrow v^3 = 216 \cdot 10^3 \Leftrightarrow v = 60\,\text{km/h}.$$

Since

$$C''(v) = s\left(0.002 + \frac{864}{v^3}\right) > 0,$$

the velocity $v = 60\,\text{km/h}$ minimises the transportation cost by the second derivative test.   □

Problem 5.47. Fermat's Principle in Optics states that light travels from one point to another along a path which minimises the time of travel. Find the path that a ray of light follows from a point A in air, where the speed of light is c_1, to a point B in water, where its speed is c_2.

Solution: The times t_1 required for light to travel from A to P and t_2 required for light to travel from P to B are given by

$$t_1 = \frac{AP}{c_1} = \frac{\sqrt{a^2 + x^2}}{c_1}, \quad t_2 = \frac{PB}{c_2} = \frac{\sqrt{b^2 + (d - x)^2}}{c_2}.$$

Hence the combined time t to travel from A to B equals

$$t = t_1 + t_2 = \frac{\sqrt{a^2 + x^2}}{c_1} + \frac{\sqrt{b^2 + (d - x)^2}}{c_2}.$$

Differentiating the above formula in x, we obtain

$$\frac{dt}{dx} = \frac{x}{c_1 \sqrt{a^2 + x^2}} - \frac{d - x}{c_2 \sqrt{b^2 + (d - x)^2}},$$

or in terms of the angles θ_1 and θ_2

$$\frac{dt}{dx} = \frac{\sin \theta_1}{c_1} - \frac{\sin \theta_2}{c_2}.$$

It follows that (notice that $\theta_1 = 0$ if $x = 0$ and $\theta_1 = 0$ if $x = d$). It is clear from Fig 5.9 that θ_1 increases when x increases and θ_2 decreases when x increases. Hence $\frac{dt}{dx}$ is an increasing function on $[0, d]$. By the Intermediate Value Theorem there is exactly one value of x in $(0, d)$ where $dt/dx = 0$. At this unique point we have

$$\boxed{\frac{\sin \theta_1}{c_1} = \frac{\sin \theta_2}{c_2}.}$$

This equation is called the **Law of Refraction** or **Snell's Law**. $\qquad \square$

Problem 5.48. A farm produces an expensive cheese whose market price is 36 euro per kilo. The cost function of this farm is given by the formula

$$C(q) = \frac{q^3}{3} - 3q^2 + 20q + 50,$$

where $C(q)$ is measured in euro and q is measured in kilos. Maximize the profit.

Solution: Since this farm is small it cannot influence the market price. It follows that the revenue of the farm is given by $R(q) = 36q$. Then the profit is

$$\Pi(q) = R(q) - C(q) = -\frac{q^3}{3} + 3q^2 - 20q - 50 + 36q = -\frac{q^3}{3} + 3q^2 + 16q - 50.$$

We have

$$C'(q) = q^2 - 6q + 20 > 0, \quad C''(q) = 2(q - 3) > 0 \ \text{ for } \ q > 3;$$

$$\Pi'(q) = -q^2 + 6q + 16 = -(q^2 - 6q - 16) = -(q + 2)(q - 8), \quad \Pi''(q) = -2(q - 3).$$

It follows that $q = 8$ kg maximises the profit of this farm. It indeed provides the maximal profit by the second derivative test: $\Pi''(8) = -10$. A simple calculation shows that $\Pi(8) = 99.33$ Euro. $\qquad\qquad\square$

Problems

Prob. 177 — Consider the function $f(x) = x^3 + 3x^2 - 45x + 4$. Then

  I. f is decreasing on $(-5, 3)$ and increasing on $(-\infty, -5) \cup (3, +\infty)$.

 II. f has a local minimum at $x = 3$.

III. f has a local maximum at $x = -5$.

$$\text{(A) I only} \quad \text{(B) II only} \quad \text{(C) I and II only}$$

$$\text{(D) I and III only} \quad \text{(E) I, II, and III}$$

Prob. 178 — The number of local minimums of the function $f(x) = 2\cos x + |x|$ on the interval $[-\pi, \pi]$ equals

$$\text{(A) 1} \quad \text{(B) 2} \quad \text{(C) 3} \quad \text{(D) 4} \quad \text{(E) 5}$$

Prob. 179 — Determine the absolute maximum value of $f(x) = \dfrac{5 + 2x}{x^2 + 14}$ on the interval $[-2, 4]$.

$$\text{(A) } \frac{1}{18} \quad \text{(B) } \frac{13}{30} \quad \text{(C) } \frac{8}{7} \quad \text{(D) } \frac{1}{2} \quad \text{(E) 0.75}$$

Prob. 180 — Find all the critical values of f when $f(x) = x^{4/5}(x - 5)^2$.

$$\text{(A) 0, } \frac{5}{7} \quad \text{(B) } \frac{10}{7}, 5 \quad \text{(C) } \frac{5}{7}, 5 \quad \text{(D) 0, } \frac{5}{7}, 5 \quad \text{(E) 0, } \frac{10}{7}$$

Prob. 181 — An advertisement is run to stimulate the sale of cars. After t days, $1 \le t \le 48$, the number of cars sold is given by

$$N(t) = 4000 + 45t^2 - t^3.$$

On what day does the maximum rate of growth of sales occur?

$$\text{(A) 17} \quad \text{(B) 13} \quad \text{(C) 15} \quad \text{(D) 16} \quad \text{(E) 14}$$

Prob. 182 — Let $f(x) = x \ln x$, then the minimal value attained by $f(x)$ is

(A) $-\dfrac{1}{e}$ (B) 0 (C) $\dfrac{1}{e}$ (D) -1 (E) There is no minimum

Prob. 183 — Show that for every positive x

$$1 - \frac{x^2}{2} < \cos x.$$

Prob. 184 — Prove that for any real x

$$\frac{2}{3} \leq \frac{x^2 + 1}{x^2 + x + 1} \leq 2.$$

Prob. 185 — Apply the derivative test of monotonicity to prove that although $x = 0$ is a point of local maximum of a differentiable function

$$f(x) = 2 - x^2\left(2 + \sin\frac{1}{x}\right) \text{ if } x \neq 0, \quad f(0) = 2,$$

there is no $\delta > 0$ such that f increases on $(-\delta, 0)$ and decreases on $(0, \delta)$.

Prob. 186 — Let $f(x)$ be a differentiable nonnegative function on $(-\infty, +\infty)$. Show that f and f^2 have the same critical points.

Prob. 187 — Find all positive b such that $c = \log_b c$ for some real number c.

Prob. 188 — If the sum of the squares of two positive numbers is 200, then their minimum product is

(A) 100 (B) $25\sqrt{7}$ (C) 28 (D) $24\sqrt{14}$ (E) none of these

Prob. 189 — A line is drawn through the point $(1, 2)$ forming a right triangle with the positive x-and y-axes. The slope of the line forming the triangle of least area is

(A) -1 (B) -2 (C) -4 (D) $-\dfrac{1}{2}$ (E) -3

Prob. 190 — On one side of a 2 km-wide river a power plant is placed. A small town is placed on the opposite side and 20 km apart along the river. It costs \$60 per meter to place cable under the river and \$20 per meter to lay it over land. Find the cheapest solution.

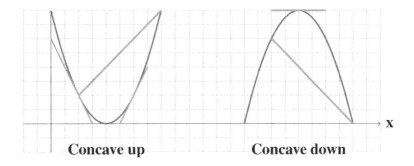

Figure 5.10: Concavity. Geometric Tests.

5.6. Concavity and Inflection Points

Definition 5.49. The graph of a differentiable function $y = f(x)$ on an open interval (a, b) is

(a) **concave up** on (a, b) if f' is increasing on (a, b).

(b) **concave down** on (a, b) if f' is decreasing on (a, b).

Theorem 5.50 (The Second Derivative Test for concavity). *Let $y = f(x)$ by twice-differentiable on an open interval (a, b).*

(a) *If $f'' > 0$ on (a, b), the graph of f over (a, b) is **concave up**.*

(b) *If $f'' < 0$ on (a, b), the graph of f over (a, b) is **concave down**.*

Proof. Apply Theorem 5.31 to $y = f'(x)$.   □

Theorem 5.51. *If f is a differentiable function on (a, b), which is concave up and concave down on (a, b), then f is a linear function.*

Proof. If f is differentiable and is both concave up and concave down, then its derivative f' is both increasing and decreasing, implying that $f' = k$ on (a, b), where k is a constant. By Corollary 5.18 we obtain that $f(x) = kx + b$ is a linear function.   □

The terminology **concave up** and **concave down** is well explained by the two following theorems. These theorems are also useful do determine the intervals of concavity up and down by a given graph, see Fig 5.10.

Theorem 5.52. *The graph of a concave up function is placed above any of its tangent. The graph of a concave down function is placed below any of its tangent.*

Proof. If the graph of $y = f(x)$ is concave down, then the graph of $y = -f(x)$ is concave up. Therefore, it is sufficient to consider only the concave up case. The equation of the tangent to the graph of $y = f(x)$ at the point $(a, f(a))$ is given by $y = f'(a)(x - a) + f(a)$. Let H be an auxiliary function measuring the height of the graph of f over the tangent line:

$$H(x) = f(x) - f'(a)(x - a) - f(a) \Rightarrow H'(x) = f'(x) - f'(a).$$

Hence $x = a$ is a critical point for $y = H(x)$. Since $y = f(x)$ is concave up, the derivative $f'(x)$ increases, implying that $H'(x)$ increases as well. Since $H'(a) = 0$, the point a is a point of absolute minimum for $y = H(x)$ by Theorem 5.39. Since $H(a) = 0$, the graph of $f(x)$ is always above the tangent line at a. □

Theorem 5.53. *The graph of a concave up function is placed below any of its chord. The graph of a concave down function is placed above any of its chord.*

Proof. The point-slope equation of the chord passing through $(a, f(a))$ and $(b, f(b))$, where $a < b$, is given by the formula

$$L(x) = \frac{f(b) - f(a)}{b - a}(x - a) + f(a), \quad a \le x \le b. \tag{5.7}$$

Suppose that f is concave up and consider an auxiliary function

$$G(x) = f(x) - L(x) \Rightarrow G'(x) = f'(x) - \frac{f(b) - f(a)}{b - a}.$$

It is clear that $G(a) = G(b) = 0$ and that G is concave up as well, implying that $G'(x)$ increases. By Theorem 3.37 the function G being continuous takes its maximal value on $[a, b]$ at some point c. The number c cannot be in (a, b) since this contradicts Theorem 5.39 (2). Hence either $c = a$ or $c = b$. In both cases $G(c) = 0$, implying that $G(x) \le 0$ on $[a, b]$. If f is concave down, then $-f$ is concave up, which completes the proof. □

The converse statement is also true. To prove it we need the following lemma.

Lemma 5.54. *Let $f(x)$ be a differentiable function on (a, b), $a < c < b$, and $L(x) = k(x - c) + f(c)$ be a linear function.*

(a) If $f(x) \le L(x)$ for $c < x$, then $f'(c) \le k$;

(b) If $f(x) \le L(x)$ for $x < c$, then $f'(c) \ge k$.

Proof. In case (a) we have

$$f'(c) = \lim_{x \to c^+} \frac{f(x) - f(c)}{x - c} \le \lim_{x \to c^+} \frac{L(x) - f(c)}{x - c} = \lim_{x \to c^+} \frac{L(x) - L(c)}{x - c} = k.$$

In case (b) we have

$$f'(c) = \lim_{x \to c^-} \frac{f(x) - f(c)}{x - c} = \lim_{x \to c^-} \frac{f(c) - f(x)}{c - x} \geq \lim_{x \to c^+} \frac{L(c) - L(x)}{c - x} = k. \qquad \square$$

Theorem 5.55. *Let f be a differentiable function on an interval and let its graph be below (above) any of its chord. Then f is concave up (down).*

Proof. For $a < b$ the equation of the chord passing through $(a, f(a))$ and $(b, f(b))$ is given by (5.7). Since $f(x) \leq L(x)$ for $a \leq x \leq b$, we conclude by Lemma 5.54 that

$$f'(a) \leq \frac{f(b) - f(a)}{b - a} \leq f'(b),$$

implying that the function $f'(x)$ increases. To consider the case of a concave down function replace f with $-f$. $\qquad \square$

Theorem 5.56. *Let f be a differentiable function on an open interval such that its graph is above (below) any of its tangent. Then f is concave up (down).*

Proof. Suppose that the graph of f is above any of its tangent. If the graph of f is below any of its chord, then f is concave up by Theorem 5.55. If it is not the case, we use the equation of a chord through $(a, f(a))$ and $(b, f(b))$, which is given by (5.7). Since the graph of $L(x)$ is not above the graph of f over (a, b), the maximum of the continuous function $G(x) = f(x) - L(x)$ is positive. Since $G(a) = G(b) = 0$ the maximum is taken at some point c, $a < c < b$. By Fermat's Theorem $G'(c) = 0$, implying that

$$f'(c) = L'(c) = \frac{f(b) - f(a)}{b - a}. \tag{5.8}$$

Let $l(x) = f'(c)(x - c) + f(c)$ be the equation of the tangent to $f(x)$ at $x = c$. By (5.8) the tangent and the chord have equal slopes, which shows that

$$l(x) - L(x) = l(c) - L(c) = f(c) - L(c) = \max_{a \leq x \leq b} \{f(x) - L(x)\} \geq f(x) - L(x) \tag{5.9}$$

for $a \leq x \leq b$. By our assumption $f(x) \geq l(x)$ for every x, Hence by (5.9) we have

$$f(x) - L(x) \geq l(x) - L(x) \geq f(x) - L(x)$$

for $a \leq x \leq b$. It follows that $l(x) = f(x)$ on (a, b). But $f(a) = L(a)$ and $f(b) = L(b)$. It follows that $f(x) = l(x) = L(x)$, which contradicts to the assumption that the maximum on (a, b) of $G(x) = f(x) - L(x)$ is positive. The second case is reduced to already considered by the sign change: $f \to -f$. $\qquad \square$

The following theorem is an application of Darboux' Theorem (see Theorem 5.22).

Theorem 5.57. *Let f be a differentiable convex (convex up or down) function on an interval (a, b). Then its derivative is continuous on (a, b).*

Proof. Since f is differentiable, its derivative satisfies the intermediate value property. Since f is concave, the derivative f' is monotonic. Hence by Theorem 3.29 the derivative f' is continuous on (a, b). □

The geometric condition that the graph of a function is placed below any of its chord has an equivalent analytic restatement. For any x_1 and x_2 in any interval inside the domain of f and for any α, $0 \le \alpha \le 1$, the following inequality holds:

$$f(\alpha x_1 + (1 - \alpha)x_2) \le \alpha f(x_1) + (1 - \alpha)f(x_2). \tag{5.10}$$

Problem 5.58. Show that for any positive a and b

$$\sqrt{ab} \le \frac{a + b}{2}.$$

Solution: Since $(-\ln x)'' = x^{-2} > 0$, the function $y = -\ln x$ is concave up. Let $\alpha_1 = \alpha_2 = 0.5$, $x_1 = a$, $x_2 = b$. Then (5.10) implies that

$$-\ln\left(\frac{a + b}{2}\right) \le -\frac{\ln a + \ln b}{2} \Leftrightarrow \ln\left(\frac{a + b}{2}\right) \ge \frac{\ln a + \ln b}{2} = \ln \sqrt{ab}.$$

Observing that the function $y = \ln x$ increases, we obtain the result. □

Definition 5.59. A point where the graph of a function **has a tangent line** and where the concavity changes is a **point of inflection**.

Example 5.60. The function $y = \sqrt[3]{x - 1}$ has an inflection point at $x = 0$, see Fig 5.11.

Solution: Indeed, if $x \ne 1$, then

$$y'(x) = \frac{1}{3}(x - 1)^{-2/3} \Rightarrow \lim_{x \to 1^+} y'(x) = \lim_{x \to 1^+} y'(x) = +\infty.$$

It follows that there is a vertical tangent to the graph of $y = \sqrt[3]{x - 1}$ at $x = 1$. The derivative $y'(x)$ increases for $x < 1$ and decreases for $x > 1$, which implies that $x = 1$ is an inflection point for the graph of $y = \sqrt[3]{x - 1}$. □

Example 5.60 shows that inflection points, being defined geometrically rather than algebraically, require a special attention in AP Calculus exams. The point c in Problem 5.61, for example, is not an inflection point since there is no tangent at c. The requirement of existence of tangents at inflection points allows one to exclude from consideration misleading cases of functions of the following type:

$$y = |x + 1| - 2|x| + |x - 1|.$$

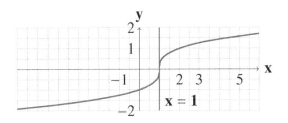

Figure 5.11: $y = \sqrt[3]{x - 1}$.

This function is both concave up and concave down on each interval $(-\infty, -1)$, $(-1, 0)$, $(0, 1)$, $(1, +\infty)$. Therefore, it is impossible to decide if it changes its concavity at $x = -1, 0, 1$. With the definition given above this function is just excluded from consideration, since there is no tangent at $(-1, 0)$, $(0, 2)$, $(1, 0)$.

Problem 5.61. Let $f(x)$ be a continuous function on $(-\infty, +\infty)$, twice differentiable on $(-\infty, c)$ and on $(c, +\infty)$ such that

$x < c$	$c < x$
$f'(x) < 0$	$0 < f'(x)$
$0 < f''(x)$	$f''(x) < 0$

Show that $f(x)$ is not differentiable at $x = c$.

Solution: The function $y = f(x)$ decreases ($f'(x) < 0$) and is concave up ($f''(x) > 0$) on $(-\infty, c)$. Similarly, $y = f(x)$ increases ($f'(x) > 0$) and is concave down ($f''(x) < 0$) on $(c, +\infty)$. So, the graph of f looks like:

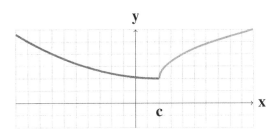

which makes it clear graphically that $f(x)$ is not differentiable at $x = c$. Since $y = f(x)$ decreases on $(-\infty, c)$, (implying that $f(x) \geq f(c)$),

$$\lim_{x \to c^-} \frac{f(x) - f(c)}{x - c} \leq 0$$

if the limit exists. Similarly,

$$\lim_{x \to c^+} \frac{f(x) - f(c)}{x - c} \geq 0.$$

if the limit exists, implying that $f'(c) = 0$ if f is differentiable at $x = c$. Since $f''(x) < 0$ for $x > c$, the derivative $f'(x)$ strictly decreases on $(c, +\infty)$, implying that $f'(x) < f'(c) = 0$, which contradicts to the condition that $f'(x) > 0$ for $x > c$. $\qquad\qquad\qquad\qquad\qquad\qquad\qquad\qquad\qquad\qquad\qquad\qquad\square$

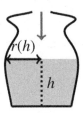

Problem 5.62. Water is poured at a constant rate into the vase shown above. Let **h(t)** be the height of the water in the vase at time **t** (assume the vase is empty when **t = 0**). Sketch a rough graph of the function **h(t)**. In particular, what happens when the water level reaches the neck of the vase?

Solution: Let $r(h)$ be the radius of the vase at height h. The increment of the volume of water in the vase for small interval of time $(t, t + \Delta t)$ is given by $\Delta V \approx \pi r^2(h)\Delta h$. The rate of volume change is constant by the condition. It follows that

$$c = \frac{dV}{dt} = \pi r^2(h)\frac{dh}{dt} \Rightarrow \boxed{\frac{dh}{dt} = \frac{c}{\pi r^2(h)}}.$$

Hence $dh/dt \downarrow$ if $r(h) \uparrow$, and $dh/dt \uparrow$ if $r(h) \downarrow$. This can also be observed from the fact that at wide parts of the vase the level increases slower than at narrow ones.

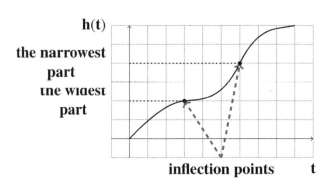

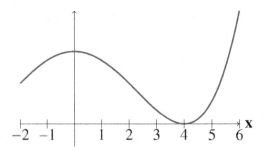

Problem 5.63. The number of the inflection points for the graph shown above is

(A) 0 (B) 1 (C) 2 (D) 3 (E) 4

Solution: The graph is above any of its chord over the interval $(-2, 2)$ and is below any of its chord over the interval $(2, 6)$. It follows that $x = 2$ is the only inflection point for this graph.
Answer: (B).

Problem 5.64. The graph of the **derivative** of f is shown above. For what values of x is the graph of $f(x)$ concave up?

(A) $-2 < x < 2$ (B) $2 < x < 6$ (C) $0 < x < 4$ (D) $4 < x < 6$

(E) $-2 < x < 0$ or $4 < x < 6$

Solution: Since we are given the graph of $y = f'(x)$, we cannot use geometric criteria for convexity. Instead we apply the definition. The graph of $f(x)$ is concave up when f' is increasing, that is when

$-2 < x < 0$ or $4 < x < 6 \Rightarrow$ Answer (E).

Problem 5.65. Which of the following statements about the function $f(x) = x^4 - x^3$ is true?

(A) f has no relative extremum.

(B) The graph of f has one point of inflection and f has two relative extremal points.

(C) The graph of f has two point of inflection and f has one relative extremum.

(D) The graph of f has two points of inflection and f has two relative extremal points.

(E) The graph of f has two points of inflection and f has three relative extremal points.

Solution: We see that $f(x) = x^3(x - 1)$ is positive outside $[0, 1]$ and is negative inside $(0, 1)$. Next, $f'(x) = 4x^2(x-0.75)$, implying that there is a point of minimum at $x = 0.75$. Finally $f''(x) = 12x(x-0.5)$ implying that $f''(x) > 0$ for $x < 0, f''(x) < 0$ for $0 < x < 1$. It follows that $x = 0$ is an inflection point. Similarly $f''(x)$ changes sign when x passes through $x = 0.5$. Therefore, $x = 0.5$ is the second inflection point. The point $x = 0.75$ is a unique point of relative extremum.
Answer: (C).

Problem 5.66. Consider the curve

$$y = 2x^3 - 3(k-1)x^2 - 6kx + k, \ k > 0.$$

Then on the interval $-1 < x < k$

(A) y increases and first is concave up, then concave down.

(B) y increases and first is concave down, then concave up.

(C) y decreases, and first is concave up, then concave down.

(D) y decreases, and first is concave down, then concave up.

(E) The concavity of y depends on a concrete value of k.

Solution: We have

$$y' = 6(x^2 - (k-1)x - k) = 6(x+1)(x-k) < 0 \ \text{on} \ -1 < x < k;$$

$$y'' = 12\left(x - \frac{k-1}{2}\right) \ \text{is first negative and the positive.}$$

Answer: (D).

x	-1.5	-1.0	-0.5	0	0.5	1.0	1.5
$f(x)$	-1	-4	-6	-7	-6	-4	-1
$f'(t)$	-7	-5	-3	0	3	5	7

Problem 5.67. Let f be differentiable for all real numbers. The table above gives selected values of f and its derivative f' in the closed interval $-1.5 \le x \le 1.5$. The second derivative of f has the property that $f''(x) > 0$ for $-1.5 \le x \le 1.5$.

Write an equation of the line tangent to the graph of f at the point where $x = 1$. Use this line to approximate the value of $f(1.2)$. Is this approximation greater than or less than the actual value of $f(1.2)$? Give a reason for your answer.

Solution: The graph of $y = f(x)$ is concave up on the interval $-1.5 \le x \le 1.5$. It follows that $f(1.2) > L(1.2)$, where $L(x) = f'(1)(x-1) + f(1)$ is the linearization of $y = f(x)$ at $x = 1$. Then

$$f(1,2) \approx L(1.2) = 5(1.2 - 1) - 4 = -3.$$

Answer: $f(1.2) \approx -3$ and -3 is less than the actual value.

Problems

Prob. 191 — Find the points of inflections for the function $y = \exp(-x^2)$.

Prob. 192 — Let f be a twice differentiable function for $0 \le x < +\infty$ such that $f(0) < 0$, $f'(0) > 0$, $f''(x) > 0$ for $x > 0$. Then the equation $f(x) = 0$ has a unique solution in $(0, -f(0)/f'(0))$.

Prob. 193 — Show that the function $y = x \ln x$ is concave up.

Prob. 194 — Prove that for any positive a and b

$$(a + b) \ln\left(\frac{a + b}{2}\right) < a \ln a + b \ln b.$$

Prob. 195 — Determine the intervals of concavity and all inflection points for $y = x^2 - x^{5/3}$.

Prob. 196 — Let f be a twice differentiable function on (A, B) such that $f''(c) \ne 0$, where $A < c < B$. Then there are numbers $a < b$ in (A, B) such that

$$\frac{f(b) - f(a)}{b - a} = f'(c).$$

Prob. 197 — If $f(x)$ is twice differentiable at any x, $x \ne 0$, and $f''(x) < 0$ for $x \ne 0$, then f is not differentiable at $x = 0$.

Prob. 198 — The function f, with $f'(x) = (x - 2)^2(x - 7)^3$, has an inflection point at $x =$

(A) 4 only (B) 7 only (C) 2 and 4 only (D) 2 and 4 only

(E) 2 and 4 and 7 only

Prob. 199 — An equation of the line tangent to the graph of $y = x^3 + 3x^2 + 2$ at its point of inflection is

(A) $y = -3x + 1$ (B) $y = -3x - 7$ (C) $y = x + 5$

(D) $y = 3x + 1$ (E) $y = 3x + 7$

5.7.   The Shape of a Graph

In plotting graphs it is convenient first to plot a graph about its critical points c, as well as about the points of x-intercept and of y-intercept. As soon as we know the values $f(c)$ or, what is better, the behaviour of the graph of $y = f(x)$ about c, we can easily sketch the graph using Theorem 5.31.

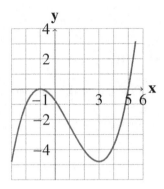

Figure 5.12: The graph of $y = 0.15(x^3 - 3x^2 - 9x - 5)$.

Problem 5.68. Using critical points sketch the graph of

$$f(x) = 0.15(x^3 - 3x^2 - 9x - 5),$$

and identify the intervals on which f is increasing and on which f is decreasing.

Solution: Using Horner's Rule, we find the roots of $x^3 - 3x^2 - 9x - 5$:

$$
\begin{array}{r|rrrr}
-1| & 1 & -3 & -9 & -5 \\
& & -1 & 4 & 5 \\
\hline
& 1 & -4 & -5 & \mathbf{0}
\end{array}
$$

It follows that

$$x^3 - 3x^2 - 9x - 5 = (x + 1)(x^2 - 4x - 5) = (x + 1)^2(x - 5). \tag{5.11}$$

Observing that

$$\lim_{x \to -1}(x - 5) = -6, \quad \text{and} \quad \lim_{x \to 5}(x + 1)^2 = 36,$$

we conclude by (5.11) that

$$f(x) \sim \begin{cases} 0.15 \cdot (-6)(x + 1)^2 = -0.9(x + 1)^2 & \text{about } x = -1, \\ 0.15 \cdot 36(x - 5) = 5.4(x - 5) & \text{about } x = 5, \end{cases}$$

which allows us to sketch the plot of the graph about points $x = -1$ and $x = 5$. We can do the same about the critical points if we find them. We have

$$f'(x) = 0.15(3x^2 - 6x - 9) = 0.45(x^2 - 2x - 3) = 0.45(x + 1)(x - 3).$$

By Theorem 5.31 we conclude that $f(x)$ strictly increases on $(-\infty, -1)$, strictly decreases on $(-1, 3)$, and again strictly increases on $(3, +\infty)$. Hence by Theorem

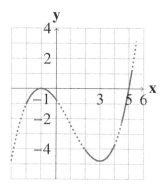

Figure 5.13: Plotting the graph of $y = 0.15(x^3 - 3x^2 - 9x - 5)$.

5.39 $x = -1$ is a point of local maximum, and $x = 3$ is a point of local minimum. The value of $f(x)$ at the critical point 3 is important to know. Applying Horner's Rule again, we find that

$$
\begin{array}{r|rrrr}
3| & 1 & -3 & -9 & -5 \\
 & & 3 & 0 & -27 \\
\hline
 & 1 & 0 & -9 & \mathbf{-32}
\end{array}
\Rightarrow f(3) = -32 \cdot 0.15 = \boxed{-4.8}.
$$

Connecting already constructed parts of the graph in Fig 5.13 by "dotted lines", we obtain the graph of $y = f(x)$, see Fig 5.12.   □

There is one yet not clarified part in plotting the graph of the function in Problem 5.68. There is no indication in the solution presented above regarding the **shapes** of parts of the graph.

Problem 5.69. Using Theorem 5.50, investigate concavity of

$$f(x) = 0.15(x^3 - 3x^2 - 9x - 5).$$

Solution: Since
$$f''(x) = 0.9(x - 1),$$

the graph of $y = f(x)$ is concave down for $x < 1$ and concave up for $x > 1$.   □

Here is a typical PVA (Position-Velocity-Acceleration) problem.

Problem 5.70. A particle is moving along a horizontal coordinate line (positive to the right) with position function

$$s(t) = 2t^3 - 12t^2 + 18t - 4, \quad 0 \le t \le 4,$$

where t is measured in seconds and s is measured in meeters. Find the velocity and acceleration, and describe the motion of the particle.

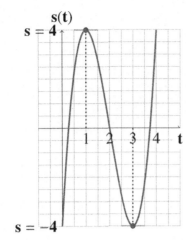

Figure 5.14: The position of a particle.

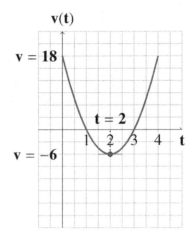

Figure 5.15: The velocity of a particle.

Solution: The velocity and acceleration are given by:

$$v(t) = s'(t) = 6t^2 - 24t + 18 = 6(t-1)(t-3),$$
$$a(t) = v'(t) = s''(t) = 12t - 24 = 14(t-2).$$

It follows that the particle starts from the initial position $s(0) = -4$ with the initial velocity $v(0) = 18$ m/sec. We apply Horner's Rule to $2t^3 - 12t^2 + 18t - 4$ to evaluate $s(1)$, $s(3)$, and $s(4)$:

$$
\begin{array}{r|rrrr}
1| & 2 & -12 & 18 & -4 \\
  &   & 2 & -10 & 8 \\
\hline
  & 2 & -10 & 8 & 4
\end{array}
\Rightarrow s(1) = \boxed{4}.
$$

$$
\begin{array}{r|rrrr}
3| & 2 & -12 & 18 & -4 \\
  &   & 6 & -18 & 0 \\
\hline
  & 2 & -6 & 0 & -4
\end{array}
\Rightarrow s(3) = \boxed{-4}.
$$

$$
\begin{array}{r|rrrr}
4| & 2 & -12 & 18 & -4 \\
  &   & 8 & -16 & 8 \\
\hline
  & 2 & -4 & 2 & 4
\end{array}
\Rightarrow s(4) = \boxed{4}.
$$

Using the critical points $(1, 4)$ and $(3, -4)$ of $s(t)$ we plot its graph, see Fig 5.14. The graph of the velocity is the graph of the parabola $v = 6(t-1)(t-3)$, see Fig 5.15. The point is at rest at two moments $t = 1$ sec and $t = 3$ sec. At these very points the particle changes its direction.

The greatest distance of the particle from the starting position are given by $s(1) - s(0) = 8$, $|s(3) - s(1)| = 8$, $s(4) - s(3) = 8$.

The total distance covered by the particle for $0 \le t \le 4$ is

$$|s(1) - s(0)| + |s(3) - s(1)| + |s(4) - s(3)| = 8 + 8 + 8 = \boxed{24\,\text{m}}.$$

The average **speed** of the particle is

$$\textbf{Average Speed} = \frac{24}{4} = \boxed{6\,\text{m/sec}}.$$

The average **velocity** of the particle is

$$\frac{s(4) - s(0)}{4} = \frac{4 - (-4)}{4} = \boxed{2\,\text{m/sec}}.$$

The instant velocity of the particle equals the average velocity twice:

$$v(t) = 2 \Leftrightarrow 6(t-1)(t-3) = 2 \Leftrightarrow 3t^2 - 12t + 8 = 0 \Leftrightarrow t_{1,2} = \frac{2}{3}(3 \pm \sqrt{3}).$$

The velocity of the particle decreases for $0 \le t \le 2$ and increases for $2 \le t \le 4$. $\square$

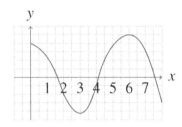

Problem 5.71. Fill in the table with signs of the first two derivatives of the function with the graph shown above:

x in	$0 < x < 2$	$2 < x < 3$	$5 < x < 6$	$6 < x < 7$	$7 < x < 8$
$f'(x)$					
$f''(x)$					

Solution: The function f decreases on $[0, 3]$ and $[6, 8]$. It is increases on $[3, 6]$. It follows that $f' < 0$ on $(0, 3)$ and $(6, 8)$, and $f' > 0$ on $(3, 6)$. The graph of the function f is concave down on $[0, 2]$ and $[4, 8]$. It is concave up on $[2, 4]$. It follows that $f'' < 0$ on $(0, 2)$ and $(4, 8)$, and $f'' > 0$ on $(2, 4)$.

x in	$0 < x < 2$	$2 < x < 3$	$5 < x < 6$	$6 < x < 7$	$7 < x < 8$
$f'(x)$	-	-	+	-	-
$f''(x)$	-	+	-	-	-

Problems

Prob. 200 — Graph a function f with the following properties:

- $f(x)$ has critical points at $x = 2$ and $x = 5$;
- $f'(x)$ is positive to the left of 2 and positive to the right of 5;
- $f'(x)$ is negative between 2 and 5.

Prob. 201 — Consider the function $f(x) = x^3 + 3x^2 - 45x + 4$. Then

I. f is decreasing on $(-5, 3)$ and increasing on $(-\infty, -5) \cup (3, +\infty)$.

II. f has a local minimum at $x = 3$.

III. f has a local maximum at $x = -5$.

(A) **I** only (B) **II** only (C) **I** and **II** only

(D) **I** and **III** only (E) **I, II,** and **III**

Prob. 202 — The number of local minimums of the function $f(x) = 2\cos x + |x|$ on the interval $[-\pi, \pi]$ equals

(A) 1 (B) 2 (C) 3 (D) 4 (E) 5

Prob. 203 — Determine the absolute maximum value of $f(x) = \dfrac{5 + 2x}{x^2 + 14}$ on the interval $[-1, 3]$.

(A) $\dfrac{1}{18}$ (B) $\dfrac{13}{30}$ (C) $\dfrac{8}{7}$ (D) $\dfrac{1}{2}$ (E) 0.75

Prob. 204 — Find all the critical values of f when $f(x) = x^{4/5}(x - 5)^2$.

(A) $0, \dfrac{5}{7}$ (B) $\dfrac{10}{7}, 5$ (C) $\dfrac{5}{7}, 5$ (D) $0, \dfrac{5}{7}, 5$ (E) $0, \dfrac{10}{7}$

Prob. 205 — An advertisement is run to stimulate the sale of cars. After t days, $1 \le t \le 48$, the number of cars sold is given by

$$N(t) = 4000 + 45t^2 - t^3.$$

On what day does the maximum **rate of growth** of sales occur?

(A) 17 (B) 13 (C) 15 (D) 16 (E) 14

Prob. 206 — Let $f(x) = x \ln x$, then the minimal value attained by $f(x)$ is

(**A**) $-\dfrac{1}{e}$ (**B**) 0 (**C**) $\dfrac{1}{e}$ (**D**) -1 (**E**) There is no minimum

Prob. 207 — The function f, with $f'(x) = (x-2)^2(x-7)^3$, has an inflection point at $x =$

(**A**) 4 only (**B**) 7 only (**C**) 2 and 4 only

(**D**) 2 and 4 only (**E**) 2 and 4 and 7 only

Prob. 208 — It is expected that in t weeks after 100 fish are released into a pond, the average weight of an individual fish (in pounds) for the first 24 weeks is given by $w(t) = 20 + 4t - 0.05t^2$. The proportion of the fish that are still alive after t weeks is

$$p(t) = \frac{10}{20 + t}.$$

The yield $Y(t)$ of the fish in t weeks is the total weight of the fish that are still alive. When is $Y(t)$ the largest?

(**A**) 4 (**B**) 8 (**C**) 12 (**D**) 20 (**E**) 22

Prob. 209 — Consumer demand for a certain product is changing over time, and the rate of change of this demand, $f'(t)$, in units/week, is given, in week t, in the following table.

t	0	1	2	3	4	5	6	7	8	9	10
$f'(t)$	12	10	4	-2	−3	−1	3	7	11	15	10

a. When is the demand for this product increasing? When is it decreasing?

b. Approximately when is demand at a local maximum? A local minimum?

Prob. 210 — Is there a polynomial $ax^3 + bx^2 + cx + d$, which has a local maximum at $(-1, 2)$ and local minimum at $(2, -1)$?

Prob. 211 — Find the critical points of $f(x) = x^{1/3}(1-x)^{3/2}$. Identify the intervals on which f is increasing and decreasing. Find the function's local extreme values.

Prob. 212 — Identify the function's local extreme values

$$y = \frac{x+2}{x^2 - 1}.$$

Prob. 213 — Plot the graph of the function

$$y = \frac{x}{\sqrt[3]{1 - x^2}}.$$

Prob. 214 — Plot the graph of the function $y = \sqrt[3]{x + 1} - \sqrt[3]{x - 1}$.

Prob. 215 — Plot the graph of the function $y = x - 1 - 3\sqrt[3]{x - 1}$.

Prob. 216 — Plot the graph of the function

$$y = x - 1 + \frac{x}{\sqrt{1 + x^2}}.$$

Prob. 217 — Plot the graph of the function $y = \arcsin(1 - \sqrt[3]{x^2})$.

Prob. 218 — Plot the graph of the function $y = \ln x - \arctan x$.

Prob. 219 — Plot the graph of the function $y = \ln(1 + x^2) - x$

5.8.   The Shapes of Implicit Functions Graphs

Since implicit functions are defined by functions $f(x, y)$ in two variables, we need the definition of differentiability of such functions.

Definition 5.72. A function $f(x, y)$ defined in an open square centered at (a, b) is called separately differentiable at (a, b) if $x \to f(x, y)$ is differentiable at $x = a$ in x and $y \to f(x, y)$ is differentiable at $y = b$ in y. The corresponding derivatives are called **partial** derivatives of f and are denoted by $f'_x(a, b)$ and $f'_y(a, b)$.

Definition 5.73. A function $f(x, y)$ defined in an open square centered at (a, b) is called differentiable at (a, b) if there are constants A and B such that

$$f(a + \Delta x, b + \Delta y) = f(a, b) + A\Delta x + B\Delta y + h_1\Delta x + h_2\Delta y, \qquad (5.12)$$

where h_1, h_2 tend to zero as soon as Δx and Δy tend to zero

Putting $\Delta y = 0$ first and then $\delta x = 0$, we obtain that any differentiable function at (a, b) is separately differentiable and

$$A = f'_x(a, b), \quad B = f'_y(a, b).$$

The inverse statement is not true but still holds under certain conditions, which we are going to consider now.

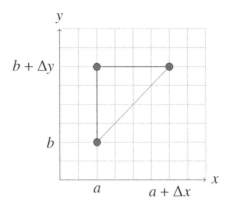

Figure 5.16: Proof of Theorem 5.74.

Theorem 5.74. *Let $f(x, y)$ be a function defined about (a, b) such that its partial derivatives $f'_x(x, y)$ and $f'_y(x, y)$ exist about (a, b) and are continuous at (a, b). Then $f(x, y)$ is differentiable at (a, b).*

Proof. Assuming that Δx and Δy are small enoght so that the partial derivatives of f exist at every point of the triangle shown on Fig 5.16, we can write applying Lagrange's Theorem separately in x and y

$$f(a + \Delta x, b + \Delta y) - f(a, b) =$$
$$\{f(a + \Delta x, b + \Delta y) - f(a, b + \Delta y)\} + \{f(a, b + \Delta y) - f(a, b\} =$$
$$f'_x(a + \theta_1 \Delta x, b + \Delta y)\Delta x + f'_y(a, b + \theta_2 \Delta y)\Delta y, \quad 0 < \theta_1, \theta_2 < 1.$$

Since both partial derivatives $f'_x(x, y)$ and $f'_y(x, y)$ are continuous at (a, b), we see that

$$f'_x(a + \theta_1 \Delta x, b + \Delta y) = f'_x(a, b) + h_1,$$
$$f'_y(a, b + \theta_2 \Delta y) = f'_y(a, b) + h_2,$$

where h_1, h_2 tend to zero as soon as Δx and Δy tend to zero. It follows that

$$f(a + \Delta x, b + \Delta y) - f(a, b) = f'_x(a, b)\Delta x + f'_y(a, b)\Delta y + h_1 \Delta x + h_2 \Delta y, \quad (5.13)$$

which means that f is differentiable at (a, b). $\qquad\square$

Theorem 5.75. *Let $f(x, y)$ be a function defined about (a, b) such that*

(1) *the partial derivative $f'_x(x, y)$ exists about (a, b);*

(2) *the partial derivative $f'_y(x, y)$ exists and is continuous about (a, b);*

(3) *$f'_y(a, b) \neq 0$;*

(4) $f(a, b) = 0$.

Then there is a positive δ such that the equations $f(x, y(x)) = 0$, $y(a) = b$, have a unique continuous solution $y(x)$ on $(a - \delta, a + \delta)$ differentiable at $x = a$. Moreover,

$$y'(a) = -\frac{f'_x(a, b)}{f'_y(a, b)}. \tag{5.14}$$

Proof. By (1) the function $x \to f(x, y)$ is continuous in x about (a, b). Similarly, by (2) the function $y \to f(x, y)$ is continuous in y about (a, b). Hence, $f(x, y)$ is separately continuous about (a, b) and, therefore, is continuous about (a, b) by Theorem 3.46.

By (2) and (3) the function $y \to f(x, y)$ is monotonic for x close to a. By Theorem 3.45 the equations $f(x, y(x)) = 0$, $y(a) = b$ have a unique continuous solution $y = y(x)$ on $(a - \delta, a + \delta)$ for some $\delta > 0$.

By Theorem 5.74 the function $f(x, y)$ is differentiable at (a, b). It follows that (5.13) is true. If $|\Delta x| < \delta$, then the increment $\Delta y = y(a + \Delta x) - y(a)$ is small, since $y(x)$ is continuous at $x = a$. Substituting these Δx and Δy in (5.13), we obtain that

$$0 = f'_x(a, b)\Delta x + f'_y(a, b)\Delta y + h_1\Delta x + h_2\Delta y \Rightarrow \frac{\Delta y}{\Delta x} = -\frac{f'_x(a, b) + h_1}{f'_y(a, b) + h_2}.$$

Passing to the limit $\Delta x \to 0$, we obtain (5.14). $\qquad\square$

Problem 5.76. Plot the graph of the Folium of Descartes

$$x^3 + y^3 = 9xy \tag{5.15}$$

and determine its shape.

Solution: We can represent (5.15) in the form of an algebraic equation of the third degree in y with coefficients depending on x:

$$f(x, y) = y^3 - 9xy + x^3 = 0. \tag{5.16}$$

We arrange the roots of (5.16) in increasing order, so that $y_1(x)$ is the minimal, $y_3(x)$ is the maximal, and $y_2(x)$ is the intermediate root. It is assumed that if some of these roots does not exist, then the corresponding function to this root is not defined. In applications of the Intermediate Value Theorem below we use the following obvious formulas:

$$\lim_{y \to -\infty} f(x, y) = -\infty, \quad \lim_{y \to +\infty} f(x, y) = +\infty. \tag{5.17}$$

To determine the domains for $y_1(x)$, $y_2(x)$, $y_3(x)$, we apply Differential Calculus to functions $y \to f(x, y)$. The derivative

$$f'_y(x, y) = 3(y^2 - 3x) \tag{5.18}$$

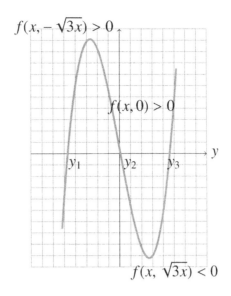

Figure 5.17: Plots of $y \to y^3 - 9xy + x^3$.

is nonnegative for $x \le 0$. This shows that $y \to f(x, y)$ strictly increases when $x \le 0$. By the Intermediate Value Theorem and by (5.17) the equation (5.16) has only one root $y_1(x)$ if $x \le 0$. Since

$$f(x, y) = y^3 + 9(-x)y + x^3 < 0 \quad \text{if} \ \ x < 0 \ \ \text{and} \ \ y \le 0,$$

we obtain that $y_1(x) > 0$ for $x < 0$. For $x = 0$ we have the unique root $y_1(0) = 0$.

If $x > 0$, then there are two points $y = \pm\sqrt{3x}$, where the derivative $f'_y(x, y)$ vanishes, see Fig 5.17. We have

$$\begin{aligned} f(x, -\sqrt{3x}) &= (-\sqrt{3x})^3 + 9x\sqrt{3x} + x^3 = x^3 + 6x\sqrt{3x} > 0, \\ f(x, \ \sqrt{3x}) &= (\sqrt{3x})^3 - 9x\sqrt{3x} + x^3 = x^3 - 6x\sqrt{3x}. \end{aligned} \tag{5.19}$$

Since $f''_{yy}(x, y) = 6y$, we obtain that

$$f''_{yy}(x, \ \sqrt{3x}) = -18\sqrt{x} < 0, \quad f''_{yy}(x, \ \sqrt{3x}) = 18\sqrt{x} > 0,$$

which implies by the second derivative test that $y = -\sqrt{3x}$ is a point of local maximum and $y = \sqrt{3x}$ is a point of local minimum. Simple algebra shows that

$$f(x, \ \sqrt{3x}) = x^3 - 6x\sqrt{3x} < 0 \Leftrightarrow 0 < x < 3\sqrt[3]{4}. \tag{5.20}$$

To get bounds for the solutions of (5.16) we apply the Intermediate Value Theorem. Since $f(x, -\sqrt{3x}) > 0$, by the Intermediate Value Theorem there is a solution $y_1(x)$,

$$y_1 < -\sqrt{3x}. \tag{5.21}$$

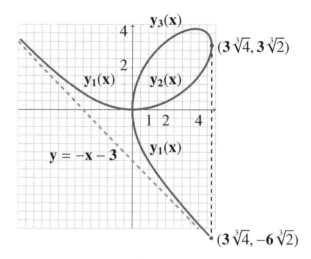

Figure 5.18: The Folium of Descartes.

Since $f(x, 0) = x^3 > 0$, the Intermediate Value Theorem shows that there are two solutions y_2 and y_3 satisfying

$$0 < y_2 < \sqrt{3x} < y_3, \tag{5.22}$$

if $0 < x < 3\sqrt[3]{4}$. If $x = 3\sqrt[3]{4}$, then $y_1 = y_2$. Finally, if $x > 3\sqrt[3]{4}$, then there are no solutions y_2 and y_3.

It follows that the function $y_1(x)$ is defined on the whole real line, whereas $y_2(x)$ and $y_3(x)$ are defined on $(0, 3\sqrt[3]{4}]$. To prove that these functions are differentiable we apply Theorem 5.75. By (5.18) $f_y'(x, y) = 0$ if and only if $y^2 = 3x$. By Theorem 5.75 the function $y_1(x)$ is differentiable everywhere except for $x = 0$. The inequalities (5.22) show that y_2 and y_3 are differentiable everywhere on $(0, 3\sqrt[3]{4})$. If $x = 3\sqrt[3]{4}$ then $y_1(x) = y_2(x) = \sqrt{3x}$, which shows that Theorem 5.75 cannot be applied at $(3\sqrt[3]{4}, 3\sqrt[6]{4})$.

To determine the intervals, where the functions $y_i(x)$ are monotonic, we apply implicit differentiation. By (5.14)

$$y'(x) = -\frac{f_x'(x, y)}{f_y'(x, y)} = -\frac{3(x^2 - 3y)}{3(y^2 - 3x)} = \frac{3y - x^2}{y^2 - 3x}. \tag{5.23}$$

For $x < 0$ the denominator $y^2 - 3x$ is positive. To determine the sign of $3y - x^2$ we evaluate

$$f\left(x, \frac{1}{3}x^2\right) = \frac{x^6}{27} - 9x\frac{x^2}{3} + x^3 = \frac{x^6}{27} - 2x^3, \tag{5.24}$$

which is obviously positive if $x < 0$. Hence by the Intermediate Value Theorem we obtain that

$$0 < y_1(x) < \frac{1}{3}x^2 \Rightarrow 3y_1 - x^2 < 0. \tag{5.25}$$

By (5.23) the derivative of $y_1(x)$ is negative, implying that $y_1(x)$ is strictly decreasing on $(-\infty, 0)$.

For $x > 0$ the function $y_1(x) < 0$ is negative. Hence the numerator $3y_1 - x^2$ is negative too. By (5.21) $y_1^2 > 3x$ and the denominator $y_1^2 - 3x$ is positive. It follows that $y_1'(x) < 0$ and $y_1(x)$ is strictly decreasing on $(0, +\infty)$.

We investigate now the branches $y_2(x)$ and $y_3(x)$ defined on $(0, 3\sqrt[3]{4}]$. Since $f(x, 3\sqrt{x}) = x^3 > 0$ and $f(x, \sqrt{3x}) < 0$, see (5.20), we conclude that

$$0 < y_2(x) < \sqrt{3x} < y_3(x) < 3\sqrt{x}.$$

By Theorem 3.57

$$\lim_{x \to 0^+} y_2(x) = \lim_{x \to 0^+} y_3(x) = \lim_{x \to 0^+} 3\sqrt{x} = 0.$$

It follows that both functions are continuous at $x = 0$ if we define $y_2(0) = y_3(0) = 0$.

To prove that both $y_2(x)$ and $y_3(x)$ are continuous at $x = 3\sqrt[3]{4}$ we apply Vieta's formulas for the algebraic equation (5.16):

$$\begin{cases} y_2 + y_3 & = -y_1 \\ y_2 y_3 & = -\dfrac{x^3}{y_1} \end{cases} \Rightarrow (y_3 - y_2)^2 = (y_3 + y_2)^2 - 4y_2 y_3 = \frac{y_1^3 + 4x^3}{y_1}.$$

Since $y_1(x)$ is continuous on $(0, +\infty)$, we conclude that

$$\lim_{x \to (3\sqrt[3]{4})^-} (y_3(x) - y_2(x))^2 = \left. \frac{y_1^3(x) + 4x^3}{y_1(x)} \right|_{x=3\sqrt[3]{4}}.$$

By Vieta's formulas

$$y_1(3\sqrt[3]{4}) = -\frac{(3\sqrt[3]{4})^3}{3^2(\sqrt[3]{4})} = -3\sqrt[3]{16} \Rightarrow y_1(3\sqrt[3]{4})^3 = \left. -4x^3 \right|_{x=3\sqrt[3]{4}}.$$

It follows that

$$\lim_{x \to (3\sqrt[3]{4})^-} (y_3(x) - y_2(x)) = 0. \tag{5.26}$$

Since by (5.22)

$$0 < \sqrt{3x} - y_2(x) < y_3(x) - y_2(x) \underset{x \to (3\sqrt[3]{4})^-}{\longrightarrow} 0,$$

we obtain by Theorem 3.57 that

$$\lim_{x \to (3\sqrt[3]{4})^-} y_2(x) = \lim_{x \to (3\sqrt[3]{4})^-} \sqrt{3x} = 3\sqrt[3]{2} = y_2(3\sqrt[3]{4}).$$

It follows that $y_2(x)$ is continuous at $x = 3\sqrt[3]{4}$. By (5.26) the function $y_3(x)$ is continuous on the closed interval $[0, 3\sqrt[3]{4}]$.

Formula (5.23) shows that $y'(x) = 0$ at $(x, y) \neq (0,0)$ on Descartes' Folium if and only if

$$\begin{cases} 3y & = x^2 \\ y^3 - 9xy + x^3 & = 0 \end{cases} \Leftrightarrow \frac{x^6}{27} - 3x^3 = 0 \Leftrightarrow x = 3\sqrt[3]{2}, \ y = 3\sqrt[3]{4}.$$

Since $\sqrt{3 \cdot 3\sqrt[3]{2}} = 3\sqrt[6]{2} < 3\sqrt[3]{4}$ inequalities (5.22) show that $(3\sqrt[3]{2}, 3\sqrt[3]{4})$ is placed on the graph of $y_3(x)$. Since $y_2(3\sqrt[3]{4}) = 3\sqrt[3]{2} > 0 = y_2(0)$, the function $y_2(x)$ increases on its domain by Theorem 5.38. Applying Theorem 5.38 to $y_3(x)$ on the intervals $[0, 3\sqrt[3]{2}]$ and $[3\sqrt[3]{2}, 3\sqrt[3]{4}]$, we obtain that $y_3(x)$ increases on the first and decreases on the second. Hence $x = 3\sqrt[3]{2}$ is the point of a local maximum for $y_3(x)$.

To determine the shape of Descartes' Folium we find the second derivative of y. Formula (5.23) shows that y' is a rational function of y and x. Hence, we can find $y'(x)$ by Differentiation Rules:

$$y''(x) = \left(\frac{3y - x^2}{y^2 - 3x} \right)' = \frac{(3y' - 2x)(y^2 - 3x) - (3y - x^2)(2yy' - 3)}{(y^2 - 3x)^2} =$$

$$\frac{y'(2yx^2 - 3y^2 - 9x) + 3x^2 - 2xy^2 + 9y}{(y^2 - 3x)^2} \overset{(5.23)}{=}$$

$$\frac{2xy(x^3 - 9xy + y^3 + 27)}{(y^2 - 3x)^3} \overset{x^3 - 9xy + y^3 = 0}{=} \frac{54xy}{(y^2 - 3x)^3}.$$

It follows that $y_1''(x) > 0$ for $x < 0$. Hence $y_1(x)$ is concave up on $(-\infty, 0)$. For $x > 0$ the function $y_1(x)$ satisfies (5.21). Hence $y_1''(x) > 0$ for $x > 0$, implying that $y_1(x)$ is concave up on $(0, +\infty)$. Finally, by (5.22), the function $y_3(x)$ is concave down and the function $y_2(x)$ is concave up.

Solution by parametric plotting. We observe that the line $y = t \cdot x$ with slope t intercepts Descartes' Folium at a single point $(x(t), y(t))$ determined by the equations:

$$\begin{cases} y & = tx \\ x^3 + y^3 & = 9xy \end{cases} \Leftrightarrow \boxed{\mathbf{x(t)} = \frac{9t}{1 + t^3}, \ \mathbf{y(t)} = \frac{9t^2}{1 + t^3}}.$$

The equations obtained give the parametrization of Descartes' Folium. Therefore, we may think about Descartes' Folium as the path of a particle moving continuously according the equations found above. Both functions $x(t)$ and $y(t)$ have the vertical asymptote $x = -1$:

$$\lim_{t \to -1^-} x(t) = +\infty, \quad \lim_{t \to -1^+} x(t) = -\infty \, ;$$

$$\lim_{t \to -1^-} y(t) = -\infty, \quad \lim_{t \to -1^+} x(t) = +\infty.$$

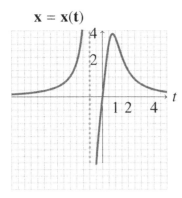

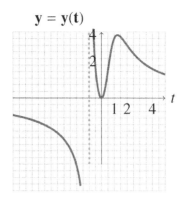

Figure 5.19: Descartes' Folium: **x = x(t)**.

Figure 5.20: Descartes' Folium: **y = y(t)**.

It is also clear that $\lim_{t\to\pm\infty} x(t) = \lim_{t\to\pm\infty} y(t) = 0$. It follows that the branches of Descartes' Folium approach infinity only if $t \to -1^{\pm}$. Taking into account the fact that t is the slope of the line $y = tx$, we conclude that there is an oblique asymptote with slope -1: $y = -x - b$. Since

$$y(t) + x(t) = \frac{9t^2}{1 + t^3} + \frac{9t}{1 + t^3} = \frac{9t}{t^2 - t + 1} \underset{t\to-1}{\to} -3,$$

we find that $b = \lim_{t\to-1} y(t) + x(t) = -3$, implying that

$$\boxed{y = -x - 3}$$

is an oblique asymptote of Descartes' Folium. Since

$$y(t) + x(t) + 3 = 3\frac{t^2 + 2t + 1}{t^2 - t + 1} = 3\frac{(t + 1)^2}{t^2 - t + 1} > 0,$$

we see that Descartes' Folium is placed above its oblique asymptote.

To complete the finite part of this folium we plot the graphs of $x = x(t)$ and $y = y(t)$, see Fig 5.19 and Fig 5.20. Using Differential Rules, we find

$$x'(t) = 9\frac{1 - 2t^3}{(1 + t^3)^2}, \quad x''(t) = \frac{54t^2(t^3 - 2)}{(1 + t^3)^3};$$
$$y'(t) = 9\frac{t(2 - t^3)}{(1 + t^3)^2}, \quad y''(t) = \frac{18(t^6 - 7t^3 + 1)}{(1 + t^3)^3}. \tag{5.27}$$

It follows that $x(t)$ increases on $(-\infty, -1)$, on $(-1, \sqrt[3]{0.5})$, and decreases on $(\sqrt[3]{0.5}, +\infty)$. The function $y(t)$ decreases on $(-\infty, -1)$, on $(-1, 0)$, increases on $(0, \sqrt[3]{2})$, and decreases again on $(\sqrt[3]{2}, +\infty)$.

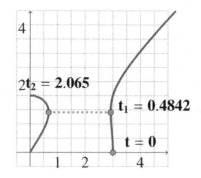

Figure 5.21: A Part of the Devil's Curve.

For t about $-\infty$ the point $(x(t), y(t))$ is about the origin. It moves right and down to infinity as t approaches -1 from the left. This part of the folium is represented by the lower infinite branch, see Fig 5.18. For $-1 < t < 0$ the point $(x(t), y(t))$ slides along the upper infinite branch. Notice that $x(0) = y(0) = 0$. When t increases from 0 to $\sqrt[3]{0.5}$ both x and y increase from 0 to $x(\sqrt[3]{0.5}) = 4.7622$ and $y(\sqrt[3]{0.5}) = 3.78$. Finally, at $t = \sqrt[3]{0.5}$ the point turns back to the origin completing the Folium of Descartes.

By (5.27)

$$\frac{dy}{dx} = \frac{y'}{x'} = \frac{t(2 - t^3)}{1 - 2t^3}, \quad \frac{d^2y}{dx^2} = \frac{2}{9}\frac{(1 + t^3)^4}{(1 - 2t^3)^3}.$$

We incorporate the calculations in the following table

t	$(-\infty, -1)$	$(-1, 0)$	$(0, \sqrt[3]{0.5})$	$(\sqrt[3]{0.5}, +\infty)$
x	$0 < x < +\infty$	$-\infty < x < 0$	$0 < x < x(\sqrt[3]{0.5})$	$0 < x < x(\sqrt[3]{0.5})$
$\frac{dy}{dx}$	< 0	< 0	> 0	$> 0 <$
$\frac{d^2y}{dx^2}$	> 0	> 0	> 0	< 0
Shape	decreasing concave up	decreasing concave up	increasing concave up	concave down

Problem 5.77 (Gabriel Cramer, 1750). Plot the graph of the Devil's Curve

$$y^4 - 4y^2 = x^4 - 9x^2.$$

Solution: Since the equation of the Devil's Curve is invariant under sign changes $x := \pm x$, $y := \pm y$, it is sufficient to plot its graph in the first quadrant, see Fig 5.21. Let $y = tx$. Then

$$y^4 - 4y^2 = x^4 - 9x^2 \Leftrightarrow x^2 = \frac{9 - 4t^2}{1 - t^4} \text{ and } y^2 = t^2\frac{9 - 4t^2}{1 - t^4}.$$

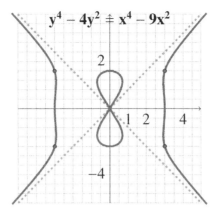

Figure 5.22: The Devil's Curve.

It follows that

$$\frac{dx^2}{dt} = \frac{-4t(2t^4 - 9t^2 + 2)}{(t^4 - 1)^2} \Rightarrow \frac{dx}{dt} = \frac{1}{x(t)} \cdot \frac{-2t(2t^4 - 9t^2 + 2)}{(t^4 - 1)^2},$$

$$\frac{dy^2}{dt} = \frac{2t(9t^4 - 8t^2 + 9)}{(t^4 - 1)^2} \Rightarrow \frac{dy}{dt} = \frac{1}{y(t)} \cdot \frac{2t(9t^4 - 8t^2 + 9)}{(t^4 - 1)^2}.$$

Finally,

$$\frac{dy}{dx} = -\frac{x(t)}{y(t)} \frac{9t^4 - 8t^2 + 9}{2t^4 - 9t^2 + 2} = -\frac{9t^4 - 8t^2 + 9}{t(2t^4 - 9t^2 + 2)}.$$

Since the discriminant of the polynomial $9X^2 - 8X^2 + 9$ is negative, we have $9t^4 - 8t^2 + 9 > 0$ for every t. Positive roots of the polynomial $2t^4 - 9t^2 + 2$ are

$$t_{1,2} = \frac{\sqrt{9 \pm \sqrt{65}}}{2} \Rightarrow \begin{cases} t_1 = & 0.484185 \\ t_2 = & 2.06532 \end{cases}$$

Notice that

$$2 = 9t_i^2 - 2t_i^4 \Rightarrow y^2(t_i) = t^2 \frac{9t_i^2 - 4t_i^4}{1 - t_i^4} = 2 \Rightarrow y(t_i) = \sqrt{2}, i = 1, 2.$$

Since

$$0 \leq x^2 = \frac{4t^2 - 9}{t^4 - 1} = \frac{4(t + 1.5)(t - 1.5)}{(t - 1)(t + 1)(t^2 + 1)},$$

and $0 \leq t < +\infty$ in the first quadrant, there are only two possible intervals for t: $[0, 1)$ and $[1.5, +\infty)$.

We indicate the moments of time t when the tangent to the Devil's Curve is vertical ($dy/dx = \infty$). Between these moments both $x(t)$ and $y(t)$ are monotonic.

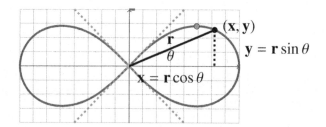

Figure 5.23: Lemniscate of Bernoulli.

As result we find the shape of the Devil's curve shown on the picture. Reflecting these pieces about the coordinate axis, we obtain the complete curve, see Fig 5.22.
Since

$$\lim_{t \to 1^-} x(t) = +\infty \ \text{and} \ \lim_{t \to 1^-} \frac{y(t)}{x(t)} = \lim_{t \to 1^-} t = 1,$$

the Devil's curve has an oblique asymptote with slope 1. We have

$$x(t) - y(t) = (1 - t) \sqrt{\frac{9 - 4t^2}{(1 - t)(1 + t)(1 + t^2)}} > 0 \ \text{for} \ 0 < t < 1,$$

which implies that $\lim_{t \to 1^-} x(t) - y(t) = 0$. It follows that the Devil's curve is placed between its oblique asymptotes $y = \pm x$.

Problem 5.78 (Jakob Bernoulli, 1694). Sketch the graph of the lemniscate of Bernoulli

$$(x^2 + y^2)^2 = x^2 - y^2. \tag{5.28}$$

Justify its shape.

Solution: To sketch the graph we apply **pollar coordinates**. Given a point (x, y) on the coordinate plane different from the origin we connect it to the origin by a straight segment. Let $r > 0$ be the length of this segment and θ be the angle it makes with the x-axis, see Fig 5.23. Hence

$$x = r \cos \theta, \ \ y = r \sin \theta, \ \ r = \sqrt{x^2 + y^2}. \tag{5.29}$$

Then (5.28) in polar coordinates is given by

$$r = \sqrt{\cos^2 \theta - \sin^2 \theta} = \sqrt{\cos 2\theta}. \tag{5.30}$$

This equation has a simple geometrical sense. When θ increases from 0 to $\pi/4$ the point (x, y) approaches the origin. So, the plot of the lemniscate of Bernoulli must look as it is shown on Fig 5.23.

To justify the shape of the curve we apply the theory of implicit functions. The curve is obtained from its part in the first quadrant by reflections with respect to the coordinate axis. Therefore, it is sufficient to justify the plot only in the first quadrant. The lemniscate of Bernoulli is the zero set of the curve $f(x, y) = (x^2 + y^2)^2 - x^2 + y^2$. We consider $f(x, y)$ as a polynomial in y with coefficients depending on x:

$$f(x, y) = y^4 + (2x^2 + 1)y^2 + x^4 - x^2.$$

Since $x^4 - x^2 = x^2(x^2 - 1)$, by Descates' Rule of signs this polynomial has one positive root for $0 < x < 1$ and no positive roots for $x > 1$. It is clear that $y = 0$ if $x = 0$ or $x = 1$.

The function $f(x, y)$ is separately continuous everywhere on the plane. The function $y \to f(x, y)$ strictly increases on the interval $(0, +\infty)$ for every x. Hence it is continuous everywhere. By Theorem 3.45 there is a unique continuous function $y(x)$ on $(0, 1)$ satisfying the equation $f(x, y(x)) = 0$. Since $f(x, y)$ is separately differentiable everywhere and the partial derivatives are continuous, the function $f(x, y)$ is differentiable. By Theorem 5.75 the function $y(x)$ is differentiable on $(0, 1)$. By (5.14)

$$y'(x) = -\frac{x}{y}\frac{2x^2 + 2y^2 - 1}{2x^2 + 2y^2 + 1}.$$

It follows that $y'(x) = 0$ on $(0, 1)$ if and only if $x = 0.25\sqrt{6}$, $y = 0.25\sqrt{2}$. Simple algebra shows that for $0 < x < 1$

$$f(x, 0) = x^4 - x^2 < 0, \quad f(x, x) = 2x^4 > 0, \quad f(x, \sqrt{1 - x^2}) = 2(1 - x^2) > 0.$$

By the Intermediate Value Theorem it follows that

$$0 < y(x) < x, \quad 0 < y(x) < \sqrt{1 - x^2}.$$

By Theorem 3.57

$$\lim_{x \to 0^+} y(x) = 0 = y(0) = y(1) = 0 = \lim_{x \to 1^-} y(x).$$

Hence $y(x)$ is continuous on $[0, 1]$ and is differentiable on $(0, 1)$. By Theorem 5.38 the function $y(x)$ is strictly increasing on $[0, 0.25\sqrt{6}]$ and strictly decreasing on $[0.25\sqrt{6}, 1]$.

By (5.29) and (5.29) on the lemniscate of Bernoulli

$$y'(x) = -\cot\theta\frac{2\cos 2\theta - 1}{2\cos 2\theta + 1} = -\cot\theta\frac{\cos^2\theta - 3\sin^2\theta}{3\cos^2\theta - \sin^2\theta} = \frac{3u - u^3}{3u^2 - 1},$$

where $u = \cot\theta$. By the Chain Rule

$$y''(x) \cdot \frac{dx}{d\theta} = \frac{d}{du}\left(\frac{3u - u^3}{3u^2 - 1}\right) \cdot \frac{du}{d\theta} = \frac{3(u^2 + 1)^2}{(3u^2 - 1)^2} \cdot \frac{1}{\sin^2\theta} > 0.$$

Since $x(\theta) = \sqrt{\cos 2\theta} \cdot \cos \theta$ is a strictly decreasing function, we see that $y''(x) < 0$, which proves that the graph of the lemniscate is concave down in the first quadrant as shown on Fig 5.23. □

Problem 5.79. Evaluate the differential dy of the implicit function

$$3x^2 - x^2 y^3 + 4y = 3.$$

Use differentials to approximate the change Δy if x changes from 1 to 0.98 and $y(1) = 2$.

Solution: Using the Rules of Differentials, see Theorem 4.34, we obtain

$$0 = d(3) = 3d(x^2) - d(x^2 y^3) + 4dy = 6xdx - 2xy^3 dx - 3x^2 y^2 dy + 4dy =$$

$$(4 - 3x^2 y^2)dy + (6x - 2xy^3)dx \Rightarrow dy = \frac{6x - 2xy^3}{3x^2 y^2 - 4}dx.$$

Since $(1, 2)$ is a point of the curve,

$$\Delta y = y(1 + (-0.02)) - y(1) \approx dy\bigg|_{(1,2)} = \frac{6x - 2xy^3}{3x^2 y^2 - 4}\bigg|_{(1,2)} dx = \frac{-5}{4} \cdot (-0.02),$$

implying that $\Delta y \approx 0.025$. □

Problems

Prob. 220 — Plot the implicit function $y = 3x \arctan(y/x)$.

Prob. 221 — Plot the implicit function $x^2 y^2 + x^2 + y^2 - 1 = 0$.

Prob. 222 — Plot the eight shaped curve $y^4 = y^2 - x^2$.

Prob. 223 — Plot the cissoid of Diocles $y^2(2 - x) = x^3$.

Prob. 224 — Plot the curve $x^2 + y^2 = x^4 + y^4$.

Prob. 225 — Plot the curve $x^2 y^2 = x^3 - y^3$.

Prob. 226 — Plot the four-leaf rose: $(x^2 + y^2)^3 = 4x^2 y^2$.

Prob. 227 — Plot the three-leaf rose: $(x^2 + y^2)^2 + 3x^2 y = y^3$.

Prob. 228 — Plot the curve $4xy = x^3 + y^3$.

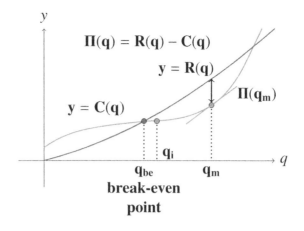

Figure 5.24: The Cost and Revenue Functions.

Prob. 229 — Sketch the plot of the implicit function $y^x = y^x$. Evaluate y' if $y \neq x$.

Prob. 230 — A point is moving along the curve $4xy = x^3 + y^3$. When the point is at $x = y = 2$, its y-coordinates is increasing at speed of 2 units per second. What is the speed of the x-coordinate at this moment?

Prob. 231 — The variables y and x are related by the equation $xy^3 - yx^3 = 6$. Using the linearization find an approximate value of $y(1.01)$ for y satisfying $y(1) = 2$.

5.9. Applications: Cost Function, Revenue, Profit

The **cost function** $C(q)$ gives the total cost of production of q units of a commodity. The values of $C(q)$ are measured in some currency units, whereas q is measured in units of production, tenth of units, thousand of units, etc. The value $C(0)$ is called the **fixed cost**. It includes the costs, for instance, of utility bills and rent, which must be paid independent of the production level.

The **revenue** $R(q)$ indicates the total income the company gets when q units of the product are produced. Revenue $R(q)$ depends on the situation on the market as well as on the efforts of the marketing department of the company. The revenue for equal quantities of product produced on different levels $q_1 < q_2$ of production must satisfy the inequalities:

$$\frac{R(q_1 + \Delta q) - R(q_1)}{\Delta q} \leq \frac{R(q_2 + \Delta q) - R(q_2)}{\Delta q}.$$

This means that the average revenue on level q_2 is not less than the average revenue on level $q_1 < q_2$. Passing to the limit $\Delta q \to 0$, we obtain that $R'(q)$ increases, implying that the graph of $y = R(q)$ is **concave up**.

The cost function $C(q)$ of an efficient company must be **convex down** for relatively small production levels q. Indeed, the cost $C(q + \Delta q) - C(q)$ must decrease in q to make the root q_{be} of equation $C(q) = R(q)$ as small as possible. The root q_{be} is called the **break-even point**. It is the minimal level of production which guarantees a nonnegative **profit** $\Pi(q) = R(q) - C(q)$. Due to the limits of resources, it is impossible to keep the cost function $C(q)$ to be convex down about all levels of production. So, there must be an inflection point q_i. For $q > q_i$ the cost functions is concave up, which makes expenses grow with increasing rate. Therefore, to be on the safe side an efficient company must keep the break-even point q_{be} less than the inflection point q_i.

Definition 5.80. A twice differentiable increasing convex up function $y = R(q)$, defined for $q \geq 0$, satisfying $R(0) = 0$, is called the **revenue of an efficient company**. A twice differentiable increasing function $C(q)$, $C(0) > 0$, is called the **cost function of an efficient company** if

(a) $C(q)$ is strictly increasing function,

(b) $C(q)$ is convex down on $(0, q_i)$,

(c) $C(q)$ is convex up for $q > q_i$,

(d) there is a solution q_{be} to the equation $R(q) = C(q)$ satisfying the inequality $0 < q_{be} < q_i$.

(e) there is a solution q_b to the equation $R(q) = C(q)$ satisfying the inequality $q_b > q_i$,

(f) $\max_{q_{be} \leq q \leq q_b} \{R(q) - C(q)\} > 0$.

Typical graphs of the revenue and cost function of an efficient company are pictured on Fig 5.24. Condition (a) says that the total cost of production of q_2 units is always greater than the cost of production of q_1 units if $q_1 < q_2$. Condition (b) says that any efficient company minimizes the rate of change of its production function until it is possible. Condition (c) says that the limitation of initial investments, product resources, and market demands on the product produced inevitably lead to the change of convexity at some level of production q_i. Condition (d) says that the beak-even point of any efficient company must be reached inside the area $0 < q_{be} < q_i$ of comfortable production. Condition (e) says that there exists a level of production q_b implying the bankruptcy of the company. Condition (f) says that the maximal profit of the company is positive on the interval $q_i \leq q \leq q_b$.

Lemma 5.81. *Let $C(q)$ be the cost function of an efficient company. Then $C'(q) > 0$ for every $q \neq q_i$.*

Proof. Since $C(q)$ strictly increases and the graph of $y = C(q)$ is concave down on $(0, q_i)$, i.e. $C'(q)$ decreases, $C'(q)$ cannot vanish in $(0, q_i)$. Indeed, otherwise,

$$C'(a) = 0 \Rightarrow C'(q) = 0 \text{ for } a < q < q_i,$$

implying that $C(q)$ is constant on (a, q_i), which is not the case. Since $C(q)$ strictly increases on $[q_i, q_b]$ and its graph is concave up on (q_i, q_b), i.e $C'(q)$ increases, we conclude that $0 \le C'(q_i) \le C'(q)$ for $q > q_i$. So,

$$C'(b) = 0 \Rightarrow C'(q) = 0 \text{ for } q_i < q < b.$$

It follows that the only possibility for $C'(q)$ to vanish on $(0, q_b)$ is $q = q_i$. □

Lemma 5.82. *Let $R(q)$ be the revenue of an efficient company. Then the q-intercept of any tangent to the graph of $R(q)$ is positive.*

Proof. Since $R(0) = 0$, and $R(q)$ increases, we obtain that

$$0 \le \lim_{q \to 0^+} \frac{R(q) - R(0)}{q - 0} = R'(0).$$

Since the graph of the revenue $R(q)$ is concave up, we obtain that

$$\frac{R(q)}{q} = \frac{R(q) - R(0)}{q - 0} = R'(q_e) < R'(q) \Leftrightarrow q > \frac{R(q)}{R'(q)}. \tag{5.31}$$

Since the equation of the tangent to $R(q)$ at q is $y = R'(q)(x - q) + R(q)$, its q-intercept equals

$$x = q - \frac{R(q)}{R'(q)} > 0,$$

see (5.31). □

The q-intercept $f(q)$ of the tangent line to the curve $y = C(q)$ at $(q, C(q))$ is given by the formula

$$f(q) = q - \frac{C(q)}{C'(q)} \tag{5.32}$$

with understanding that $f(q)$ is undefined if $C'(q) = 0$.

Definition 5.83. Given a total cost $C(q)$ of production, the average cost of production is defined by

$$A(q) = \frac{C(q)}{q}.$$

Lemma 5.84. *Let $C(q)$ be a positive differentiable function on $(0, +\infty)$. Then a point $q > 0$ is a critical point of $A(q)$ if and only if*

$$C'(q) = A(q). \tag{5.33}$$

The later happens if and only if the tangent line to the graph of the cost function $y = C(x)$ at $x = q$ passes through the origin $(0, 0)$.

Proof. By the Differentiation Laws we have

$$A'(q) = \frac{C'(q)}{q} - \frac{C(q)}{q^2} = \frac{C'(q) - A(q)}{q}. \tag{5.34}$$

This shows that the critical points of $A(q)$ are solutions to the equation (5.33). Inserting $C'(q) = A(q)$ into the equation (5.32), we obtain that q is a critical point of $A(q)$ if and only if $f(q) = 0$, i.e. the tangent to the curve $y = C(q)$ at this point q passes through the origin. □

Formula (5.34) allows one to express the marginal cost $C'(q)$ in terms of the average cost and the marginal average cost:

$$\boxed{C'(q) = A(q) + qA'(q).} \tag{5.35}$$

Lemma 5.85. *For an efficient company the function $f(q)$ defined by (5.32) decreases on $(0, q_i)$ and increases on (q_i, q_b).*

Proof. Differentiating $f(q)$, we obtain

$$f'(q) = 1 - \frac{C'(q)}{C'(q)} + \frac{C(q)}{C'(q)^2}C''(q) = \frac{C(q)}{C'(q)^2}C''(q),$$

which obviously implies the statement by the properties (**b**) and (**c**) of the cost function of an efficient company. □

Theorem 5.86. *All critical points of the average cost $A(q)$ of an efficient company are the points of the absolute minimum of $A(q)$. These points make a closed interval $I_e = [c, d]$ inside (q_i, q_b), which may reduce to one point. If a level of production q_m maximises the profit, then $d < q_m$.*

Proof. By Lagrange's Theorem (see Theorem 5.9)

$$\frac{C(q) - C(0)}{q - 0} = C'(q_{av}),$$

where $0 < q_{av} < q$. Since $C(0) > 0$ and $C(q)$ is concave down on $(0, q_i)$, we have for $0 < q \leq q_i$:

$$A(q) = \frac{C(q)}{q} > \frac{C(q) - C(0)}{q - 0} = C'(q_{av}) \geq C'(q).$$

It follows that any solution q to the equation (5.33) satisfies $q > q_i$. Since both $A(q)$ and $C'(q)$ are continuous about $q = q_i$, we conclude that there is a positive number δ such that

$$A(q) > C'(q) \text{ for } 0 < q \le q_i + \delta. \tag{5.36}$$

By (5.32)

$$f(q) = q - \frac{C(q)}{C'(q)} = q\left\{1 - \frac{A(q)}{C'(q)}\right\} \tag{5.37}$$

By (5.36) and (5.37) $f(q) < 0$ for $0 < q \le q_i + \delta$. By Lemma 5.82 any tangent to the graph of $R(q)$ intercepts the q-axis to the right of $q = 0$. If q_m maximizes the profit $\Pi(q) = R(q) - C(q)$, then q_m satisfies the equation $R'(q) = C'(q)$. Hence the slope of the tangent to the graph of $C(q)$ at $q = q_m$ equals $R'(q_m)$. Since $R(q_m) > C(q_m)$, we obtain that the tangent to the graph of $C(q_m)$ intercepts the q-axis to the right of the intercept of the tangent to the graph of $R(q)$ at q_m, i.e $f(q_m) > 0$. By Lemma 5.85 $f(q)$ increases on (q_i, q_b). Since extremal points of $A(q)$ are the zeros of $f(q)$, we conclude that any extremal point q_a satisfies $q_a < q_m$. Since $f(q)$ is continuous on $[q_i + \delta, q_b]$ and increases, its zero set ie either a single point or a closed interval $I_e = [c, d]$. The function $f(q)$ is negative for $q < c$ and is positive for $q > d$. By (5.34) we obtain that

$$A'(q) = \frac{C'(q) - A(q)}{q} \begin{cases} < 0 & \text{if } q < c \\ > 0 & \text{if } q > d \end{cases}$$

implying that every critical point of $A(q)$ is a point of absolute minimum. $\qquad\square$

Theorem 5.86 indicates a good strategy to achieve the maximal profit. The company must control its average cost $A(q)$ of production. Until $A(q)$ decreases there is no reason to control other parameters. When the level of production providing the minimal value of $A(q)$ is passed, it is necessary to control the ratio

$$m(q) = \frac{R(q + \Delta q) - R(q)}{C(q + \Delta q) - C(q)} \approx \frac{R'(q)}{C'(q)},$$

where Δq is a relatively small positive number. The increase in production must be stopped as soon as $m(q)$ becomes close to 1.

This theory can be simplified for a small efficient company.

Definition 5.87. An efficient company is called **small** if its greatest possible production level cannot influence the market price of the product produced.

Let p_e be the equilibrium price of the unit of a product on the market. Then the revenue of a small efficient company producing this product equals $R(q) =$

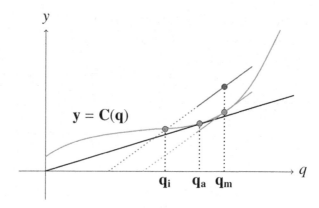

Figure 5.25: The Average Cost.

$p_e q$. Since in this case $R'(q) = p_e$, the equation for the level of production q_m maximizing the profit becomes

$$C'(q_m) = p^*. \qquad (5.38)$$

Let p_a be the minimal average cost of product produced by the company, which is attained on the production level q_a. Since the company is efficient, we see that $q_a < q_m$. Since $C'(q)$ increases on (q_i, q_b), we see that

$$p_a = C'(q_a) \le C'(q_m) = p^*.$$

It follows that the minimal average cost of production of a small efficient company cannot exceed the market price, see Fig 5.25.

Let us consider the example of a small company of Problem 5.48.

Example 5.88. Remind that the cost function of the farm in Problem 5.48 is given by

$$C(q) = \frac{q^3}{3} - 3q^2 + 20q + 50. \qquad (5.39)$$

Lemma 5.89. *A small company with the cost function* (5.39) *can operate on the market only if the market price* p^* *is greater than 22.26 Euro. It will be an efficient company if* $p^* > 30.67$.

Proof. Since

$$C'(q) = q^2 - 6q + 20 = (q - 3)^2 + 11 > 0,$$

the cost function $C(q)$ is strictly increasing. Since $C''(q) = 2(q - 3)$, the cost function $C(q)$ is convex down on $(0, 3)$ and is convex up on $(3, +\infty)$. The tangent line to the graph of $y = C(q)$ passes through the origin if and only if

$$0 = f(q) = q - \frac{C(q)}{C'(q)} \Leftrightarrow C'(q) = A(q) \Leftrightarrow A'(q) = 0.$$

Since

$$A(q) = \frac{q^2}{3} - 3q + 20 + \frac{50}{q} \Rightarrow A'(q) = \frac{2}{3}q - 3 - \frac{50}{q^2}, \qquad (5.40)$$

the equation $A'(q) = 0$ has the unique solution $q_a = 6.35631$. This level of production makes the average cost $A(q_a) = 22.26$ minimal. By (5.40) the slope of this tangent is $C'(q_a) = A(q_a) = 22.26$, implying that the graph of the revenue $y = p^*q$ will be below this tangent and hence below the graph of the cost function if $p^* \leq 22.26$. This small company, therefore, may make a profit only if $p^* > 22.26$.

In order this farm be efficient it is necessary and sufficient that the line of revenue $y = p^*q$ be higher the line through the origin and the point of inflection $(q_i, C(q_i))$. Since $q_i = 3$, and $C(3) = 92$, we obtain the lowest bound for the market price until the farm remains efficient:

$$p^* > \frac{92}{3} \approx 30.67. \qquad \qquad \square$$

Assuming as in Problem 5.48 that $p^* = 36$, we obtain the equation for the break-even and bankruptcy points:

$$0 = C(q) - R(q) = \frac{q^3}{3} - 3q^2 - 16q + 50.$$

This equation has three solutions:

$$q_1 \approx -5.32052, \quad q_2 \approx 2.35645, \quad q_3 \approx 11.9641.$$

Dropping the negative root and keeping two positive roots, we obtain that:

$$q_{be} \approx 2.35645 < q_i = 3 < q_b \approx 11.9641.$$

It was shown in Problem 5.48 that

$$99.33 \cdots = \max_{q_{be} \leq q \leq q_b} \{R(q) - C(q)\} = \Pi(8) > 0.$$

By (5.40) $q_a = 6.35631$. This level of production makes the average cost minimal. If the farmer will produce this amount of cheese, his profit becomes $\Pi(6.35631) = 87.305$, which is 87.9% of the maximal possible profit. So, increasing the level of production by 26%, the farmer increases his profit by 13%.

To determine the optimal level q_m of production for a small company, one can use the following empirical method. First of all one determines the increment $\Delta q > 0$ and define the sequence

$$q_0 = q_{be}, \quad q_1 = q_0 + \Delta q, \quad q_2 = q_1 + \Delta q, \quad \ldots, \quad q_n = q_{n-1} + \Delta q.$$

Using (5.35), one evaluates $C'(q_k)$:

$$A(q_k), \quad A'(q_k) \approx \frac{A(q_{k+1}) - A(q_k)}{\Delta q}, \quad C'(q_k) = A(q_k) + q_k A'(q_k).$$

It is not necessary evaluate $C'(q_k)$ if $A'(q_k) < 0$. Then the optimal level of production is determined by the inequality

$$A(q_k) + q_k A'(q_k) \leq p^* < A(q_{k+1}) + q_{k+1} A'(q_{k+1})$$

The calculations can be conveniently arranged into a table. We demonstrate them on the Example 5.88 of a small company.

q	2	3	4	5	6	**7**	8	9
$A(q)$	40.33	30.67	25.83	23.33	22.33	22.47	23.58	25.56
$A'(q)$	−9.67	−4.84	−2.5	-1	0.14	1.11	1.98	
$C'(q)$					22.33	**30.24**	39.42	

Problem 5.90 (Average Costs). Let $C(q)$ be the total cost of producing a q units of commodity and $A(q) = C(q)/q$ be the average cost. Then the marginal cost $C'(q_0)$ can be find graphically:

- Construct the tangent line t_1 to $y = A(q)$ at some q_0.

- Let t_2 be the line with the same vertical intercept as t_1 but with the doubled slope of the line t_1.

Then $C'(q_0)$ is the distance shown on Fig 5.26.

Solution: We first write the equations of the lines:

$$t_1(q): \quad y_1 = A'(q_0) \cdot (q - q_0) + A(q_0);$$
$$t_2(q): \quad y_2 = 2A'(q_0) \cdot q + A(q_0) - q_0 \cdot A'(q_0)$$

The intercept of t_2 with the vertical line $q = q_0$ is

$$y_2(q_0) = 2A'(q_0) \cdot q_0 + A(q_0) - q_0 \cdot A'(q_0) = A'(q_0) \cdot q_0 + A(q_0)$$

Finally,

$$q \cdot A'(q) + A(q) = q \left(\frac{C(q)}{q} \right)' + \frac{C(q)}{q} = q \frac{C'(q)q - C(q)}{q^2} + \frac{C(q)}{q} = C'(q). \quad \square$$

Fig 5.26 shows how one can determine the optimal level of production using an empirical average cost function. In $\triangle EFG$ the line EK is a mediant and at the same time is tangent to $y = A(q)$.

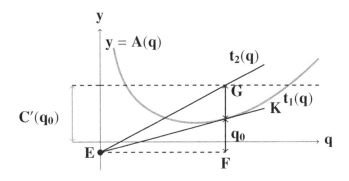

Figure 5.26: Average and Marginal Costs.

Exercise

Prob. 232 — Consider a small company with the cost function

$$C(q) = \frac{q^3}{3} - 2q^2 + 4q + 10.$$

Using a calculator,

(a) determine the lowest price on the market with which this company may survive;

(b) determine the lowest price on the market with which this company is efficient;

(c) determine the break-even and bankruptcy levels of production if the market price for a unit of product is 10;

(d) determine the maximal profit of this company if the market price for a unit of product is 10.

5.10. Lorenz Curves

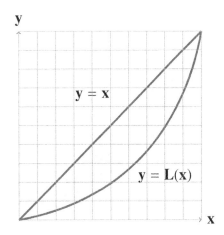

The Lorenz curve was introduced in 1905 by an American economist Max Otto Lorenz to describe income inequality.

On the graph above the variable x represents the proportion of members in a given community whose income is less or equal than $L(x) \cdot I_0$, where I_0 is the total income of the community considered. It is common to construct the Lorenz curve for a particular country.

For example, $L(0.40) = 0.12$ for the Lorenz curve above means that the bottom 40% of families received 12% of the total income I_0 for all families in a given year, i.e. they received $0.12I_0$. Similarly, $L(0.60) = 0.27$ means that the bottom 60% of families received 27% of the total income for all families in the same year. Namely, they received $0.6I_0$.

It is clear that the families with the cumulative income **I**, satisfying

$$0.12I_0 < I \le 0.27I_0$$

make $0.60 - 0.40 \cdot 100\% = 20\%$ of all families. Hence, the Lorenz curve makes it easy to evaluate the total income distribution in a society.

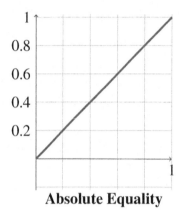

Absolute Equality

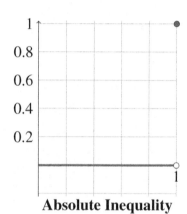

Absolute Inequality

Theorem 5.91. *Any Lorenz curve is concave up.*

Proof. Let $0 < a < b < 1$ and Δx is a small positive number such that $\Delta x < \min\{(b - a), 1 - b\}$. Then

$$\frac{L(a + \Delta x) - L(a)}{\Delta x} \quad \text{and} \quad \frac{L(b + \Delta x) - L(b)}{\Delta x}$$

are average incomes of the families in the slots $(a, a + \Delta x)$ and $(b, b + \Delta x)$ correspondingly. □

Proof. Since the second slot is placed to the right, we have

$$\frac{L(a + \Delta x) - L(a)}{\Delta x} \le \frac{L(b + \Delta x) - L(b)}{\Delta x}.$$

Passing in this inequality to the limit as $\Delta x \to 0^+$, we obtain that

$$L'(a) \leq L'(b),$$

implying the concavity of $y = L(x)$.   □

Theorem 5.92. *Let $y = L(x)$ be a Lorenz curve. Then*

(a) $0 \leq L(x) \leq 1$.

(b) $L(0) = 0$.

(c) $L(1) = 1$.

(d) $L(x) \leq x$.

Proof. **(a)** holds since $100 \cdot L(x)\%$ is a percent of the total income.

(b) holds since no wages are earned when no wage-earners are employed.

(c) holds since 100% of wages are earned by 100% of the wage-earners.

(d) The graph of $y = L(x)$ is concave up. Therefore the chord through $(0, 0)$ and $(1, 1)$ is placed above the graph or on it.

□

Robin Hood Index is the number

$$\mathbf{RH} = \max_{0 < x < 1} [x - L(x)] = c - L(c). \tag{5.41}$$

Since L is continuous and concave up such a c exists. Moreover, the set of all c satisfying (5.41) is a closed segment which may reduce to a set of one number.

Let us indicate how the Lorenz curve may be constructed. We have a big but finite family of citizens, consisting of n people with a total annual income I_0. We arrange this people so that their incomes (in proportion to the total income I_0) increase:

$$x_1 \leq x_2 \leq \cdots \leq x_n, \quad x_1 + x_2 + \cdots + x_n = 1.$$

Given these numbers, we define

$$L\left(\frac{k}{n}\right) = x_1 + \cdots + x_k.$$

For any positive integer k, $k \leq n$, we have

$$\frac{k}{n} - L\left(\frac{k}{n}\right) = \left(\frac{1}{n} - x_1\right) + \left(\frac{1}{n} - x_2\right) + \cdots + \left(\frac{1}{n} - x_k\right).$$

Since $1 = L(1)$, we see that

$$\left(\frac{1}{n} - x_1\right) + \left(\frac{1}{n} - x_2\right) + \cdots + \left(\frac{1}{n} - x_n\right) = 0. \tag{5.42}$$

Since the sequence $\{x_k\}$ increases, there is a positive integer r such that

$$x_{r-1} < \frac{1}{n} \leq x_r.$$

We refer citizens with numbers less than r to poor people and the citizens with numbers not less than r to rich people. By (5.42) we obtain that the deficit of income of poor citizens below the average income $1/n$ equals the excess of income of reach people above the average income $1/n$:

$$\underbrace{\left(\frac{1}{n} - x_1\right) + \cdots + \left(\frac{1}{n} - x_{r-1}\right)}_{\textit{the deficit of income of poor}} = \underbrace{\left(x_r - \frac{1}{n}\right) + \cdots + \left(x_n - \frac{1}{n}\right)}_{\textit{the excess of income of reach}} \tag{5.43}$$

and this equals the Robin Hood Index.

5.11.   Applications: Elasticity

In Economics the dependence of sales on the change in price is measured by the **elasticity of demand**:

$$\varepsilon(p) = -\frac{q'p}{q} = -\frac{p}{q}\frac{dq}{dp} \approx -\frac{p}{q}\frac{\Delta q}{\Delta p} = -\frac{\frac{\Delta q}{q}}{\frac{\Delta p}{p}}.$$

According to **Weber-Fenchler Law** the quantities noticeable by companies and by consumers are the quotients

$$\boxed{\frac{\Delta q}{q}} \quad \text{and} \quad \boxed{\frac{\Delta p}{p}}$$

expressed therefore usually in percents.

Since the demand curve decreases, the elasticity is positive. If consumers consider the change in price insignificant, which means that they are ready to buy for a greater price $p + \Delta p$, i.e by the Weber-Fenchler Law they ignore $|\Delta p/p|$, then the number of sales q will not decrease much, meaning that $|\Delta q/p|$ is smaller than $|\Delta p/p|$. In other words, in this case $\varepsilon(p) < 1$, and we say that the the demand is **inelastic** at price p. We say that the demand is **elastic** (at price p) if $\varepsilon(p) \geq 1$.

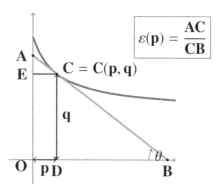

Figure 5.27: Elasticity of Demand Geometrically.

Theorem 5.93 (The Revenue Theorem). *The revenue increases if $\varepsilon(p) < 1$ and decreases if $\varepsilon(p) > 1$.*

Proof. We apply the product rule to relate the rate of change of the revenue with elasticity. The formula for the revenue is given by $R(p) = p \cdot q(p)$. Then

$$R'(p) = (p)'q + pq' = q + pq' = q\left(1 + \frac{p}{q}\frac{dq}{dp}\right) = q(1 - \varepsilon(p)).$$

Hence $R'(p) > 0$ ($R(p)$ increases at p) if $\varepsilon(p) < 1$. Similarly, $R'(p) < 0$ ($R(p)$ decreases at p) if $\varepsilon(p) > 1$. □

Theorem 5.94 (Geometric Illustration of Elasticity of Demand). *The elasticity of demand at price p is the quotient of the length of the segment of tangent, defined by its y-intercept and the tangency point, to the length of the segment of tangent, defined by its tangency point and its x-intercept.*

Proof. See Fig 5.27. The equation of the tangent line to the demand curve at $p = a$ is

$$q = q'(a)(p - a) + q(a) = 0 \Leftrightarrow p = a - \frac{q(a)}{q'(a)}.$$

It follows that

$$|AO| = q(a) - aq'(a), \quad |OB| = a - \frac{q(a)}{q'(a)}.$$

Since $\triangle ABO \backsim \triangle CBD$, we obtain

$$\frac{|AC|}{|CB|} = \frac{|AB|}{|CB|} - 1 = \frac{|OB|}{|DB|} - 1 = \frac{a - \frac{q(a)}{q'(a)}}{-\frac{q(a)}{q'(a)}} - 1 = -a\frac{q'(a)}{q(a)} = \varepsilon(a).$$

The above arguments can also be arranged as follows:

$$\frac{|AC|}{|CB|} = \frac{|OD|}{|DB|} = \frac{p}{q\cot\theta} = \frac{p}{q}\tan\theta = -\frac{p}{q}\frac{dq}{dp} = \varepsilon(p). \qquad \square$$

Theorem 5.95 (The First Elasticity Theorem). *Let $q = q(p)$ be a decreasing direct demand function continuously differentiable on the closed interval $[0, a]$, where a satisfies $q(a) = 0$. Then there is a price p_e in the open interval $(0, a)$ such that $\varepsilon(p_e) = 1$.*

Remark 5.96. Theorem 5.95 states that under very general restrictions on the direct demand function there always exists a price with the elasticity of demand equal 1.

Proof of the First Elasticity Theorem. First, we observe that

$$\lim_{p\to 0^+} \varepsilon(p) = -\frac{\lim_{p\to 0^+} p}{\lim_{p\to 0^+} q(p)} \cdot \lim_{p\to 0^+} \frac{dq}{dp}(p) = -\frac{0}{q(0)}q'(0) = 0.$$

Since $\varepsilon(p)$ is continuous on $[0, a)$ we complete the proof by the Intermediate Value Theorem if we can show that there exists a point p in $(0, a)$ such that $\varepsilon(p) > 1$. Indeed, then we just apply this theorem to $\varepsilon(p)$ on the interval (a, p). Suppose to the contrary that $\varepsilon(p) < 1$ on $(0, a)$. Then by the Revenue Theorem the Revenue $R(p) = p \cdot q(p)$ increases. But this contradicts to the equality:

$$\lim_{p\to a^+} p \cdot q(p) = a \cdot q(a) = 0. \qquad \square$$

Another Proof of the First Elasticity Theorem. Consider the revenue $R(q) = p \cdot q(p)$. Then $R(0) = R(a) = 0$ and $q(p) > 0$ on $(0, a)$. By Rolle's Theorem there is c in $(0, a)$ such that $R'(c) = 0$. But by the Revenue Theorem (observe that $q(p) > 0$ on $(0, a)$) this means the $\varepsilon(c) = 1$. We can put $p_e = c$. $\qquad \square$

Theorem 5.97 (The Second Theorem on Elasticity of Demand). *Let $q = q(p)$ be a decreasing direct demand function continuously differentiable on the closed interval $[0, a]$, where a satisfies $q(a) = 0$. And let $q(p)$ be concave down on $[0, a]$. Then there is a unique price p_e in the open interval $(0, a)$ such that $\varepsilon(p_e) = 1$.*

Proof. The existence of p_e is guaranteed by the First Theorem on Elasticity of Demand. We prove that $\varepsilon(p)$ increases. Then there is only one p_e with $\varepsilon(p_e) = 1$.

Since $q'' \le 0$ on $(0, a)$ (it is concave down) and $-q' > 0$ on $(0, a)$ (q decreases)

$$\varepsilon'(p) = -\left(\frac{p}{q}\right)' \cdot q' - \frac{p}{q}q'' = -\frac{q - pq'}{q^2} \cdot q' - \frac{pq''}{q} =$$
$$\frac{p(q')^2 + q(-q') + pq(-q'')}{q^2} > 0. \qquad \square$$

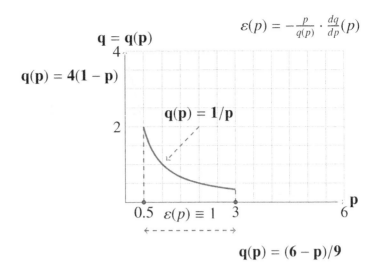

Figure 5.28: $\varepsilon(p) = 1$ on an interval.

Example 5.98. There exists a concave up demand function $q(p)$ on an interval $[0, a]$ such that its elasticity of demand equals 1 on a closed interval $[c, d]$, $0 < c < d < a$.

Solution: The elasticity of demand of a hyperbolic demand function $q(p) = 1/p$ is identically 1. We define $q(p)$ to be equal $1/p$ on $[c, d]$ and linear outside of $[c, d]$:

$$q(p) = \begin{cases} - & p/c^2 + 2/c \text{ if } 0 \leq c < d \\ & 1/p \text{ if } c \leq p \leq d \\ - & p/d^2 + 2/d \text{ if } p > d \end{cases}$$

We chose $d = a/2$ so that $q(a) = 0$. The construction is illustrated by Fig 5.28. The graphs of $\varepsilon(p)$ and $R(p)$ in this case are shown on Fig 5.29.

Theorem 5.99 (Concavity of the Inverse Demand Function $\mathbf{p^D(q)}$). *Let $y = f(x)$ be a decreasing twice differentiable function on $[a, b]$. Then the inverse function $y = f^{-1}(x)$ has the same concavity as $y = f(x)$.*

Proof. By the definition of the inverse function $f^{-1}(f(x)) = x$. Differentiating both sides and applying the Chain Rule we get:

$$(f^{-1})'(f(x)) \cdot f'(x) = 1 \Rightarrow (f^{-1})'(f(x)) = \frac{1}{f'(x)}.$$

Differentiating the identity obtained by the Chain rule we get

$$(f^{-1})''(f(x))f'(x) = -\frac{1}{(f'(x))^2}f''(x) \Rightarrow (f^{-1})''(f(x)) = -\frac{1}{(f'(x))^3}f''(x).$$

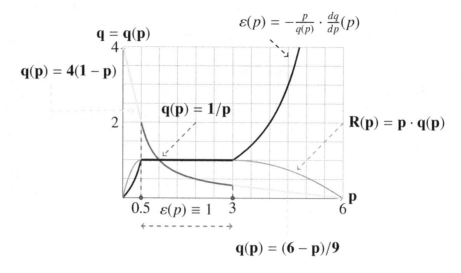

Figure 5.29: $\varepsilon(p) = 1$ on an interval.

Since $f'(x) < 0$, the result follows by the Second Derivative Test for Concavity.

$\square$

Problem 5.100 (Elasticity of Demand for a products with many substitutes). A company producing cheese A estimates its demand by the formula:

$$q^D(p) = 4 - 0.001 \cdot p^4,$$

where p is measured in pounds of sterling and **q** is counted in thousands of units produced per day. Give an economical explanation.

Solution: We find that

$$\frac{dq}{dp} = -4 \cdot 10^{-3} \cdot p^3 < 0 \quad \frac{d^2q}{dp^2} = -12 \cdot 10^{-3} \cdot p^2 < 0,$$

implying that the demand is concave down and decreasing. We find that

$$\varepsilon(p) = -\frac{p}{q}\frac{dq}{dp} = \frac{4 \cdot 10^{-3} \cdot p^4}{4 - 10^{-3} \cdot p^4} = 1 \Leftrightarrow p = (800)^{1/4} \approx \mathbf{5.3183}$$

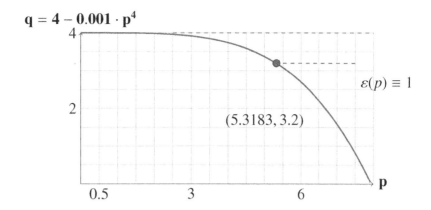

$$q = 4 - 0.001 \cdot p^4$$

For $0 \le p \le 3$ the demand curve is almost constant, since all consumers of substitutes for cheese A will by it for these prices. Starting with $p = 3$, more and more consumers will buy substitutes for A with increase of p. The price $p = 5.829$, corresponding $\varepsilon(p) = 1$, provides the maximal revenue $R(p)$ for cheese A. The curve shows that the sales at this price make $q = 2.6667$, i.e. approximately 2/3 of all possible sales. On the price interval $6 \le p \le 7.5$ the curve goes steep down, since only people very devoted to cheese A will buy it for such a price.

Conclusion: The concave down shape of the demand curve reflects a great number of substitutes for a product for selling price. Notice that as we already showed it does not matter whether it is a direct or inverse demand curve.

5.12.   L'Hospital's Rule

Theorem 5.101 (Indeterminate Form 0/0)**.** *Let f and g be differentiable functions on an open interval I with an end-point c, where c is either a real number or $\pm\infty$. Suppose that*

(**1**) $\lim_{x \to c} f(x) = \lim_{x \to c} g(x) = 0$,

(**2**) $g'(x) \ne 0$ *on some open sub-interval J of I with the end-point c.*

Then

$$\lim_{x \to c} \frac{f'(x)}{g'(x)} = L \Rightarrow \lim_{x \to c} \frac{f(x)}{g(x)} = L.$$

Here L may be finite or infinite.

Remark 5.102. Notice that by (**2**) and by Theorem 5.38 the function $g(x)$ is strictly monotonic on J. In particular, $g(x)$ does not vanish in J about c.

Problem 5.103. Using L'Hospital's Rule evaluate

$$\lim_{x \to 0} \frac{x - \sin x}{x^3}.$$

Solution: Both functions $f(x) = x - \sin x$ and $g(x) = x^3$ are differentiable on $(-\infty, +\infty)$ and $g'(x) = 3x^2 \neq 0$ if $x \neq c = 0$. It follows that

$$\lim_{x \to 0} \frac{x - \sin x}{x^3} = \lim_{x \to 0} \frac{1 - \cos x}{3x^2},$$

if the second limit exists. Both functions $f(x) = 1 - \cos x$ and $g(x) = 3x^2$ are differentiable on $(-\infty, +\infty)$ and $g'(x) = 6x \neq 0$ if $x \neq c = 0$. It follows that

$$\lim_{x \to 0} \frac{1 - \cos x}{3x^2} = \lim_{x \to 0} \frac{\sin x}{6x} = \frac{1}{6}$$

by Theorem 3.72. Notice, that it is not a very good idea to evaluate

$$\lim_{x \to 0} \frac{\sin x}{x} = 1$$

by L'Hospital's Rule. The reason is that this very limit is used to find the derivative of $\sin x$. However, being applied in this situation, it gives a correct answer. Therefore, L'Hospital's Rule can be applied in multiple choice questions if necessary.

In practice the above calculations can be arranged in one line:

$$\lim_{x \to 0} \frac{x - \sin x}{x^3} = \lim_{x \to 0} \frac{1 - \cos x}{3x^2} = \lim_{x \to 0} \frac{\sin x}{6x} = \frac{1}{6}.$$

When the chain of limits is finished, it is necessary to read it backward to verify that all conditions of L'Hospital's Rule are satisfied at each step made. □

Problem 5.104. Evaluate

$$\lim_{x \to 0} \frac{1 - \cos x}{x + x^2}$$

Solution: Be careful to apply L'Hospital's Rule correctly

$$\lim_{x \to 0} \frac{1 - \cos x}{x + x^2} = \lim_{x \to 0} \frac{\sin x}{1 + 2x} = \frac{0}{1} = 0.$$

Up to now the calculation is correct, but if we continue to differentiate in an attempt to apply L´Hôpital's Rule once more, we get

$$\lim_{x \to 0} \frac{\cos x}{2} = \frac{1}{2},$$

which is not the correct limit. **L'Hospital's Rule can only be applied to limits in indeterminate forms**, and 0/1 is not an indeterminate form. □

Problem 5.105. Find the limit

$$\lim_{x \to 0} \left(\frac{1}{\sin x} - \frac{1}{x} \right)$$

Solution: Since

$$\frac{1}{\sin x} - \frac{1}{x} = \frac{x - \sin x}{x \sin x},$$

we apply L'Hospital's Rule:

$$\lim_{x \to 0} \left(\frac{1}{\sin x} - \frac{1}{x} \right) = \lim_{x \to 0} \frac{x - \sin x}{x \sin x} =$$

$$= \lim_{x \to 0} \frac{1 - \cos x}{\sin x + x \cos x} = \lim_{x \to 0} \frac{\sin x}{2 \cos x - x \sin x} = \frac{0}{2} = 0. \quad \square$$

The proof of L'Hospital's Rule is based on Cauchy's Theorem.

Theorem 5.106 (Cauchy). *Let f, g be continuous functions on a closed interval $[a, b]$, differentiable in the open interval (a, b). Suppose that $g'(x) \neq 0$ for every x, $a < x < b$. Then there is a point c in (a, b) such that*

$$\frac{f(b) - f(a)}{g(b) - g(a)} = \frac{f'(c)}{g'(c)}. \tag{5.44}$$

Remark 5.107. Notice that if $g(x) = x$, Cauchy's Theorem follows by Lagrange's Theorem. It is not surprise, therefore, that the proof of Cauchy's Theorem follows the same lines as the proof of Lagrange's Theorem.

Proof of Cauchy's Theorem. First we observe that $g(a) \neq g(b)$. Otherwise $g'(c) = 0$ for some c, $a < c < b$ by Rolle's Theorem, which contradicts the assumption that $g'(x) \neq 0$ for every x, $a < x < b$. Let us consider an auxiliary function

$$\Pi(x) = f(x) - f(a) - \frac{f(b) - f(a)}{g(b) - g(a)} \cdot \{g(x) - g(a)\}.$$

Being a linear combination of differentiable functions $\Pi(x)$ is differentiable on (a, b). Similarly, it is continuous on $[a, b]$. Since $\Pi(a) = \Pi(b) = 0$, we can apply of Rolle's Theorem to $\Pi(x)$. It follows that there is c in (a, b) such that

$$0 = \Pi'(c) = f'(c) - \frac{f(b) - f(a)}{g(b) - g(a)} g'(c),$$

which completes the proof since $g'(c) \neq 0$. $\quad \square$

Proof Theorem 5.101. First, we assume that c is a real number and that $x \to c^+$. Then $J = (c, d)$. By (**1**) both functions f and g can be extended to continuous functions on $[c, d)$ if we put $f(c) = g(c) = 0$. Decreasing d, if necessary, we can assume that f and g are continuous on $[c, d]$. Let $c < x < d$. Then by Theorem 5.106 there is a number $\xi(x)$, $c < \xi(x) < x$ such that

$$\frac{f(x)}{g(x)} = \frac{f(x) - f(c)}{g(x) - g(c)} = \frac{f'(\xi)}{g'(\xi)}.$$

If $x \to c^+$, then $\xi(x) \to c^+$ by Sandwich Theorem. It follows that

$$\lim_{x \to c^+} \frac{f'(\xi(x))}{g'(\xi(x))} = \lim_{x \to c^+} \frac{f'(x)}{g'(x)}$$

Hence

$$\lim_{x \to c^+} \frac{f(x)}{g(x)} = \lim_{x \to c^+} \frac{f(x) - f(c)}{g(x) - g(c)} = \lim_{x \to c^+} \frac{f'(x)}{g'(x)},$$

as stated. The case $x < c$ for a real number c is considered similarly.

Let now $c = +\infty$. Then

$$\lim_{x \to +\infty} \frac{f(x)}{g(x)} \stackrel{t=1/x}{=} \lim_{y \to 0^+} \frac{f(1/y)}{g(1/y)} = \lim_{y \to 0^+} \frac{-f'(1/y)/y^2}{-g'(1/y)/y^2} \stackrel{x=1/y}{=} \lim_{x \to +\infty} \frac{f'(x)}{g'(x)}.$$

The case $x \to -\infty$ is considered similarly. □

Theorem 5.108 (Indeterminate Form ∞/∞). *Let f and g be differentiable functions on an open interval I with an end-point c, where c is either a real number or $\pm\infty$. Suppose that*

(**1**) $\lim_{x \to c} f(x) = \lim_{x \to c} g(x) = \infty$,

(**2**) $g'(x) \neq 0$ *on some open sub-interval J of I with the end-point c.*

Then

$$\lim_{x \to c} \frac{f'(x)}{g'(x)} = L \Rightarrow \lim_{x \to c} \frac{f(x)}{g(x)} = L.$$

Here L is finite or infinite.

Proof. We suppose that $J = (d, c)$, where $d < c$ and c is either finite or $c = +\infty$. By (**2**) and Theorem 5.38 $g(x)$ is strictly monotonic on J. In particular, $g(x)$ does not vanish in J about c and $g'(x)$ does not change sign on (d, c). For any $d < t < x < c$ by Cauchy's Theorem we have

$$\frac{f(x)}{g(x)} = \frac{f(x) - f(t)}{g(x) - g(t)} \cdot \underbrace{\left\{ \frac{1 - \dfrac{g(t)}{g(x)}}{1 - \dfrac{f(t)}{f(x)}} \right\}}_{} = \underbrace{\frac{f'(\xi)}{g'(\xi)}}_{A} \cdot \underbrace{\left\{ \frac{1 - \dfrac{g(t)}{g(x)}}{1 - \dfrac{f(t)}{f(x)}} \right\}}_{B}, \tag{5.45}$$

$t < \xi < x$. Given ε, $0 < \varepsilon < 1$ we determine t so that

$$L - \frac{\varepsilon}{2} < \frac{f'(s)}{g'(s)} < L + \frac{\varepsilon}{2} \Rightarrow |A - L| < \frac{\varepsilon}{2}. \tag{5.46}$$

for every s in (t, c). For this t we find by (1) a number x_t such that

$$|B - 1| < \frac{\varepsilon}{2|L| + \varepsilon}.$$

Then for every x in (x_t, c) we have

$$\left| \frac{f(x)}{g(x)} - L \right| = |AB - L| = |A(B-1) + A - L| \le |A||B - 1| + |A - L|.$$

By (5.46)

$$|A| \le |A - L| + |L| < |L| + \frac{\varepsilon}{2}.$$

It follows that for any x in (x_t, c)

$$\left| \frac{f(x)}{g(x)} - L \right| \le \frac{2|L| + \varepsilon}{2}|B - 1| + \frac{\varepsilon}{2} = \varepsilon,$$

which completes the proof in case of a finite L.

If L is infinite, then either $L = +\infty$ or $L = -\infty$. If $f'(x)$ has infinitely many zeros x_n approaching c, then

$$\lim_n \frac{f'(x_n)}{g'(x_n)} = 0,$$

which contradicts the assumption that this limit is infinite. By Theorem 5.38 f is strictly monotonic about c. Then we may apply already proved part of Theorem 5.108 to the quotient $g(x)/f(x)$ with $L = 0$. By the Algebraic Rules for limits the quotient $f(x)/g(x)$ has infinite limit.   □

The condition that $g'(x) \ne 0$ in two theorems above is important. The following example was first found by O. Stolz (1879). We present a simplified version of R. Boas. See [1, pp. 138-140] for more examples and comments.

Example 5.109. Let
$$f(x) = x + \cos x \sin x,$$
$$g(x) = e^{\sin x}(x + \cos x \sin x).$$
Then $\lim_{x \to +\infty} f'(x)/g'(x) = 0$, but $\lim_{x \to +\infty} f(x)/g(x)$ does not exist.

Solution: We have $f'(x) = 1 + \cos 2x = 2\cos^2 x$, and

$$g'(x) = e^{\sin x} \cos x \{x + \cos x \sin x + 2 \cos x\}.$$

It follows that

$$\lim_{x \to +\infty} \frac{f'(x)}{g'(x)} = \lim_{x \to +\infty} \frac{2\cos^2 x}{e^{\sin x} \cos x \{x + \cos x \sin x + 2\cos x\}} =$$

$$\lim_{x \to +\infty} \frac{2\cos x e^{-\sin x}}{x + \cos x \sin x + 2\cos x} = 0.$$

Since $f(x)/g(x) = e^{-\sin x}$ oscillates about $+\infty$ between e and $1/e$, the limit of $f(x)/g(x)$ as $x \to +\infty$ does not exist. □

Example 5.110. Find the limit

$$\lim_{x \to +\infty} \frac{x}{\sqrt{x^2 + 1}}.$$

Solution: Using simple algebra, we find by Algebraic Rules for limits that

$$\lim_{x \to +\infty} \frac{x}{\sqrt{x^2 + 1}} = \lim_{x \to +\infty} \frac{x}{x} \cdot \frac{1}{\sqrt{1 + \frac{1}{x^2}}} \overset{y = 1/x^2}{=} \frac{1}{\sqrt{1 + \lim_{y \to 0} y}} = 1.$$

However, the following natural attempt to apply l'Hopital's Rule fails. Let $f(x) = x$ and $g(x) = \sqrt{x^2 + 1}$. Then

$$\frac{f'(x)}{g'(x)} = \frac{1}{\dfrac{x}{\sqrt{x^2 + 1}}} = \frac{\sqrt{x^2 + 1}}{x}. \quad □$$

Example 5.111. Evaluate the limit

$$\lim_{x \to +\infty} \frac{x - \sin x}{x + \sin x}.$$

Solution: Applying the Algebraic rules, we have

$$\lim_{x \to +\infty} \frac{x - \sin x}{x + \sin x} = \lim_{x \to +\infty} \frac{1 - \dfrac{\sin x}{x}}{1 + \dfrac{\sin x}{x}} = \frac{1 - \lim_{x \to +\infty} \dfrac{\sin x}{x}}{1 + \lim_{x \to +\infty} \dfrac{\sin x}{x}} = \frac{1 - 0}{1 + 0} = 1.$$

We cannot apply l'Hopital's Rule since

$$\frac{(x - \sin x)'}{(x + \sin x)'} = \frac{1 - \cos x}{1 + \cos x}$$

has no limit at $+\infty$. □

Theorem 5.108 can be used to compare the growth of functions of different nature.

Problem 5.112. Let $a > 1$ and $\alpha > 0$. Show that

$$\lim_{x \to +\infty} \frac{x^\alpha}{a^x} = 0.$$

Solution:

$$\lim_{x \to +\infty} \frac{x^\alpha}{a^x} \overset{\text{continuity of } x^\alpha}{=} \left(\lim_{x \to +\infty} \frac{x}{a^{x/\alpha}} \right)^\alpha = \left(\lim_{x \to +\infty} \frac{1}{a^{x/\alpha} \ln a^{1/\alpha}} \right)^\alpha = 0^\alpha = 0. \quad \square$$

Problem 5.113. Show that for every $\alpha > 0$

$$\lim_{x \to +\infty} \frac{\ln x}{x^\alpha} = 0.$$

Solution:

$$\lim_{x \to +\infty} \frac{\ln x}{x^\alpha} = \lim_{x \to +\infty} \frac{1/x}{\alpha x^{\alpha-1}} = \lim_{x \to +\infty} \frac{1}{\alpha x^\alpha} = 0. \quad \square$$

Problem 5.114. Show that for every $\alpha > 0$

$$\lim_{x \to 0^+} x^\alpha \ln x = 0.$$

Solution:

$$\lim_{x \to 0^+} x^\alpha \ln x = \lim_{x \to 0^+} \frac{\ln x}{x^{-\alpha}} = \lim_{x \to 0^+} \frac{1/x}{-\alpha x^{-\alpha-1}} = \lim_{x \to 0^+} \frac{x^\alpha}{-\alpha} = 0. \quad \square$$

Problem 5.115. Evaluate the limit

$$\lim_{x \to 1^+} (x-1)^{\ln x}.$$

Solution: Applying Euler's formula and continuity of e^x, we find:

$$\lim_{x \to 1^+} (x-1)^{\ln x} = \lim_{x \to 1^+} e^{\ln x \cdot \ln(x-1)} = e^{\lim_{x \to 1^+} \ln x \cdot \ln(x-1)}.$$

To find the later limit we apply Theorem 5.108:

$$\lim_{x \to 1^+} \ln x \cdot \ln(x-1) = \lim_{x \to 1^+} \frac{\ln(x-1)}{\frac{1}{\ln x}} = \lim_{x \to 1^+} \frac{\frac{1}{x-1}}{-\frac{1}{x \ln^2 x}} = -\lim_{x \to 1^+} \frac{x \ln^2 x}{x-1} =$$

$$-\lim_{x \to 1^+} \frac{(x \ln^2 x)'}{1} = -\lim_{x \to 1^+} (\ln^2 x + 2 \ln x) = -(\ln^2 1 + 2 \ln 1) = 0. \quad \square$$

Problems

Prob. 233 — Evaluate the limits

$$\lim_{x \to 4} \frac{x^2 - 16}{x62 + x - 20}, \quad \lim_{x \to a} \frac{x^3 - ax^2 - a^2 x + a^3}{x^2 - a^2}.$$

Prob. 234 — Evaluate the limits

$$\lim_{x \to 0} \left(\frac{\sin x}{x} \right)^{\frac{1}{x}}, \quad \lim_{x \to \pi} \frac{\cot 2x}{\cot 3x}, \quad \lim_{x \to 0} \left(\frac{1}{x(1 + x)} - \frac{\ln(1 + x)}{x^2} \right).$$

Prob. 235 — Find the limits

$$\lim_{x \to +\infty} x \ln \frac{x - a}{x + a}, \quad \lim_{x \to 0} x^x, \quad \lim_{x \to +\infty} (1 + x)^{\frac{1}{x}}, \quad \lim_{x \to 0} \left(\frac{\tan x}{x} \right)^{\frac{1}{x^2}}.$$

Prob. 236 — Let $f(x)$ be a differentiable function on $(0, +\infty)$ such that $\lim_{x \to +\infty} f'(x) = m$. Prove that

$$\lim_{x \to +\infty} \frac{f(x)}{x} = m.$$

Midterm

Multiple Choice Questions, Part IA

Problem 1. Which of the following functions could have the graph sketched above?

$$\textbf{A } y = xe^x \quad \textbf{B } y = xe^{-x} \quad \textbf{C } y = \frac{e^x}{x} \quad \textbf{D } y = \frac{x}{1 + x^2} \quad \textbf{E } y = \frac{x^2}{x^3 + 1}$$

Problem 2. The curve

$$y = \frac{x^2}{4 - x^2} \text{ has}$$

(A) two horizontal asymptotes

(B) two horizontal asymptotes and one vertical asymptote

(C) two vertical asymptotes but no horizontal asymptotes

(D) one horizontal and one vertical asymptote

(E) one horizontal and two vertical asymptotes

Problem 3. A function $y = f(x)$ is defined by

$$f(x) = \begin{cases} x^3 & \text{if } 0 \le x \le 1 \\ 0 & \text{if } x = 2 \end{cases}$$

Which of the following is true?

A $\lim_{x \to 2} f(x) = 0$ **B** $\lim_{x \to -1} f(x) = 0$ **C** $\lim_{x \to 0^-} f(x) = -1$

D $\lim_{x \to 2^-} f(x) = 0$ **E** $\lim_{x \to 2} f(x)$ does not exist.

Problem 4. Since January 1, a bottle of soda has been rising in price at a constant rate of 2 cents per month. Price reached $1.56 per bottle by November 1. Determine the price at the beginning of the year.

A $1.36 **B** $1.34 **C** $1.38 **D** $1.26 **E** $1.16

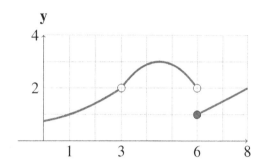

Problem 5. The graph of $y = f(x)$ is plotted above. Which of the following statements about f is true?

A $\lim_{x \to 3} f(x) = \lim_{x \to 6} f(x)$ **B** $\lim_{x \to 3} f(x) = 2$ **C** $\lim_{x \to 6} f(x) = 2$

D $\lim_{x \to 6} f(x) = 2$ **E** $\lim_{x \to 3} f(x)$ doesn't exist

Problem 6. If

$$f(x) = x^{-2/3}(x - 2)^{2/3} + x^{1/3}(x - 2)^{-1/3},$$

then the natural domain of f is:

A $\{x : x \neq 0\}$ **B** $\{x : x > 0\}$ **C** $\{x : 0 \leq x \leq 2\}$

D $\{x : x$ is a real number$\}$ **E** $\{x : x \neq 0$ and $x \neq 2\}$

Problem 7. Which of the following is the range of $f(x) = 5\cos(2x - \pi) + 3$?

A $(-\infty, +\infty)$ **B** $[-2, 4]$ **C** $[2, 8]$ **D** $[-2, 8]$ **E** $[-0.4, 1.6]$

Problem 8. Which of the following statements is true?

A $\log_{\frac{1}{2}} 2 < \log_{\frac{1}{\sqrt{2}}} 2$ **B** $\log_{\frac{1}{2}} 2 > \log_{\frac{1}{2}} 4$ **C** $\log_3(2 + 4) = \log_3 2 + \log_3 4$

$$\textbf{D } \log_{\frac{1}{5}}(5\sqrt{5}) = \frac{3}{2} \quad \textbf{E } \log_{\frac{1}{2}} 2 - \log_{\frac{1}{2}} 4 = \log_{\frac{1}{2}} 2$$

Problem 9. A missile starts vertically upward from an underground tunnel so that in t seconds after the start it is $s(t)$ feet above the ground. Here $s(t) = -16t^2 + 1600t - 75$. Determine when the missile is at its highest point.

$$\textbf{A } 20 \text{ sec} \quad \textbf{B } 30 \text{ sec} \quad \textbf{C } 40 \text{ sec} \quad \textbf{D } 50 \text{ sec} \quad \textbf{E } 60 \text{ sec}$$

Problem 10. If

$$f(g(x)) = \frac{2x+1}{4x+5} \quad \text{and} \quad f(x) = \frac{1}{2x+1},$$

then $g(x) =$

$$\textbf{A } \frac{x+2}{2x+1} \quad \textbf{B } \frac{1}{x+4} \quad \textbf{C } \frac{2x+1}{x+2} \quad \textbf{D } \frac{x}{2x+1} \quad \textbf{E } x+2.$$

Problem 11. If $\ln x - \ln\left(\frac{1}{x}\right) = 6$, then $x =$

$$\textbf{A } \frac{1}{e^3} \quad \textbf{B } \frac{1}{e} \quad \textbf{C } e \quad \textbf{D } e^3 \quad \textbf{E } 2e.$$

Problem 12. If $f(x) = \frac{x}{1-x^2}$ is a function defined on $(-1, 1)$, then the inverse function f^{-1}, is given by $f^{-1}(x) =$

$$\textbf{A } \frac{2x}{1+\sqrt{1+4x^2}} \quad \textbf{B } -\frac{1+\sqrt{1+4x^2}}{2x} \quad \textbf{C } \frac{1+\sqrt{1+4x^2}}{2x}$$

$$\textbf{D } -\frac{2x}{1+\sqrt{1+4x^2}} \quad \textbf{E } \text{Doesn't exist}$$

Problem 13.

$$\lim_{x \to 3} \frac{\sqrt{x^2 - 2x + 6} - \sqrt{x^2 + 2x - 6}}{x^2 - 4x + 3} =$$

$$\textbf{A } \frac{3}{4} \quad \textbf{B } \frac{5}{8} \quad \textbf{C } -\frac{1}{2} \quad \textbf{D } \frac{3}{2} \quad \textbf{E } -\frac{1}{3}.$$

Problem 14.

$$\lim_{x \to 0} \frac{\sqrt[3]{x^3 + 2x^4}}{\ln(1+2x)} =$$

$$\textbf{A } 2 \quad \textbf{B } \frac{1}{6} \quad \textbf{C } \frac{1}{3} \quad \textbf{D } \frac{1}{2} \quad \textbf{E } \text{Doesn't exist}.$$

Problem 15.

$$\lim_{x \to -\infty} \frac{\ln(1+e^x)}{x} =$$

$$\mathbf{A} \ 1 \quad \mathbf{B} \ 0 \quad \mathbf{C} \ 1/e \quad \mathbf{D} \ e \quad \mathbf{E} \ \frac{1}{2}.$$

Problem 16.

$$\lim_{x \to 0} \left(\frac{1}{x} \ln \sqrt{\frac{1+x}{1-x}} \right) =$$

$\mathbf{A} \ e \quad \mathbf{B} \dfrac{1}{e} \quad \mathbf{C} \ 1 \quad \mathbf{D} \ 0 \quad \mathbf{E}$ does not exist.

Problem 17.

$$\lim_{x \to 1} \left(\frac{1}{1-x} - \frac{3}{1-x^3} \right) =$$

$\mathbf{A} \ -1 \quad \mathbf{B} \dfrac{1}{3} \quad \mathbf{C} \ 0 \quad \mathbf{D} \dfrac{1}{6} \quad \mathbf{E}$ does not exist.

Problem 18.

$$\lim_{x \to 0} \left(\frac{x^2 - 2x + 3}{x^2 - 3x + 2} \right)^{\frac{2x}{\sin x}} =$$

$\mathbf{A} \dfrac{2}{3} \quad \mathbf{B} \dfrac{3}{2} \quad \mathbf{C} \dfrac{9}{4} \quad \mathbf{D} \ 1 \quad \mathbf{E}$ does not exist.

Problem 19.

$$\lim_{x \to 0^+} (\sin x)^{\frac{1}{x^2}}$$

$\mathbf{A} \ \sqrt{e} \quad \mathbf{B} \dfrac{1}{\sqrt{e}} \quad \mathbf{C} \ 0 \quad \mathbf{D} \ -\dfrac{1}{\sqrt{e}} \quad \mathbf{E}$ does not exist.

Problem 20.

$$f(x) = \begin{cases} 2x + 4 & \text{if } x < -1 \\ x^2 & \text{if } x \geq -1 \end{cases} \qquad g(x) = \begin{cases} x - 3 & \text{if } x < 2 \\ x^2 - 4 & \text{if } x \geq 2 \end{cases}$$

If $a = \lim_{x \to 2^-} f(g(x))$ and $b = \lim_{x \to 2^+} f(g(x))$ then

$$\mathbf{A} \ a = 2, b = 1 \quad \mathbf{B} \ a = 2, b = 0 \quad \mathbf{C} \ a = 0, b = 0$$

$$\mathbf{D} \ a = -2, b = -1 \quad \mathbf{E} \ a = 1, b = -1.$$

Problem 21. Let

$$f(x) = \begin{cases} x^2 + 4x + a & \text{if } x \leq -1 \\ ax + b & \text{if } -1 < x < 1 \\ 2bx - 1 & \text{if } x \geq 1 \end{cases}$$

be a continuous function. Then

$\mathbf{A} \ a = 2, b = 1 \quad \mathbf{B} \ a = 4, 0 \quad \mathbf{C} \ a = 4, b = 5 \quad \mathbf{D} \ a = 5, b = 4 \quad \mathbf{E} \ a = 1, b = -5.$

Problem 22. A tank with oil was emptied in 40 minutes. The table below indicates the volume of oil (in liters) which remained in the tank in t minutes the draining took the place.

t(min)	0	5	10	15	20	25	30	35	40
v(liters)	6700	4500	3000	2200	1800	1200	600	300	0

During which of the following 10-minutes intervals is the average speed of oil draining the least?

A $t = 0$ to $t = 10$ minutes **B** $t = 10$ to $t = 20$ minutes

C $t = 15$ to $t = 25$ minutes **D** $t = 25$ to $t = 35$ minutes

E $t = 30$ to $t = 40$ minutes

Problem 23.

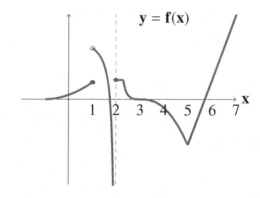

Which of the following is true about the graph above?

A $f(x)$ has a removable discontinuity at $x = 1$.

B $f(x)$ is not continuous at $x = 5$.

C $f(x)$ has a jump discontinuity at $x = 2$.

D $f(x)$ has an essential discontinuity at $x = 2$.

E $f(x)$ has an essential discontinuity at $x = 1$.

Problem 24. According to the Gutenberg-Richter Law the number N of yearly earthquakes in a region of Richter's magnitude at least M satisfies an approximate relation $\log_{10} N = a - M$ for some constant a. There is one earthquake of magnitude $M \geq 8$ per year. How many earthquakes of magnitude $M \geq 7$ occur per year?

A 10 **B** 20 **C** 100 **D** 200 **E** 1000.

Problem 25. If the function f is defined by $f(x) = x^5 - 1$, then $f^{-1}(x)$, the inverse function of f, is defined by $f^{-1}(x) =$

A $\dfrac{1}{\sqrt[5]{x+1}}$ **B** $\dfrac{1}{\sqrt[5]{x+1}}$ **C** $\sqrt[5]{x-1}$ **D** $\sqrt[5]{x} - 1$ **E** $\sqrt[5]{x+1}$

Problem 26. A continuous function $f(x)$ on $[-1, 11]$ takes values specified in the following table.

x	0	2	6	10	12
$f(x)$	-2	4	k	6	-1

For which values of the parameter k the equation $f(x) = 2$ has at least four solutions in $(-1, 11)$?

A $2 < k < 3$ **B** $k < 2$ **C** $k > 2$ **D** $k = 2$ **E does not exist**.

Problem 27. Consider the function:

$$f(x) = \begin{cases} x^2 + 1 & \text{if } -1 \le x < 1 \\ -x + 1 & \text{if } 1 \le x < 2 \\ -1 & \text{if } x > 2 \end{cases}$$

The points in the domain of f at which f is continuous are

A $(-1, 1), (1, \infty)$ **B** $[-1, 1), (1, \infty)$ **C** $(-1, 1), (1, 2), (2, \infty)$

D $[-1, 1), (1, 2), (2, \infty)$ **E** $(-1, 2), (2, \infty)$.

Problem 28. Which of the following graphs represents the statement:"f is continuous at $x = a$ and $\lim_{x \to a} f(x) = L$"?

A
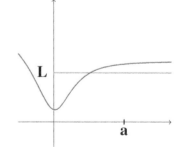

B

C
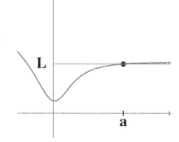

D

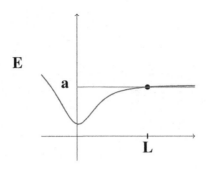

Problem 29. Consider the functions, $f(x) = \sin\left(\frac{1}{x}\right)$, $x \neq 0$, and $g(x) = x\sin\left(\frac{1}{x}\right)$, $x \neq 0$. Which of the following describes the behavior of f and g as $x \to 0$?

A $\lim_{x\to 0} f(x) = 0$ and $\lim_{x\to 0} g(x) = 0$.

B $\lim_{x\to 0} f(x)$ and $\lim_{x\to 0} g(x)$ do not exist.

C $\lim_{x\to 0} f(x) = 0$ and $\lim_{x\to 0} g(x)$ does not exist.

D $\lim_{x\to 0} f(x)$ does not exist and $\lim_{x\to 0} g(x) = 0$.

E $\lim_{x\to 0} f(x) = \infty$ and $\lim_{x\to 0} g(x) = 0$.

Problem 30. The curve $16y^2 + 32y - 4x^2 - 24x = 84$ determines

A an ellipse   **B** a parabola   **C** an y – directed hyperbola

D an x – directed hyperbola   **E** empty curve.

Free Response Questions, Part IIA

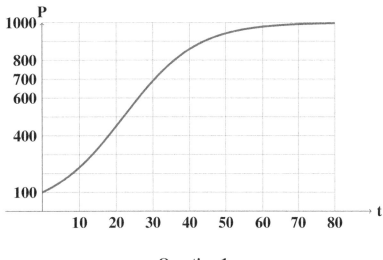

Question 1.

The graph pictured above shows a function $P = f(t)$, where P is the population of a group of rabbits in some forest after t months.

a. Estimate $f(30)$ and explain what this quantity represents in the context of this problem.

b. For $h = 10$ estimate

$$\frac{f(30 + h) - f(30)}{h}$$

and explain what this quantity represents in the context of this problem.

c. Estimate the average rate of change of the rabbit population during the first 30 months. Include appropriate units with your answer.

d. What is the rabbit population in the long run?

Question 2.

The function $f(x)$ is given by the formula

$$f(x) = \frac{4x^2 - 5x}{x^3 + 1}.$$

a. Determine the number of x-intercepts of the graph $y = f(x)$.

b. Find the y-intercept of the graph $y = f(x)$.

c. List all asymptotes of the graph $y = f(x)$.

d. Sketch an approximate graph of $y = f(x)$.

Question 3.

An airplane traveling at speed of 820 km/h encounters a slight headwind that slows it to 780 km/h. In few minutes, the headwind eases and the plane's speed increases to 800 km/h.

a State the Intermediate Value Theorem.

b Explain why the plane's speed is $790 km/h$ at least twice during the flight.

c State the definition of a strictly increasing function.

d Show that the equation $x^3 + x^2 - x - 2 = 0$ has only one real root.

Question 4.

The functions $y = f(x)$ and $y = g(x)$ are given by their graphs plotted below

y = f(x)	**y = g(x)**
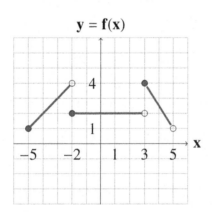	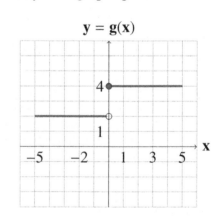

a. Find the ranges of $f(x)$ and $g(x)$.

b. Determine the set of all points of non-removable discontinuity for the function $f(x)$.

c. Write a piece-wise formula for the function $y = f(x)$.

d. Plot the graph of $f(g(x))$.

Midterm I, Solutions

Problem 1. Solution: The case **C** is not possible since the function in **C** is not defined at $x = 0$. The case **E** must be excluded since the function in **E** is not defined at $x = -1$. The function in **D** is odd. The graph plotted above is not symmetric with respect to the origin. Therefore, we also exclude **D**. We exclude **A** since the function $y = xe^x$ increases on $(0, +\infty)$. **Answer: B**

Problem 2. Solution: Since

$$\lim_{x \to \pm\infty} \frac{x^2}{4 - x^2} = \lim_{x \to \pm\infty} \frac{1}{\dfrac{4}{x^2} - 1} = -1,$$

the graph has only one horizontal asymptote $y = -1$. The function is unbounded about $x = \pm 2$ and

$$\lim_{x \to -2^-} \frac{x^2}{4 - x^2} = -\infty \qquad \lim_{x \to 2^-} \frac{x^2}{4 - x^2} = +\infty$$

$$\lim_{x \to -2^+} \frac{x^2}{4 - x^2} = +\infty \qquad \lim_{x \to 2^+} \frac{x^2}{4 - x^2} = -\infty$$

implying that the lines $x = -2$ and $x = 2$ are vertical asymptotes.

Answer: E

Problem 3. Solution: Let us recall the definition of the limit $\lim_{x \to x_0} f(x) = L$ of a function $y = f(x)$ defined on an open interval about x_0:

For every number $\varepsilon > 0$ there is $\delta = \delta(\varepsilon)$ such that for all x,

$$0 < |x - x_0| \Rightarrow |f(x) - L| < \varepsilon.$$

It is assumed in this definition that $f(x)$ must be defined on some interval about a except possibly at a itself. This restriction is made, since in Calculus limits are mostly used to find the slope of the tangent at $x = a$ as the limit of slopes of secants. To run this process it is necessary that $f(x)$ be defined in some interval

229

$(a - \delta, a + \delta)$. In our case $f(x)$ is not defined about $x = 2$. Therefore, the limit does not exist. **Answer: E**

Problem 4. Solution: Let x be the number of months elapsed since January 1. Let $y = y(x)$ be the price of a bottle in cents at x. Since the rate of change of y is constant, the function $y = y(x)$ must be linear, implying that its graph is a straight line. Since the price y increases by 2 each time x increases by 1, the slope of the line must be 2. The fact that the price was 156 cents ($1.56) in November 1, which is 10 months later of January 1, implies that this line passes through $(10, 156)$. By the point-slope equation

$$y - y_0 = m(x - x_0)$$

with $m = 2$, $x_0 = 10$, $y_0 = 156$. Hence

$$y - 156 = 2(x - 10) \quad \text{or} \quad y = 2x + 136.$$

Notice that the y intercept is $(0, 136)$, which implies that the price of soda at the beginning of the year was $1.36 per bottle. **Answer: A**

Problem 5. Solution: Since

$$\lim_{x \to 3^-} f(x) = 2 = \lim_{x \to 3^+} f(x),$$

the limit of $f(x)$ exists and equals 2. **Answer: B**

Problem 6. Solution: Since $x^{-2/3}$ is defined for every real number $x \neq 0$ and $(x - 2)^{-1/3}$ is defined for every $x \neq 2$, the correct answer is **Answer: E**

Problem 7. Solution: Given a real number y, the equation $y = 5\cos(2x - \pi) + 3$ in x has a solution if and only if

$$-1 \leq \frac{y - 3}{5} = \cos(2x - \pi) \leq 1 \Leftrightarrow -5 \leq y - 3 \leq 5 \Leftrightarrow -2 \leq y \leq 8.$$

Answer: D

Problem 8. Solution:

$$\begin{cases} \log_{\frac{1}{2}} 2 & = \frac{1}{\log_2 \frac{1}{2}} = -1 \\ \log_{\frac{1}{\sqrt{2}}} 2 & = \frac{1}{\log_2 2^{-1/2}} = -2 \end{cases} \Rightarrow \text{A is wrong!}$$

$$\begin{cases} \log_{\frac{1}{2}} 2 & = \frac{1}{\log_2 \frac{1}{2}} = -1 \\ \log_{\frac{1}{2}} 4 & = 2\log_{\frac{1}{2}} 2 = 2\frac{1}{\log_2 2^{-1}} = -2 \end{cases} \Rightarrow \text{B is true!}$$

$$\log_3(2 + 4) = \log_3 6 < \log_3 2 \cdot 4 = \log_3 2 + \log_3 4 \Rightarrow \text{C is wrong!}$$

$$\log_{\frac{1}{5}}(5\sqrt{5}) = \log_{\frac{1}{5}} 5^{3/2} = \frac{3}{2}\log_{\frac{1}{5}} 5 = -\frac{3}{2} \Rightarrow \textbf{D is wrong!}$$

$$\log_{\frac{1}{2}} 2 - \log_{\frac{1}{2}} 4 = \log_{\frac{1}{2}}\frac{2}{4} = \log_{\frac{1}{2}}\frac{1}{2} = 1 \neq -1 = \log_{\frac{1}{2}} 2 \Rightarrow \textbf{E is wrong!}$$

Answer: B

Problem 9. Solution:

$$s(t) = -16t^2 + 1600t - 75 = -16\left(t^2 - 100t\right) - 75 = -16\left((t-50)^2 - 50^2\right) - 75 =$$
$$-16(t-50)^2 + 16\cdot 50^2 - 75 = 39925 - 16(t-50)^2.$$

Answer: D

Problem 10. Solution: We have

$$\frac{2x+1}{4x+5} = f(g(x)) = \frac{1}{2g(x)+1} \Rightarrow 2g(x) + 1 = \frac{4x+5}{2x+1} \Rightarrow g(x) = \frac{x+2}{2x+1}.$$

Answer: A

Problem 11. Solution: By the properties of logarithms we have

$$\ln x - \ln\left(\frac{1}{x}\right) = \ln x + \ln x = 2\ln x \Rightarrow 2\ln x = 6 \Rightarrow \textbf{x} = \textbf{e}^3.$$

Answer: D

Problem 12. Solution: Let y be a real number. Then the equation

$$y = \frac{x}{1-x^2} \Leftrightarrow yx^2 + x - y = 0$$

has a unique solution $x = 0$ if $y = 0$ and has two solutions if $y \neq 0$:

$$x_1 = \frac{-1+\sqrt{1+4y^2}}{2y}, \quad x_2 = \frac{-1-\sqrt{1+4y^2}}{2y}.$$

The solution x_2 satisfies

$$|x_2| = \frac{1+\sqrt{1+4y^2}}{2|y|} > \frac{\sqrt{1+4y^2}}{2|y|} > \frac{\sqrt{4y^2}}{2|y|} = 1,$$

implying that x_2 is not in the domain of $f(x)$. The solution x_1 satisfies

$$|x_1| = \frac{\sqrt{1+4y^2}-1}{2|y|} = \frac{4y^2}{2|y|\sqrt{1+4y^2}+1} = \frac{2|y|}{\sqrt{1+4y^2}+1} < \frac{2|y|}{\sqrt{4y^2}} < 1,$$

implying that x_1 is in the domain of $f(x)$. Since

$$x = \frac{-1 + \sqrt{1 + 4y^2}}{2y} = \frac{4y^2}{2y(1 + \sqrt{1 + 4y^2})} = \frac{2y}{1 + \sqrt{1 + 4y^2}},$$

we obtain after the substitution $x \rightleftarrows y$, that

$$y = \frac{2x}{1 + \sqrt{1 + 4x^2}}$$

is the inverse function for $f(x)$. **Answer: A**

Problem 13. Solution:

$$\frac{\sqrt{x^2 - 2x + 6} - \sqrt{x^2 + 2x - 6}}{x^2 - 4x + 3} = \frac{12 - 4x}{(x^2 - 4x + 3)\left(\sqrt{x^2 - 2x + 6} + \sqrt{x^2 + 2x - 6}\right)} =$$

$$\frac{4(3 - x)}{(x - 1)(x - 3)\left(\sqrt{x^2 - 2x + 6} + \sqrt{x^2 + 2x - 6}\right)} =$$

$$\frac{4}{(1 - x)\left(\sqrt{x^2 - 2x + 6} + \sqrt{x^2 + 2x - 6}\right)} \to \frac{4}{-2\left(\sqrt{3^2 - 2 \cdot 3 + 6} + \sqrt{3^2 + 2 \cdot 3 - 6}\right)} =$$

$$\frac{-2}{6} = -\frac{1}{3}.$$

as $x \to 3$. **Answer: E**

Problem 14. Solution:

$$\frac{\sqrt[3]{x^3 + 2x^4}}{\ln(1 + 2x)} = \frac{x\sqrt[3]{1 + 2x}}{\ln(1 + 2x)} = \frac{\sqrt[3]{1 + 2x}}{2\dfrac{\ln(1 + 2x)}{2x}} \Rightarrow$$

$$\lim_{x \to 0} \frac{\sqrt[3]{x^3 + 2x^4}}{\ln(1 + 2x)} = \frac{\lim_{x \to 0} \sqrt[3]{1 + 2x}}{2\lim_{x \to 0} \dfrac{\ln(1 + 2x)}{2x}} = \frac{1}{2}$$

Answer: D

Problem 15. Solution:

$$\frac{\ln(1 + e^x)}{x} = \frac{\ln(1 + e^x)}{e^x} \cdot \frac{e^x}{x} \Rightarrow \lim_{x \to -\infty} \frac{\ln(1 + e^x)}{x} = \lim_{x \to -\infty} \frac{\ln(1 + e^x)}{e^x} \cdot \lim_{x \to -\infty} \frac{e^x}{x} =$$

$$\lim_{y = e^x \to 0} \frac{\ln(1 + y)}{y} \cdot \lim_{y = e^x \to 0} y \cdot \lim_{x \to -\infty} \frac{1}{x} = 1 \cdot 0 \cdot 0 = 0.$$

Answer: B

Problem 16. Solution:

$$\frac{1}{x} \ln \sqrt{\frac{1+x}{1-x}} = \frac{\ln(1+x) - \ln(1-x)}{2x} = \frac{\ln(1+x)}{2x} + \frac{\ln(1-x)}{-2x}.$$

It follows that

$$\lim_{x \to 0} \left(\frac{1}{x} \ln \sqrt{\frac{1+x}{1-x}} \right) = \frac{1}{2} \lim_{x \to 0} \frac{\ln(1+x)}{x} + \frac{1}{2} \lim_{x \to 0} \frac{\ln(1-x)}{-x} = \frac{1}{2} \cdot 1 + \frac{1}{2} \cdot 1 = 1.$$

Answer: C

Problem 17. Solution:

$$\frac{1}{1-x} - \frac{3}{1-x^3} = \frac{1}{1-x} \left(\frac{1+x+x^2-3}{1+x+x^2} \right) = \frac{1}{1-x} \frac{x-1+x^2-1}{1+x+x^2} =$$

$$\frac{-1-x-1}{1+x+x^2} x \underset{\to}{\to} 1 = \frac{-3}{3} = -1.$$

Answer: A

Problem 18. Solution:

$$\left(\frac{x^2 - 2x + 3}{x^2 - 3x + 2} \right)^{\frac{2x}{\sin x}} = \exp \left\{ 2 \frac{x}{\sin x} \ln \left(\frac{x^2 - 2x + 3}{x^2 - 3x + 2} \right) \right\}.$$

Since

$$\lim_{x \to 0} \frac{x}{\sin x} = 1 \text{ and } \lim_{x \to 0} \frac{x^2 - 2x + 3}{x^2 - 3x + 2} = \frac{3}{2},$$

the limit equals

$$\exp \left\{ 2 \ln \left(\frac{3}{2} \right) \right\} = \frac{9}{4}$$

Answer: C

Problem 19. Solution: For $0 < x < \pi/6$

$$0 < (\sin x)^{\frac{1}{x^2}} = \exp \left\{ \frac{\ln \sin x}{x^2} \right\} \le \exp \left\{ \frac{-\ln 2}{x^2} \right\}.$$

We have:

$$\lim_{x \to 0^+} \frac{-\ln 2}{x^2} = -\infty \Rightarrow \lim_{x \to 0^+} \exp \left\{ \frac{-\ln 2}{x^2} \right\} = 0.$$

By the Sandwich Theorem

$$\lim_{x \to 0^+} (\sin x)^{\frac{1}{x^2}} = 0.$$

Answer: C

Problem 20. Solution:

$$\lim_{x \to 2^-} f(g(x)) = \lim_{x \to 2^-} f(x-3) \overset{y=x-3}{=} \lim_{y \to -1^-} f(y) = \lim_{y \to -1^-} (2y+4) = 2;$$

$$\lim_{x \to 2^+} f(g(x)) = \lim_{x \to 2^+} f(x^2-4) \overset{y=x^2-4}{=} \lim_{y \to 0^+} f(y) = \lim_{y \to 0^+} y^2 = 0.$$

Answer: B

Problem 21. Solution: Since $f(x)$ is continuous at $x = -1$, we have:

$$\lim_{x \to -1^-} f(x) = \lim_{x \to -1^-} (x^2 + 4x + a) = a - 3 = \lim_{x \to -1^+} f(x) = \lim_{x \to -1^+} (ax+b) = b - a,$$

implying that

$$a - 3 = b - a \Leftrightarrow \mathbf{2a - b = 3}.$$

Since $f(x)$ is continuous at $x = 1$, we have:

$$\lim_{x \to 1^-} f(x) = \lim_{x \to 1^-} (ax+b) = a + b = \lim_{x \to 1^+} f(x) = \lim_{x \to 1^+} (2bx - 1) = 2b - 1,$$

implying that

$$a + b = 2b - 1 \Leftrightarrow \mathbf{a - b = -1}.$$

Now

$$\begin{cases} 2a - b &= 3 \\ a - b &= -1 \end{cases} \Leftrightarrow \begin{cases} a &= 4 \\ b &= 5 \end{cases}$$

Answer: C

Problem 22. Solution: We evaluate the average rates of decrease during specified intervals of time:

$$\frac{v(10) - v(0)}{10} = \frac{3000 - 6700}{10} = -370$$

$$\frac{v(20) - v(10)}{10} = \frac{1800 - 3000}{10} = -120$$

$$\frac{v(25) - v(15)}{10} = \frac{1200 - 2200}{10} = -100$$

$$\frac{v(35) - v(25)}{10} = \frac{300 - 1200}{10} = -90$$

$$\frac{v(40) - v(30)}{10} = \frac{0 - 600}{10} = -60$$

The least average sped is 60. The correct answer is **Answer: E**

Problem 23. Solution: Since the following limits exist, are finite, and are not equal:

$$\lim_{x \to 1^-} f(x) \neq \lim_{x \to 1^+} f(x),$$

$f(x)$ has a jump discontinuity at $x = 1$, which cannot be removed. Hence **A** and **E** are false. Since $\lim_{x \to 5} f(x) = f(5)$, the function $f(x)$ is continuous at $x = 5$. Hence **B** is false. Since $\lim_{x \to 2^-} f(x) = -\infty$, the point $x = 2$ is not a jump discontinuity. Hence **C** is false and **D** is true. The point $x = 2$ is a point of an essential discontinuity of $f(x)$. **Answer: D**

Problem 24. Solution: Since there is $N = 1$ earthquake of magnitude $M \geq 8$ per year, we obtain

$$0 = \log_{10} 1 = a - 8 \Rightarrow a = 8.$$

It follows that the number N of earthquakes of magnitude $M \geq 7$ per year satisfies

$$\log_{10} N = 8 - 7 \Rightarrow N = 10^1 = 10.$$

Answer: A

Problem 25. Solution:

$$y = x^5 - 1 \Leftrightarrow x^5 = y + 1 \Leftrightarrow x = \sqrt[5]{y+1} \overset{x \leftrightarrows y}{\Leftrightarrow} y = \sqrt[5]{x+1}$$

Answer: E

Problem 26. Solution:

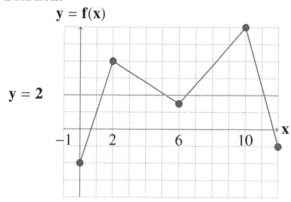

When $k < 2$ then by the Intermediate Value Theorem the equation $f(x) = 2$ has at least 4 roots. The example above shows that it is may be not the case if $k \geq 2$.
Answer: B

Problem 27. Solution: Since $f(t) = t^2 + 1$ function $f(t$ is continuous at every point of $[-1, 1)$ by the Theorem on Algebraic Rules for continuous functions. By the same reason it is continuous at every point of $(1, 2)$ and $(2, +\infty)$. If $t = 1$ then

$$\lim_{t\to 1^-} f(t) = \lim_{t\to 1^-}(t^2 + 1) = 2 \neq 0 = \lim_{t\to 1^+}(-t + 1) = \lim_{t\to 1^+} f(t),$$

implying that $f(t)$ has a jump discontinuity at $t = 1$. Similarly,

$$\lim_{t\to 2^-} f(t) = \lim_{t\to 2^-}(-t + 1) = -1 = \lim_{t\to 2^+}(-1) = \lim_{t\to 2^+} f(t).$$

However, since $f(x)$ is not defined at $x = 2$ it cannot be continuous at $x = 2$.
Answer: D

Problem 28. Solution: All functions on the graph are continuous implying that $\lim_{x\to a} f(x) = f(a)$. The function in **A** satisfies $f(a) < L$ whereas in **B** it satisfies $f(a) > L$. In **C** the point **a** is placed on the vertical axis but even if we consider it on the horizontal axis we see that $L > f(a)$. In **E** again $f(a) < L$. The correct picture is **D**. **Answer: D**

Problem 29. Solution: We observe first that the limit $\lim_{x\to 0} f(x)$ does not exist since $f(x) = 0$ at points $1/\pi n$ and $f(x) = 1$ at points $1/(0.5\pi + 2\pi n)$ for every positive integer n. Therefore, $f(x)$ takes both values 0 and 1 in any interval $(-\delta, +\delta)$. It follows that if we take $\epsilon = 0.1$, for instance, then the box with horizontal side $(-\delta, +\delta)$ and the vertical side $(L - 0.1, L + 0.1)$ cannot contain the graph of $y = f(x)$ whatever L is taken. Notice that the distance between 0 and 1 is 1 and the vertical length of the box is 0.2. This observation eliminate all cases except for **D** and **B**. Since

$$-|x| \leq g(x) \leq |x| \text{ and } \lim_{x\to 0} |x| = 0,$$

we conclude by the Sandwich Theorem that $\lim_{x\to 0} g(x) = 0$ implying **D**. **Answer: D**

Problem 30. Solution: Since

$$0 = 16y^2 + 32y - 4x^2 - 24x - 84 = 16(y^2 + 2y) - 4(x^2 + 2 \cdot 3 \cdot x) - 84 =$$
$$16(y^2 + 2y + 1) - 16 - 4(x^2 + 2 \cdot 3 \cdot x + 9) + 4 \cdot 9 - 84 =$$
$$16(y + 1)^2 - 4(x + 3)^2 - 64 \Rightarrow \boxed{\frac{(y + 1)^2}{2^2} - \frac{(x + 3)^2}{4^2} = 1}.$$

the curve is a hyperbola centered at $(-3, -1)$. Its standard equation is

$$\frac{y^2}{2^2} - \frac{x^2}{4^2} = 1 \Rightarrow y = \pm\frac{2}{4}\sqrt{x^2 + 16}.$$

The asymptotes of the hyperbola are $y = \pm 0.5x$. As it is clear from the formula the graph of the parabola in the upper half-plane is placed above both asymptotes $y = \pm 0.5x$. It follows that the axis of the hyperbola is parallel to the y axis.
Answer: C.

Question 1. Solution:

a.

$$f(30) \approx 690 \text{ rabbits live in the forest.}$$

b.

$$\frac{f(30+10) - f(30)}{10} \approx \frac{860 - 690}{10} = 17 \text{ rabbits per month}$$

is the average rate of increase of rabbit's population between the 30th and 40th months.

c.

$$\frac{f(30) - f(0)}{30} \approx \frac{690 - 100}{30} \approx 19.7 \text{ rabbits per month}$$

d. The level $L = 1000$ is the horizontal asymptote for the graph of $P = P(t)$. Hence $\lim_{t \to +\infty} P(t) = 1000$.

Question 2. Solution:

a. A point c is an x-intercept of the graph $y = f(x)$ if and only if $x = c$ is a zero of the polynomial $p(x) = 4x^2 - 5x = 4x(x - 5/4)$. It follows that there are only two x-intercepts of the graph $y = f(x)$ at $x = 0$ and $x = 5/4$.

b. $f(0) = 0$, implying that there is only one y-intercept of the graph $y = f(x)$ at $y = 0$.

c. Since

$$\lim_{x \to \infty} \frac{4x^2 - 5x}{x^3 + 1} = 0,$$

we see that $y = 0$ is a horizontal asymptote for the graph of $y = f(x)$. For big positive values of x the graph of $y = f(x)$ is placed **above** the asymptote and for $x \to -\infty$ it is placed **below**. There is also one vertical asymptotes $x = -1$. We have

$$\lim_{x \to -1^+} f(x) = \lim_{x \to -1^+} \frac{4x^2 - 5x}{x^3 + 1} = \frac{4 \cdot (-1)^2 - 5 \cdot (-1)}{\lim_{x \to -1^+}(x^3 + 1)} = +\infty;$$

$$\lim_{x \to -1^-} f(x) = \lim_{x \to -1^-} \frac{4x^2 - 5x}{x^3 + 1} = \frac{4 \cdot (-1)^2 - 5 \cdot (-1)}{\lim_{x \to -1^-}(x^3 + 1)} = -\infty;$$

d Using asymptotes, x- and y-intercepts we first plot the graph about the points of x-intercepts, about ∞, and about $x = -1$, the vertical asymptote of the graph. Then using the principle **Simple Formula $\Rightarrow$ Simple Graph** we connect the curves obtained by a smooth line.

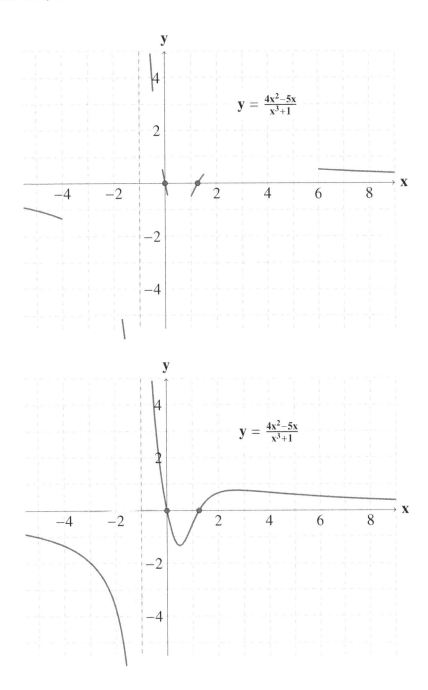

$$y = \frac{4x^2 - 5x}{x^3 + 1}$$

$$y = \frac{4x^2 - 5x}{x^3 + 1}$$

Question 3. Solution:

a The Intermediate Value Theorem

Let f be a continuous function on a closed interval $[a, b]$ and $f(a) \neq f(b)$. If y is any number between $f(a)$ and $f(b)$, then there is at least one number c in the open interval (a, b) such that $f(c) = y$.

b Let $v(t)$ be the speed of the airplane as a function of time t, t_1 be any moment when the speed of the airplane equals $820\,km/h$, $t_2 > t_1$ be any moment when the speed of the airplane equals $780\,km/h$, and $t_3 > t_2$ be any moment when the speed of the airplane equals $800\,km/h$. Since $780 < 790 < 820$, the Intermediate Value Theorem guarantees that $f(c_1) = 790$ for some c_1, $t_1 < c_1 < t_2$. Since $780 < 790 < 800$, by the Intermediate Value Theorem there is c_2, $t_2 < c_2 < t_3$ such that $f(c_2) = 790$.

c Definition

A function f is strictly increasing on an interval I, if, for any choice of x_1 and x_2 in I, with $x_1 < x_2$, we have $f(x_1) < f(x_2)$.

d The function

$$f(x) = x^3 + x^2 - x - 2$$

is continuous on $(-\infty, +\infty)$ by the Algebraic Rules for continuous functions. Since $f(1) = -1$, $f(2) = 8$, the function $f(x)$ must vanish in the open interval $(1, 2)$. Since

$$f(x) = x^2(x + 1) - (x + 1) - 1 = (x + 1)(x^2 - 1) - 1 = (x - 1)(x + 1)^2 - 1,$$

the function $f(x)$ takes only negative values for $x \le 1$. If $x_2 > x_1 > 1$, then

$$f(x_2) - f(x_1) = x_2^3 - x_1^3 + x_2^2 - x_1^2 - (x_2 - x_1) =$$
$$(x_2 - x_1)\left[x_2^2 + x_2 x_1 + x_1^2 + x_1 + (x_2 - 1)\right] > 0,$$

implying that $f(x)$ increases on $[1, +\infty)$. It follows that the equation $f(x) = 0$ has only one root, which is placed in the open interval $(1, 2)$.

Question 4. Solution:

a. The horizontal line test shows that the range of f is $[1, 4]$, and the range of g is $\{2, 4\}$.

b. These are the **jump points**: $x = -2, 3$.

c. The graph of $y = f(x)$ is made of three line segments. The slope of the first is $(4 - 1)/(-2 - (-5)) = 1$, the second line segment is horizontal, the slope of the third is $(1 - 4)/(5 - 3) = -1.5$. Using the point-slope equations, we obtain the formula:

$$f(x) = \begin{cases} x + 6 & \text{if } -5 \le x < -2 \\ 2 & \text{if } -2 \le x < 3 \\ -1.5x + 8.5 & \text{if } 3 \le x < 5 \end{cases}.$$

d.

$$f(g(x)) = \begin{cases} f(4) & \text{if } 0 \le x \\ f(2) & \text{if } x < 0 \end{cases} = \begin{cases} 2.5 & \text{if } 0 \le x \\ 2 & \text{if } x < 0 \end{cases}$$

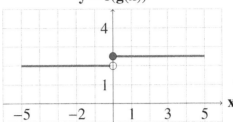

y = f(g(x))

MidTerm
The Table.

N	CL	N	CL
1	B	24	A
2	E	25	E
3	E	26	B
4	A	27	D
5	B	28	D
6	E	29	D
7	D	30	C
8	B	31	♠
9	D	32	♠
10	A	33	♠
11	D	34	♠
12	A	35	♠
13	E	36	♠
14	D	37	♠
15	B	38	♠
16	C	39	♠
17	A	40	♠
18	C	41	♠
19	C	42	♠
20	B	43	♠
21	C	44	♠
22	E	45	♠
23	D		

Mock Exam 1

Section IA, 30 questions, 60 min, No Calculators

Problem 1. What is
$$\lim_{x \to 1} \left(\frac{1}{1-x} - \frac{3}{1-x^3} \right)?$$
(A) -2 (B) -3 (C) 0,   (D) -1 (E) **the limit does not exist.**

Problem 2. If $f(x) = e^x - e^{1/x}$, then $f'(x) =$

(A) $e^x + \dfrac{e^{1/x}}{x^2}$ (B) $xe^x + e^{-1/x}$ **C** $e^x - e^{1/x}$

(D) $e^x - \dfrac{e^{1/x}}{x^2}$ (E) $e^x + e^{-1/x}$.

Problem 3. The function
$$f(x) = x^2 - e^{-3x}$$

is invertible on $(-\infty, +\infty)$. Give the slope of the normal line to the graph of f^{-1} at $x = -1$.

(A) $-\dfrac{1}{3}$ (B) -6 (C) $\dfrac{1}{3}$ (D) 3 (E) -3

Problem 4. Determine
$$\lim_{x \to \infty} x^2 \cdot \sin^2\left(\frac{2}{x} \right).$$

(A) 2 (B) 4 (C) 16 (D) $\dfrac{1}{2}$ (E) **Does not exists.**

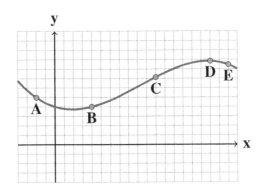

Problem 5. At which of the five points on the above graph are dy/dx and d^2y/dx^2 of opposite sign?

(**A**) A (**B**) B (**C**) C (**D**) D (**E**) E.

Problem 6. A curve has the property that the slope of the tangent at any its point (x, y) equals $2x + 3$. Find the equation of the curve if it is known that it passes through $(1, 2)$.

(**A**) $y = 5x - 3$ (**B**) $y = x^2 + 1$ (**C**) $y = x^2 + 3x$

(**D**) $y = x^2 + 3x - 2$ (**E**) $y = x^2 + 3x - 3$

Problem 7. The graph of $f'(x)$ the **derivative** of f, is shown below. At which values of x does the graph of $y = f(x)$ have points of inflection?

(**A**) x_1 and x_3 (**B**) x_2 and x_5 (**C**) x_1 and x_2 (**D**) x_4 (**E**) x_2, x_4 and x_5

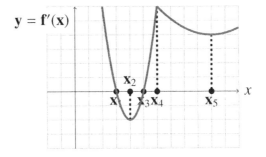

$$y = \mathbf{f}(\mathbf{x})$$

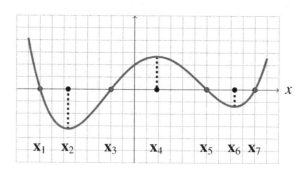

$x_1 \quad x_2 \qquad x_3 \qquad x_4 \qquad x_5 \quad x_6 \; x_7$

Problem 8. The graph of $y = f(x)$ is shown above. Determine the zeros of the derivative $f'(x)$.

(A) x_1, x_3, x_5, x_7 (B) x_1, x_3, x_4 (C) x_4, x_6 (D) x_2, x_4, x_6 (E) x_2, x_3

Problem 9. Which of the following statements about the function given by $f(x) = x^4 - 2x^3$ is true?

A f has no relative extremum.

B The graph of f has one point of inflection and f has two relative extremal points.

C The graph of f has two point of inflection and f has one relative extremum.

D The graph of f has two points of inflection and f has two relative extremal points.

E The graph of f has two points of inflection and f has three relative extremal points.

Problem 10. The function

$$f(x) = \frac{1 + cx^3}{(2x + 3 + 2\sin(x))^3}$$

has a horizontal asymptote $y = 1$ as x approaches $+\infty$. What is the value of c?

(A) 1 (B) 8 (C) 27 (D) 16 (E) $\dfrac{1}{2}$

Problem 11. The position of a particle moving along a line is given by $s(t) = 2t^3 - 24t^2 + 90t + 7$ for $t \geq 0$. For what values of t is the speed of the particle increasing?

(A) $3 < t < 4$ only (B) $t > 4$ only (C) $t > 5$ only

(D) $0 < t < 3$ and $t > 5$ **(E)** $3 < t < 4$ and $t > 5$

Problem 12. A function $f(x)$ is differentiable everywhere. Some of its values are specified in the following table.

x	0.0	0.5	1.0	1.5	2.0	2.5
$f(x)$	1.4	1.5	1.5	1.2	1.1	1.0

Let $g(x) = f(f(x))$. Estimate $g'(1.5)$.

     (A) 1   **(B)** -0.12 **(C)** 0.5   **(D)** 0.24   **(E)** 0.12.

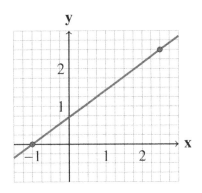

Problem 13. The figure above shows the graph of the **derivative** of f. Given that $f(0) = 1$, find the y-intercept of the tangent to the graph of $y = f(x)$ at $x = -1$.

     (A) $\dfrac{9}{14}$ **(B)** $\dfrac{3}{2}$ **(C)** 1   **(D)** $-\dfrac{1}{14}$ **(E)** $-\dfrac{9}{14}$

Problem 14. The position of a particle moving along the x-axis at time t is given by $x(t) = \cos^2(4\pi t)$. At which of the following values of t the particle changes direction?

     (I) $t = \dfrac{1}{8}$ (II) $t = \dfrac{1}{6}$ (III) $t = 1$ (IV) $t = 2$

   (A) (I), (II) and (III)   **(B)** (I) and (II)   **(C)** (I), (III) and (IV)

     (D) (II), (III) and (IV)   **(E)** (III) and (IV)

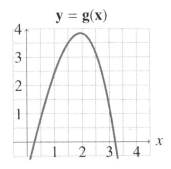

$y = g(x)$

Problem 15.   The graph of $y = g(x)$ is shown above. Which of the graphs pictured below is a possible graph of **$y = g'(\mathbf{x})$**?

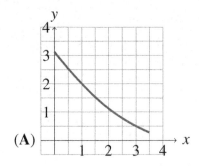

(A)

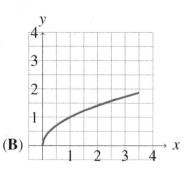

(B)

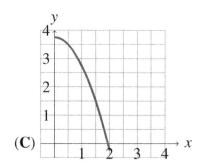

(C)

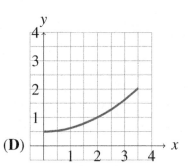

(D)

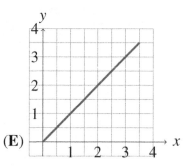

(E)

Problem 16. Select the **TRUE** statement associated with the function

$$f(x) = \frac{\sin(x)}{x^2}$$

A The graph of f is symmetric about the x-axis.

B The function f does not have a horizontal asymptote.

C The graph of f passes through the origin.

D The graph of f is always concave up.

E The function f has a vertical asymptote at $x = 0$.

(**A**) *A*   (**B**) *B*   (**C**) *C*   (**D**) *D*   (**E**) *E*.

Problem 17. The slope of the tangent to the curve $y^3 x + y^2 x^2 = 6$ at $(2, 1)$ is

(**A**) $-\dfrac{3}{2}$ (**B**) $-\dfrac{5}{14}$ (**C**) $-\dfrac{2}{3}$ (**D**) $\dfrac{14}{5}$ (**E**) 0

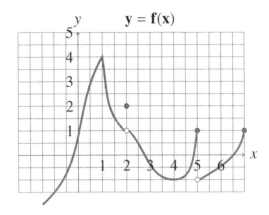

Problem 18. The graph of a function f is shown above. If $\lim_{x \to b} f(x)$ exists and f is not continuous at b, then $b =$

(**A**) 7   (**B**) 5   (**C**) 1   (**D**) 2   (**E**) 0

x	2.2	2.3	2.4	2.5
$f(x)$	3.14	3.32	3.48	3.63

Problem 19. Let f be a function such that $f''(x) < 0$ for all x in the closed interval $[2, 3]$. Selected values of f are shown in the table above. Which of the following holds for $f'(2.4)$?

(**A**) $f'(2.4) < 0$ (**B**) $0 < f'(2.4) < 1.5$ (**C**) $1.5 < f'(2.4) < 1.6$

(**D**) $1.6 < f'(2.4) < 1.8$ (**E**) $f'(2.4) > 1.8$

Problem 20. Find the angle at which the rates of change of sine and cosine are the same.

(**A**) $\pi \cdot n$ (**B**) $2\pi \cdot n$ (**C**) $\dfrac{\pi}{4} \cdot (4n - 1)$ (**D**) $\pi \cdot (2n - 1)$ (**E**) does not exist

Problem 21. The graph of the **derivative** of f is shown below.

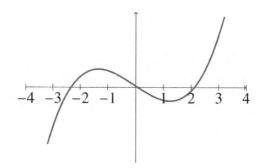

Give the number of values of x in the interval $[-3, 3]$ where the graph of f has inflection.

(A) 1   (B) 2   (C) 0   (D) 3   (E) 4

Problem 22.   A toll road has $25,000$ cars per day in average. The charge is $0.50 per car. According to a research made every $0.05 increase in the toll reduces the number of cars passed by 250. Find the toll which maximizes the revenue.

(A) $0.50   (B) $1.59   (C) $2.95   (D) $3   (E) $2.75

Problem 23.   A differentiable function f satisfies the conditions $f(5) = 2$ and $f'(5) = 1$. Using linearization estimate $f(4.9)$.

(A) 2.2   (B) 1.9   (C) 3.4   (D) 3.8   (E) 4.6

Problem 24.   Find the derivative of $g(x) = 5\sin^2(6x) + 5\cos^2(6x)$ in x.

(A) $30\cos^2(6x) - 30\sin^2(6x)$ (B) $5\cos^2(6x) - 5\sin^2(6x)$ (C) $120\sin(6x)\cos(6x)$

(D) 30   (D) 0

Problem 25.   A company's revenue $R(x)$ from the sale of its product and the cost $C(x)$ of its production are given by formulas:

$$R(x) = 60x - \frac{x^2}{25000}, \quad C(x) = 10 + 0.5x,$$

where x is the number of gallons of the product produced each week and both $R(x)$, $C(x)$ are measured in dollars. The production increases 50 gallons per week. Find the rate of change of the company's profit when the production level is $x = 100$.

(A) 2 974.60   (B) 2 000   (C) 2 489.40   (D) 69.59   (E) 1 865.10

Problem 26. A particle moves along the x-axis as described by $2t^3 - 3t^2$. Find the acceleration of the particle at the time when the velocity has local minimum.

$$(A) -1 \quad (B) 0 \quad (C) -2 \quad (D) 1 \quad (E) 1.1$$

Problem 27. The derivative of $f(x) = x^{-x}$ equals:

$$(A) -xx^{-x} - x^{-x}\ln(x) \quad (B) -xx^{-x-1} + x^{-x}\ln(x) \quad (C) -xx^{-x-1} - x^{-x}\ln(x)$$

$$(D) xx^{-x-1} + x^{-x}\ln(x) \quad (E) -xx^{-x-1}$$

Problem 28. Determine

$$\lim_{x \to 0} \frac{7x - \sin x}{x^2 + \sin(3x)} =$$

$$(A) 6 \quad (B) 2 \quad (C) 1 \quad (D) \frac{3}{2} \quad E\ 0$$

Problem 29. If $f(x) = \sin(\ln(2x))$, then $f'(x) =$

$$(A) \frac{\sin(\ln(2x))}{2x} \quad (B) \frac{\cos(\ln(2x))}{x} \quad (C) \frac{\cos(\ln(2x))}{2x}$$

$$(D) \frac{\sin(\ln(2x))}{x} \quad (E) \cos\left(\frac{1}{2x}\right)$$

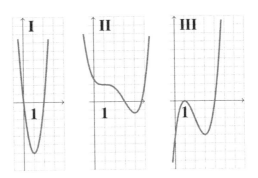

Problem 30. Three graphs labelled I, II, and III are shown above. One is the graph of f, one is the graph of f', and one is the graph of f''. Which of the following correctly identifies each of the three graphs?

	(A)	(B)	(C)	(D)	(E)
f	I	II	II	III	III
f'	II	I	III	I	II
f''	III	III	I	II	I

Section IB, 15 questions, 45 min, calculators are allowed

Problem 76. Let f be a function differentiable on $(0, +\infty)$. If

$$f'(x) = 1 + \ln\left(x + \sqrt{1 + x^2}\right)$$

on $(0, +\infty)$ and $f(1.1) = 1$, then what is an approximate value of $f(1)$ obtained by the linear approximation centered at 1.1? Is this value smaller or greater than $f(1)$?

(A) $0.808 > f(1)$ (B) $0.901 < f(1)$ (C) $0.808 < f(1)$

(D) $0.805 > f(1)$ (E) $0.7 > f(1)$

Problem 77. Find the minimal value of the function $f(x) = 3x^3 - 5x + 9$ for $x \ge 0$.

(A) 6.515 (B) 2.368 (C) 3.258 (D) 4.175 (E) -2.349

Problem 78. The height h, in meters, of an object at time t is given by

$$h(t) = 24t + 24t^{3/2} - 16t^2.$$

What is the height (in meters) of the object at the instant when it reaches its maximum upward velocity?

(A) 2.545 (B) 10.263 (C) 34.125 (D) 54.889 (E) 89.005

Problem 79. Let f be the function defined by $f(x) = x + \ln x$. What is the value of c for which the instantaneous rate of change of f at $x = c$ is the same as the average rate of change of f over $[1, 4]$?

(A) 0.456 (B) 1.244 (C) 2.164 (D) 2.342 (E) 2.452

Use the graph shown below to solve two following problems.

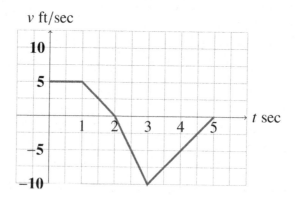

Problem 80. The object attains its maximum speed when $t =$

(A) 0 (B) 1 (C) 2 (D) 3 (E) 5

Problem 81. During $2 < t < 3$ the object's acceleration (in ft/sec^2) is

(A) -10 (B) -5 (C) 0 (D) 5 (E) 10

Problem 82. The derivative of the function f is given by

$$f'(x) = -\frac{x}{3} + \cos\left(x^2\right).$$

At what values of x does f have a relative minimum on the interval $0 < x < 3$?

(A) 1.094 and 2.608 (B) 1.798 (C) 2.372 (D) 2.493 (E) 2.608

Problem 83. Let f be the function given by $f(x) = x^2 - 2x + 3$. The tangent line to the graph of f at $x = 1$ is used to approximate values of $f(x)$. Which of the following is the greatest value of x for which the error resulting from this tangent line approximation is less than 0.1?

A 1.32 B 1.51 C 1.21 D 1.71 E 1.81

Problem 84. The function f is differentiable on the interval $[0, 1]$ and $g(x) = f(3x)$. The table below gives some values of f:

x	0.1	0.2	0.3	0.4	0.5	0.6
$f(x)$	1.01	1.042	1.180	1.298	1.486	1.573

What is the approximate value of $g'(0.1)$

A 2.21 B 3.84 C 4.14 D 3.54 E 5.64

Problem 85. The **derivative** of f is graphed below.

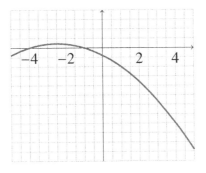

Give a value of x where f has a local maximum.

A 1   **B** no value   **C** $-\dfrac{5}{2}$ **D** -1 **(E)** -4

Problem 86. A rectangle has both a changing height and a changing width, but the height and width change so that area of the rectangle is always 300 square feet. Give the rate of change of the width (in ft/sec) when the height is 11 feet, if the height is decreasing at that moment at the rate of $11/10\, ft/sec$.

(A) $\dfrac{-30}{11}$ **(B)** $\dfrac{30}{11}$ **(C)** $\dfrac{11}{300}$ **(D)** $\dfrac{11}{400}$ **(E)** 311

Problem 87. A thin metal cable has length $L = 10$ cm when the temperature is $T = 20°C$. Estimate the change in length in cm when T rises to $22°C$ assuming that
$$\frac{dL}{dT} = kL,$$
where the coefficient k of thermal expansion equals 1.7×10^{-5}.

(A) 6.12×10^{-4} **(B)** 2×10^{-4} **(C)** 3.4×10^{-4} **(D)** 2×10^{-5} **(E)** 0.006

Problem 88. A study shows that the concentration $C(t)$ (in micrograms per milliliter) of antibiotic in a patient's blood serum after t hours is
$$C(t) = 120(e^{-0.1t} - e^{-bt}),$$
where $b \geq 1$ is a constant depends on the particular combination of antibiotic agents used. Solve numerically for the value of b (to two decimal places) for which maximum concentration occurs at $t = 1$ hour.

(A) 2.86   **(B)** 3.2   **(C)** 1.97   **(D)** 0.1   **(E)** 3.71495

Problem 89. The temperature, in degrees Fahrenheit ($°F$), of water in a pond is modeled by the function H, given by
$$H(t) = 55 - 9\cos\left(\frac{2\pi}{365}(t + 10)\right),$$
where t is the number of days since January 1 ($t = 0$). What is the instantaneous rate of change of the temperature of the water at time $t = 90$ days?

(A) $0.114°F/day$ **(B)** $0.153°F/day$ **(C)** $50.252°F/day$

(**D**) $56.350°\text{F/day}$ (**E**) $-0.114°\text{F/day}$

Problem 90. The second derivative of a function g given by

$$g''(x) = 2^{-x^2} + \cos x + x.$$

For $-5 < x < 5$, on what open intervals is the graph of g concave up?

(**A**) $-5 < x < -1.016$ only (**B**) $-1.016 < x < 5$ only

(**C**) $0.463 < x < 2.100$ only

(**D**) $-5 < x < 0.463$ and $2.100 < x < 5$ (**E**) do not exist

IIB, 2 questions, 45 min, calculators are allowed

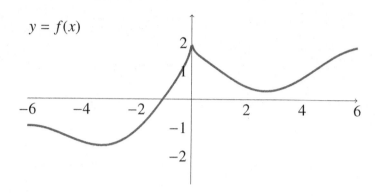

$y = f(x)$

Problem 1. The graph of
$$f(x) = \frac{x + 2\cos x}{1 + \sqrt[3]{x^2}}$$
is shown above. The function $y = g(x)$ satisfies $g'(x) = f(x)$ for every x and $g(0) = 2$.

(a) 3pts Write the equation of the tangent line to the graph of $y = g(x)$ at $x = 0$.

(b) 3pts Find the x-coordinates of all points of local extremum of $y = g(x)$ on the interval $[-6, 6]$.

(c) 3pts Find the x-coordinates of all points of inflection of the graph of $y = g(x)$ on the interval $[-6, 6]$.

Problem 2.

(a) 3pts Using a calculator, determine an appropriate window, and sketch the graph of
$$f(x) = x^4 + 6x^3 - 24x^2 + 24.$$

(b) 3pts Find all points of local extremum of the function f and indicate them on the graph.

(c) 3pts Find all inflection points of the graph of $y = f(x)$ and indicate them on the graph.

IIA, 4 questions, 60 min, No Calculators are allowed

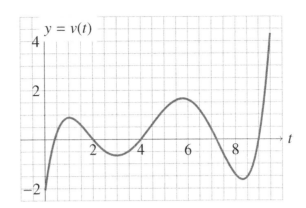

Problem 3. The graph above shows the velocity $v = s'(t)$ of a particle moving along a straight line. The positive direction on the line is to the right.

(a) **2pts** What happens with the particle at time $t = 1$? Is it moving to the left, right, or not moving at all? Justify your answer.

(b) **2pts** Find approximately the moments of time t when the particle is not accelerating and is moving to the right. Justify your answer.

(c) **2pts** Using the graph, determine the number of when the particle is at rest. Justify your answer.

(d) **3pts** Using the graph, estimate the average acceleration when $6 \leq t \leq 8$. Indicate approximately the moment when this average acceleration equals the instant acceleration. Justify your answer.

Problem 4. A car P starts at the very instant when car Q passes it by in the same direction along a straight road. The velocity of P is given by

$$v_P(t) = 5\left(\sqrt{1 + 8t} - 1 \right) \text{ feet per second.}$$

The velocity of Q is shown in the graph below

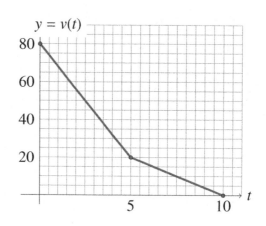

(a) **3pts** Determine the number of moments t, when $v_P(t) = v_Q(t)$. Which of two intervals $(0, 5)$, $(5, 10)$ contains such moments if they exist. Justify your arguments.

(b) **3pts** Determine the average acceleration of car Q for $0 < t < 10$. Is there a moment, when the average acceleration equals the instantaneous acceleration? Justify your arguments.

(c) **3pts** Determine the average acceleration of car P. Find the moment of time when the instantaneous acceleration equals the average acceleration.

Problem 5. A company determines that in t months, $S(t)$ hundred widgets will be sold, where

$$S(t) = \frac{6}{t+1} - \frac{7}{(t+1)^2} + 4.$$

(a) **3pts** Using Calculus, sketch the graph of $S(t)$.

(b) **3pts** When will sales be maximized? What is the maximum level of sales?

(c) **3pts** It is planned to terminate the advertising campaign when the sales rate is minimized. When does this occur? What are the sales level and sales rate at this time?

Problem 6. To stimulate economy, the Parliament adopted a program of unemployment reduction. In t months after the program begins, the number $N(t)$ of thousands of unemployed people is given by the formula:

$$N(t) = -t^3 + 12t^2 + 144t + 1\,024.$$

(a) **5pts** Determine the maximal number of unemployed people. Determine the moment of the greatest level of unemployment.

(b) 4pts To avoid over stimulation of the economy the program must be terminated as soon as the rate of unemployment begins to decline. Evaluate this moment of time. Determine the number of unemployed people at this moment.

Mock I, Solutions

Problem 1. Solution: We have

$$\frac{1}{1-x} - \frac{3}{1-x^3} = \frac{1}{1-x}\left(1 - \frac{3}{1+x+x^2}\right) = \frac{1+x+x^2-3}{(1-x)(1+x+x^2)} =$$
$$\frac{(x-1)+x^2-1}{(1-x)(1+x+x^2)} = -\frac{1+x+1}{1+x+x^2} \xrightarrow[x\to 1]{} -1$$

Answer: D.

Problem 2. Solution: By the Chain Rule

$$f'(x) = \frac{df}{dx} = e^x - e^{1/x}\frac{d\left(\frac{1}{x}\right)}{dx} = e^x + \frac{e^{1/x}}{x^2}.$$

Answer: A.

Problem 3. Solution: We have $f(0) = -1$ implying that $f^{-1}(-1) = 0$. By the formula for the derivative of the inverse function

$$x = f\left(f^{-1}(x)\right) \Rightarrow 1 = f'\left(f^{-1}(x)\right) \cdot \left(f^{-1}\right)'(x) \Rightarrow \left(\mathbf{f^{-1}}\right)'(\mathbf{x}) = \frac{1}{\mathbf{f'\left(f^{-1}(x)\right)}}.$$

Then the slope of the tangent line is

$$k = \left(f^{-1}\right)'(-1) = \frac{1}{f'(0)} = \frac{1}{\left.(2x+3e^{-3x})\right|_{x=0}} = \frac{1}{3}.$$

So, the slope of the tangent k is $1/3$. Since $k \cdot k_1 = -1$, we obtain that $k_1 = -3$. It follows that the slope of the normal is -3.

Answer: E.

259

Problem 4. Solution:

$$\lim_{x \to \infty} x^2 \cdot \sin^2\left(\frac{2}{x}\right) = \lim_{x \to \infty} 4 \frac{\sin^2\left(\frac{2}{x}\right)}{\left(\frac{2}{x}\right)^2} \overset{y=1/x}{=} 4 \lim_{y \to 0} \left(\frac{\sin(y)}{y}\right)^2 = 4.$$

Answer: B.

Problem 5. Solution: We have $dy/dx = 0$ at D, since it is a point of local maximum, $d^2y/dx^2 = 0$ at C, since it is an inflection point. We have $dy/dx > 0$ and $d^2y/dx^2 > 0$ at B, since the function $y = y(x)$ increases and is concave up about B. We have $dy/dx < 0$ and $d^2y/dx^2 < 0$ at E, since the function $y = y(x)$ decreases and is concave down about E. Finally, $dy/dx < 0$ about A, since the function $y = y(x)$ decreases about A, and $d^2y/dx^2 > 0$ at A, since the graph of $y = y(x)$ is concave up about A. **Answer: A.**

Problem 6. Solution: Let $y = f(x)$ be the function which defines this curve. Since

$$\frac{d(x^2 + 3x)}{dx} = 2x + 3,$$

we conclude that $f(x) = x^2 + 3x + C$, where C is a constant. Since $f(1) = 2$, we obtain that

$$2 = f(1) = 1^2 + 3 \cdot 1 + C \Rightarrow C = -2.$$

Answer: D.

Problem 7. Solution: A point $x = a$ is an inflection point of the graph of $y = f(x)$ if the graph changes the direction of its concavity at this point and the function is continuous at this point. The function $y = f(x)$ being differentiable is continuous at every point indicated. The derivative $y = f'(x)$ decreases ($f''(x) < 0$) on $(0, x_2)$, (x_4, x_5), and increases ($f''(x) > 0$) on (x_2, x_4), $x > x_5$. It follows that the points of inflections are x_2, x_4, x_5. **Answer: E.**

Problem 8. Solution: The derivative vanishes at the points x corresponding to the horizontal tangent. These are x_2, x_4, x_6.

Answer: D.

Problem 9. Solution:

$$y = \mathbf{f(x)}$$

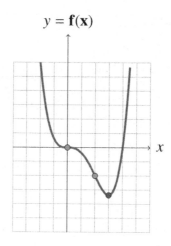

The function $f(x) = x^3(x - 2)$ is positive outside $[0, 2]$ and is negative inside $(0, 2)$. Next, $f'(x) = 2x^2(2x - 3)$, implying that there is a point of minimum at $x = 1.5$. Finally, $f''(x) = 12x(x - 1)$ implying that $f''(x) > 0$ for $x < 0$, $f''(x) < 0$ for $0 < x < 1$. It follows that $x = 0$ is an inflection point. Similarly, $f''(x)$ changes sign when x passes through $x = 1$. Therefore, $x = 1$ is the second inflection point. The point $x = 1.5$ is a unique point of relative extremum. **Answer: C**.

Problem 10. Solution:

$$1 = \lim_{x \to +\infty} \frac{1 + cx^3}{(2x + 3 + 2\sin(x))^3} = \lim_{x \to +\infty} \frac{x^3}{x^3} \frac{c + 1/x^3}{(2 + \frac{3}{x} + \frac{\sin(x)}{x})^3} = \frac{c}{8}.$$

Answer: B.

Problem 11. Solution: The speed is given by the formula:

$$\mathbf{speed} = \left| \frac{ds}{dt} \right| = |6t^2 - 48t + 90| = 6|t^2 - 8t + 15| = 6|t - 3)(t - 5)|.$$

Since the graph of $y = |6(t-3)(t-5)|$ on $(3, 5)$ is a parabola with vertex at $(3+5)/2 = 4$, we obtain that the speed decreases on $(-\infty, 3)$, increases on $(3, 4)$, decreases on $(4, 5)$ and again increases on $(5, +\infty)$.

$$\mathbf{speed} = |ds/dt|$$

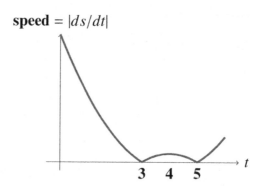

Answer: E.

Problem 12. Solution: By the Chain Rule

$$g'(x) = f'(f(x)) \cdot f'(x) \Rightarrow g'(1.5) = f'(f(1.5)) \cdot f'(1.5) = f'(1.2) \cdot f'(1.5) \approx$$
$$\frac{f(1.5) - f(1)}{1.5 - 1} \cdot \frac{f(2) - f(1)}{2 - 1} = \frac{1.2 - 1.5}{0.5}(1.1 - 1.5) = (-0.6) \cdot (-0.4) = 0.24.$$

Answer: D.

Problem 13. Solution: The slope of the line on the graph is

$$\frac{2.5 - 0}{2.5 - (-1)} = \frac{5}{7}.$$

Since this line intercepts the x-axis at $x = -1$, we conclude that

$$f'(x) = \frac{5}{7}x + \frac{5}{7}.$$

for all values of x. Notice that

$$g(x) = \frac{5}{14}x^2 + \frac{5}{7}x$$

has the same derivative as f on $(-\infty, +\infty)$. By the corollary to Rolle's theorem $f(x) = g(x) + C$ for all x. Since $f(0) = 1$ and $g(0) = 0$, we see that $C = 1$. Hence

$$f(x) = \frac{5}{14}x^2 + \frac{5}{7}x + 1 \Rightarrow f(-1) = \frac{5}{14} - \frac{5}{7} + 1 = \frac{9}{14}.$$

Then the equation of the tangent line to the graph of $y = f(x)$ at $x = -1$ is given by

$$y = f'(-1)(x + 1) + f(-1) = 0 \cdot (x + 1) + \frac{9}{14} = \frac{9}{14}.$$

Therefore, this line intercepts the y-axis at $9/14$. **Answer: A.**

Problem 14. Solution: The derivative

$$\frac{dx}{dt} = -2\cos(4\pi t)\sin(4\pi t)(4\pi) = -4\pi \sin(8\pi t)$$

changes its sign at $t = 1/8$, $t = 1$ and $t = 2$ and it is positive about $t = 1/6$.

Answer: C.

Problem 15. Solution: Since $x = 2$ is a point of local maximum for $y = g(x)$, we see that $g'(2) = 0$. The only graph satisfying this property is **C**.

Answer: (C).

Problem 16. Solution:

$$f(x) = \frac{1}{x} \cdot \frac{\sin(x)}{x}.$$

Since

$$\lim_{x \to 0} \frac{\sin(x)}{x} = 1$$

$f(x)$ behaves like the hyperbola $y = 1/x$ about $x = 0$ implying that $x = 0$ is a vertical asymptote of $f(x)$. Other statements are wrong.

Answer: E.

Problem 17. Solution: The point $(2, 1)$ is on the curve

$$(y^3 x + y^2 x^2)\Big|_{\substack{y=1 \\ x=2}} = 2 + 4 = 6.$$

Differentiating the equation implicitly, we obtain

$$3y^2 y' x + y^3 + 2yy' x^2 + 2y^2 x = 0 \Rightarrow y' = -\frac{y^2(y + 2x)}{yx(3y + 2x)} \Rightarrow$$

$$y'\Big|_{\substack{y=1 \\ x=2}} = -\frac{y^2(y + 2x)}{yx(3y + 2x)}\Big|_{\substack{y=1 \\ x=2}} = -\frac{5}{14}.$$

Answer: B.

Problem 18. Solution: We see that $f(b) \neq \lim_{x \to b} f(x)$ if $b = 2$. The limit does not exist at $b = 5$. All other points are the points of continuity. **Answer: D.**

Problem 19. Solution: Since $f'' < 0$ the function f' decreases. Then by Lagrange's theorem

$$1.5 = \frac{f(2.5) - f(2.4)}{0.1} = f'(c_1) < f'(2.4) < f'(c_2) = \frac{f(2.4) - f(2.3)}{0.1} = 1.6.$$

Answer: C.

Problem 20. Solution: We have

$$\frac{d(\sin x)}{dx} = \cos x = \frac{d(\cos x)}{dx} = -\sin x \Rightarrow \cos x = -\sin x \Leftrightarrow \tan x = -1.$$

Answer: C.

Problem 21. Solution: There are exactly TWO points ($x_1 \approx -1.3$ and $x_2 \approx +1.3$) where f'' changes sign:

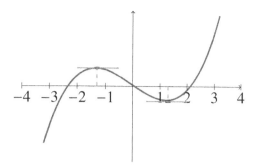

Answer: B.

Problem 22. Solution: If x is the number of five cents increases in the toll, then the number of cars passed decreases by $250x$. The revenue is a function of x:

$$R(x) = (0.50 + 0.05x)(25\,000 - 250x) = 0.05 \cdot 250 \cdot (10 + x)(100 - x) =$$
$$= 12.5(10 + x)(100 - x) = 12.5(1000 + 90x - x^2).$$

It is clear that $R''(x) = -12.5 < 0$. It follows that the maximal revenue is obtained at x satisfying

$$R'(x) = 0 \Leftrightarrow 2x = 90 \Leftrightarrow x = 45.$$

The price in this case is $p = 0.5 + 45 \cdot 0.05 = 2.75$. **Answer: E**.

Problem 23. Solution: The equation of the tangent to the graph of $f(x)$ at the point $(5, 3)$ is

$$y = (x - 5) + 2 \Rightarrow f(4.9) \approx L(4.9) = (4.9 - 5) + 2 = 1.9.$$

Answer: B.

Problem 24. Solution: By the trigonometric identity $g(x) = 5$. The derivative of a constant function is 0.

Answer: E.

Problem 25. Solution: The formula for the profit is:

$$\Pi(x) = R(x) - C(x) = 60x - \frac{x^2}{25000} - 10 - 0.5x = 59.5x - \frac{x^2}{25000} - 10.$$

The number of gallons $x = x(t)$ produced by the company each week depends on time t measured in weeks. Differentiating the above formula in t we obtain :

$$\frac{d\Pi}{dt} = \left(59.5 - \frac{x}{12500}\right)\frac{dx}{dt} = \left(59.5 - \frac{x}{12500}\right) \cdot 50.$$

It follows that

$$\frac{d\Pi}{dt}\bigg|_{x=100} = \left(59.5 - \frac{100}{12500}\right)50 = 59.5 \cdot 50 - 4 = 2\,974.60$$

Answer: A.

Problem 26. Solution: The acceleration is the derivative of the velocity. Therefore, by Fermat's Theorem it must be zero, when the velocity takes its local minimal value. Since $v(t) = 6t^2 - 6t$, the velocity $v(t)$ attaints its local minimum at $t = 0.5$. **Answer: B.**

Problem 27. Solution:

$$\frac{d}{dx}x^{(-x)} = \frac{d}{dx}e^{-x\ln x} = x^{-x}\frac{d}{dx}(-x\ln x) = x^{-x}(-1 - \ln x).$$

Answer: C.

Problem 28. Solution:

$$\lim_{x\to 0}\frac{7x - \sin x}{x^2 + \sin(3x)} = \lim_{x\to 0}\frac{x}{x}\frac{7 - \dfrac{\sin x}{x}}{x + \dfrac{\sin(3x)}{x}} = \lim_{x\to 0}\frac{7 - \dfrac{\sin x}{x}}{x + 3\dfrac{\sin(3x)}{3x}} =$$

$$\frac{7 - \lim_{x\to 0}\dfrac{\sin x}{x}}{\lim_{x\to 0}x + 3\lim_{x\to 0}\dfrac{\sin(3x)}{3x}} = \frac{7 - 1}{0 + 3} = 2$$

Answer: B.

Problem 29. Solution: By the Chain Rule:

$$(\sin(\ln(2x)))' = \cos(\ln(2x))(\ln(2) + \ln x)' = \frac{\cos(\ln(2x))}{x}$$

Answer: B.

Problem 30. Solution: If the graph of f is shown on I, then $f'(x) < 0$ for $x < 1$, which is not the case with II. Since $f'(x) > 0$ for $x > 1$, it is not the case for III. Therefore, I is not the graph of f.

If the graph of f is shown on III, the $f'(x) > 0$ for $x < 1$, which is not the case neither for I nor for II. Therefore, III is not the graph of f.

If the graph of $y = f(x)$ is shown on II, then $f'(1) = 0$, which is the case only if the graph of $y = f'(x)$ is shown on III. There must be an extra zero of $f'(x)$ at $x = 4$, and indeed this is true for III. The intervals, where f increases and decreases are $x > 4$ and $x < 4$ correspond to the intervals of negativity and positivity of the function shown on III. It is clear that then the graph of $y = f''(x)$ is shown on I. This choice obviously agrees with the intervals of concavity of f. So, f is shown on II, f' is shown on III, and f'' is shown on I. **Answer: C.**

Problem 76. Solution: Since

$$f''(x) = \frac{1}{\sqrt{1 + x^2}} > 0,$$

the graph of $y = f(x)$ is concave up. Hence the graph of $y = f(x)$ is placed above any of its tangent. It follows that any linear approximation gives a smaller value. Since

$$f'(1.1) = 1 + \ln(1.1 + \sqrt{1 + 1.1^2}) \approx 1.91092,$$

and $f(1.1) = 1$, we obtain that

$$f(1) \approx L(1) = f'(1.1)(1 - 1.1) + f(1.1) = 1 - 0.191092 \approx 0.80891.$$

Answer: C.

Problem 77. Solution: We have

$$f'(x) = 9x^2 - 5 = 9\left(x^2 - \frac{5}{9}\right), \quad f''(x) = 18x > 0 \Leftrightarrow x > 0.$$

Since $\lim_{x \to +\infty} f(x) = +\infty$, it follows that the minimal value of $f(x)$ on $[0, +\infty)$ is taken at the positive root of the derivative $f'(x)$:

$$x_0 = \frac{\sqrt{5}}{3} = 0.745356\ldots \Rightarrow f(x_0) \approx 6.51548.$$

Answer: A.

Problem 78. Solution: Using a calculator, we first define the functions $h(t)$, $v(t)$, $a(t)$:

$$\text{Define } h(t) = 24 \cdot t + 24 \cdot t^{\frac{3}{2}} - 16 \cdot t^2$$

$$\text{Define } v(t) = \frac{d}{dt}(h(t))$$

$$\text{Define } a(t) = \frac{d}{dt}(v(t)).$$

Using the 'solve' command, we obtain

$$\text{solve}\,(a(t) = 0, t) \Rightarrow t = \frac{81}{256}$$

Using Calculus menu, we evaluate

$$\frac{d}{dt}\,(a(t))\big|_{t=\frac{81}{256}} = \frac{-4096}{81}.$$

This shows that the second derivative of $v(t)$ is negative at the moment $t = 81/256$ and its first derivative $a(t)$ is zero at this moment. Hence the maximal velocity occurs at the moment $t = 81/256$.

$$h\left(\frac{81}{256}\right) = \frac{42039}{4096} \approx 10.2634.$$

Answer: B.

Problem 79. Solution: Using a calculator, we define the function f and find the required average rate of change

$$\text{Define } f(x) = x + \ln(x)$$
$$\frac{f(4) - f(1)}{4 - 1} \Rightarrow \frac{2 \cdot \ln(2) + 3}{3} \approx 1.4621.$$

Using Ctrl + C we copy the answer to the buffer. It is clear that $f'(x) = 1 + 1/x$. Inserting a more accurate value into 'solve' command with Ctrl + V, we find that

$$\text{solve}\left(1 + \frac{1}{x} = 1.4620981203733, x\right) \Rightarrow x = 2.16404$$

Answer: C.

Problem 80. Solution: The maximum of $|v(t)|$ is attained at $t = 3$.

Answer: D.

Problem 81. Solution: The acceleration equals

$$\frac{v(3) - v(2)}{3 - 2} = -10.$$

Answer: A.

Problem 82. Solution: First we define the function $g(x)$ using calculator:

$$\text{Define } g(x) = \frac{-x}{3} + \cos\left(x^2\right).$$

Using calculator, we find the zeros of g by $nSolve(g(x) = 0, x)$. The calculator gives the solution

$$x = -1.9961 \text{ or } x = -1.43914 \text{ or } x = 1.09427 \text{ or } 2.3715 \text{ or } x = 2.60774.$$

Next, we define

$$\text{Define } h(x) = \frac{d}{dx}(g(x)),$$

and evaluate

$$h(2.60774) = -2.91177, \quad h(2.3715) = 2.57158, \quad h(1.09427) = -2.37109.$$

Since

$$f'(2.3715) = g(2.3715) = 0, \text{ and } f''(2.3715) = h(2.3715) = 2.57158 > 0,$$

we conclude by the second derivative test that $x = 2.3715$ is the only point of the local minimum on $(0, 3)$. **Answer: C**.

Problem 83. Solution: We have $f(1) = 2$, $f'(1) = 2(1 - 1) = 0$. It follows that $L(x) = 2$. Observing that $f''(x) = 2 > 0$, we see that the graph of $y = f(x)$ is concave up and therefore is placed above the tangent. Finally,

$$f(x) - L(x) = (x^2 - 2x + 3) - 2 = x^2 - 2x + 1 = (x - 1)^2$$

It follows that

$$(x - 1)^2 < 0.1 \Leftrightarrow |x - 1| < \sqrt{0.1} = 0.316228\ldots \Rightarrow x < 1.32.$$

Answer: A.

Problem 84. Solution: By the Chain Rule $g'(x) = f'(3x) \cdot 3$. Hence $g'(0.1) = 3f'(0.3)$. Now we calculate:

$$3\frac{f(0.3) - f(0.2)}{0.1} = 3\frac{1.180 - 1.042}{0.1} = 4.14,$$

$$3\frac{f(0.4) - f(0.3)}{0.1} = 3\frac{1.298 - 1.180}{0.1} = 3.54.$$

Both results are present in the answers. However a better approximation can be obtained by

$$3\frac{f(0.4) - f(0.2)}{0.2} = 3\frac{1.298 - 1.042}{0.2} = 3.84,$$

which is placed between the two above values. The values in **A** and **E** are too far from the found values. **Answer: B**.

Problem 85. Solution: As it is clear from the graph the derivative f' changes its sign from + to − only at −1. In other words f increases when x increases to −1 and decreases afterwards. **Answer: D.**

Problem 86. Solution: The width $w = w(t)$ and the height $h = h(t)$ are related by the equation $w = 300/h$. Applying the Chain Rule, we obtain:

$$\frac{dw}{dt} = -\frac{300}{h^2}\frac{dh}{dt} \Rightarrow \left.\frac{dw}{dt}\right|_{h=11} = -\frac{300}{11\cdot 11}\cdot\frac{-11}{10} = \frac{30}{11}.$$

Answer: B.

Problem 87. Solution:

$$\Delta L \approx dL = \left.\frac{dL}{dT}dT\right|_{L=10} = \left.kLdT\right|_{L=10} = k\times 10\times(22-20) = 20k = 3.4\times 10^{-4}.$$

Answer: C.

Problem 88. Solution: We have $C(0) = 0$ and $\lim_{t\to+\infty} C(t) = 0$. Since C is continuous it attains its maximal value at some critical point which is a solution to the equation:

$$0 = C'(t) = 120(be^{-bt} - 0.1e^{-0.1t}) \Leftrightarrow 10b = e^{(b-0.1)t}.$$

This equation has a solution $b = 0.1$ which does not satisfy the conditions of the problem since it is smaller than 1. Assuming that $b \neq 0.1$, we find that $t = \frac{\ln(10b)}{b-0.1} > 0$. Since there is only one critical point it must be the point of maximum. To find the required value of b we put $t = 1$ and solve the equation $e^{(b-0.1)} - 10b = 0$ in b:

$$\text{solve}(e^{x-0.1} - 10\cdot x = 0, x)$$

gives the required value of $b = 3.71495$
Answer: E.

Problem 89. Solution: We define the function $h(t)$ in the calculator and evaluate its derivative:

$$\text{Define } h(t) = 55 - 9\cdot\cos\left(\frac{2\cdot\pi\cdot(t+10)}{365}\right)$$

$$\frac{d}{dt}(h(t))|_{t=90} \Rightarrow \frac{18\cdot\cos\left(\frac{7\pi}{146}\right)\cdot\pi}{365} \approx 0.153174$$

Answer: B.

Problem 90. Solution: We define the second derivative of g:

$$\text{Define } h(x) = 2^{-x^2} + \cos x + x$$

We find the zeros of h, i.e. the inflection points of g:

$$\text{Solve } (h(x) = 0, x) \Rightarrow x = -1.01589.$$

Since $\lim_{x \to -\infty} h(x) = -\infty$, $\lim_{x \to +\infty} h(x) = +\infty$, the function $h(x)$ changes its sign from $-$ to $+$, when x goes through -1.01589 in the positive direction. It follows that g is concave up in $(-1.01589, 5)$.

Answer: B.

Question 1 (9 pts)

Solution: (a) $y = g'(0)x + g(0) = f(0)x + 2 = 2x + 2$.

(**b**) The graph of $f(x) = g'(x)$ shows that there is only one root of the derivative of $g(x)$:

$$\text{Define } f(x) = \frac{x + 2 \cdot \cos x}{1 + \sqrt[3]{x^2}}$$

$$\text{solve } (f(x) = 0, x) \Rightarrow x = -1.02987.$$

Since $f(x) < 0$ for $x < -1.02987$ and $f(x) > 0$ for $x > -1.02987$, this point is a point of local minimum.

(**c**) It is clear from the graph of $f(x)$ that there are at least two points, where the tangents to the graph are horizontal. They are located about -3 and 3. We find them with the calculator:

$$\text{solve} \left(\frac{d}{dx}(f(x)) = 0, x \right).$$

The results are:

$$x = -97.5655, \quad x = -5.95147, \quad x = -3.27378,$$
$$x = 2.70002, \quad x = 6.44606, \quad x = 28.0524.$$

Of these points only three are in $[-6, 6]$:

$$\mathbf{x = -5.95147, \quad x = -3.27378, \quad x = 2.70002}.$$

Since $f(x) = g'(x)$ increases on $(-1, 0)$, the function $g(x)$ is concave up on $(-1, 0)$. Since $f(x) = g'(x)$ decreases on $(0, 1)$, the function $g(x)$ is concave down on $(0, 1)$. Since $f(x)$ is continuous at $x = 0$, the tangent to the graph $y = g(x)$ at $x = 0$ exists (see (**a**)). Hence $x = 0$ is an inflection point.

Question 2 (9 pts)

Solution: (a) We first determine the size of the graph.

$$f'(x) = 4x^3 + 18x^2 - 48x = 2x(2x^2 + 9x - 24).$$

The roots of $f'(x) = 0$ are 0 and

$$\frac{-9 \pm \sqrt{81 + 192}}{4} = \begin{cases} 1.880675 \\ -6.3806775 \end{cases}.$$

Using the calculator, we find that

$$f(0) = 24, \quad f(-6.3806775) = -854.222, \quad f(1.880675) = -8.4656.$$

So, using **Window Settings**, we change the default values of yMin to −900 and yMax to 40. After that we get the following graph:

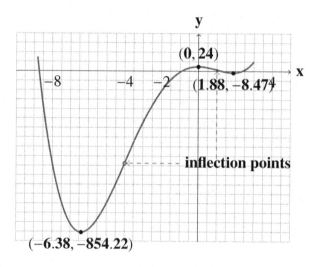

(b)

$$\begin{array}{ccc} (-6.381, -854.22) & (0, 24) & (1.881, -8.466) \\ \downarrow & \downarrow & \downarrow \\ \textbf{loc min} & \textbf{loc max} & \textbf{loc min} \end{array}$$

(c) Since

$$f''(x) = 12x^2 + 36x - 48 = 12(x + 4)(x - 1),$$

we obtain that

$$\begin{array}{cc} (-4, -488) & (1, 7) \\ \downarrow & \downarrow \\ \textbf{inflection} & \textbf{inflection} \end{array}$$

Question 3 (9 pts)

Solution:
(a) Since $v(1) > 0$, the particle is moving to the right.

(b) The acceleration $a(t) = v'(t)$ vanishes at the moments, when the tangent to the graph of $y = v(t)$ is horizontal. Since it is also required that the particle moves in the positive direction, there must be $v(t) > 0$ at these moments. Both conditions are satisfied at $t \approx 1$, $t \approx 5.75$.

(c). The particle is at rest when it is not moving ($v(t) = 0$). This happens for **FIVE** values of t: at $t \approx 0.4$, $t = 2$, $t = 4$, $t \approx 7.2$, $t = 9$.

(d) We have

$$a(c) = \frac{v(8) - v(6)}{8 - 6} \approx \frac{-1.5 - 1.5}{2} = -1.5.$$

The required instant acceleration equals the slope of the chord connecting the points $(6, 1.5)$ and $(8, -1.5)$. Using the graph of $v(t)$, we estimate that this happens at $t \approx 6.6$.

Question 4 (9 pts)

Solution: (a) Since

$$\frac{d}{dt} v_P(t) = \frac{5 \cdot 8}{2\sqrt{1 + 8t}} = \frac{20}{\sqrt{1 + 8t}} > 0,$$

the velocity $v_P(t)$ strictly increases, whereas the velocity $v_Q(t)$ strictly decreases. The continuous function $f(t) = v_Q(t) - v_P(t)$ satisfies

$$f(0) = 80, \quad f(5) = 20 - 5\left(\sqrt{41} - 1\right) < 20 - 5(6 - 1) = -5.$$

By the Intermediate Value Theorem the function $f(t)$ vanishes somewhere in $(0, 5)$. Since $f'(t) = v'_Q(t) - v'_P(t) < 0$, there is only one moment of time such that $v_Q(t) = v_P(t)$. This moment is located in $(0, 5)$.

(b). The average acceleration of car Q is given by

$$\frac{v_Q(10) - v_Q(0)}{10 - 0} = -8 \, \text{ft/sec}^2.$$

The acceleration of car Q takes only two values:

$$\frac{v_Q(5) - v_Q(0)}{5 - 0} = -12 \, \text{ft/sec}^2, \quad \frac{v_Q(10) - v_Q(5)}{10 - 5} = -4 \, \text{ft/sec}^2.$$

The function $v_Q(t)$ is not differentiable at $t = 5$. So, Lagrange's Theorem cannot be applied in this case. There is no a moment, when the average acceleration equals the instantaneous acceleration.

(c) The average acceleration of car P is

$$\frac{v_P(10) - v_P(0)}{10 - 0} = \frac{5 \cdot (\sqrt{81} - 1)}{10} = 4 \, \text{ft/sec}^2.$$

Then

$$\frac{d}{dt}v_P(t) = \frac{20}{\sqrt{1 + 8t}} = 4 \Leftrightarrow t = 3.$$

Question 5 (9 pts)

Solution: (a)

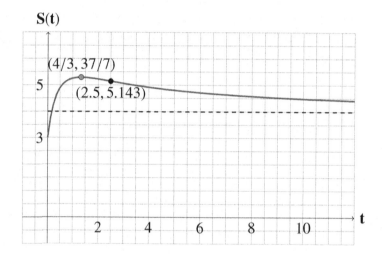

We differentiate:

$$\frac{dS}{dt} = 2\frac{4 - 3t}{(t + 1)^3}, \quad \frac{d^2S}{dt^2} = 6\frac{2t - 5}{(t + 2)^4}.$$

Since the derivative of S is positive on $(0, 4/3)$ and is negative for $t > 4/3$, we see that $t = 4/3$ is the point of maximum. We find $S(4/3) = 37/7 \approx 5.29$. The point of inflection is

$$\frac{d^2S}{dt^2} = 6\frac{2t - 5}{(t + 2)^4} = 0 \Leftrightarrow t = \frac{5}{2} = 2.5.$$

To sketch the graph we apply the method of graph sketching by important points. It is easy to see that $S(0) = 3$ and that $S = 4$ is a horizontal asymptote for $S = S(t)$:

$$\lim_{t \to +\infty} S(t) = 4 + \lim_{t \to +\infty} \frac{6}{t + 1} - \lim_{t \to +\infty} \frac{7}{(t + 1)^2} = 4 + 0 - 0 = 4.$$

Since

$$S(t) - 4 = \frac{6}{t+1} - \frac{7}{(t+1)^2} = \frac{6t+6-7}{(t+2)^2} = \frac{6t-1}{(t+1)^2},$$

the graph of $S = S(t)$ intercepts the asymptote $S = 4$ at $t = 1/6$ and remains above $S = 4$ for $t > 1/6$.

(b) The sales will be maximal at $t = 4/3$. So, $S(4/3) = 5 + 2/7$.

(c) The sales rate is $S'(t)$. Therefore, it will be minimal at the inflection point $t = 2.5$. We find: $S(2.5) = 5.143$, $S'(2.5) = -0.16$.

Question 6 (9 pts)

Solution: (a) We have

$$N'(t) = -3t^2 + 24t + 144 = -3(t^2 - 8t - 48), \quad N''(t) = 24 - 6t.$$

We see that the maximum of unemployment occurs at the positive root of the equation:

$$0 = t^2 - 8t - 48 = (t+4)(t-12).$$

This means that the maximum number of unemployed will be

$$
\begin{array}{r|rrrr}
12| & -1 & 12 & 144 & 1024 \\
& & -12 & 0 & 1728 \\
\hline
& -1 & 0 & 144 & \mathbf{2752}
\end{array}
\Rightarrow N(12) = 2\,752 \text{ thousand.}
$$

This happens in 12 months after the decision, i.e in one year.

(b) The rate of unemployment begins decline when $N''(t) = 24 - 6t = 0$, i.e in 4 months. And at this time the number of unemployed will be

$$
\begin{array}{r|rrrr}
4| & -1 & 12 & 144 & 1024 \\
& & -4 & 32 & 704 \\
\hline
& -1 & 8 & 176 & \mathbf{1728}
\end{array}
\Rightarrow N(4) = 1\,728 \text{ thousand.}
$$

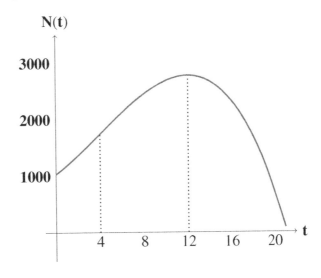

Final

Section IA, 30 questions, 60 min, No Calculators

Problem 1. Find the instantaneous rate of change of the function

$$f(x) = \left(\frac{1}{3}\right)^x$$

at $x = 3$.

(A) $\dfrac{\ln 3}{27}$ (B) $\dfrac{1}{27}$ (C) $\dfrac{-\ln 3}{27}$ (D) $-27\ln 3$ (E) $\dfrac{-1}{27}$

Problem 2. The function

$$f(x) = x^3 - e^{-x}$$

is invertible on $(-\infty, +\infty)$. Find the slope of the normal line to the graph of the inverse function f^{-1} at $x = -1$.

(A) -1 (B) $\dfrac{-1}{3}$ (C) 3 (D) $3 + e$ (E) 1

Problem 3. The minimum value of the function

$$f(x) = \frac{1}{\sqrt{9 - x^2}}, \text{ is}$$

(A) 3 (B) -3 (C) $\dfrac{1}{3}$ (D) $\dfrac{-1}{3}$ E none of these

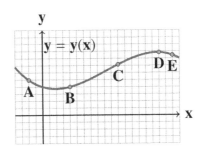

276

Problem 4. At which x-coordinates of the five points on the above graph are dy/dx and d^2y/dx^2 both positive?

(A) A (B) B (C) C (D) D (E) E.

Problem 5. Let $y = \dfrac{x^2}{\ln x}$. Then $y' =$

(A) $\dfrac{2x}{\ln x} - \dfrac{x}{(\ln x)^2}$ (B) $\dfrac{2x \ln x + x}{(\ln x)^2}$ (C) $2x \cdot \dfrac{1}{\ln x} - \dfrac{x^2}{(\ln x)^2}$

(D) $2x \cdot \dfrac{1}{\ln x} + \dfrac{x^2}{(\ln x)^2}$ (E) **none of these**.

Problem 6. If $g(x) = \dfrac{2x+3}{x^2 - 5x + 5}$, then $g'(x) =$

(A) $\dfrac{2x^2 + 6x - 25}{(x^2 - 5x + 5)^2}$ (B) $-\dfrac{2x^2 + 6x - 25}{(x^2 - 5x + 5)^2}$ (C) $\dfrac{2}{(2x - 5)}$

(D) $\dfrac{6x^2 - 14x - 5}{(x^2 - 5x + 5)^2}$ (E) $-\dfrac{6x^2 - 14x - 5}{(x^2 - 5x + 5)^2}$.

Problem 7. The range of the function $y = \sqrt{x - x^3}$ is given by

(A) $[0, +\infty)$ (B) $\left[0, \sqrt{\dfrac{2}{3\sqrt{3}}}\right]$ (C) $\left[\sqrt{\dfrac{2}{3\sqrt{3}}}, +\infty\right)$ (D) $(0, +\infty)$ (E) $\left(0, \sqrt{\dfrac{2}{3\sqrt{3}}}\right)$.

Problem 8. Evaluate
$$\lim_{x \to 0}\left(\frac{1}{\sin^2 x} - \frac{1}{x^2}\right) =$$
(A) 3 (B) $\dfrac{1}{3}$ (C) 0,   D $-\dfrac{1}{3}$,   (E) **the limit does not exist**.

Problem 9. If $y = x + \ln x$, then $\dfrac{dx}{dy} =$

(A) $\dfrac{x}{1 + x}$ (B) $\dfrac{1 + x}{x}$ (C) $\dfrac{y}{1 + y}$ (D) $\dfrac{x}{1 + y}$ (E) $\dfrac{y}{1 + x}$

Problem 10. If $y = (\sin x)^x$, then $y' =$

(A) $x(\sin x)^{x-1} \cos x$ (B) $(\sin x)^x \ln \sin x$ (C) $(\sin x)^x (\ln \sin x + x \tan x)$

(D) $(\sin x)^x (\ln \sin x + x \cot x)$ (E) $x(\sin x)^{x-1} \sin x$

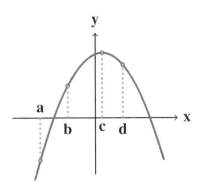

Problem 11. The figure above shows the graph of a function f. Which of the following has the greatest value?

(A) $f(a)$ (B) $f'(c)$ (C) $f'(a)$ (D) $f(d) - f(c)$ (E) $\dfrac{f(b) - f(a)}{b - a}$

Problem 12. A gun sends a bullet straight up. In t seconds it reaches a height of

$$s(t) = 180t - 16t^2.$$

What is the acceleration in ft/sec^2 of the bullet at $t = 2$?

(A) 16   (B) -32 (C) 32   (D) -16 (E) 0

Problem 13. If f is differentiable function such that $f(2) = 1$ and $f'(2) = 2$, which of the following statements could be **false**?

(A) $\lim\limits_{x \to 2} f(x) = 1$ (B) $\lim\limits_{x \to 2} f'(x) = 2$ (C) $\lim\limits_{x \to 2} \dfrac{f(x) - 1}{x - 2} = 2$

(D) $\lim\limits_{h \to 0} \dfrac{f(2 + h) - 1}{h} = 2$ (E) $\lim\limits_{x \to 2^+} f(x) = \lim\limits_{x \to 2^-} f(x)$

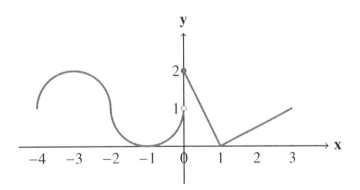

Problem 14. The graph of the piecewise-defined function f is shown in the figure above. The graph has a vertical tangent line at $x = -2$ and horizontal tangent lines at $x = -3$ and $x = -1$. What are all values of x, $-4 < x < 3$, such that f is continuous but not differentiable at x?

(A) $x = 1$ (B) $x = -2$ and $x = 0$ (C) $x = -2$ and $x = 1$

(D) $x = 0$ and $x = 1$ (E) $x = 0, x = 1$ and $x = -2$

Problem 15. Evaluate

$$\lim_{x \to \pi} \frac{\cos x + \sin(2x) + 1}{x^2 - \pi^2}.$$

(A) $\dfrac{1}{2\pi}$ (B) $\dfrac{1}{\pi}$ (C) 1 (D) 0 (E) nonexistent

Problem 16. Which of the following functions has exactly one point of inflection?

(A) $f(x) = -15x + 3$ (B) $f(x) = 3x^2 - 10x + 20$ (C) $f(x) = 10x^4 - 4x^3 + 3$

(D) $f(x) = x^3 - x - 1$ (E) $f(x) = -12e^{-x} + 7$

x	$f(x)$	$f'(x)$
0	3	−1
1	2	5
2	−4	3

Problem 17. Let f and g be differentiable functions such that $g(x) = f^{-1}(x)$. Some values of f and f' are given in the table above. What is the value of $g'(2)$?

(A) -1 (B) $\dfrac{1}{5}$ (C) $\dfrac{1}{3}$ (D) $\dfrac{1}{2}$ (E) cannot be determined

Problem 18. The curves $y = -x^2 + 6x$ and $y = -2x + k$ are tangent. What is k?

(A) 0 (B) 4 (C) 6 (D) 8 (E) 16

x	$f(x)$	$g(x)$	$f'(x)$	$g'(x)$
4	6	5	−3	9
5	5	4	−5	9
6	4	6	4	5

Problem 19. The table above shows some of the values of two differentiable functions f and g and their derivatives. If $h(x) = f(x)g(x)$, then $h'(5) =$

(**A**) -45 (**B**) -32 (**C**) 25 (**D**) -3 (**E**) 4

Problem 20. Use the table of the previous problem to find $h'(4)$, where $h(x) = f(g(x))$.

(**A**) -45 (**B**) -27 (**C**) -15 (**D**) 0 (**E**) 25

Problem 21. Let $f(x)$ be a differentiable function for $x > 0$ satisfying $f(3) \approx 1.099$, $f(3.03) \approx 1.109$. Using linearization determine which of the following is closest to $f'(3)$?

(**A**) 0.368 (**B**) 0.371 (**C**) 0.4 (**D**) 0.333 (**E**) 0.6

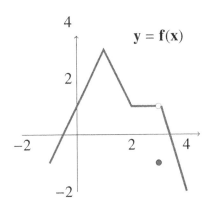

Problem 22. The graph of f is shown above. Which of the following statements is true?

(**A**) f is continuous at $x = 3$ (**B**) f is differentiable at $x = 3$

(**C**) f is undefined at $x = 3$ (**D**) $\lim\limits_{x \to 3} f(x)$ exists (**E**) $\lim\limits_{x \to 3} f(x) = -1$

Problem 23. What is the slope of the tangent line to the curve

$$y = \frac{e^x}{x + 4} \quad \text{at} \quad x = 1?$$

(**A**) $-\dfrac{e}{5}$ (**B**) $-\dfrac{4e}{25}$ (**C**) $\dfrac{4e}{25}$ (**D**) $\dfrac{4e}{5}$ (**E**) $\dfrac{6e}{5}$

Problem 24. The function f is defined by

$$f(x) = \begin{cases} \dfrac{3x^2 + 4x + 1}{4(x + 1)} & \text{when } x \neq -1 \\ m & \text{when } x = -1 \end{cases}$$

For what value of m is f continuous at $x = -1$.

(A) -1 (B) 0.75 C 0 D -0.5 E 1

Problem 25. A particle moves along the x-axis as described by $3t^2 - 2t^3$. Find the acceleration of the particle at the time when the velocity is maximal.

A -1 B 1 C -2 D 0 E 1.1

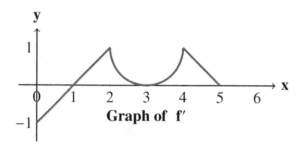

Graph of f'

Problem 26. The graph of f', the derivative of the function f, is shown above. Which of the following could be the graph of f?

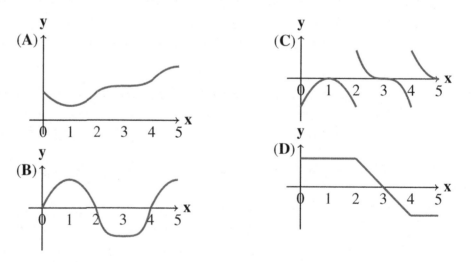

Problem 27. An ice sphere melts so that it maintains its spherical shape. The volume of the sphere is decreasing at a constant rate of 2π cubic meters per hour.

At what rate, in square meters per hour, is the surface area of the sphere decreasing at the moment when the radius is 5 meters?

$$(A) \; \frac{4\pi}{5} \quad (B) \; 40\pi \quad (C) \; 80\pi^2 \quad (D) \; 100\pi \quad (E) \; 200\pi$$

Problem 28. The area of the largest rectangle with one side along the x-axis and the two vertices on the curve of $y = e^{-|x|}$ is

$$A \; \sqrt{\frac{2}{e}} \quad B \; \sqrt{2e} \quad C \; \frac{2}{e} \quad D \; \frac{1}{\sqrt{2e}} \quad (E) \; \frac{2}{e^2}$$

Problem 29. If f is a differentiable function such that $f(0) = -4$ and $f(5) = 5$, then which of the following must be true?

I. There exists c in $(0, 5)$ where $f(c) = 0$.

II. There exists d in $(0, 5)$ where $f'(d) = 0$.

III. There exists d in $(0, 5)$ where $f'(k) = \frac{9}{5}$.

(A) I only (B) II only (C) I and III only (D) I and II only (E) I, II and III only

Problem 30. Evaluate the limit:

$$\lim_{x \to 0} (\cos 2x)^{\frac{3}{x^2}}$$

(A) 1 (B) e^{-6} (C) e only (D) e^{-1} (E) I, does not exist

Section IB, 15 questions, 45 min, calculators are allowed

Problem 76. An object moves along the y-axis with coordinate position $y(t)$ and velocity

$$v(t) = \sqrt{t} - \cos(e^t)$$

for $t \geq 0$. At time $t = 1$, the object is moving

(**A**) downward with negative acceleration (**B**) upward with negative acceleration

(**C**) downward with positive acceleration

(**D**) upward with positive acceleration (**E**) at rest

Problem 77. Find the point(s) on the interval $(0, 2)$ at which the tangent line to the curve $y = e^x - \sin x$ is parallel to the chord connecting the endpoints of this curve.

(**A**) 0.147 (**B**) 1.148 (**C**) 1.356 (**D**) 1.756 (**E**) none of these points

Problem 78. The graph of

$$y = e^{\sin x} - 2$$

crosses the x-axis at one point in the interval $(0, 1)$. What is the slope of the graph at this point?

(**A**) 0.506   (**B**) -1 (**C**) 1.442   (**D**) 1.961   (**E**) 2.347

Problem 79. If $f'(x) = \sqrt{x^2 + 2} + x^2 - 2x$, then f has a local minimum at $x =$

(**A**) -0.333 (**B**) 0.362 (**C**) 0.370 (**D**) 0.919 (**E**) none of these

Problem 80. The derivative of a function f is given by

$$f'(x) = e^{\sin x} - \cos x - 1, \quad \text{for } 0 < x < 9.$$

On what intervals is f decreasing?

(**A**) $0 < x < 0.633$ and $4.115 < x < 6.916$

(**B**) $0 < x < 1.947$ and $5.744 < x < 8.230$

(**C**) $0.633 < x < 4.115$ and $6.916 < x < 9$

(**D**) $1.947 < x < 5.744$ and $8.230 < x < 9$ (**E**) none of these

Problem 81. The curve defined by $x^3 + xy - y^2 = 1$ has a horizontal tangent line when $x =$

(**A**) 1 or -0.5 (**B**) 1.037 (**C**) 0.923 (**D**) 1.196 (**E**) none of these.

Problem 82. How many asymptotes does the curve

$$y = \frac{2x^2}{4 - x^2}$$

have?

(**A**) two horizontal (**B**) two horizontal and one vertical

(**C**) two vertical and no horizontal (**D**) one horizontal and one vertical

(**E**) one horizontal and two vertical

Problem 83. A twice differentiable function f satisfies

$$f(3) = 2, \quad f'(3) = 5, \quad f''(3) = -2. \quad \text{Then} \quad \frac{d^2}{dx^2}\left(f^2(x)\right)\bigg|_{x=3} =$$

(**A**) 42 (**B**) 10 (**C**) 20 (**D**) 38 (**E**) -20

Problem 84. Suppose f is a differentiable function on the interval $[0, 1]$ and $g(x) = f(2x)$. The table below gives some values of f:

x	0.1	0.2	0.3	0.4	0.5	0.6
$f(x)$	1.01	1.042	1.180	1.298	1.486	1.573

What is the approximate value of $g'(0.2)$

(**A**) 2.21 (**B**) 2.36 (**C**) 3.06 (**D**) 3.76 (**E**) 5.64

Problem 85. For $f(x) = x^2 e^{-x}$ find values c in $[0, 1]$ satisfying the Mean Value Theorem (= Lagrange's Theorem) for f on $[0, 2]$.

(**A**) $c = 0.19618$ (**B**) $c = 0.87734$ (**C**) $c = 0.12533$

(**D**) $c = 0.17731$ (**E**) $c = 0.17735$

Problem 86. Find the smallest possible a such that the function $f(x) = x^4 + 2e^x$ is invertible on $(a, +\infty)$:

(**A**) 1.389 (**B**) 0.641 (**C**) -0.538 (**D**) -0.641 (**E**) **does not exist**

Problem 87. Consider the function

$$P(t) = 500t^2 - 500\ln(t + 1)$$

for $t > -1$. Which of the following statements is true?

(**A**) $P(t)$ increases, then decreases, then increases indefinitely as $t \to \infty$.

(**B**) $P(t)$ decreases indefinitely as $t \to \infty$.

(**C**) $P(t)$ increases indefinitely as $t \to \infty$.

(**D**) $P(t)$ decreases, then increases indefinitely as $t \to \infty$.

(**E**) $P(t)$ increases, then decreases indefinitely as $t \to \infty$.

Problem 88. If the derivative of f is $f'(x) = \ln(x + 1) - 2$, at which of the following values of x does f have an absolute minimal value on $(-1, +\infty]$?

(A) 2.53 (B) 6.39 (C) 2.12 (D) 4.44 (E) 1.72

Problem 89. A function $f(x)$ has the following additional properties on its domain:

I. $f''(x) > 0$ for $x > 3$ **II.** $f''(x) < 0$ for $x < 3$ **III.** $f'(x) < 0$ for $x > 3$

IV. $f'(x) < 0$ for $x < 3$ **V.** $f(3.1) > f(2.9)$

Which of the following could be a property of f?

(**A**) f has a vertical asymptote at $x = 3$ (**B**) f is decreasing at $x = 3$

(**C**) f is continuous at $x = 3$ (**D**) $x = 3$ is a point of inflection for f

(**E**) all of the above

Problem 90. The position of a particle on a line is given by

$$s(t) = t^3 - 6t^2 + 9t - 1?$$

Then its minimal velocity equals

(A) -3 (B) 0 (C) 3 (D) 6 (E) 9

IIB, 2 questions, 45 min, calculators are allowed

Question 1 (9 pts)

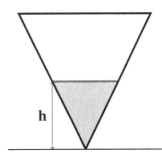

The height of the water level in a right conical storage tank, shown above, (the radius of its base equals its height) is modeled by a differentiable function h, where $h(t)$ is measured in meters and t is measured in hours. At time $t = 0$, the height of the water in the tank is 25.1 meters. The height is changing at the rate

$$h'(t) = 2 - \frac{24e^{-0.025t}}{t + 4}$$

meters per hour for $0 \le t \le 24$.

(a) 3pts At what rate is the volume of water changing at time $t = 0$? Indicate units of measure.

(b) 3pts When does the minimal height of the water during the time period $0 \le t \le 24$ occur? Justify your answer.

(c) 3pts Is it true that the height is always positive? Justify your answer.

Question 2 (9 pts)

Consider the curve defined by

$$9x^2 + 4y^2 - 54x + 16y + 61 = 0.$$

(a) 2 pts Using implicit differentiation, evaluate dy/dx.

(b) 2 pts Write the equation for each vertical tangent to the curve.

(c) 2 pts The points $(3, -5)$ and $(5, -2)$ are on the curve. Write the equation for the secant line through these points.

(d) 3 pts Write the equation for lines tangent to the curve and parallel to the secant line from part **(c)**.

IIA, 4 questions, 60 min, No Calculators are allowed

Question 3 (9 pts)

The graph of the derivative, f', of some function f is shown below.

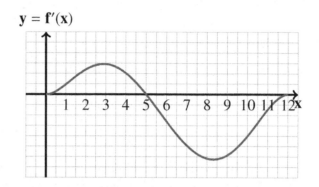

y = f'(x)

(a) **2pts** At what value of x does f achieve a local maximum? Justify your arguments.

(b) **2pts** Does f have any point of inflection? If so, what are they?

(c) **2pts** Determine the concavity of the curve about the point $x = 2$.

(d) **3pts** Arrange the values $f(5), f(7), f(10)$ in the increasing order.

Question 4 (9pts)

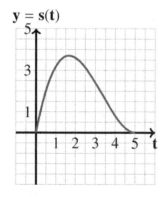

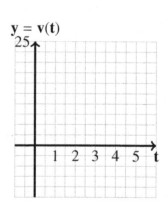

A particle is moving along a horizontal line. The graph of its position $s = s(t)$ is shown above.

(a) **2pts** Determine the moments of time when the particle is not moving. Justify your answer.

(b) **2pts** On what interval of time is the particle moving backward? Justify your answer.

(c) **3pts** On the coordinate axes provided above sketch the graph of the velocity, $v(t)$, of this particle.

(d) **2pts** Estimate the distance travelled by the particle for the fist three seconds.

Question 5 (9pts)

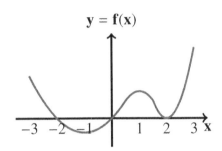

y = f(x)

The graph of a differentiable function f on $[-3, 3]$ is shown above. It has horizontal tangents at $x = -1$, $x = 1$, and $x = 2$. It is also known that $f'(0) = 1$. The function g is the antiderivative of f satisfying $g(0) = -1$.

(a) **2pts** Find all values of x on the open interval $-3 < x < 3$ such that g has a relative minimum at x. Justify your answer.

(b) **2pts** Determine open subintervals in $-3 < x < 3$ where the graph of g is concave down. Give reasons for your answer.

(c) **2pts** Find the value of

$$\lim_{x \to -1} \frac{g(x + 1) + 1}{(x + 1)^2},$$

or show that it does not exist. Give reasons for your answer.

(d) **3pts** Let h be the function defined by

$$h(x) = 2f(2x + 1) + 1.$$

Evaluate $h'(-0.5)$.

Question 6 (9pts)

A demographic study shows that

$$P(r) = (0.25r + 2)e^{-0.1r} \text{ hundred people}$$

live r miles from the city center.

(a) **2pts** Determine the population at the city center.

(b) **2pts** For what values of r is $P(r)$ increasing? For what values is it decreasing?

(c) **2pts** At what distance from the city center is the population largest? Using Taylor's formula estimate the largest population.

(d) **3pts** Sketch the graph of $P(r)$ for $r \geq 0$. Determine all asymptotes and the intervals of monotonicity.

Final, Solutions

Problem 1. Solution:

$$f'(x) = \frac{df}{dx} = \left(\frac{1}{3}\right)^x \ln\frac{1}{3} \Rightarrow f'(3) = \frac{-\ln 3}{27}.$$

Answer: C.

Problem 2. Solution: We have $f(0) = -1$ implying that $f^{-1}(-1) = 0$. By the formula for the derivative of the inverse function

$$x = f\left(f^{-1}(x)\right) \Rightarrow 1 = f'\left(f^{-1}(x)\right) \cdot \left(f^{-1}\right)'(x) \Rightarrow \left(\mathbf{f^{-1}}\right)'(\mathbf{x}) = \frac{\mathbf{1}}{\mathbf{f'\left(f^{-1}(x)\right)}}.$$

Then

$$k = \left(f^{-1}\right)'(-1) = \frac{1}{f'(0)} = \frac{1}{\left.(3x^2 + e^{-x})\right|_{x=0}} = 1.$$

So, the slope of the tangent k is 1. Since $k \cdot k_1 = -1$, we obtain that $k_1 = -1$. It follows that the slope of the normal is -1.

Answer: A.

Problem 3. Solution: We have

$$f'(x) = -\frac{1}{2}(9 - x^2)^{-3/2}(-2x) = 0 \Leftrightarrow x = 0.$$

Answer: C.

Problem 4. Solution: $dy/dx > 0$ on the part of the graph which goes up. Therefore we have a choice between B, C and D. About B the graph is concave up implying that $d^2y/dx^2 > 0$ whereas about D it is concave down implying $d^2y/dx^2 < 0$. We have $dy/dx = 0$ for D. The point C is an inflection point.

Answer: B.

Problem 5. Solution: We have

$$\left(\frac{x^2}{\ln x}\right)' = \frac{2x \ln x - x^2(\ln x)'}{(\ln x)^2} = \frac{2x \ln x - x}{(\ln x)^2}.$$

Answer: A.

Problem 6. Solution:

$$g'(x) = \left(\frac{2x+3}{x^2-5x+5}\right)' = \frac{2\cdot(x^2-5x+5)-(2x+3)\cdot(2x-5)}{(x^2-5x+5)^2} =$$
$$\frac{-2x^2-6x+25}{(x^2-5x+5)^2}.$$

Answer: B.

Problem 7. Solution: Since $x-x^3 = (1+x)x(1-x)$, the polynomial $p(x) = x-x^3$ is non-negative on the intervals $(-\infty, -1]$ and $[0, 1]$. We have $p'(x) = 1-3x^2$. It follows that p decreases on the interval $(-\infty, -1)$ to $p(-1) = 0$. Hence $y = \sqrt{p(x)}$ also decreases. Being continuous, this functions assumes every nonnegative value exactly once. Since the values of y on $[0, 1]$ are non-negative, we conclude that the range of the function $y = \sqrt{x-x^3}$ is $[0, +\infty)$.

Answer: A.

Problem 8. Solution:

$$\lim_{x\to0}\left(\frac{1}{\sin^2 x}-\frac{1}{x^2}\right) = \lim_{x\to0}\frac{x^2-\sin^2 x}{x^4}\frac{x^2}{\sin^2 x} = \lim_{x\to0}\frac{x^2-\sin^2 x}{x^4}\cdot\lim_{x\to0}\frac{x^2}{\sin^2 x} =$$
$$\lim_{x\to0}\frac{x^2-\sin^2 x}{x^4}\cdot\frac{1}{\left(\lim_{x\to0}\frac{\sin x}{x}\right)^2} = \lim_{x\to0}\frac{x^2-\sin^2 x}{x^4} = \lim_{x\to0}\frac{\left(x^2-\sin^2 x\right)'}{4x^3} =$$
$$\lim_{x\to0}\frac{2x-2\sin x\cos x}{4x^3} = \lim_{x\to0}\frac{2x-\sin 2x}{4x^3} = \lim_{x\to0}\frac{2-2\cos 2x}{12x^2} =$$
$$\lim_{x\to0}\frac{1-\cos 2x}{6x^2} = \lim_{x\to0}\frac{2\sin 2x}{6\cdot2x} = \frac{1}{3}.$$

Answer: B.

Problem 9. Solution: We differentiate in y the implicit equation $y = x + \ln x$:

$$1 = \frac{dx}{dy}+\frac{1}{x}\frac{dx}{dy} = \frac{dx}{dy}\left(1+\frac{1}{x}\right) \Rightarrow \frac{dx}{dy} = \frac{x}{1+x}.$$

Answer: A.

Problem 10. Solution:

$$\ln y = x \ln \sin x \Rightarrow \frac{y'}{y} = \ln \sin x + x(\ln \sin x)' = \ln \sin x + x\frac{\cos x}{\sin x} \Rightarrow$$
$$y' = y(\ln \sin x + x \cot x) = (\sin x)^x (\ln \sin x + x \cot x).$$

Answer: D.

Problem 11. Solution: From the graph we have

$$f(a) < 0, \quad f(d) - f(c) < 0, \quad f'(a) > 0, \frac{f(b) - f(a)}{b - a} > 0.$$

Since $x = c$ is the point of maximum, we conclude that $f'(c) = 0$. So, the choice is between **C** and **E**. By the intermediate value theorem for derivatives, there is t, $a < t < b$ such that
$$\frac{f(b) - f(a)}{b - a} = f'(t).$$

Since the graph of $y = f(x)$ is convex down, the derivative $f'(x)$ decreases, which implies that
$$\frac{f(b) - f(a)}{b - a} = f'(t) < f'(a).$$

Answer: C.

Problem 12. Solution: We have

$$v(t) = \frac{ds}{dt} = 180t - 32t \Rightarrow a(t) = \frac{dv}{dt} = -32.$$

Answer: B.

Problem 13. Solution: Since f is differentiable, it is continuous. It follows that **A** and **E** are true. **C** and **D** mean that $f'(2) = 2$. Hence both of them are true. The derivative of a function may be discontinuous as the following example shows. Let

$$h(x) = \begin{cases} x^2 \sin\left(\frac{1}{x}\right) & \text{if } x \neq 0 \\ 0 & \text{if } x = 0 \end{cases}$$

Then

$$h'(0) = \lim_{x \to 0} \frac{h(x)}{x}, \quad h'(x) = 2x \sin\left(\frac{1}{x}\right) - \cos\left(\frac{1}{x}\right), \quad x \neq 0.$$

Clearly, the limit

$$\lim_{x \to 0} h'(x) = 0 - \lim_{x \to 0} \cos\left(\frac{1}{x}\right)$$

does not exist. Now we put $f(x) = h(x - 2) + 2x$.

Answer: B.

Problem 14. Solution: The function f is not differentiable at $x = -2, 0, 1$. It is continuous at $x = -2, 1$.

Answer: C.

Problem 15. Solution: We have

$$\lim_{x \to \pi} \frac{\cos x + \sin(2x) + 1}{x^2 - \pi^2} \overset{x=\pi+y}{=} \lim_{y \to 0} \frac{\cos(y + \pi) + \sin(2y + 2\pi) + 1}{y(y + 2\pi)} =$$

$$\lim_{y \to 0} \frac{1 - \cos(y) + \sin(2y)}{y(y + 2\pi)} = \lim_{y \to 0} \frac{1 - \cos(y)}{y} \cdot \frac{1}{y + 2\pi} + \lim_{y \to 0} 2 \cdot \frac{\sin(2y)}{2y} \cdot \frac{1}{y + 2\pi} =$$

$$0 \cdot \frac{1}{2\pi} + 2 \cdot 1 \cdot \frac{1}{2\pi} = \frac{1}{\pi}.$$

Answer: B.

Problem 16. Solution: A is false since $f''(x) = 0$ for every $x \in \mathbb{R}$. **B** is false since $f''(x) = 6 > 0$ for every $x \in \mathbb{R}$. **C** is false since

$$f''(x) = 120x^2 - 24x = 120x(x - 0.2).$$

This formula shows that there are two points of sign change of f: $x = 0$ and $x = 0.2$.

Since

$$f''(x) = (3x^2 - 1)' = 6x$$

changes sign only in $x = 0$, we conclude that **D** is true.

E is false since

$$f''(x) = -12e^{-x} < 0, \quad x \in \mathbb{R}.$$

Answer: D.

Problem 17. Solution:

$$x = f(g(x)) \Rightarrow 1 = f'(g(x)) \cdot g'(x) \Rightarrow g'(2) = \frac{1}{f'(g(2))} = \frac{1}{f'(1)} = \frac{1}{5}.$$

Answer: B.

Problem 18. Solution: The slope of $y = -2x + k$ at x is -2 and of the parabola $y = -x^2 + 6x$ equals

$$\left(-x^2 + 6x\right)' = -2x + 6 \Rightarrow -2x + 6 = -2 \Leftrightarrow x = 4.$$

Then the equation of the tangent to $y = -x^2 + 6x$ at $x = 4$ is:

$$y = -2(x - 4) + 8 = -2x + 16 \Rightarrow \mathbf{k = 16}.$$

Answer: E.

Problem 19. Solution:

$$h'(5) = f'(5) \cdot g(5) + f(5)g'(5) = (-5) \cdot 4 + 5 \cdot 9 = \mathbf{25}.$$

Answer: C.

Problem 20. Solution:

$$h'(4) = f'(g(4))g'(4) = f'(5)g'(4) = (-5) \cdot 9 = \mathbf{-45}.$$

Answer: A.

Problem 21. Solution: Since

$$f(x) \approx L(x) = f(3) + f'(3)(x - 3),$$

we obtain for $x = 3.03$ that

$$1.109 = f(3.03) \approx L(3.03) = 1.099 + f'(3) \cdot 0.03 \Rightarrow f'(3) \approx \frac{0.01}{0.03} \approx \mathbf{0.333}.$$

Answer: D.

Problem 22. Solution: Answer: D.

Problem 23. Solution: We have

$$\mathbf{slope} = \left(\frac{e^x}{x + 4} \right)' \bigg|_{x=1} = \frac{e^x(x + 4) - e^x}{(x + 4)^2} \bigg|_{x=1} = \frac{4e}{25}$$

Answer: C.

Problem 24. Solution: Since $x = -1$ is a root of the polynomial $y = 3x^2 + 4x + 1$, we conclude by the long division of polynomials that

$$3x^2 + 4x + 1 = (x + 1)(3x + 1) \Rightarrow \lim_{x \to -1} \frac{(x + 1)(3x + 1)}{4(x + 1)} = \frac{-2}{4} \Rightarrow m = -0.5.$$

Answer: D.

Problem 25. Solution: The acceleration is the derivative of the velocity. Therefore it must be zero when the velocity takes its maximal value by Fermat's Theorem.

Answer: D.

Problem 26. Solution: Since the graph in **C** represents a discontinuous function, it cannot be differentiable. The derivative of the function represented by **D** is zero on the interval $(0, 2)$, which excludes this function from consideration.

The graph of f' shows that $f'(x) \geq 0$ for $1 < x < 5$ and $f'(x) < 0$ for $0 \leq x < 1$. This implies that function $y = f(x)$ increases on $(1, 5)$ and decreases on $(0, 1)$.

Answer: A.

Problem 27. Solution: Since

$$V = \frac{4}{3}\pi r^3, \ A = 4\pi r^2,$$

we see that

$$-2\pi = \frac{dV}{dt} = 4\pi r^2 \frac{dr}{dt} \Rightarrow \left.\frac{dr}{dt}\right|_{r=5} = -\frac{2\pi}{4\pi 5^2} = -\frac{1}{50} \Rightarrow \frac{dA}{dt} = 8\pi r \frac{dr}{dt} \Rightarrow$$

$$\left.\frac{dA}{dt}\right|_{r=5} = 8\pi \cdot 5 \cdot \left(-\frac{1}{50}\right) = -\frac{4\pi}{5}.$$

Answer: A.

Problem 28. Solution:

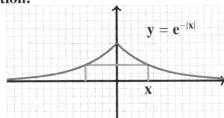

The area $A(x)$, $x > 0$, of the rectangle is $2xe^{-x}$. Also, $A(0) = 0$. Then

$$\lim_{x \to \pm\infty} A(x) = 0, \quad A'(x) = 2e^{-x} - 2x \cdot (-x) = 2e^{-x}(1 - x).$$

We see that $A'(x) = 0$ if and only if $x = 1$. Then

$$A(1) = 2 \cdot 1 \cdot e^{-1} = \frac{2}{e}.$$

Answer: C.

Problem 29. Solution: We plot the graph of the linear function satisfying $f(0) = -4, f(5) = 5$:

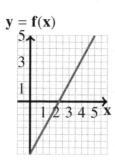

Since $f(0) < 0$ and $f(5) > 0$, the continuous function f must vanish at some point c in $(0, 5)$. So, **I** is true. By the Intermediate Value Theorem for derivatives

$$\frac{9}{5} = \frac{f(5) - f(0)}{5 - 0} = f'(k) \text{ for some } k \in (0, 5).$$

Hence, **III** is true.

The statements **II** is **False**, as the example of the graph above shows.

Answer: C.

Problem 30. Solution: We have

$$(\cos 2x)^{\frac{3}{x^2}} = e^{\frac{3\ln(\cos 2x)}{x^2}}.$$

The L'Hospital Rule gives

$$\lim_{x \to 0} \frac{3\ln(\cos 2x)}{x^2} = \lim_{x \to 0} \frac{3\,(\ln(\cos 2x))'}{(x^2)'} = \lim_{x \to 0} \frac{6(-\sin 2x)}{2x\cos(2x)} = -6\lim_{x \to 0} \frac{\sin 2x}{2x} \cdot \frac{1}{\cos(2x)} = -6.$$

Answer: B.

Problem 76. Solution: Observing that $\pi/2 < e = 2.71828\ldots < \pi = 3.1415\ldots$, we obtain that

$$\begin{aligned} v(t) &= \sqrt{t} - \cos(e^t) \\ a(t) &= \frac{1}{2\sqrt{t}} + e^t \cdot \sin(e^t) \end{aligned} \Rightarrow \begin{aligned} v(1) &= 1 - \cos(e) > 0 \\ a(1) &= \frac{1}{2} + e \cdot \sin(e) > 0 \end{aligned}$$

Answer: D.

Problem 77. Solution: First, using the calculator, we define Define $f(x) = e^x - \sin(x)$. Next, we define

$$\text{Define } k = \frac{f(2) - f(0)}{2 - 0}.$$

Finally,

$$\text{solve}\left(\frac{d}{dx}f(x) = k,\ x\right) \Rightarrow x = 1.14758$$

Answer B.

Problem 78. Solution: Using the calculator, we define the function $f(x)$: Define $f(x) = e^{\sin x} - 2$. To find the solution of the equation $f(x) = 0$ in the interval $(0, 2)$ we apply "**nSolve**" command, which gives only one solution

$$\text{nSolve}\,(f(x) = 0, x, 0, 2) \Rightarrow 0.765846$$

in contrast to "**solve**" command, which lists all solutions on the real line. Finally,

$$\frac{d}{dx}(f(x))|_{x=0.765846} = 1.44159$$

Answer: C.

Problem 79. Solution: Since

$$f'(x) = \sqrt{x^2 + 2} + x^2 - 2x = (x - 1)^2 + \sqrt{x^2 + 2} - 1 \geq \sqrt{2} - 1 > 0,$$

the function f increases, implying that there are no local minimum points.
Answer: E.

Problem 80. Solution: First, we define

$$g(x) = e^{\sin x} - \cos x - 1.$$

Next. we plot the graph of this function in the window $-2 < x < 10,\ -3 < y < 3$:

y = f(x)

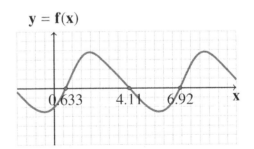

Finally, we locate the zeros of g using "analyze graph" option.
Answer: A.

Problem 81. Solution : Differentiating implicitly, we obtain

$$3x^2 + y + xy' - 2yy' = 0 \Rightarrow y' = \frac{3x^2 + y}{2y - x}.$$

If $y' = 0$ then $y = -3x^2$. Then the required x is a root of the equation $-27x^6 - 3x^3 - 9x^4 - 1 = 0$:

$$\textbf{solve}\left(-27x^6 - 3x^3 - 9x^4 - 1 = 0, x\right) \Rightarrow \text{false},$$

implying that there are no such points on the curve. **Answer E.**

Problem 82. Solution : We define

$$f(x) = \frac{2 \cdot x^2}{4 - x^2},$$

and using a calculator evaluate the following limits:

$$\lim_{x \to \infty}(f(x)) = -2, \quad \lim_{x \to 2^+}(f(x)) = -\infty, \quad \lim_{x \to 2^-}(f(x)) = \infty.$$

The first limit shows that $y = -2$ is a unique horizontal asymptote. The second and the third limits show that $x = \pm 2$ are vertical asymptotes.

Answer: E.

Problem 83. Solution: We have

$$\frac{d^2}{dx^2}\left(f^2(x)\right)\bigg|_{x=3} = \frac{d}{dx}(2f(x)f'(x))\bigg|_{x=3} = 2\left((f'(x))^2 + f(x)f''(x)\right)\bigg|_{x=3} =$$
$$2\left((f'(3))^2 + f(3)f''(3)\right) = 2(25 - 2 \cdot 2) = 42.$$

Answer: A.

Problem 84. Solution: By the Chain Rule $g'(x) = f'(2x) \cdot 2$. Hence $g'(0.2) = 2f'(0.4)$. Now we calculate:

$$g'(0.2) \approx 2\frac{f(0.4) - f(0.3)}{0.1} = 2\frac{1.298 - 1.180}{0.1} = 2.36,$$

$$g'(0.2) \approx 2\frac{f(0.5) - f(0.4)}{0.1} = 2\frac{1.486 - 1.298}{0.1} = 3.76.$$

Both results are present in the answers. However, a better approximation can be obtained by

$$g'(0.2) \approx 2\frac{f(0.5) - f(0.3)}{0.2} = 2\frac{1.486 - 1.180}{0.2} = 10 \cdot 0.306 = 3.06,$$

which is placed between the two above values. The values in **A** and **E** are too far from the found values. **Answer: C.**

Problem 85. Solution: The number c is the solution to the equation in $[0, 2]$:

$$\frac{f(2) - f(0)}{2 - 0} = \frac{2}{e^2} = f'(c) = e^{-c}(2c - c^2).$$

The graph of $y = 2e^{x-2} - 2x + x^2$ plotted with the graphic calculator shows that there are only two intercepts with the line $y = 2$, the first is slightly to the right from $x = 0$ and the second is in $[1, 2]$.

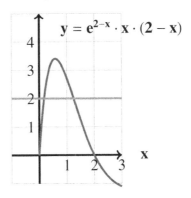

Using the command nSolve($2e^{x-2} - 2x + x^2 = 0, x, 0, 1$) of the graphic calculator we find that $c_1 = 0.17731$. **Answer: D.**

Problem 86. Solution: Using a calculator, we define Define $f(x) = x^4 + 2 \cdot e^{-x}$ and then

$$\frac{d}{dx}(f(x)) \Rightarrow 4 \cdot x^3 - 2 \cdot e^{-x}, \quad \text{solve}\left(4 \cdot x^3 - 2 \cdot e^{-x} = 0, x\right) \Rightarrow x = 0.641005$$

which gives the required value of $a = 0.641005$. **Answer: B.**

Problem 87. Solution: Notice that $f(t) = 0.002 \cdot P(t)$ is a constant multiple of $P(t)$ with positive constant. Hence, they both increase or decrease in the same way. Using **TI-nspire CX CAS**, we define the function $f(x)$: Define $f(x) = x^2 - \ln(x + 1)$. After that we press **Ctrl+Doc** keys to add graphs and plot the graph of $y = f(x)$:

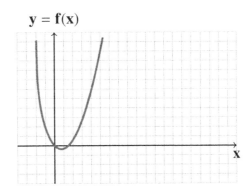

Answer: D.

Problem 88. Solution: The graph of $f'(x)$ looks as follows:

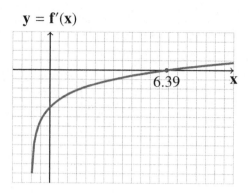

y = f'(x)

6.39

Answer: B.

Problem 89. Solution: The function $y = f(x)$ decreases for $x < 3$ as well as for $x > 3$. Hence

$$f(3.1) \le f(x_2) \text{ for } 3 < x_2 < 3.1, \text{ and } f(x_1) \le f(2.9) \text{ for } 2.9 < x_1 < 3.$$

Since $f(3.1) > f(2.9)$, we see that

$$f(x_2) - f(x_1) \ge f(3.1) - f(2.9) > 0 \tag{47}$$

for any x_2, $3 < x_2 < 3.1$ and for any x_1, $2.9 < x_1 < 3$. Hence $f(x)$ cannot be continuous at $x = 3$, since otherwise the equality

$$\lim_{x_2 \to 3^-} f(x_2) = \lim_{x_1 \to 3^+} f(x_1),$$

contradicts to (47). Thus **C** must be excluded. Any point of inflection is a point of continuity. This excludes **D** and **E**.

f cannot decrease at $x = 3$ since otherwise $f(x_1) \ge f(x_2)$ for $3 - \delta < x_1 < 3 < x_2 < 3 + \delta$ for some positive δ, which is not the case as the inequality (47) shows. Thus **B** must be excluded.

Only **A** remains. But it is true as the example $f(x) = 1/(x-3)$ shows. **Answer: A**.

Problem 90. Solution: Clearly,

$$v(t) = \frac{ds}{dt} = 3t^2 - 12t + 9 = 3(t^2 - 4t + 3) = 3(t - 1)(t - 3).$$

The minimum of $v(t)$ on $[1, 3]$ is attained at $t = \frac{1+3}{2} = 2$ and equals $v(2) = -3$. **Answer: A**.

Question 1 (9 pts)

Solution: (a) We have

$$\frac{dV}{dt} = \frac{d}{dt}\left(\frac{1}{3}\pi h^3(t)\right) = \pi h^2 \frac{dh}{dt} \Rightarrow \left.\frac{dV}{dt}\right|_{t=0} = \pi(25.1)^2 \left.\frac{dh}{dt}\right|_{t=0} = \pi \cdot 630.1 \cdot (-4) =$$

$$- 2520.04\pi = -7916.94\,\text{meter}^3/\text{hour}.$$

Answer: -7916.94 meter^3/hour.

(b) Using a graphic calculator, we plot the graph of the derivative h':

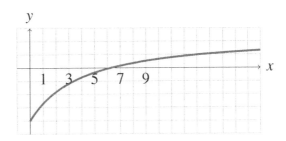

The graph shows that there is only one zero of $y = h'(t)$ on $0 < t < 24$. We find this zero with the **Solve** command: $t = 6.26126$ hours. Since the function $h'(t)$ changes sign from $-$ to $+$ at $t = 6.26126$, it is a point of local minimum of h.

(c) The second derivative of h is

$$h''(t) = \frac{0.6(t + 44) \cdot (0.97531)^t}{(t + 4)^2} > 0,$$

which implies that the graph of $y = h(t)$ is concave up. It follows that the graph is above any tangent to the graph, including the tangent at $t = 0$:

$$y = -4t + 25.1 \Rightarrow y(6.26126) = 0.054976 > 0.$$

It follows that $h(6.26126) > 0$, implying the result.

Question 2 (9 pts)

Solution: First, we extract the full squares:

$$9x^2 + 4y^2 - 54x + 16y + 61 = 9(x - 3)^2 + 4(y + 2)^2 - 36.$$

Hence the curve given is an ellipse:

$$\frac{(x - 3)^2}{2^2} + \frac{(y + 2)^2}{3^2} = 1.$$

(a) Differentiating the above equation implicitly in x, we obtain

$$\frac{x-3}{2} + 2\frac{y+2}{9}\cdot\frac{dy}{dx} = 0 \Rightarrow \frac{dy}{dx} = \frac{27-9x}{4y+8}.$$

(b) The tangent is vertical at $y = -2$, which happens if and only if $x = 3 \pm 2$. In other words, the vertical tangents are given by $\mathbf{x = 1}$, $\mathbf{x = 5}$.

(c) The slope is

$$\frac{(-2)-(-5)}{5-3} = \frac{3}{2} \Rightarrow y = \frac{3}{2}(x-3) - 5 \Rightarrow \mathbf{y = 1.5x - 9.5}.$$

(d) We have

$$\frac{dy}{dx} = \frac{3}{2} \Leftrightarrow \frac{27-9x}{4y+8} = \frac{3}{2} \Leftrightarrow 9 - 3x = 2y + 4 \Leftrightarrow y = \frac{-3x+5}{2}$$

We substitute this expression for y into the equation of the curve:

$$1 = \frac{(x-3)^2}{2^2} + \frac{(y+2)^2}{3^2} = \frac{(x-3)^2}{2^2} + \frac{(x-3)^2}{2^2} \Leftrightarrow x_{1,2} = 3 \pm \sqrt{2} = \begin{cases} 4.41421 \\ 1.58579 \end{cases}.$$

$$\begin{cases} y + 4.121 = 1.5(x - 4.414) \\ y - 0.121 = 1.5(x - 1.586) \end{cases}$$

Question 3 (9 pts)

Solution: **(a)** Since f' changes its sign from $+$ to $-$ at $x = 5$, the point $x = 5$ is the point of local maximum.

(b) The points of inflection are the points at which the graph of $y = f(x)$ changes its concavity. Since f' increases on $(0, 3)$, and decreases on $(3, 8.25)$, the point $x = 3$ is a point of inflection. Since f' increases on $(8.25, 12)$ the point $x = 8.25$ is the second point of inflection.

(c) The derivative f' of f increases about $x = 2$, which implies that the graph is concave up about $x = 2$.

(d). The derivative $f'(x) < 0$ on $(5, 11]$ and the function f being differentiable at $x = 5$ is continuous at $x = 5$. It follows that $y = f(x)$ decreases on $[5, 11]$. Hence $f(10) < f(7) < f(5)$.

Question 4 (9pts)

Solution: (**a**) The particle does not move when its velocity $v(t) = s'(t)$ equals zero. This happens when the tangent to the graph of $s(t)$ is horizontal. Estimating with the graph, we find that the tangent is horizontal at $t \approx 1.7$.

(**b**) The particle moves backward when its velocity is negative. The velocity is negative on the interval, where the function $s(t)$ decreases. Estimating with the graph, we find that this interval is $(1.7, 5)$.

(**c**) Using the information obtained in (**a** – **b**), we plot the graph:

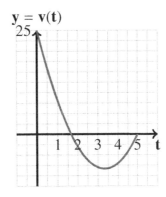

(**d**). The distance travelled by the particle is:

$$|s(1.7) - s(0)| + |s(3) - s(1.7)| \approx= 3.7 + 3.7 - 2.3 = 5.1.$$

Question 5 (9pts)

Solution: (**a**) A differentiable function g has a local minimum at x if $f(x) = g'(x) = 0$ and if f changes its sign from $-$ to $+$ at x. Analyzing the graph of f, we see that $x = 0$ is the only point with such a property.

(**b**) The graph of g is concave down on the intervals, where $g''(x) = f'(x) \le 0$. This happens on the intervals on which f decreases. Hence, g is concave down on $(-3, -1) \cup (1, 2)$.

(**c**) Since $g(0) = -1$ and $f(0) = 0$, we may apply l'Hospital Rule twice:

$$\lim_{x \to -1} \frac{g(x+1) + 1}{(x+1)^2} \overset{y=x+1}{=} \lim_{y \to 0} \frac{g(y) + 1}{y^2} \lim_{y \to 0} \frac{(g(y) + 1)'}{2y} = \lim_{y \to 0} \frac{f(y)}{2y} = \frac{f'(0)}{2} = \frac{1}{2}.$$

(**d**) Applying the Chain Rule, we obtain

$$h'(x)\Big|_{x=-0.5} = 4f'(2x+1)\Big|_{x=-0.5} = 4f'(0) = 4.$$

Question 6 (9pts)

Solution: (a)

$$P(0) = (0.25 \cdot 0 + 2)e^{-0.1 \cdot 0} = 2 \text{ hundred of people} = \textbf{200 people}.$$

(**b**)

$$P'(r) = 0.25e^{-0.1r} - (0.25r + 2)0.1e^{-0.1r} = (0.05 - 0.025r)e^{-0.1r}.$$

Since $P'(r) > 0$ for $0 < r < 2$, the function increases on $(0, 2)$. Since $P'(r) < 0$ for $2 < r < +\infty$, the function decreases on $(1, +\infty)$.

(**c**) The population is the largest at $r = 2$ miles, since $P'(2) = 0$ and since $P(r)$ increases for $0 < r < 2$ and decreases for $2 < r < +\infty$.

$$P(2) = 2.5e^{-0.2} \approx 2.5\left(1 - 0.2 + \frac{(-0.2)^2}{2!}\right) = 2.05 \text{ hundred} = \textbf{205 people}$$

(**d**)

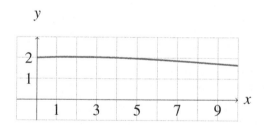

There is only one horizontal asymptote $y = 0$:

$$\lim_{r \to +\infty} P(r) = 0.$$

The intervals of monotonicity are $(0, 2)$ and $(2, +\infty)$.

Final Exam
The Key to the Solutions

1	C	24	D
2	A	25	D
3	C	26	A
4	B	27	A
5	A	28	C
6	B	29	C
7	A	30	B
8	B	76	D
9	A	77	B
10	D	78	C
11	C	79	E
12	B	80	A
13	B	81	E
14	C	82	E
15	B	83	A
16	D	84	C
17	B	85	D
18	E	86	B
19	C	87	D
20	A	88	B
21	D	89	A
22	D	90	A
23	C		

References

1. R.P.Boas, *Lion Hunting and Other Mathematical Pursuits*: the Mathematical Association of America, 1995.

2. K.C. Ciesielski, and D. Miller, "A continuous tale on continuous and separately continuous functions," *Real Analysis Exchange*, vol. 41, no. 1, 19-54, 2016.

3. R. Descartes, *The Geometry of Rene Descartes*: Dover, 1954.

4. R. Descartes, *Discourse on the Method*: Oxford University Press, 2006.

5. L. Euler, *Foundations of Differential Calculus*: Springer, 2000.

6. E. Goursat, *A Course in Mathematical Analysis*: vol 1, Ginn and Co, 1904.

7. V.J. Katz, *A History of Mathematics*: Addison-Wesley, 1998.

8. R.L. Kruse, and J.J. Deely, "Joint Continuity of Monotonic Functions", *Amer. Math. Monthly*, vol 76, pp. 74-76, January 1969.

9. E. Maor, *e. The Story of a Number*: Princeton, 1994.

10. J.A. Stedall, *The Arithmetic of Infinitisimals, John Wallis 1965*: Springer, 2004.

11. D.T. Whiteside, *The Mathematical Papers of Isaac Newton*: vol V, Cambridge University Press, 1972.

12. W.H. Young, "A note on monotonic functions", *Quarterly Journal of Pure and Applied Mathematics*, vol. 41, pp. 79-87, 1910.

Subject index